Guitar Tone:
Pursuing the Ultimate Guitar Sound

Mitch Gallagher

Course Technology PTR
A part of Cengage Learning

COURSE TECHNOLOGY
CENGAGE Learning®

Australia, Brazil, Japan, Korea, Mexico, Singapore, Spain, United Kingdom, United States

COURSE TECHNOLOGY
CENGAGE Learning®

**Guitar Tone: Pursuing the
Ultimate Guitar Sound
Mitch Gallagher**

**Publisher and General Manager,
Course Technology PTR:**
Stacy L. Hiquet

Associate Director of Marketing:
Sarah Panella

Manager of Editorial Services:
Heather Talbot

Marketing Manager:
Mark Hughes

Acquisitions Editor:
Orren Merton

Project and Copy Editor:
Catheen D. Small

Interior Layout:
Shawn Morningstar

Cover Designer:
Luke Fletcher

Indexer:
Larry Sweazy

Proofreader:
Megan Belanger

For product information and technology assistance, contact us at
Cengage Learning Customer & Sales Support, 1-800-354-9706

For permission to use material from this text or product,
submit all requests online at **cengage.com/permissions**
Further permissions questions can be emailed to
permissionrequest@cengage.com

Library of Congress Control Number: 2010926276

ISBN-13: 978-1-4354-5615-0

ISBN-10: 1-4354-5615-7

Course Technology, a part of Cengage Learning
20 Channel Center Street
Boston, MA 02210
USA

Cengage Learning is a leading provider of customized learning solutions with office locations around the globe, including Singapore, the United Kingdom, Australia, Mexico, Brazil, and Japan. Locate your local office at: **international.cengage.com/region.**

Cengage Learning products are represented in Canada by Nelson Education, Ltd.

For your lifelong learning solutions, visit **courseptr.com.**

Visit our corporate Web site at **cengage.com.**

Printed in the United States of America
1 2 3 4 5 6 7 13 12 11

For Mom and Dad, who bought me my first guitar.

Acknowledgments

It would be remiss to begin this book without wondering where we would be without the original "Icons of Tone." There is no way to repay the immeasurable debt of gratitude owed to Leo Fender, Adolph Rickenbacker, Ted McCarty, Seth Lover, Paul Bigsby, Les Paul, Jim Marshall, Fred Gretsch, and the many other forward-thinking innovators and visionaries who launched the wonderful world of electric guitar that we enjoy today.

Many thanks to Orren Merton, the acquisitions editor behind this book, for his extensive input and brainstorming, plus a ton of wonderful guitar conversation! Thanks to Mark Garvey and everyone at Course Technology PTR for their interest in and enthusiasm for publishing this book.

It was a great pleasure to once again work with Cathleen Small as my editor on this project—her edits and corrections are always exactly on the mark. Thanks, Cathleen!

Special thanks to Bob Bailey, Tom Menrath, Tom Castonzo, Marc Silver, and Mike Ross for the multitudinous guitar-centric conversations that ultimately spawned the idea for this book.

Finally, this book is for Felicia, the most patient and supportive wife ever. I love you!

About the Author

MITCH GALLAGHER has been chasing guitar tone for more than 30 years. He holds a Bachelor of Arts degree in music from Moorhead State University (now called Minnesota State University - Moorhead). His graduate studies at the University of Missouri in Kansas City included music composition and classical guitar. He taught hundreds of guitar lessons to students of all ages and in all styles.

He toured as a lead guitarist/vocalist in rock and country bands and has played with big bands, with fusion and experimental music groups, and as a classical and steel-string guitar soloist. As a classical guitarist, he studied with Michael Coates and Douglas Niedt, and he currently studies with Jason Vieaux and Denis Azabagic. He has performed in master classes with William Kanengiser of the Los Angeles Guitar Quartet and Lorenzo Micheli of Italy's SoloDuo.

As a music technology specialist, he has taught college courses, lectured, given clinics, consulted with manufacturers, and spoken at festivals, conventions, and conferences around the world. Publications such as the *Washington Post* consult him as a technology expert. He is a respected recording, live sound, and mastering engineer.

As a composer, he studied with Henry Gwiazda, Gerald Kemner, and James Mobberley. His compositions cover genres from classical to experimental to heavy metal. *Prophecy #1: At First Glance*, an experimental percussion ensemble/synthesizer work based on the Fibonacci number series, received a 1991 NARAS (Grammy) award in the Best New Music/New Classical category. He was a featured artist at the 1994 International Computer Arts Festival in Sofia, Bulgaria, where he lectured on and performed his *Prophecy* series of electronic music compositions.

The former senior technical editor of *Keyboard* magazine and former editor-in-chief of *EQ* magazine, Gallagher has published well over 1,000 articles in publications such as *Premier Guitar, Guitar Player, Acoustic Guitar, Guitars & Gear, Performing Songwriter, EQ, EQ en Español, Keyboard, Pro Sound News, Select, Sweetnotes, ProGear, Government Video, Extreme Groove, Music Technology Buyer's Guide, Videography, Strings*, and *Microphones & Monitors*. He is also the former editor of *Church Sound* magazine and served as associate editor at *Live Sound* magazine. His monthly column, "Guitar Tracks," appears in *Premier Guitar* magazine. He is featured in well over 100 videos on YouTube.

His books include *Make Music Now!* (Backbeat Books), *Pro Tools Clinic* (Music Sales/Schirmer Trade Books), *The Studio Business Book, 3rd Edition* (Course Technology PTR), *Acoustic Design for the Home Studio* (Course Technology PTR), *Mastering Music at Home* (Course Technology PTR), and *The Music Tech Dictionary* (Course Technology PTR). *Project Studio Mastering* (Multi-Platinum Pro Tools) is his first instructional DVD.

In addition to freelance writing and editing, he is an adjunct faculty member at Indiana University/Purdue University Fort Wayne; he operates The Sound Sauna/MAG Media Productions, a recording and mastering studio; and he is the editorial director for Sweetwater Sound in Fort Wayne, Indiana.

Visit Mitch Gallagher online at www.mitchgallagher.com.

Table of Contents

Chapter 9 Cabinets and Enclosures 137

Part II
The Icons of Tone   265

Chapter 17 Jeff Beck   269

Chapter 18 Larry Carlton   273

Chapter 19 Eric Clapton   277

Chapter 20 The Edge   285

Chapter 21 Robben Ford   289

Chapter 22 David Gilmour   293

Introduction

Is there anything finer than plugging a tasty electric guitar into a stellar amp and bathing in the sonic bliss of a fabulous tone washing over you?

There's just nothing else quite like it: the bright twang of a Tele, the rich sparkle of a Blackface, the unbridled roar of a Plexi, the thick crunch of a Les Paul, the chime of an AC30, the wail of a Strat, the singing sustain of a Boogie, the on-the-verge-of-meltdown scream of an amp pushed beyond its limit, the visceral impact of a cranked stack....

These are the things we live for, the things that make us grin with pure excitement. And it all comes down to one thing: *tone*. In the beginning, it may have been the hope of attracting the opposite sex or dreams of fame or fortune that started us playing electric guitar. But in the end, it's the *sound* that keeps us coming back to caress those six shiny strings.

What is it about the sound of an electric guitar that means so much to us? What makes us spend our lives striving for better and better tone? Why does it feel so *good* to wring every last bit of luscious sonic goodness out of that instrument?

To take a small step back, few would argue that the point of playing guitar (or any instrument) is to play music—to create sounds, notes, and phrases that stimulate an emotional, physical, or intellectual response in the listener. But if that guitar (or voice or other instrument) doesn't have good sound—if it isn't toneful and desirable to hear—then no one is going to listen for long. So, it could be argued that tone may be the primary factor upon which the success of any musical performance is built. (Yeah, that's it!)

But what is tone—or, more specifically, what is *good* tone? And how does a guitarist go about achieving good tone?

If you're like me, then these two questions consume a big portion of your mind, time, and (unfortunately) disposable income. My quest for the ultimate guitar sound began in the mid-1970s. I had somehow acquired a potent case of pneumonia and ended up out of school for a couple of weeks. As consolation for missing out on the joys of school (as if I need consoling for that!), my mom brought home a fresh new copy of an album (this was back in the good ol' days when an "album" was only available on vinyl and maybe cassette tape)—KISS *Alive*. From the moment I heard (and felt—I quickly discovered that it was necessary to play it *loud* to get the proper effect) the first crunching riff of "Deuce," I was hooked on the sound of electric guitar. While I might not now point to that album as an iconic example of stellar audio quality or prototypical guitar tones, and despite the fact that the band and engineer/producer Eddie Kramer have since stated that the album was heavily doctored in the studio after the fact, it doesn't matter. The damage was done, and my life was changed forever—and I like to think it was changed for the better—by Ace Frehley's screaming tobacco-sunburst Gibson Les Paul Standard (with rewound, hotter lead pickup) and stacks of Marshall Super Lead amps (with 6550 power tubes instead of the more common EL34 tubes).

From there, it was a short step to Ted Nugent's ridiculously cool hollow-body Gibson Byrdland through a wall of Fender Dual Showman amps madness; Jimi Hendrix's and Ritchie Blackmore's cranked Strats through Marshalls; Eddie Van Halen's eye-, and ear-, and mind-opening modified Strat-style guitar through modified Marshall stack revolution; the fixed-wah wail of Michael Schenker's Flying V and Marshalls; Angus Young's crunching Gibson SG through Marshall stacks assault—and on and on. The love of music drove me, but it was the *sound* of the guitar that grabbed me and wouldn't let go.

Since then, I've gone through (and continue to go through) scads of amps, piles of guitars, a crate-load of pickups and hardware, a small mountain of stompboxes, and miles of cables, and I even became a recording engineer, all for the purpose of chasing the sound of the electric guitar and the myriad types of music you can make with it. It's a never-ending quest—perhaps a prototypical example of the philosophy that it's the journey that should be enjoyed and not the destination, since there is no enduring final destination in this quest! Each seeming arrival is an evanescent illusion; moments later, satisfaction flutters away, and the search is on again.

To anthropomorphize for just a moment, tone is a difficult quarry to hunt: baffling, frustrating, elusive, mercurial—the smallest change in any of so many tiny things can chase her away. A change in the temperature of a single component can cause her to scurry back into hiding. When you do pin her down, even if you walk away with her firmly ensconced in your memory, her countenance will have changed when you return.

There are several reasons why tone is so difficult to pin down. With electric guitar, many components go into creating a sound. On the macro level, we have the guitar, the amp, and any effects that may be processing the signal. And, as we dig deeper, we find that each of those macro elements consists of many smaller elements. For example, an electric guitar is made of strings, pickups, hardware, various types of wood or other materials, electronic components, and more things, not least of which is the physical design and construction of the instrument. Likewise, an amplifier has tubes, transistors, capacitors, resistors, transformers, potentiometers, other electronic components, speaker drivers (which in turn are composed of a number of smaller elements), the physical speaker cabinet and its design and construction, and more. So it continues, through effects, even the cables used to connect everything together, and on down to the picks used to put the strings in motion. The smallest change in nearly any component in an electric guitar system—and it is, after all, a system—can affect the tone produced to a more or less audible degree. Some components in the system make a huge difference, and some make a minor or negligible difference, but all make their contribution to the tone.

But the tonal equation goes beyond the sound-generating equipment being used. The tone produced by an electric guitar system (or any instrument, for that matter) is at the mercy of the environment in which the sound is created—sound reflections from the walls, floor, and ceiling change the perceived tone. How the room resonates or passes vibrations on to the outside world affects the tone. The furniture, floor coverings, and other items in the room absorb or reflect sound and affect the tone. Even factors of climate, such as the humidity and atmospheric pressure, can change the perceived attributes of a sound.

As if all of this weren't enough to make it difficult to figure out how to achieve good tone, we must consider perhaps the most important—and most capricious—element in the system of all: the player.

From the physical—how the player puts the string into motion, how each note is fretted, where each note is fretted, any vibrato or other right- or left-hand articulation added—to the metaphysical—the mood, the mindset, and the emotion being expressed behind each note—the player and his fingers are the ultimate keys to the production of sound on the guitar. As the player changes from moment to moment, so changes his guitar tone.

So, where does this leave us when considering electric guitar tone? Of all the factors we can explore, for many of us, it comes back to gear—guitars, amps, effects, cables, picks, and more. Equipment inspires us, delights us, changes our playing, affects our music, and is at the heart of our own personal sound.

Most of us who find ourselves embroiled in tone quests are semi-obsessed with gear. (Maybe "*fanatically obsessed*" is a better description!) We think about it, we lust for it, we debate the merits of it, we experiment, we tinker, we change things, we research, we test, we compare, we modify, we purchase, we sell, we trade, we fill the virtual world with the din of online discussion forum chatter—gear is our hobby, gear is our pastime, gear is the cornerstone of the tonal temple at which we worship.

The uninitiated may scoff, but what's wrong with loving gear? It's fun! It's rewarding! It's educational! It's expensive!

And, hopefully, ultimately, this gear fixation leads us to the aural equivalent of the Holy Grail: *tone*. That indescribable, visceral sonic envelopment that is our bliss as we make music.

Whether you play rock, jazz, country, metal, fusion, blues, punk, or atmospheric sonic washes—or even just strum "cowboy" chords while sitting on the front porch like a modern-day Andy Griffith—as guitar players, we all have one thing in common: Our diverse and individual tones define us and the music we make. Which, in a meandering sort of way, brings us full circle, back to two of the questions posed near the beginning of this exposition:

What is tone?

And,

How do we get *good* tone?

When considering the first question, there are academic definitions for the way in which we use the word *tone*, such as "the quality of a musical or vocal sound," "the particular quality of brightness, deepness, or shade of a [sonic] color," and there is also a list of synonyms, including "timbre," "sound," "color," and more. There are even musical definitions, such as a "whole-step interval"—but none of these tells the complete story. "Great tone" is a combination of many things electronic, acoustic, musical, physical, emotional, cerebral—each player assembles and manipulates those components into his own special blend, creating his own unique sonic stew.

As for the second question, the only answer for most of us is a lifetime of pursuit that is at once equal parts joyous and frustrating—but always rewarding. A big part of succeeding in that pursuit is an understanding of what goes into making a great tone. And that's where this book comes in; we'll find our way toward our goal by exploring the gear we love, examining the approaches various players take, and defining the requirements necessary to achieve the sounds of particular genres. We'll look at vintage and new, boutique and factory, modern and retro. Along the way, we'll attempt to sort out the facts versus the myths versus the opinions, and we'll figure out how each component contributes to the overall tone of our guitars and other gear.

The search for tone may not have a definitive conclusion for most of us, but that doesn't make the journey any less worth taking. It's not easy to achieve great tone, but the reward—the joy of wallowing in the luscious sound of strings resonating in concert with your musical desires—is a reward greater than any other.

Better tone awaits—turn the page and let's get started!

Part I

The Tools of Tone

YOU'VE PROBABLY HEARD THE OLD CLICHÉ ABOUT TONE coming from your fingers. And from our own personal experience, we can probably each verify that there's truth to it—the player is the source of his own tone in many respects. It's a very common experience: We hear a guitarist playing through his or her rig and achieving a certain sound. Then we pick up the exact same guitar, with the same amp and effects and all the same settings…but the sound is very different. And often, the better and more accomplished the players involved are, the more noticeable the sonic difference is. But how is that possible?

The most obvious facet of this is that how you play the instrument affects the sound you create. If you pick hard, then you'll get a certain snappy, bright, loud sound. If you brush the strings gently, then the sound will be different—softer, more ethereal, quieter. How hard you squeeze the strings against the fingerboard and the frets may change the sound, and where you attack the strings—near the bridge, near the neck—will certainly impact the tone. How you bend notes, the vibrato you add (or don't add), where on the neck you choose to fret a particular note—all of these things physically combine to alter the sound your guitar and your other equipment produces.

There's another connection to this "tone is in your fingers" idea that's a bit less obvious at first glance—and that can sometimes be much more subtle sonically. The tone you create and how you produce that tone comes about because you have an aural picture in your mind of the sound you want your hands and your instrument to create—fat, thin, bright, or dark, the sound you make is in direct relation to the sound you *want* to make. Now, before you write me off as a complete wacko, this is not to say that if you conjure a mental image of your tone as a twangy surf sound and you're playing a hot-rodded shred-metal machine through a super-gain amp stack cranked to 11 that the sound you make is going to match your mental image, but you might be surprised by how much what you *want* to hear is what you *do* hear—at least in some respects. Much of this goes back to what I said before: How you play affects the tone, and your playing will certainly change based on what you want to hear and what you want to produce from a musical standpoint. Your tone is in your hands, and consciously or subconsciously, through habit, inspiration, or intent, your mind controls what your hands do.

Still, back here on Earth, the guitar you play, the amp you use, and the effects you plug in will have the largest impact on your sound. Each of these tools and the components that comprise it makes a difference in the sound. From the most major to the least consequential, it all matters.

There is a caveat, though. Although we can change many things about the tools we use, it's important to remember that the whole thing is an interactive system—or actually, several systems joined together to make a larger, complete chain. The guitar influences the amp in certain ways, the effects change the relationship, the cables affect the amp and the guitar, and so on. So, even though we'll examine each of our tone tools and the components that make it up separately, keep the systems and the chain as a whole in mind.

One more thing to keep in mind: The gear you use doesn't matter. (Yow, I'll be banned from every guitar discussion forum on the planet after committing that statement permanently to print!) Here's what I mean: Cheap or expensive, factory or boutique, new or vintage, road-scarred or pristine, it's not the gear that you own and use—it's what you *do* with the gear you own and use. And, what style of music you play and what sound you're trying to create. And, of course, what you like and enjoy using. Your own personal preference in tones and music will determine what you use. Never let anyone tell you that the gear you have is wrong or not the best. If it works for you, no matter what it is, then it's the best! *Vive la différence!*

Guitar Types and Construction

ALTHOUGH THERE ARE MANY PLACES FROM WHICH we can launch our quest for tone, the beginning for most of us is the guitar itself. After all, it's the guitar we love. We can be fond of amplifiers and stompboxes, we can be enamored of a certain type of strings or whatever, but it all comes back to the guitar. That's where the magic begins.

One of the larger factors in the tone of an electric guitar is its type—its design and how it is constructed. How the guitar is designed affects how it resonates, how the vibrations are presented to the pickup, how the instrument sustains, the harmonic quality of the sound (whether the tone of the guitar is bright or dark), how susceptible the guitar is to feedback at high volume levels, and so on.

The earliest "electric guitars" were simply acoustic guitars to which a pickup of a primitive sort was attached so that the guitar could be heard over the powerful big bands of the day—there was no way an unamplified acoustic guitar could compete. But all of that changed when several innovators came up with ideas for solidifying and electrifying the instrument, including Adolph Rickenbacker with his "Frying Pan" lap steel guitars (the first production electric guitar, introduced in 1931), Lloyd Loar with his Vivi Tone solid-body and acoustic-electric guitars (created after he left Gibson, around 1935), Paul Bigsby with his proto-Tele shaped solid-body (conceived by Merle Travis and built by Bigsby in 1946), and Les Paul with his famous "Log"—a 4-inch by 4-inch chunk of pine attached to a Gibson neck and flanked by an Epiphone acoustic guitar body that had been sawed in half—which he built circa 1939. This all led up to Leo Fender changing the world with the launch of his Esquire and Broadcaster solid-body electric guitars in 1949. (The Broadcaster name was later changed to Telecaster in response to a trademark conflict with Gretsch, which made a line of drums under the name Broadkaster.) Gibson soon leapt into the fray by joining forces with Les Paul to create his namesake solid-body guitar in 1952…and the era of the electric solid-body guitar was underway.

But, of course, the solid-body isn't the only electric guitar type; the guitar world is also populated with a plethora of hollow bodies and semi-hollow bodies. Each type has its own tonal characteristics.

Hollow-Body

The electric guitar type that is closest to the traditional acoustic guitar and that was the earliest type of "electrified" guitar is the hollow-body. There are varying degrees of how close a hollow-body guitar model might be to a true acoustic guitar. On one end of the spectrum, certain arch-top hollow-body electric guitars are identical to arch-top acoustic guitars, with the exception of the addition of a pickup or pickups and volume and tone controls. In many cases, the pickup is suspended over the body of the instrument from a mount attached to the neck or pick guard. The idea behind "floating" the pickup is to prevent its weight from damping the natural resonance and vibration of the guitar's top. The volume and tone controls may be mounted to the top of the guitar or, in some cases, mounted to the pick guard to prevent the weight of the controls and the mounting holes in the top from impeding the top from freely vibrating in response to the strings' motion.

The physical design of the guitar, from the bracing of the soundboard (or top) and back to how the sides are bent and attached to the top and back, are the same as with an all-acoustic flat-top or arch-top guitar. A hollow-body electric guitar may use a wooden bridge base, similar to an acoustic guitar bridge base, to which a metal bridge is attached (in place of the bone or synthetic saddle used on many acoustic guitars). In many cases, the bridge isn't even glued down or attached to the top of the guitar; it is held in place by downward pressure from the strings (as is also the case with some acoustic guitars and mandolins).

Typically the guitar's strings anchor to a suspended or floating "trapeze" tailpiece that attaches to the endpin of the guitar and that doesn't require mounting posts through the guitar top. The concept behind using all of this floating hardware is to keep the necessary electric components from affecting the acoustic performance of the instrument as much as possible. The result is a guitar that performs well acoustically—though that isn't the primary goal—and that also performs well as an electric. In other words, the primary goal is to capture the resonance and natural sound of the ostensibly acoustic guitar with a pickup and to make that sound louder, so it is audible in a big band or a jazz combo setting.

At the other end of the hollow-body spectrum are guitars with somewhat thicker, carved tops that cap a hollow-body. These guitars often use similar hardware and hardware mounting schemes to solid-body electric guitars, rather than the hardware of true acoustic guitars. The acoustic performance of the guitar may be compromised, but the goal with these designs is more about the electric tone heard through the amp. How the guitar performs acoustically isn't the primary concern, although it contributes significantly to the richness, depth, and flavor of the sound.

But most hollow-body guitars fall somewhere in the middle of these two extremes. From a woodworking and design standpoint, they are largely constructed as arch-top acoustic guitars, but the pickups are mounted into holes cut in the guitar's top, and the volume and tone controls are mounted to holes that likewise pierce the top. The thin top may be made from laminated wood, from a single solid sheet of wood, or from two book-matched sheets of wood. Most players and manufacturers agree that solid tops (versus laminates) generally provide better performance, vibrating more like a high-quality acoustic guitar. This increased ability to vibrate translates to more richness and resonance than a laminated top—the tradeoff is the cost of the instrument, as quality pieces of wood for solid tops are usually more expensive than equivalent laminated pieces of wood. Another tradeoff is that solid tops can be more prone to cracking than laminated tops in low humidity or other stressful situations. In other words, laminate tops are generally more durable than solid tops.

In most cases, the neck of a hollow-body guitar is glued into a slot in the end of the guitar's body, in similar fashion to how an acoustic guitar is constructed. This allows for good transfer of vibrations among the neck, the neck/body joint, and the body of the instrument.

Solid-Body

A solid-body guitar features a body carved from a single solid piece of wood or from two or more solid pieces that have been glued together to create the blank from which the guitar body will be shaped. The difference between the two approaches can vary from minor to significant. For example, a typical Telecaster- or Stratocaster-style guitar might feature a body made from a single hunk of wood a couple of inches thick, and wide and long enough to form the body. In some cases, two or more pieces of wood, each a couple of inches thick, each long enough for the body, but not wide enough to make the body on their own, are glued side by side to create a blank that is wide enough to form a body. There may be a small amount of tonal benefit from a one-piece body versus one that is made from two or more pieces. The purest resonance will come from a single piece of wood, though when multiple pieces of wood are glued together the result may be increased strength and rigidity, which can enhance sustain and make the guitar slightly brighter sounding.

A Les Paul–style guitar, on the other hand, generally features a thick back of one type of wood (usually mahogany) capped by a thick top, which is usually carved from a slab of maple. This results in a very different tone compared to a body made from one piece of wood, as the qualities of the different types of woods used for the back and top are combined—most noticeably, the thick maple cap provides a bright, articulate top end to the darker tone of the mahogany back. (See the next chapter for much more on the wood types used for guitar construction and their tonal impacts.)

Don't be fooled, though; there are a couple of ways for manufacturers to create a guitar that looks as if it has a true carved maple top without using an expensive, thick piece of highly figured maple—even if the guitar has a stained or natural finish that reveals the grain of the wood.

> ▷ Less expensive guitars that appear to have a thick maple top may in fact have a thin veneer of figured maple that has been glued to the thick back of the guitar. This could be the case even if the guitar appears to have a carved top; the underlying wood of the back of the guitar may be shaped into the contour of a carved top, and then a thin veneer of figured maple is vacuum shaped and glued to that contour. Although this provides the look of a true carved maple top, the thin wood of the veneer does not provide the tonal benefits of a real, thick, carved maple top.

> ▷ The guitar body may actually feature three layers: a thick back; a carved top made from less-expensive, un-figured (plain) maple; and then a very thin veneer of highly figured maple. In this case, the tone may be similar to using a true carved top of maple, with the appearance of a carved maple top, but at a more affordable price.

Chambering versus Weight Relief

Beginning in the mid-1990s, some manufacturers, such as Gibson, began offering "weight-relieved" and "chambered" guitars. The idea behind both concepts is the same: Portions of the interior of a solid-body guitar are drilled, routed, or carved away. But technically there is a difference between chambering and weight relief.

Weight relief is simply carving away a portion of the body's interior wood to reduce the overall weight of the guitar. Though the wood removal may not be random, it isn't done with an eye toward preserving or enhancing the innate tone and resonance of the instrument—often holes are simply routed or drilled in the interior of the body to remove wood before a top or cap is put on to complete the body.

With chambering, on the other hand, the wood is removed in specific places from inside the guitar body in order to add resonance to the body and improve the sound of the guitar.

Although it is clear that weight relief works—it does what it's supposed to do—the weight of the guitar is reduced compared to if it were non–weight relieved—many guitarists feel that removing wood in a non-specific way from the guitar body may have a negative impact on the sustain and tone of the instrument. (Though I've played weight-relieved Gibson Les Paul Traditional model guitars, for example, that were spectacular.)

By contrast, many guitarists find that chambering can have a positive effect on the tone and resonance of the guitar. For example, I have a guitar I built using a body made with a chambered mahogany back with a thick maple top. The result is a lightweight guitar that is lively and responsive, with good resonance and sustain. I've played other guitars that were chambered that felt somewhat dead. There are a variety of factors that can contribute to this, including the types of wood, the particular piece of wood, the thickness of the wood, the amount of chambering, and so on.

Would you know if you were playing a weight-relieved or chambered guitar versus one made from lightweight woods? There can be a difference; the resonance may be different, and there may be a "feel" difference in how the resonance occurs throughout the instrument. Plus (pardon me for stating the obvious), a chambered/weight-relieved instrument will feel lighter than if it were made from a solid piece of wood. You can also tap on the guitar front and back in various places. If it's chambered or weight relieved, you'll sometimes hear when you hit a hollow spot versus when you hit a solid spot.

Carved versus Flat Tops

A solid-body electric guitar may have a flat top, or it may have a top that has been carved to have a shape that is thicker in the middle and thinner toward the rim of the guitar. In most cases, the actual carving doesn't directly affect the tone, except in one potential way: If there is, for example, a maple top on the guitar, and the top thickness is greater at the center of the guitar, the thicker maple may increase the amount of brightness that the top wood contributes to the tone more than if the top were thinner and of constant thickness across the width of the guitar.

In some cases, a guitar made from a single slab of wood (without a different type of wood as a top) will have a top that is carved. Since the top wood is the same as the main body wood (and may even comprise the same slab of wood), there will be no tonal impact resulting from the top or the carving—the tone will be the same as a slab of wood as thick as the carved section.

In other cases, the body may be shaped in a specific way; for example, a Fender Stratocaster has a *belly cut* or *tummy cut*, where wood is removed from the upper back of the guitar, and a *forearm cut*, where wood is removed from the front upper bout where the player's pick arm rests. These cuts (also known as a *comfort cuts*) are added purely to enhance the playing comfort of the guitar and are not intended to impact the tone of the instrument (though removing any amount of body wood may alter the tone somewhat). Other guitars, such as Paul Reed Smith instruments, often have shaped cutaways. Once again, this is to improve access to the upper frets and to enhance playing comfort; the carving is not intended to affect the tone of the instrument. None of these "shaping" examples would be considered a carved top or a carved guitar, even though the instrument has certainly been shaped.

Solid-Body Construction

There are three basic ways in which a solid-body guitar may be constructed, beyond how the body itself is made. The first two construction methods date back to the original Fender and Gibson solid-body electric guitars.

Set Necks

Gibson used (and continues to use) a "traditional" method for constructing the guitar, similar to how many acoustic guitars are built, where the neck is glued into a slot that is cut into the body. This is called *set-neck* construction. Gibson (along with many other manufacturers, such as Paul Reed Smith) uses this method for most of its electric guitars to this day. A *tenon*, or a protruding piece of wood on the end of the neck that slips farther into the guitar body—in some cases, as far as under the neck pickup—may be used to reinforce the body/neck joint. Opinions vary on how the length of a tenon affects the tone of a guitar; debates flare up about the virtues of long-tenon Les Pauls and short-tenon (also known as *rocker* tenon) Les Pauls, though many players agree that logically a long tenon makes for a more solid joint (more wood surface for gluing and support), and therefore, all other things being equal, could impact tone and sustain positively. Of course, a long tenon requires a longer piece of wood for the neck blank (not a trivial matter in these days of increasingly scarce tonewoods) and more time/work—not only must the tenon be shaped and the neck positioned correctly (which is easier with a short tenon), the tenon often must be routed or reshaped later, after being installed in the guitar, to allow for the neck pickup cavity—so it is therefore more expensive to manufacture.

For a short time in the late 1960s through 1974 or early 1975, Gibson also made Les Pauls with *trans* tenons (also known as *transitional* tenons or *modified long* tenons), which were essentially long tenons with the "tongue" cut off. You can tell which sort of tenon a set-neck guitar has by taking out the neck pickup. If you can see the neck wood running into and under the pickup cavity, it's a long tenon. If you can see the end of the tenon on the neck side of the pickup cavity, then it is a trans tenon. If you can't see any neck wood, it's likely a short tenon, or the guitar doesn't have a tenon.

In the end, there have been great guitars made with all three tenon styles—and with no tenon. Although the type of tenon could make a difference in the tone, it probably is not a substantial contributor to the sound or sustain a guitar produces.

Bolt-On Necks

Leo Fender took a different path in his quest for a guitar that was analogous to Henry Ford's Model T—one where any part could be easily, quickly, and affordably replaced by anyone with a basic skill set and access to common hand tools. He used bolts (technically, wood screws) to fasten the neck into a "pocket" cut into the body of the guitar. Fender and many other manufacturers continue to rely on this type of bolt-on neck construction for their guitars.

Tight Fit

For the best sustain, vibration transfer, resonance, and tone, the heel of a bolt-on guitar's neck must fit as tightly as possible into the guitar body's neck pocket. Extra space around the neck heel can reduce vibration transfer and affect the guitar's performance. A smooth, level surface on both the bottom of the neck heel and the bottom of the neck pocket is necessary for maximum contact. Some players feel that paint or other finish in the neck pocket and heel can prevent firm contact between the two pieces of wood and affect sustain and tone.

Likewise, if shims are required in the neck pocket to get the neck set to the correct angle related to the body, this reduces the amount of contact between the neck and body. If a shim is required, it is best to use a resonant material, such as hardwood, rather than paper or other material, which might, in fact, damp the transfer of vibrations between the neck and the body.

The screws used to hold the neck onto the guitar body need to be cinched down as tightly as possible, making the best physical connection between the body and neck, so that the two can function as one solid unit. (Fender used four screws to mount their guitars' necks through 1971, when the number was reduced to three, and a "Micro Tilt" feature—a small screw that could be used to adjust the neck angle—was added. By 1980, Fender had returned to four neck screws for most models and ditched the Micro Tilt.)

There are about 6-1/2 square inches of contact space between the bottom of the neck heel and the bottom of the neck pocket of a Strat- or Tele-style guitar, and with the four screws firmly tightened down, more than three-quarters of a ton of pressure can be applied to the contact area between the two pieces of wood. This can, according to some builders, result in a stronger, more resonant join than a set neck or even a neck-through design. (See the "Neck Through" section later in this chapter for more on neck-through guitar construction.)

Generally, when the guitar is first assembled, accomplishing this tight fit is not a problem, though a wood screw will rarely be able to hold as tightly as a true bolt/nut; in most cases, the wood will strip first. The problem is that some bolt-on neck guitars (such as many Strat- and Tele-style instruments) have their truss rod adjustment at the heel (body end) of the neck, necessitating removing—or at least loosening—the neck screws each time the neck relief is adjusted and sometimes when the frets must be worked on. And each time those wood screws are loosened, they potentially won't go back and hold quite as firmly as they did before being loosened. When the screws don't grab on as tightly, the tone and sustain can be affected. It's not usually a severe problem, but it can be an issue with vintage guitars, and it can become an issue as a bolt-on guitar ages.

Some manufacturers have countered this by installing metal inserts in the neck-heel mounting holes and then using true bolts rather than wood screws to hold the neck on. There are also after-market parts companies, such as Onyx Forge Guitars, that offer retrofittable metal insert/bolt combinations that can be installed in almost any bolt-on neck guitar. These inserts allow the bolts to be tightened more firmly than wood screws and for the neck to be repeatedly removed and reattached without loosening the connection between the neck and body.

Another solution to this problem is Warmoth's Pro Strat- and Tele-style replacement necks, which employ a side-adjust mechanism for their truss rod, along with a regular end-of-neck truss-rod adjustment. Though this type of neck may still need to be removed for fret or other work or for major truss-rod adjustments, for minor truss-rod adjustments there is no need to remove the neck.

Still another solution is Fender's *bullet* truss rod, which has its adjustment at the headstock end of the neck, under the nut. With this type of setup, there is no need to remove the neck to adjust the truss rod.

Various manufacturers have come up with different approaches to bolt-on neck construction, each designed to provide the most solid, stable connection between the neck heel and the body's neck pocket. Two-bolt with wedge, three-bolt, three-bolt with neck angle adjust, four-bolt, five-bolt, super-tight pockets, shaped neck heels—all of these are believed by their respective designer/manufacturer/luthier to provide the optimum connection between the guitar's neck and its body for maximum sustain and tone. Do they all work equally well, or do some excel over the others? In many cases it's a question of taste, as each is slightly different. In other words, it's hard to judge without trying the specific instrument. For example, you might think the two-bolt with wedge pocket (as designed and used by Tom Anderson Guitars) might not be as strong as, say, a five-bolt design. But when you see someone doing chin-ups from the neck of an Anderson guitar (as has been shown on the Anderson website), your opinion might change.

What doesn't change is that, regardless of the method used for securing the neck to the body, the important thing is that the fit is tight and stable. The neck mustn't shift, or it won't play well or stay in tune. And if the neck and body don't become one rigid unit, sustain and tone will be affected.

Neck Through

The third method of guitar construction is *neck through* (or *neck thru*), where the neck and the center portion of the body are constructed from one long piece (or side-by-side long laminated pieces) of wood and then solid "wings" are glued to the neck/center body section to fill out the shape of the body. In this case, the majority of the tone is developed based on the type of wood used for the neck/center body section, with a certain amount of influence from the type of wood(s) used for the body's wings.

Neck-through guitar design and construction is the closest you can come to the arguable ideal of making a complete solid-body guitar body/neck from a single piece of wood (which doesn't happen very often, though I have seen photos of an amazing—and amazingly expensive—solid-body electric bass made entirely from one single piece of flamed maple).

Necks and Tone

There are tonal differences among the three guitar construction approaches; how the neck is attached affects how vibrations are passed between the body and neck of the guitar. It's probably obvious, but neck-through construction carries vibrations through a single, contiguous piece of wood. Many guitarists feel this type of construction provides the best sustain of any of the three types; some also feel that neck-through construction enhances the tone, due to the stronger and uninterrupted transfer of vibrations.

With set-neck construction, a tight, glued-in joint between the neck and the guitar body provides an excellent transfer of vibrations. This type of construction can also provide excellent sustain—the glued-in neck/body joint is nearly as solid as a true neck-through design. After all, the Gibson Les Paul is renowned for having some of the best sustain of any electric guitar model, glued-in neck and all!

All things being equal, it would seem as though a bolt-on-necked guitar would have the least transfer of vibrations from neck to body (and vice versa)—and many guitarists would argue that this is true based on their own experience. (Just compare the sustain of a Telecaster to a Les Paul or a neck-through guitar—though, of course, there are other differences besides the type of neck joint on these disparate models.) However, a tight neck-pocket-to-neck fit and cinched-down neck bolts can result in a guitar that is quite efficient at transferring vibrations. It can function nearly as well as—or some would say better than—the other two types. (Refer to the "Tight Fit" sidebar earlier in this chapter.)

So, what about tonal differences among the three? Many players feel that bolt-on designs tend to have a brighter, spankier tone—the Fender Telecaster and Stratocaster being the prime examples. Set-neck and neck-through designs often are described as thicker sounding with more sustain; the Les Paul is cited as the prototypical example. As with most things related to guitar tone, there are no hard-and-fast rules—I've heard bolt-on guitars with excellent sustain and thick tone, and there certainly are examples of neck-though guitars that don't ring all that well. However, as a general rule, it is safe to say that the more solid the joint between the neck and body, the better the vibrations will transfer and the stronger the tone will be, whether the guitar is a bolt-on, a set-neck, or a neck-through design.

Semi-Hollow-Body

In the late 1950s, Gibson, under the guiding hand of then-president, the late Ted McCarty (who is credited with completing Gibson's deal with Les Paul and with designing the radical-for-the-time Gibson Flying V and Explorer and the never-officially produced Moderne model) set about creating a guitar that would combine the best features of a solid-body with some of the aspects of a hollow-body. The result was the ES-335 semi-hollow-body guitar, which spawned numerous siblings (the ES-345 and ES-355 and later the ES-336 and ES-339, among others), as well as competitors from companies such as Epiphone. Fender even got into the game with the Telecaster Thinline, Starcaster, and other models.

Semi-hollow-body guitars are generally about as deep as a solid-body guitar (that is to say, substantially thinner than most true hollow-body guitars) and feature a solid block of wood that runs through the center of the guitar from the neck to the end pin, with hollow sides or wings. Most often, the neck is set or glued into the central body block, though a semi-hollow-body guitar could also have a neck-through design with hollow wings attached. (That's essentially what Les Paul's original Log guitar was.)

The result is a guitar that has aspects of a solid-body—good sustain, brighter sound, resistance to feedback— with some of the resonance and richness of a hollow-body guitar. Various models feature a center section that is more or less solid. In some cases, the wood core fills the space between the thin top of the guitar and the thin back; in other cases, the core doesn't extend all the way to the back of the guitar, allowing the back of the guitar to vibrate as in a hollow-body. And, in some cases, the wood core stops behind the guitar's bridge, rather than extending all the way to the bottom rim/end pin of the instrument. As a general rule, the smaller or less extensive the wood core and the less completely it fills the center portion of the instrument, the more like a hollow-body the guitar will be. The thicker and more complete the core is, the more like a solid-body the guitar will be.

Table 1.1   The Properties of Guitar Types

	Hollow-Body	Semi-Hollow-Body	Solid-Body
Sustain	As long as, or slightly less than, a similar acoustic guitar.	Longer sustain than an acoustic guitar.	Long sustain.
Brightness	Typically dark or acoustic guitar-like.	Medium bright.	Typically quite bright compared to other types, but depends on species and densities of the neck and body woods, any chambering or weight relief, and how the guitar is constructed.
Resonance	About the same as, or slightly less than, a similar acoustic guitar.	Medium resonance.	Comparatively little resonance compared to other types, but depends on species and densities of the neck and body woods, any chambering or weight relief, and how the guitar is constructed.
Durability	About the same as a similarly designed acoustic guitar.	Nearly as durable as a solid-body.	Very durable.
Overall Acoustical Tone	Round, rich, nearly as deep and full as a similar acoustic guitar.	Full, rich, with some acoustic guitar qualities and some solid-body guitar qualities.	Thinner compared to other types, but depends on species and densities of woods, any chambering or weight relief, and how the guitar is constructed.
Feedback Resistance	Little resistance to feedback.	Moderate resistance to feedback.	Good resistance to feedback.

Neck Construction

In the past few years, I've built several solid-body guitars. In the process, I swapped out the necks on the instruments a number of times, trying different neck thicknesses, shapes, and carves and different neck and fingerboard woods. It will come as no surprise that each change made a difference, and of course, the thicknesses and the wood species were primary factors in those differences. But what I was quite surprised to notice was how much of the overall tone of the instrument came from the neck. Had you asked me before, I would have said that the majority of the sound came from the body of the guitar, with a lesser percentage from the neck. Now, my opinion is quite different. In fact, I would rate the neck as at least an equal contributor with the body in producing the tone of a guitar—solid-body, hollow-body, or semi-hollow-body, but especially with solid bodies.

So, does the construction of a neck affect its tonal contribution or have any other effect? Though guitar necks are almost all made in similar fashion—they're carved in one way or another from a rough wooden neck blank —(excluding necks that aren't made from wood, of course!)—what differs is how that blank is constructed. A neck blank may be a single piece of wood including the fingerboard or with a separate fingerboard on top, or it might be laminated from multiple side-by-side pieces of wood usually with a separate fingerboard on top. The headstock may be part of the same piece(s) of wood as the neck, or it may be attached to the neck shaft with a glue joint. If the neck has a separate fingerboard, the truss rod is probably installed behind it. If there is no separate fingerboard, the truss rod is usually installed from the back of the neck, with a wooden strip added later to cover the slot required for the installation.

Although a neck made from multiple pieces of wood might be stronger than one carved from a single piece of wood (excluding the fingerboard), many players feel that a single-piece neck resonates better and produces better tone. Taking this one step further, how the wood for the neck is cut may influence its tone, resonance, and sustain. Although most neck wood is flat sawn (cut parallel to the tree's growth rings), many players and builders believe that quarter-sawn wood (cut at 90 degrees to the tree's growth rings) is superior from a tonal standpoint. We'll look at more about this in the next chapter.

Neck Carve and Size

The thickness of the neck shaft can also make a difference in the tone. Although a slim, super-fast neck may be comfortable to shred on, it will have a different tone from a thick, fat, "baseball bat"–carve neck shaft. As a general rule (there are always exceptions), the fuller and rounder the shape of the neck shaft, the fuller and rounder the guitar's tone will be, with all other things being equal (though "all other things" never are equal). Likewise, the thicker the fingerboard is—say, a thick slab of rosewood on a maple neck versus a thin sheet of rosewood on the same maple neck—the more it will contribute to the tone.

The actual carve of the neck—whether it is a half-circle "C" shape that doesn't diminish in size from the body to the nut, a "V" shape that starts thin at the nut and gets increasingly thicker as it approaches the body, or some other shape entirely—doesn't affect the tone, other than from the standpoint that certain carves result in more overall wood being used to make the neck versus others. In other words, it's not the shape of the neck that affects the tone, it's the amount of wood required to make that shape that makes a difference.

But the tradeoff with neck thicknesses is playing comfort. Players with smaller hands generally don't enjoy a huge neck carve, for example. And, thick or thin, you have to feel comfortable with a neck shape in order to play well on the guitar. The goal is to arrive at a compromise: Find a neck shape and size that fits your hand well, while still having as much wood as possible for tone production and sustain.

Truss Rod

Virtually all electric guitars include a truss rod of some sort—a threaded metal rod or other assembly inside a channel in the neck shaft that can be tightened or loosened to help stabilize the neck against the considerable tension of the strings and to help straighten the neck should it bow due to humidity changes. Tonally, there's not much you can do with or about a truss rod (without major surgery or completely changing the neck), but it is worth being aware that certain truss-rod types—such as those that use side-adjust mechanisms or multiple rods—may add weight/mass to the neck, which can change the balance of the guitar and how the neck resonates.

Scale Length

The scale length of a guitar—defined as the distance from where the strings contact the nut to where they contact the bridge—can play a factor in the feel of a guitar and the string tension, but it also makes a tonal difference. There are two common scale lengths in use by manufacturers today: 24¾ inches, which is the standard Gibson scale length; and 25½ inches, which is the standard Fender scale length. The vast majority of guitar manufacturers use one of these scale lengths on their various models, with one exception; many of Paul Reed Smith's guitar models use a 25-inch scale length. (A few of the company's models use 24¾-inch or 25½-inch scale lengths.) Beyond this, other scale lengths have been used, such as 22.5 inches on the Fender Duo-Sonic, 23.5 inches on the Gibson Byrdland, and 24.6 inches on the Gretsch 6120. "Specialty" guitars such as baritone guitars, can have 27-inch or even longer scale lengths.

You wouldn't think that a difference of less than an inch between the two industry-standard scale lengths could make that much of a difference in the tone or feel of a guitar, but it certainly does. As a general rule, given the same string gauges, a shorter scale length will result in lower string tension than a longer scale length. With a longer scale length, a given string has to be pulled tighter to produce a certain pitch versus achieving the same pitch with the same gauge string at a shorter scale length. This has implications for playing comfort, sustain, and ease of string bending/finger vibrato, but it also has tonal implications. With a longer scale length and therefore (all other things being equal) higher tension, the result will be a brighter sound and a tighter bottom end. Scale length and the resulting string tension difference is a part of why Les Pauls have that classic, thick, low-end "chunk" and Strats and Teles have that wonderful bright "twang."

Synthetics and Other Materials

Although most guitars are constructed of wood, it's not true that *every* guitar is made from wood. The body and/or the neck might be made from synthetics, such as carbon fiber or Lucite, from metal, or from a combination of these materials along with wood. From Dan Armstrong clear Lucite guitars to Travis Bean guitars with metal necks, from all-aluminum Velenos to hollow metal Trussarts with wood necks, from wood Zemaitis guitars with engraved metal tops to carbon-fiber reinforced Parkers, from synthetic Steinbergers to Moses graphite necks, nontraditional materials have been used to construct guitars and guitar bodies and necks for decades.

Each of these materials has its own sound—whether it contributes a tonal color or its contribution is to remain tonally neutral—and other characteristics. For example, materials such as solid metal can add a substantial amount of sustain and brightness to the tone. Synthetics may be used on their own for guitar components or used to strengthen wooden components. Typically, synthetics don't have a significant amount of tonal color of their own; this allows them to be a neutral platform for the strings to vibrate upon and for the pickups to work from. Many players enjoy this, as it gives them a clean base from which to build a tonal palette, especially where a lot of effects processing will be employed.

Pickup Placement and Routing

Other guitar design and construction parameters can influence the final tone produced by the guitar. On the design side, where the pickups are placed under the strings has a big impact. For the bridge pickup (if there is one), the closer to the bridge the pickup is located, the brighter and thinner the tone will be. Moving that pickup farther away from the bridge will add beef to the tone and reduce high-frequency content. Angling the bridge pickup, as is traditionally done with Strat- and Tele-style guitars and as Eddie Van Halen pioneered when he built his first humbucker-equipped Strat-style guitars, individually changes the location on each string where the pickup senses the vibration. This usually results in the bass strings being picked up farther from the bridge for a thicker sound, and the high strings being picked up closer to the bridge for a brighter tone. Some players and manufacturers reverse the angle of the bridge pickup so that the bass strings are sensed closer to the bridge for brighter, twangier sound, and the high strings are sensed farther away for thicker sound.

Neck-pickup placement (assuming there is a neck pickup) is likewise an important consideration. There is a sweet-spot location under the strings where the best combination of harmonics will be seen by the neck pickup's magnetic aperture. The ideal location is often in the same place where the 24th fret is (or would be) on the guitar's neck. This means that the neck-pickup placement on a 24-fret guitar is arguably compromised from a tonal perspective, especially if the neck pickup is larger, such as a dual-coil humbucker design. This can be easily demonstrated with a guitar model that is offered in both 22- and 24-fret versions, such as the Paul Reed Smith Custom 22 and Custom 24—basically the same guitar, just with two extra frets and, by necessity, a slightly relocated neck pickup on the Custom 24 model. On the 22-fret version the neck pickup is a bit farther from the bridge and will have a slightly rounder tone with a different harmonic composition from the neck pickup on the 24-fret guitar. The tonal difference is apparent to some players; other players don't hear a huge difference, and still others are willing to overlook the difference in order to have the extra two frets on a full two-octave fingerboard.

Middle pickups are sometimes simply centered between the neck and bridge pickups, though there is a harmonically optimum location for that pickup as well. Going a step beyond that, how the guitar is routed for the pickups—with routs just large enough to contain the pickups or with a "swimming pool" rout that removes a much larger amount of wood from the body—along with the control cavity rout or routs can definitely impact the tone and resonance of a solid-body electric guitar.

Other Design Considerations

The design and construction considerations don't stop there. The hardware selection used, such as the type of bridge, frets, and tuners; the materials the nut and frets are made from—all of these items and more go into determining the tone produced by a guitar. And how that hardware is installed, such as how much of the body must be carved away in order to install a tremolo tailpiece, is certainly also a factor in the sound of the instrument. We'll be discussing all of these items in greater detail in the next few chapters.

Table 1.2   Guitar Types and Construction Tonal Factors

Tone Factor	Tonal Contribution
Guitar type, design, and construction	Major
Chambering/weight relief	Moderate
Carved versus flat top	Subtle to major, depending on guitar construction
Set neck/bolt-on neck/neck through	Moderate
Neck construction	Moderate
Neck carve and size	Moderate
Truss rod	Subtle
Scale length	Major
Body/neck materials	Major
Pickup placement	Moderate

Wood

THOUGH GUITARS HAVE BEEN MADE FROM MANY DIFFERENT TYPES of materials—aluminum, synthetics, carbon fiber, steel, Lucite, and more—the vast majority are made from one or more varieties of woods. A wide array of woods is used for guitar construction, each of which offers a luthier or manufacturer a tonal color, and in many cases a visual option, that he or she can use when crafting an instrument.

Tracheids

Where would guitars be without tracheids? Much more limp, for one thing! A tracheid is a long, thick-walled, tubular cell in a vascular plant (such as a tree) that carries water and nutrients from the roots to the rest of the plant, and that provides structural support. Part of how a tree grows and supports itself involves how the tracheids (and other cells) die, dry out, and ultimately become building blocks for the structure for the plant. How the tracheids resonate and carry vibrations is one of the characteristics of a tonewood, which is said to contribute to the sound of an instrument.

There are four primary places where wood makes an appearance on and contributes to the tone of most electric guitars.

▷ **Body back.** The back of a solid-body is typically the largest piece of wood in the instrument, and it contributes greatly to the overall tone. In fact, the "back" may comprise the entire guitar body, if there is no separate top glued on the body. In semi-hollow-body and even more so in hollow-body guitars, the back works in conjunction with the top to develop resonance and tone in the instrument.

▷ **Body top.** When a solid-body guitar has a separate top, there could be two reasons for it. First, the top may be purely cosmetic; a highly figured piece of wood may be used to give the guitar a beautiful appearance. Second, the top could be a different type of wood from the back, providing a different tonal response. For example, a maple top (with a brighter sound) might be combined with a mahogany back (with a darker sound) to create an instrument with a balanced response. In the case of a semi-hollow-body or full hollow-body electric guitar, the top is where a lot of the tone is developed—just like on an acoustic guitar.

▷ **Neck shaft and headstock.** Because of the way in which the neck supports and carries the strings, it is responsible for contributing a large amount to the resonance and vibration of a guitar. It's immediately noticeable—in a "live" guitar, when the strings are struck you can feel the entire neck spring to life with vibration. Personally, I enjoy this; the guitar seems to give back to the tone and sustain, as opposed to simply being a platform on which the strings vibrate. Other players, however, feel that a less resonant neck may be better, that the strings may sustain longer and with a different tone if they are essentially terminated at the nut and the bridge, without transferring vibrations into the wood of the guitar. (This was a big trend in the late 1970s and into the 1980s, with guitars featuring dense woods, heavy brass bridges—some mounted to heavy brass sustain blocks inset into the body—brass nuts, and so on.) Of course, if the body and neck aren't resonating, it may be, in fact, that they are soaking up the string vibrations and therefore deadening the tone and sustain of the instrument.

▷ **Fingerboard.** Depending on how the neck is constructed, it may or may not have a separate glued-on fingerboard. And if there is a separate fingerboard, it may or may not be made from the same type of wood as the rest of the neck. This can have a noticeable effect on the tone of the instrument. For example, a one-piece maple neck might have a bright sound with strong attack. Adding an East Indian rosewood fingerboard on top of the maple neck might round out the sound and make it warmer on the top end, whereas adding an ebony fingerboard might make the sound even brighter.

A guitar designer who knows the characteristics of various types of wood can use this to his advantage to craft the tone he wants from the instrument. For example, I've used solid, one-piece East Indian rosewood necks on several instruments I've built. But even though the sound has full, punchy midrange, there can sometimes be a lack of top-end articulation. When I constructed one recent guitar, I used a one-piece rosewood neck but capped it with an ebony fingerboard, resulting in the best of both worlds: the rich midrange of rosewood with the articulation and high-end sparkle of ebony.

And as a player, if you know the tonal characteristics of woods, it can help you find a starting point for selecting the best instrument for your needs and desires. Although there is no guarantee that a piece of wood will have exactly the tone or response you expect—every tree is different, and each piece of wood made from that tree will also be unique—each species of tree still has basic characteristics that you can use as a guide for beginning a search.

Types of Wood

There are some basic characteristics of various wood types that can be taken as a fairly reliable indicator of what sort of tone a piece of wood will produce. For example, the denser the wood, the brighter the sound will likely be. Likewise, a harder wood will probably have a brighter sound than a softer wood. Each species of wood has characteristics such as its range of density, stiffness, pore size, oiliness, and so on. All of these contribute to the tone it will produce when used to make a musical instrument.

Hard or Soft?

The difference between hardwood and softwood may not be what you think. (Here's a clue: It has nothing to do with how hard the wood is.) By definition, hardwoods come from deciduous trees—that is, trees that lose their leaves each year. (Examples include maple, mahogany, ash, and many more.) Softwoods come from conifers, which have needles and usually stay green year-round. (Examples include pine, spruce, and others.)

In general terms, hardwoods tend to have higher density and are therefore heavier and harder than softwoods. However, this is just a loose rule. Some species, such as basswood, which is technically considered a hardwood (because it's deciduous), are soft and lightweight.

Both types of woods are used in electric-guitar construction, though hardwoods tend to dominate for most applications.

A quick search through any guitar-centric catalog, magazine, website, or forum will quickly reveal that the majority of guitars are made using alder, ash, and mahogany (often with maple tops) for bodies. You'll also quickly discover that the most common woods for necks are maple or mahogany with maple or rosewood fretboards. But when looking at all the guitars on the market, it becomes apparent that a wide array of woods is used in manufacturing the instruments.

In fact, the list of woods used to make guitars is steadily increasing as luthiers and manufacturers find new tonewoods and as they are forced to find substitutes for tonewoods that have become endangered or otherwise hard to come by. Of course, cost also plays a role in the woods that are selected for a specific guitar model, particularly with mass-produced or entry-level instruments.

> **Afromosia.** Afromosia is an African hardwood that is often used for countertops and butcher blocks. It is sometimes used for guitar necks, where it provides similar tone to hard maple but offers a naturally darker finish color without the need for staining.

> **Agathis.** Also known as *kauri*, this is a wood that grows in rainforests in southeast Asia and that, depending on the specific piece of wood, may have characteristics ranging from similar to alder to similar to mahogany. Typically, agathis is used for bodies for inexpensive solid-body guitars.

> **Alder.** A lightweight wood with good stiffness resulting in a balanced, full sound with tight highs and broad lows, sometimes with slightly scooped mids and strong lower mids, and also with moderate attack and good sustain. Alder has been used extensively by Fender for the bodies of Telecasters and Stratocasters and is also popular as a body wood with many other manufacturers.

> **Ash.** The type of ash used in guitars is usually northern hard ash, which is a very hard and dense (and therefore heavy) wood. (See below for soft ash, also known as *swamp ash*.) It has a bright tone with excellent sustain. It grows in the central United States and generally has a white-yellow/cream color. It has open pores, making it harder to finish. Ash is used frequently for guitar bodies and sometimes for solid-body tops.

Basswood. Basswood grows in the eastern United States, in the Great Lakes region, in Canada, and in the Appalachians. It is a lightweight, resonant, soft wood that is often used for guitar bodies, especially for "shredder" guitars, where it provides a full, warm, midrange-oriented tone that works well for high-gain styles. It first came to popularity during the "hair metal" boom of the 1980s and remains popular with manufacturers such as Ibanez.

Bloodwood. Also known as *satine* and with color ranging from orange-red to deep red (which darkens with age), this aptly named wood is sometimes used for guitar bodies, where it may be laminated with a lighter wood to combat its tendency to warp. It is also used for fingerboards and for inlays. Bloodwood is a dense, hard wood with straight, fine grain and a bright top-end tone.

Bocote. Also known as *Mexican rosewood* (though it is from the species *Cordia* and is therefore not a rosewood), Bocote is a dense, tight-grained yellowish or reddish wood with dark and light brown streaks. It has strong sustain and warm tone and is sometimes used as a neck wood in combination with complementary fingerboard woods.

Brazilwood. See *pernambuco*.

Bubinga. Also known as *African rosewood* (though it is not a true rosewood), bubinga has been used in guitar making for many years—Rickenbacker has long used it for fingerboards, and it is commonly used for bass necks and occasionally bass bodies. It is a stiff wood with balanced tone that is also used for guitar necks and sometimes guitar bodies.

Camphor burl. A wood from Southeast Asia—though it has been cultivated in certain parts of the southern United States—with a light yellowish to brownish color. It is primarily used for furniture and chests and veneers, but it is occasionally used for guitar bodies and solid-body tops, where the burl results in intense figuring. For a burl, it is remarkably stable. (See the sidebar "Types of Figured Maples" later in this chapter for more on burls.)

Canary. Also known as *arariba*, canary is a yellow wood with red streaks. It is not quite as dense, heavy, or bright sounding as maple. Canary is used for guitar necks and occasionally for fingerboards. Canary wood grows in Panama, Ecuador, and southern Brazil.

Claro walnut. *Claro* is a term that is often misused in conjunction with walnut—it is applied to black or California walnut, which is incorrect usage. The word *claro* means "bright" or "clear" in Spanish. Claro walnut actually refers to wood that comes from the lower part of the stumps of orchard walnut trees grown along the West Coast of the United States. It does not refer to a specific species, since these orchards typically are based around walnut created by grafting English walnut to either black walnut or California walnut. The wood from the lower bole (stump) of the tree, in the area where the graft took place, will have a brown and tan swirled variegated color with an appearance almost like marble. Claro walnut is often used for gunstocks as well as for guitar bodies and tops, where it has similar sonic characteristics to black walnut.

Ebony. Ebony is an extremely dense, heavy, and hard wood, with a very bright tonality. It is used mainly for guitar fingerboards, though occasionally an entire neck will be made from it. There are a variety of types, including African, Asian/Malaysian, Madagascar, Macassar, and Nigerian, which share many of the same characteristics. Ebony ranges in color from brown with dark streaks to intensely black, sometimes with brown, reddish, or yellowish streaks.

Goncalo alves. This dense wood from Brazil has a tan color with dark streaks. It is sometimes referred to as *zebrawood*, along with several other species of wood. It is used for necks and fingerboards, where it provides a balanced tone and good sustain.

Holly. Holly is said to be the whitest naturally occurring wood that is available. It is used for peghead overlays on certain Gibson Les Pauls and other models. In this application, it does not affect the tone of the instrument.

Imbuia. Also spelled *imbuya* and also known as *Brazilian walnut* (though it is not a true walnut species), this southern Brazilian wood ranges from olive-colored to dark brown, sometimes with dark streaks, burl, and deep figuring. It is a hard and heavy wood that has a bright sound with strong low end and excellent clarity. It can be used for guitar bodies and for necks.

Koa. A relatively scarce wood that grows only between 300 and 7,000 feet on five Hawaiian islands. Koa has strength and density characteristics similar to mahogany, though it tends to have a darker tonality. The wood is dark brown, with some pieces sporting dark streaks and/or flame figuring. Koa is used for necks and bodies.

Korina. Korina, also known as *limba*, grows in West Africa. It first came to prominence in the 1950s, when Gibson used it for the then-radical Explorer and Flying V guitar models. There are two varieties: white, which is light-yellow colored, and black, which is variegated, with black streaks and figuring lines. Korina is quite similar in many characteristics to mahogany, with medium weight and density. Tonally, it is also similar to mahogany, though with a bit of added depth and richness in the midrange.

Lacewood. A medium-weight Australian wood with a grain/figure that can resemble spots, lace, or reptile skin. It is most commonly used for solid-body tops or occasionally for entire bodies and necks, where it has a tone similar to alder.

Limba. See *korina*.

Mahogany. There are several varieties of mahogany used in making guitars. Tropical American mahogany is the most desired for its resonant tone, but this species is becoming increasingly scarce. As a replacement, perhaps the most prevalent variety is African mahogany (from West and Central Africa), with Honduras (from southern Mexico, Central America, and northern South America) mahogany also making a strong showing. Recently, beautiful "ribbon" and other figured varieties of mahogany have been making appearances, primarily being used for backs on solid-body guitars with figured maple tops.

Mahogany is a medium- to heavy-weight, medium-density wood with a reddish brown color. Expect a balanced, resonant tone with excellent sustain, thick bottom end, rich midrange, and controlled, warm top end. Mahogany is used for solid guitar bodies, solid-body backs, and necks, where it is always paired with a complementary fingerboard wood—usually rosewood or ebony.

Maple. Maple is a common hardwood that is used for everything from floors to furniture and from cabinets to bowling pins. It's also a primary wood in the luthier's and the guitar manufacturer's arsenal. It is commonly used for necks; fingerboards; carved and flat solid-body tops; hollow-body and semi-hollow-body sides, backs, and tops; and even for complete solid bodies, though some players might find a solid-body made from 100 percent maple to be too heavy and too bright. There are two main varieties used in making electric guitars: Eastern hard rock maple and Western maple (also known as *soft maple* or *big leaf maple*). Both types are quite strong and dense, though soft maple isn't as dense or as heavy as Eastern hard rock maple.

Eastern hard rock maple comes from New England, the Great Lakes region, and eastern Canada. It provides a very bright, crisp tone with excellent sustain and resonance. It is used for bodies, necks, and fingerboards.

Western maple comes from southern Canada and the western United States. It is also quite bright, though because it is less dense and heavy, it isn't quite as bright as Eastern hard rock maple. It is used for guitar bodies, as well as for tops. Most of the figured maple (see the following "Types of Figured Maples" sidebar) that is used in guitars is Western maple.

Figure Ratings

In some cases, a manufacturer or wood supplier may give figured pieces of maple (and some other types of figured wood) a rating that arbitrarily indicates how figured a particular piece might be. The ratings are often expressed on an "A" scale, where an A piece of wood has a certain amount of figuring, AA has more, AAA and AAAA still more, and so on. This type of "A" rating is generally subjective, based only on someone's opinion of how figured the piece of wood looks compared to other pieces of figured wood. Such ratings are purely of cosmetics and do not indicate the tonal or structural desirability of the wood.

Morado. See *pau ferro.*

Nato. Sometimes known as *Eastern mahogany*, nato is the name used for the wood from the *Mora* family of trees, which grow in Latin America, from southern Mexico to Argentina. Nato has characteristics somewhat similar to mahogany, though it is not as highly regarded as a tonewood. It is an inexpensive, plentiful wood that is available in large pieces. In guitars, it is used to make inexpensive, entry-level import instruments.

Ovangkol. Also known as *mozambique, shedua, amazoue,* and *amazakoue,* ovangkol is from the same family as bubinga. It grows in West Africa and ranges in color from yellowish to reddish brown, sometimes with darker streaks—occasionally with a purplish hue that makes it resemble rosewood. It is tonally similar to rosewood, with a bit more top-end sparkle.

Padauk. Also spelled variously as *padouk* and *paduak* (among other spellings), this African wood—it grows in Nigeria, Cameroon, and the Congo—offers a combination of a warm orangish-brown color, medium-heavy weight, and a tone that is somewhat warmer than maple. Padauk is used for guitar bodies and necks.

Pau ferro. Also known as *Santos rosewood* and *Bolivian rosewood* (though it is not a true rosewood), pau ferro grows in Bolivia and Brazil. It is an oily wood that can sometimes cause allergic reactions, though these often diminish with time/desensitization. It is used primarily for fingerboards, though occasionally for necks. Pau ferro offers feel and tone that fall somewhere between rosewood and ebony.

Types of Figured Maples

More so than perhaps any other wood used for guitar construction, maple is available with a variety of exotic-looking grains and deep figuring. An entire catalog of different types of figuring (which tend to be visual only and, according to many builders, do not affect tone) is commonly available.

Bird's-eye. Figured maple in which the pattern resembles small swirls or "eyes." Though it may look a bit like burl (see the following paragraph), there are no knots in the bird's-eye pattern. No one knows what causes bird's-eye figuring in maple, though it occurs most commonly in the Eastern hard rock variety. There are web discussion forum–spread rumors that bird's-eye maple can be unstable, but aside from its cosmetics, most players and builders find that bird's-eye maple has the same stability and tonal characteristics as unfigured maple.

Burl/burly. A burl is a deformity in the grain pattern in the tree's growth, caused by stress. This results in a very unusual, highly figured wood that can be difficult to work with due to the presence of knots. Though burls are most commonly found in redwood, some maple and other types of wood also develop burls. The color of burl maple can vary from the usual yellowish, "vanilla ice cream" maple color to darker and lighter colors, and there may be voids (gaps) in the wood.

Curly. Another name for *flame maple*.

Fiddleback. A synonym for *flame maple*, though fiddleback maple is sometimes described as having tightly striped figuring similar to that often found on the back of vintage violins.

Flame. Maple in which the figuring has become wavy and distorted into a "chatoyant" pattern. (*Chatoyancy* is an optical reflection pattern—commonly known as *cat's eye*—found in certain gemstones. In woodworking, a similar visual effect is found in finished wood where the figure has taken on a three-dimensional aspect.) Flame and other figuring is not a result of the grain of the wood. Instead, the optical pattern (figuring) shows up perpendicular to the grain of the wood, depending on how it has been cut.

In flame maple, the growth of the wood fibers results in visual waves and stripes, which can range from straight and narrow to wide, rippling, and undulating. The figuring in flame maple is entirely an optical characteristic, and therefore cosmetic, and it does not affect any other physical or tonal characteristic of the wood compared to non-figured maple.

Quilt/quilted. An optical figuring of some maple that has been flat sawn. The figure appears as a quilt pattern, often said to resemble rippling water, especially when the wood is stained. The figuring is purely cosmetic and does not affect any other physical or tonal characteristic of the wood compared to un-figured maple.

Spalted. Wood from a dead tree, or occasionally a highly stressed living tree, that has been attacked by a fungus, resulting in unusual coloring, often with accompanying black lines. Spalted wood can be soft and crumbly, so it is generally reserved for a thin top that is glued onto a thick back, though sometimes a piece will be found with enough stability to make an entire solid guitar body. In some cases, "punky" or crumbly spalted wood may be saturated in glue to stabilize it.

Tiger stripe. Another name for *flame maple*, sometimes described as having wider figuring bands (stripes).

Pernambuco. A dense Brazilian wood (it is also known as *Brazilwood*) commonly used for high-end violin bows. It is occasionally used as a neck wood for guitars. It has an orange-red, coppery color. Due to over-harvesting, pernambuco is on the endangered list, though it is not on the prohibited list as of this writing. (In fact, the shortage of pernambuco is one factor that has led to the adoption of carbon-fiber violin bows.) Pernambuco offers excellent resonance and sustain, with a rich tone similar to rosewood.

Pine. Pine is a light, soft wood that grows in the western United States. It was used for the bodies of some of the original electric guitars, including Les Paul's "Log," early Telecasters, and others, where it provided good balance and resonance but was found to be too soft to be durable enough for production instruments.

Poplar. One of the original woods used for the production of solid-body guitars, poplar grows in the eastern and southern United States. It is slightly heavier than alder, with similar tonal characteristics.

Purpleheart. A very hard, dense wood that offers good sustain and balanced tone with strong bottom end. Purpleheart is found in Central and South America. It is used for necks, bodies, and fingerboards—and it's purple!

Redwood. A wood native to Northern California, also known as *sequoia*, with a reddish color and sometimes with deep figuring, including flame or curl and burl. Though more commonly used for acoustic guitars, redwood is used for tops on solid bodies and occasionally for full bodies. It is lightweight with good stability. (There's a reason why it's used for picnic tables!) Redwood offers balanced, warm tone with solid low end.

Rosewood. Rosewood comprises the large family of *Dalbergia* species (including around 300 subspecies), members of which grow in tropical and subtropical regions in many parts of the world, including India, Indonesia, Africa, South America, and Central America. The name comes from the fact that the cut wood has an aroma similar to roses. The heartwood (the dense middle portion of the tree trunk) of rosewood trees ranges from reddish to dark brown to almost black; the sapwood (the softer, recently formed outer portion of the tree trunk, which carries nutrients throughout the plant) can be yellowish or almost white.

Rosewood is typically quite oily, which means that it does not take a finish well—rosewood necks and fingerboards are almost always left unfinished. (Some players love the feel of unfinished rosewood necks and refer to rosewood as *crackwood*—as in, once you play a guitar with an unfinished rosewood neck, nothing else feels as good, and you always want another....)

Rosewood is very dense and strong, with excellent resonance and with a well-balanced, warm tone. Within this general description, there are, of course variations among the numerous species. It is mainly used for fingerboards, although solid rosewood necks have become increasingly common from builders such as Paul Reed Smith and others, and there have even been examples of guitar bodies or entire guitars—such as a Fender Telecaster model—made from solid rosewood.

Rosewood is very slow growing, sometimes taking 300 years to reach maturity. Because of this and because of overharvesting, many species have become scarce or endangered. Some species are protected under the Lacey Act and CITES and have become extremely rare. (See the following "Types of Rosewood" sidebar.)

Types of Rosewood

African blackwood. A purplish to nearly black rosewood from East Africa, often with both darker stripes and yellowish stripes. Very dense and difficult to work. Used for fingerboards.

African rosewood. See *bubinga*.

Bois de Rose. A burgundy-colored type of rosewood from Madagascar, often with darker stripes. Used for fingerboards.

Bolivian rosewood. See *pau ferro*.

Brazilian kingwood. A species of rosewood from Brazil, often with variegated shades of purple, yellow, reddish-brown, and more. Used for binding and fingerboards.

Brazilian rosewood. An endangered species of rosewood from Brazil. Dark brown with dark streaks. Brazilian rosewood is among the most prized musical instrument woods for its rich tonality and excellent resonance. For guitars, it is mainly used for fingerboards and sometimes for entire necks. Brazilian rosewood is protected under the Lacey Act and CITES. (See the "CITES and the Lacey Act" sidebar later in this chapter.)

Brazilian tulipwood. A yellowish member of the rosewood family from Brazil that is sometimes used for fingerboards.

Cocobolo. A species of Central American rosewood. It is extremely oily—to the point of sometimes staining hands and causing allergic reactions—and therefore difficult to work or shape and to glue. Some cocobolo is so dense that it sinks in water. It has been used for bass bodies as well as for guitar fingerboards, where it adds a distinct resonance and warmth.

East Indian rosewood. A readily available type of rosewood that is harvested in India or that is grown on plantations in Indonesia, where it is known as *sonokeling*. It is used for necks and especially for fingerboards.

Guatemalan rosewood. A reddish-brown rosewood species that is used for necks and fingerboards.

Honduras rosewood. A brownish-red to purplish type of rosewood from Belize often used for making marimba keys. Sometimes used for guitar fingerboards.

Kingwood. See *Brazilian kingwood*.

Madagascar rosewood. Several species of light to dark purplish rosewood from Madagascar that can also have yellowish stripes and dark stripes. Considered to be very similar to Brazilian rosewood. Used for fingerboards.

Malagasy rosewood. Variously described as the same thing as *Madagascar rosewood*, as a subset of Madagascar rosewood, or as a rare type of rosewood from Madagascar that is similar in characteristics to *Brazilian tulipwood*, though generally more reddish-brown in color. Used for fingerboards.

Mexican rosewood. See *bocote*.

Palisander. A species of rosewood from Madagascar. It is a close match for Brazilian rosewood and is in high demand for fingerboards.

Panama rosewood. A very rare and just recently documented species of rosewood found growing only in a small region of Panama. It has been used for necks.

Santo rosewood. See *pau ferro*.

Tulipwood. See *Brazilian tulipwood*.

Voamboana. A rare type of rosewood from Madagascar, similar to *Brazilian kingwood*. Sometimes used for fingerboards.

Sapele. Like *nato*, sapele is sometimes known as *Eastern mahogany*. It grows in Nigeria and the Ivory Coast. Often used for guitar necks on inexpensive instruments, sapele has characteristics almost identical to or slightly brighter than domestic (tropical American) mahogany. The figured variety is sometimes used for bodies and backs.

Snakewood. A dense, colorful reddish-brown wood found in Central and South America that is used for binding and inlays and occasionally for fingerboards.

Spruce. Most players think of spruce as a wood used for the tops of acoustic guitars. And it's true that because it is so soft, spruce is rarely used for making solid-body electric guitars, though Parker Guitars does make models with Sitka spruce bodies. (A hard composite "shell" is put on the spruce body to strengthen and protect it.) However, spruce is also used to make the acoustic guitar–like tops and backs of some semi-hollow-body or hollow-body guitars. In this application, both solid and laminated spruce sheets are used. As with acoustic guitar soundboards, a solid spruce top (made from a single piece or two bookmatched pieces of spruce) will generally provide a richer tone. A laminated top (sort of like a sheet of plywood) made from several thin layers of spruce will be stronger but will not vibrate as freely.

There are two spruce varieties commonly used in guitar making: *Sitka* (a.k.a. *Canadian*) *spruce* and *red spruce*. Sitka is generally believed to be a superior tonewood with a bigger sound. Sitka spruce is also believed to "open up" as it ages, improving in its tone over time and as it is played.

Spruce is a soft wood but remarkably stiff, which allows it to vibrate well. It typically has full low end and fairly bright top end with softer midrange.

Swamp ash. Though swamp ash is clearly a type of *ash*, it is treated as a different type of wood for our purposes, because, well, it is a very different type of wood compared to regular hard ash. The wood grows in the wet, swampy regions of the southeastern United States (thus the name). Swamp ash is generally a light wood with large open pores, though it can vary widely in weight and density based on where it comes from on the tree. Wood that comes from near the water line will typically be lighter and more resonant (and therefore perceived as tonally better by some players), while that from higher up the tree will be heavier, with less resonance and liveliness.

Swamp ash is used for guitar bodies as well as for solid-body tops and provides a balanced, resonant tone with good attack and high end. Because swamp ash grows in the United States, builders here tend to get first pick at the available wood, meaning that often non-U.S.-made swamp ash guitars will use pieces from higher on the tree.

Walnut. Walnut offers a chocolate-brown coloring with deep, dark figuring. It is the darkest natural wood species found in North America, with black walnut and California walnut being common examples. Walnut is a heavy, dense wood that has a tonality slightly darker than maple. It is used for necks and bodies.

Wenge. Pronounced "weng-gay," this is a heavy wood from Zaire and West Africa. Wenge has a deep black or chocolate-brown color. Its density provides good sustain, with strong upper mids and articulate attack. It is used for bodies, necks, and fingerboards. Because of its heavy weight, it is often employed as a layer or for layers in a multi-piece neck or body, rather than as an entire body or neck.

Zebrawood. A name applied to a variety of wood species, including *goncalo alves*. Zebrawood gets its name from its appearance, with alternating thin light tan and dark brown or black streaks. It is a dense, heavy wood with a tone similar to maple; it comes from central Africa. Zebrawood is a threatened species due to overharvesting, but it is not prohibited as of this writing.

Ziricote. Also known as *Mexican ebony*, ziricote is a rare type of wood from the Yucatán Peninsula. Ziricote is dark brown in color with intense darker figuring. It is used mainly for fingerboards.

Cutting Wood

There are several ways in which a piece of wood can be cut from a log or a larger chunk of wood. The first is *flat sawn*, where the growth rings of the tree are parallel to the surface of the board. The second, *quarter sawn*, also known as *edge grained*, is where the wood is cut so that the growth rings are perpendicular to the board's surface. This is done by cutting a log into quarters lengthwise. Many players and manufacturers prefer quarter-sawn wood, particularly for necks, as it is believed to be more stable and toneful, with more uniform figuring and vibration characteristics. *Rift sawn* is a variation on quarter sawn, where a different angle is used to cut slabs or planks from the quartered log, resulting in less wasted wood.

Once the wood is cut into thick boards, a single piece may be large enough to make a complete part of an instrument (such as a back). With figured woods for guitar tops, it can be difficult to find a piece that is wide enough to comprise a one-piece top. (Because of this, one-piece tops often command a premium price.) In this case, two pieces are glued together side by side. The luthier or manufacturer will often slice the board in two, creating two thinner slices of wood. After slicing the board, the top piece is turned over, like opening a book, resulting in a mirror image of the figuring between the two pieces. This process is called *bookmatching* and is the standard approach used for creating two-piece figured tops, whether for solid bodies or for semi-hollow bodies or hollow bodies.

CITES and the Lacey Act

As concerns about the environment and preserving endangered species have increased, wood trading has likewise become increasingly regulated by treaties and domestic and international law. Unfortunately, several tonewoods are on the list of endangered species, most notably Brazilian and other species of rosewood.

The CITES treaty—the Convention on International Trade in Endangered Species (of wild flora and fauna)—was drafted in 1973 and provides protection for some 28,000 species of plants and 5,000 species of animals. The treaty is endorsed by 145 member nations. Since the agreement went into effect, only one of the species on the list has become extinct as a result of trade. CITES works through an international permit/authorization system that allows for the legal importation and exportation of protected species and materials to which countries voluntarily adhere. The treaty has served to significantly control trafficking in protected species, meaning that, for example, only Brazilian rosewood that can be proven to have been harvested before it was banned (which occurred in 1992) can be used to construct a guitar.

The Lacey Act, on the other hand, is a U.S. law signed into effect by President McKinley in 1900, with numerous amendments since then. Under the Lacey Act, it is illegal to import, export, sell, buy, or even transport or receive any plant or plant-derived material or any animal or animal-derived material protected under a law of the U.S., by a Native American tribe, or by a foreign law. This means that it would be illegal (with extremely harsh penalties) to, for example, sell Brazilian rosewood harvested after it was protected in 1992. The problem is proving the provenance of a piece of wood. How can a manufacturer prove when it was harvested, especially when the manufacturer probably did not harvest the wood themselves?

The Lacey Act is of grave concern for guitarists and guitar manufacturers, because it could potentially make it illegal to even *transport* a guitar made from protected materials. At the time of this writing, Gibson had just been raided and was being investigated for allegedly receiving undocumented woods. This could set an important precedent, because it is often very difficult to authenticate the origin of imported woods.

It remains to be seen how rigidly the Lacey Act will be enforced in the future. Will we need documentation to take a guitar containing a Brazilian rosewood fingerboard abroad? Will we be able to purchase or resell a guitar containing protected materials without unassailable proof of provenance? Only time will tell.

Weight

Visit a guitar forum and ask whether a light guitar or a heavy guitar is better…and then prepare yourself for a deluge of responses. You'll hear that light guitars are better, that heavy guitars are fine, and that weight really doesn't matter. Eventually, someone will point out that the iconic guitars from the classic "golden" vintage era—meaning the mid to late 1950s and early 1960s—made by Fender and Gibson typically were lighter than many of their modern counterparts. And this doesn't apply to just solid bodies; semi-hollow bodies and even hollow bodies have their own weight issues.

The theory will be put forth that today it is harder to find lightweight wood of the quality that was around back in those days. And this may be true—certainly many of the tonewoods that were commonly used in those days are much scarcer today. In certain eras, such as the 1970s, the weights of guitars went way up; Les Pauls from the 1970s often are several pounds heavier than their late-1950s counterparts. In this case, we're talking about as much as a 30 percent or 40 percent difference in weight for a guitar with very similar dimensions, meaning that the wood used has to be much denser. And, as we saw earlier in this chapter, denser wood is probably going to sound brighter, with less prominent midrange and tighter bottom end.

Still, it's very difficult to make a blanket statement about how the weight of the wood used to build a guitar affects the final tone. Wood is simply so variable in its density, weight, stiffness, pore size, and more, all of which affect the sound it creates. Having said that, many players do prefer a lighter guitar, feeling that it will resonate better and contribute positively to the sound. At the same time, many players find that heavier guitars provide excellent sustain with good punch and great clarity and top end.

In the end, though you can make generalizations about the weight of a guitar and its tone, it comes down to how the guitar functions as a whole—the wood used and its density, the other components, and that little touch of magic that seems required to make a guitar sing.

But one thing is for sure: It's definitely nicer to wear a guitar made from light wood if you're playing for hours at a time!

Finish

So you've got some great pieces of wood. They ring like a bell when struck, vibrating freely. Does it really make sense to wrap that resonating organic material in a tight skin of inert plastic or other synthetic coating? Doesn't that seem counterproductive?

There is, of course, an aesthetic aspect to a guitar's finish—raw wood can look good, but there's nothing like a beautiful finish, whether a solid color, a graphic, a sunburst, or a stain. But the main point behind a finish is more than aesthetic; it's to protect the wood and the guitar, both from wear and tear and from the effects of changing humidity. The key is to use a finish that provides adequate protection without being so thick or heavy that it damps the resonance of the wood.

There are several types of finishes in common use by luthiers and manufacturers today.

▷ **Dyes and stains.** If a guitar uses figured woods, then a stained finish is often used to bring out the grain and figuring. Stain or dye in and of itself won't affect the guitar's tone, but it's possible that a clear topcoat of another type of finish (such a polyurethane clear coat) will be applied over the stain, which may impact the tone.

▷ **Polyester.** A hard *catalyzed* (meaning the finish cures chemically rather than drying) synthetic finish used on many guitars from the 1970s through the 1990s. It is probably the hardest and toughest finish used for guitars, buffing out to a glass-like sheen, with good resistance to dings and scratches. Some players feel that the thick plastic-like finish deadens the response of the guitar—but no one says that polyester *has* to be a thick finish.

▷ **Polyurethane/urethane.** A modern synthetic finish that can be applied in quite thin coats. Urethane provides good protection and a glass-like shine and, if applied thinly enough, should not dampen the resonance of a guitar. Unfortunately, to save money, some companies put on thick poly coats, which makes the guitar easier to sand and buff, but that thick layer of finish can have a negative effect on tone and resonance.

▷ **Acrylic lacquer.** In the 1960s, Fender used acrylic lacquers—literally car paints—to finish their guitars. Acrylic lacquers use a synthetic resin, which is colorless and transparent, dissolved in thinner, resulting in a fast-drying finish. Acrylic lacquer has an advantage over nitrocellulose lacquer in that it does not yellow as it ages.

▷ **Nitrocellulose lacquer.** A solvent-based lacquer that provides a sturdy, durable finish that is easy to repair, since applying solvent will re-dissolve the finish. Many guitarists feel that nitrocellulose lacquer is ideal for supporting the tone of an instrument—in large part because almost all vintage and collectable instruments had nitro finishes. Nitro finishes wear and age nicely, in many cases improving with age.

The problem is that the way nitrocellulose lacquer finish works, the solvents evaporate as the freshly applied lacquer dries—and those solvents and fumes are hazardous and even potentially toxic. Special equipment and measures must be taken to ensure safety, which can be prohibitively expensive. Nitro was actually banned as a car finish, but it can still be legally used for furniture and some other applications.

It's worth noting that saying that a guitar has a nitrocellulose lacquer finish may or may not mean that the instrument uses only that type of lacquer. In fact, many modern nitro-finished guitars actually use the same undercoats, sealers, and/or fillers as poly-finished guitars, with the only nitro used being the top clear coats.

▷ **French polish.** A very, very thin shellac finish often used on classical guitars and violins. It is popular for delicate instruments because it can be applied thin enough not to impact the instrument's natural resonance. This may be the thinnest finish used on guitars, and it also may be the least durable. It also requires skill and practice to apply well, making it unsuitable for a production environment.

▷ **Oil.** Tung oil (which is pressed from the nut of the tung tree) is the finish that is used on gunstocks. It is sometimes used on guitars, particularly for necks. (Ernie Ball/Music Man is one manufacturer that uses an oil finish on their necks.) Technically, most oil finishes are a type of varnish, as they react to air, which cures them. Oil finishes are most commonly used on necks to provide an unfinished feel and response, but with a bit of protection from playing wear. In many cases an oil finish should be renewed (a tiny amount of oil lightly brushed on) annually to maintain the protection.

Breathable Finish

When nitrocellulose finishes are discussed with regard to guitars, someone will often say, "Nitro lets the wood breathe, since it's basically made from wood." The listeners or forum readers will nod their heads sagely at the obvious logic of this statement. Unfortunately, there's not much truth to it.

Although it's true that nitrocellulose lacquer uses cellulose, which is the same material as wood, the cellulose used actually comes from cotton, which is easier to work with.

But regardless of whether we're talking about wood or cotton, the "breathing" part is a myth. Nitrocellulose lacquer was developed by DuPont as an automotive finish that would seal and protect cars from the elements. It was intended to solidly encase the metal, not to let it "breathe," which would imply that moisture could get through and caused oxidation (rust). In the same way, nitrocellulose lacquer does not allow the wood in a guitar to "breathe."

To bust another myth, nitro finishes don't "cure" over a several-month period of time, as is popularly believed. (Nitro is not a catalyzed finish; it doesn't cure.) The finish dries as the solvents evaporate; the initial drying happens very quickly, but total evaporation of the solvents may take weeks or months. Because of this, the guitar may feel sticky to the touch until the finish is completely dry.

Many players hold out nitrocellulose lacquer as the best finish for a guitar tonally. Most manufacturers, however, state that any finish, if applied thinly enough, can be tonally transparent. The problem is that, as with many factors in the tone of a guitar, it's almost impossible to do a true apples-to-apples A/B comparison of two types of finish. The only way to do so would be to refinish the same guitar, but even then it would be impossible to have an identical performance on the instrument as the basis for the test.

Ultimately, the finish is probably a minor contributor or factor in the tone a guitar produces.

Table 2.1   Wood Tonal Factors

Tone Factor	Tonal Contribution
Body wood	Major
Neck wood	Major
Fingerboard wood	Subtle to moderate
Neck wood cut (flat sawn/quarter sawn)	Subtle
Wood weight	Subtle to moderate
Finish type and thickness	Subtle

Hardware

T HERE'S MORE TO A GUITAR THAN JUST WOOD! We need hardware to hold the strings on the guitar, to get it in tune, to divide the fretboard into discrete notes…even to hold the guitar up when we're standing (though I doubt anyone has ever debated the tonal merits of various types of strap buttons). In this chapter, we'll be looking at the hardware that comes in contact with and impacts the motion of the strings—electronics and pickups will be covered in the next chapter. Most of the hardware we'll be discussing will be made from one sort of metal or another, with one exception: the nut. Let's begin there.

String Nut

Okay, so I lied—a guitar's nut actually *can* be made of metal, which was a somewhat common practice in the late 1970s and early 1980s, when the trend was toward heavy hardware, with the idea of enhancing sustain through added mass. In those days, brass or sometimes steel nuts made their appearance, adding a bright tonality to the open strings. Nickel was also sometimes used for string nuts, and today it is possible to get a nut made from titanium. Some players and manufacturers feel that using metal for the nut makes the open strings sound more like fretted notes, because in both cases the string is terminated with metal.

A guitar may also use a roller nut, which often has round metal inserts (one per string) that rotate around a shaft or on bearings and allow the strings to move back and forth without snagging in order to improve tuning stability, especially with heavy tremolo use. There is always a danger with these types of nuts that the mechanism can vibrate or resonate in response to the string motion, which could reduce sustain and possibly damp the tone.

One other case where a guitar's nut might be metal is where a locking nut is employed to keep the strings clamped down during vigorous vibrato tailpiece use, with the best example being the Floyd Rose–style double-locking tremolo. A locking nut will change the tone of the open strings substantially, adding considerable brightness and possibly thinning out the bottom end.

But in almost every other case, a guitar's nut will be made from some sort of non-metal. The most popular materials are plastic of one type or another, Teflon- or graphite-impregnated synthetic material, Corian, artificial bone or ivory (typically a type of plastic), or real bone or ivory. Most of these sound quite similar, in fact, though there can be differences. For example, some say that Graph Tech's white TUSQ nut sounds slightly brighter than their black TUSQ nut. For another example, a wide range of plastics can be used to make string nuts; some of these function well, but others can deaden tone and sustain. Corian is a very hard material (yes, it's the same stuff that is used for many solid-surface kitchen countertops) that provides a tight, balanced tone.

I do agree with many players who feel that a bone nut offers a little something extra, tonewise. Bone and ivory are the traditional string nut materials, offering durability and a bright, full tone with excellent sustain. I have bone nuts on two of my guitars, and I was surprised by how much of a difference in tone there was between the bone nuts and the original plastic nuts they replaced.

Ostensibly, the nut only affects tone and sustain for the open strings. Once the string has been fretted, the nut is removed from the equation. But some players argue that there could still be some resonance and vibration that will pass through the nut, even for a fretted note. If there is a tonal effect on fretted notes when a different nut material is used, the effect will be minimal. On my guitars, I feel the overall sound of the guitar improved when the bone nuts were installed, but will I swear that there was a difference in the tone of the fretted notes? No—it probably was not enough for anyone to notice.

Frets

Speaking of frets, there are a couple of ways that a fret could impact the tone of a guitar. The first is the fret material. Logically, the harder the material, the brighter the tone will be, but experience does not always hold this out. For example, many players have compared stainless-steel frets versus the more traditional—and softer—nickel/silver frets, and they feel that the stainless frets sound subtly brighter. But most manufacturers do not feel that there is a noticeable change in tone when different fret materials are employed. There are other differences, such as stainless steel feeling smoother and wearing longer, but most say that fret material does not make a…well…*material* difference in the tone.

However, one Colorado-based "boutique" manufacturer, Crystal Frets, claims that their frets *do* make a big difference in the tone, stating that their pure quartz crystal frets eliminate the metal-on-metal distortion caused by steel strings on nickel or steel frets, resulting in clearer tone, longer sustain, and a warmer, fuller, more powerful tone as a result of the frets having "a density that prevents the string energy from going thru or around the fret." At this writing, only a few guitars had been made using these patented quartz frets, so the jury is still out on these claims.

Having said that, in my experience I have found that the size of the frets can have an impact on the tone. I recently re-fretted a Telecaster neck, going from the standard, small vintage-sized frets to quite large jumbo frets, and I immediately noticed that the tone was brighter with the larger frets. It wasn't a huge difference, but it was apparent to me.

Bridges and Tailpieces

A guitar's bridge and tailpiece (whether separate or as a one-piece combination) can be among the most important pieces of hardware from a string-vibration and tone-production standpoint. There are many different types of bridges and tailpieces found on electric guitars. They vary both with intended function as well as with the type of guitar on which they will be mounted. There are also many variations among each type, with commensurate tonal variations. In other words, there are lots of different bridges and tailpieces out there, each with its own sound!

Hollow-Body Bridges and Tailpieces

Most hollow-bodies use Tune-o-matic-style bridges, though the bridge will generally mount to a wooden plate that then sits on or is glued to the top of the guitar, rather than mounting directly to the guitar with thick metal studs, as on solid-body or semi-hollow-body instruments. (See the section "Tune-o-Matic" later in this chapter for more on this type of bridge.) Other hollow-bodies use bridges very similar to those found on archtop acoustic guitars, often made of ebony or rosewood, with the intent of maximizing the acoustic performance of the instrument with as little "electric" impact as possible, aside from making the organic sound louder.

Virtually all hollow-body guitars use some sort of floating trapeze tailpiece, which anchors to the endpin or end block of the guitar and extends over the face of the guitar toward the bridge. This minimizes any interference caused by the weight of a tailpiece on the top and allows the top to resonate more freely and to perform in a more acoustic guitar–like fashion. Because a trapeze tailpiece doesn't have the mass or solidity of a stop tailpiece, the tailpiece won't contribute any extra sustain to the guitar.

Even if a vibrato tailpiece is used on a hollow-body guitar, as with the Bigsby units used on many Gretsch models, the tailpiece anchors to the endpin, though it may place some weight on the guitar top.

Solid-Body and Semi-Hollow-Body Bridges

Solid-bodies and semi-hollow-bodies both use bridges that take advantage of the fact that the hardware can be rigidly mounted directly into the solid wood core of the instrument, which greatly enhances the transfer of vibrations throughout the guitar. There are three broad categories of bridges: Tele-style, Strat-style, and Tune-o-matic. Likewise, there are three broad categories of tailpieces: stop tailpieces, tremolo/vibrato tailpieces, and trapeze tailpieces (as discussed previously).

Tele-Style

Telecaster bridges use a metal plate that serves as a base for three or six bridge pieces and the bridge pickup. The strings pass over the bridge pieces and through the bridge plate and then anchor through holes extending through to the back of the guitar. The signature twangy tone of a Telecaster is a result of the combination of all these things:

> ▷ **Pickup mounting.** In almost all Tele-style guitars, the bridge pickup is suspended by screws through the bridge plate. Unlike other guitars, where the bridge and bridge pickup are mounted separately from one another, in a Tele-style guitar the bridge and bridge pickup interact, contributing to the sonic signature of the guitar.

▷ **How the base plate is formed.** A Tele-style bridge has a flat base with either a thick metal rear side or with the base bent up on the rear side. The anchor screws for the bridge pieces pass through this rear edge. On vintage-style Tele bridges, the sides of the bridge plate are also bent up, creating a three-sided tray. Manufacturers of aftermarket Tele bridges tout a number of improvements, such as thicker, more rigid bass plates, claiming improvements in sustain, volume, and note separation, as well as increased bass and control over harsh top end. The metal used (usually steel) and how the metal is formed (for example, multistage bending instead of simple bending, cold rolling, and so on) can also be tweaked for better rigidity and resonance. High-quality bridges use nickel or copper to fill voids in the steel, with plating on top of this for corrosion control.

The sides of the bridge may be lowered or removed entirely to make playing techniques, such as palm muting, easier. Some players do feel that lowering or eliminating the sides from a Tele bridge changes the tone. I've had all three kinds on the same guitar (full sides, lowered sides, no sides) and did not notice any change in tone. Those with lower sides or no sides were more comfortable to play on, though!

▷ **The type and number of bridge pieces.** Vintage Tele-style bridges used three bridge pieces, with two strings passing over each bridge piece. This allows for vibrations from one string to influence the other string sharing its bridge piece. Later models used six bridge pieces, which allowed for independent intonation adjustment for each string. More recently, several three-piece bridge saddle sets have come out with built-in intonation compensation (meaning the bridge pieces are pre-shaped to provide some correction for intonation). This allows those who go for the twangier sound of a three-piece saddle arrangement to still enjoy more accurate intonation.

Saddles can also be made from different materials. Brass saddles have a warm tone, whereas steel saddles offer more punch and sustain. Some players also mix and match saddles of different materials in the same guitar, such as steel for the bottom three strings and brass for the top three strings on a six-saddle guitar.

▷ **How the strings are anchored.** After the strings pass over the bridge saddles, on the vast majority of Tele-style bridges they pass through holes in the base plate, through holes drilled in the body, and then are anchored by metal ferrules (little cup-shaped pieces of metal that prevent the string from pulling into the wood) in the back of the guitar.

Some players, however, prefer to anchor the strings—or at least some of the strings—through additional holes drilled in the rear side of the bridge plate, rather than passing them through the guitar body. This reduces the string tension and also changes how vibrations are transferred among the strings, bridge, and body. Changing the string tension and vibration transfer in this way in turn changes the tone and may reduce the instrument's sustain.

Strat-Style

Strat-style guitars are probably available with the widest variety of bridges and tailpieces out there—fixed bridges, tremolo bridges (with seemingly endless variations), locking tremolos, separate bridges and tailpieces.... You can get an "S-style" guitar configured with just about any bridge or tailpiece type you like.

▷ **Hard tail.** Some Strat-style guitars feature *hard-tail* bridges, meaning fixed bridges instead of tremolo/vibrato tailpieces. The major difference between a hard-tail Strat bridge and a Tele-style bridge is that a Strat hard-tail bridge does not include an extended plate for mounting the bridge pickup. Another difference is that pretty much all Strat-style hard-tail bridges use six bridge pieces. As on Tele-style bridges, the strings pass through the bridge plate, through the guitar body, and anchor into the back of the body with metal ferrules.

Better...or Just Different?

Who would have thought that you could upgrade all of the hardware on a Telecaster and still not achieve the tone that you were after? If you think about it, a Tele is purely a workhorse guitar. Like all of his instruments, Leo Fender designed it to be affordable and to be easily serviceable in the field—just unscrew one part and screw on another one!

The original vintage models that everyone lusts after certainly were not precision instruments containing all the best hardware (or wood—some were made from pine) backed up by modern-day metallurgy. If you examine one closely, the parts may strike you as being quite primitive in some ways.

And here's a more modern-day example: I have a "frankentele" that I assembled from a bunch of spare parts I had lying around—a cheap MIJ (made in Japan) Squier body, a well-used neck from a reissue '62 Fender that my friend Bob traded me, some tuners that came off an old guitar, and a set of Seymour Duncan pickups. I upgraded the guitar with new frets, a custom pickguard, and a bone nut. But the six-saddle bridge I had lying around was a standard-grade, newer-style Fender unit I'd picked up somewhere. The guitar sounded and played quite well, if I do say so myself. Twangy but rich, with good sustain and tonal depth.

But I gave in to tone lust and boutique hype and purchased a very expensive aftermarket bridge with three vintage-approved bridge pieces, excellent metal, and all sorts of cool appointments. From everything I'd read, it should have sounded spectacular.

Surprise, surprise. On that particular guitar, the new bridge made the tone overly bright, thinned out the bottom end, and sounded harsh overall. I put the bridge I'd been using back on the guitar, and the guitar suddenly sprang back to life. Lesson learned: It's cool to try the latest, greatest, most boutique parts, and they will probably result in a different tone...but will it be a *better* tone? That is the question! Ultimately, only your ears can decide.

The main variation with hard-tail bridges will be the type of bridge pieces used. Vintage-style bridge pieces are made from bent strips of metal (brighter, twangier), whereas more modern units will be solid, die-cast metal, such as steel (punchy and bright) or brass (warm and round). There is a big difference in the amount of metal contained in each type of bridge piece and therefore in the tone that each produces.

▷ **Vibrato/tremolo.** When Leo Fender came up with his radical bridge/tailpiece combination for the Stratocaster, he called it a *synchronized tremolo tailpiece*, forever dooming guitarists everywhere to incorrect terminology. (Ah well, *we* know what we're talking about!) Though there are many variations available these days, the original *vibrato* tailpiece that Leo designed is still the basis for all of them and remains the baseline for tonal comparisons.

The original Fender bridge used six screws along the front "knife edge" of the bridge plate as pivot points for the bridge to rotate upon. Many players believe this still offers the best tone as compared to newer-style bridges, which often pivot on two screws. I have used both—on the same guitar—and I can't say that I heard much difference, nor did I notice much difference in the sustain or resonance of the guitar.

One place where you *can* hear a difference is changing the tremolo block—the large chunk of metal that attaches to the underside of the bridge plate and that serves as an anchor for both the strings and the springs in the back of the guitar that counterbalance the string tension. Various materials are used for tremolo blocks. Vintage units are leaded steel, which some players feel can deaden the tone. Less-expensive guitars often use zinc because it is cheaper, though the tradeoff is reduced sustain and lost clarity in the tone.

Aftermarket pure-steel blocks are available, which provide clearer tone and more sustain. A brass block is heavy and will add midrange and sustain. A titanium block will be much lighter in weight and will provide a clearer sound with a more open top end.

As with hard-tail Strat bridges, the saddle materials and design can make a big difference. A bigger difference will be found with how the bridge is set up. Many players enjoy a tremolo tailpiece set so that the unit can be pushed down in pitch as well as pulled up in pitch. But for the best tone and sustain, the bridge should be pulled tight against the body (so that it will only go down in pitch) either by screwing the springs in the back down or by adding additional springs to the unit. (Most Strat-style trem blocks and spring claws can accept up to five springs.) Eric Johnson is one player who sets his tremolos for down-only action; his signature Fender Stratocaster comes loaded with five tremolo springs installed, holding the tailpiece tightly against the guitar's top.

Another option is to firmly block the tremolo using a piece of wood wedged in the tremolo cavity in the back of the guitar. The tradeoff with blocking the tremolo is that it no longer works for raising or lowering string pitch (a definite deal breaker for most of us). The bridge in essence becomes a fixed bridge, albeit with the extra resonance and sustain provided by the metal tremolo block. As a point of reference, Eric Clapton always blocks the tremolos on his Strats.

▷ **Locking vibrato.** Among the latest developments in guitar vibrato tailpieces is the locking tremolo. (If you consider something developed 30 or so years ago "the latest," that is.) With a locking tremolo, the string is clamped at the bridge and also at the nut. Because the string can't slip or bind at the bridge or the nut, it stays in tune no matter how heavily you abuse the tremolo. There are several varieties, but most of them are based on (or even made under license from) Floyd Rose. This works great for keeping the guitar nearly welded in tune, but it can sacrifice some tone, as hard terminating the strings eliminates several sources of resonance. This can result in a thinner tone with a loss of sustain—though for heavy whammy bar users and abusers, the tradeoff is worth it.

To counter this, locking tremolos utilize tremolo blocks, similar to vintage blocks (though the strings don't pass through the block). Aftermarket companies offer upgrade blocks and bridge pieces to increase sustain and resonance.

Tune-o-Matic

Gibson has traditionally used various incarnations of their Tune-o-matic fixed bridge with a separate top-mounted stop tailpiece or (especially in the 1950s) a trapeze tailpiece for many of their solid-body and semi-hollow-body guitar models. Tune-o-matic bridges and stop tailpieces (see "Tailpieces" later in this chapter for more on stop tailpieces) mount to studs inserted into the guitar's top, providing excellent transfer of vibration.

There are actually two types of Tune-o-matic bridges in use by Gibson (and others)—the Nashville and the

Vibrato Routing

Installing a Fender-style vibrato (which includes all of the various descendants and offshoots, such as Wilkinsons, Floyd Roses, and others) requires a fair amount of routing. You must cut a large slot through the body for the tremolo block, and the back of the guitar needs a large cavity for the tension springs and the claw that attaches the springs to the guitar body.

All of that routing can certainly take some wood out of a guitar body! And, as we saw in earlier chapters, taking wood out of a guitar can reduce its resonance, sustain, and tone.

It's a tradeoff many players are willing to make, though, to have the extra expressive capability of a vibrato arm. Plus, there are those who prefer the different sort of resonance that comes from a vibrato tailpiece—particularly one with a nice tremolo block. And, by using resonant woods to build a guitar, you can dial in the tone exactly as you want—with or without a trem.

ABR-1. Though both look very similar, the Nashville Tune-o-matic has longer-throw slots for intonation adjustments on the bridge pieces (and is therefore a slightly wider bridge) and is also hollow underneath. Some players feel this weakens the bridge and may also weaken the tone. Nashville bridges also typically have studs (bridge posts) that thread into metal inserts that are mounted in the top of the guitar. ABR-1 bridges have studs that screw directly into the wood of the top, without metal inserts.

I have heard of players—and I personally have also experienced this—who had trouble with the studs of a Nashville bridge not fitting tightly into the metal top inserts. Clearly, this will result in lost tone and sustain because the pieces aren't fitting together tightly. In my case, I changed out the bridge for a new one and also installed new studs that fit the inserts very tightly. It made a tremendous difference in the tone and sustain of the guitar!

Having said all of that, the Nashville bridge was, in fact, developed to address some of the shortcomings of the older ABR-1 bridge—rattling bridge pieces, vibrating retaining wires, studs bending in the wood top, and so on. But if either bridge is installed properly, with tight-fitting parts, it is well adjusted and set up, and so on, the tonal differences between a Nashville and an ABR-1 bridge will not be major (assuming, of course, that good metal is used for each, and so on).

Where the bridge studs are concerned, there is a recent development that many players advocate: locking studs. These use either set screws or collars to lock the bridge rigidly to the stud, improving the vibration transfer, which should help tone and sustain.

Another consideration for both Nashville and ABR-1 bridges is the material used to make the bridge pieces—the little inserts inside the bridge that actually carry and intonate the strings. Various metals can be used, including steel, zinc, and brass, which, as with other types of bridges, will affect the midrange, sustain, and brightness of the tone. There are also graphite and nylon bridge pieces that can be installed to modify the tone—and there's nothing that says different types of bridge pieces can't be mixed on the same guitar. Joe Bonamassa, for example, uses steel bridge pieces for the lower three strings on his signature model Gibson Les Paul, but he uses nylon bridge pieces for the top three strings. His opinion is that the nylon pieces smooth out the tone of the plain (unwound) strings.

Tailpieces

Tune-o-matic bridges are typically paired with a separate stop tailpiece—essentially a solid metal bar that mounts to the top of the guitar using heavy studs that screw into metal inserts in the guitar body and that anchors the ball end of the strings. This type of tailpiece can offer an extremely rigid connection between the body of the guitar and the strings, providing excellent vibration transfer. For even tighter connection between the tailpiece and body, some manufacturers now offer locking tailpiece studs, which can improve sustain and tone.

As with other hardware, stop tailpieces are available in several different metals: zinc, steel, brass, titanium, and others. Aluminum was used for the original Gibson stop tailpieces in the 1950s, and there has been a resurgence of interest in these lightweight tailpieces because of their effect on the tone—more open, brighter, and more harmonic content. However, the tradeoff can be less chunky low end and reduced lower mids.

Stop tailpieces also allow string tension to be adjusted by raising or lowering the tailpiece on its studs. The higher the tailpiece is raised, the looser the strings will feel, which may also increase low end in the tone and reduce brightness a small amount. Some players also *overwrap* or *topwrap* their strings, bringing them backward through the tailpiece, wrapping them over the top of the tailpiece, and then passing them over the bridge. Some do this so that they can use heavier strings while maintaining manageable string tension; others like the way topwrapping makes their regular-gauge strings feel looser, as well as the tonal changes that can result.

There are, of course, other types of tailpieces that can be matched with Tune-o-matic-type bridges. Some solid-body and semi-hollow-body guitars use trapeze tailpieces, which are exactly the same as those found on hollow-body guitars, anchoring the strings to the endpin of the guitar. Many players end up swapping out the trapeze tailpiece on their guitar for a stop tailpiece to improve sustain and vibration transfer. For example, the late-'60s Gibson ES-335 used by Larry Carlton had its trapeze tailpiece replaced with a stop tailpiece.

There are also separate vibrato tailpieces that can be used with Tune-o-matic-style bridges. Some of these are as simple as a bent piece of metal that anchors the strings and that can be bent with a handle for pitch change. Others are as complex as Bigsby units, which feature a shaft that anchors the strings—the shaft is turned with a handle to change pitch, and a heavy spring returns the strings to their normal pitch.

All of these separate vibrato tailpieces impact tone and sustain—and may also cause tuning problems. For many players, the tradeoff is worth it to have the extra control and expression the vibrato provides.

Wraparound Bridge

Some manufacturers, such as Paul Reed Smith, use one-piece wraparound bridge/tailpiece combinations. These actually date back to the earliest Les Pauls, where the strings wrapped around a bar (secured to the end of the guitar by a trapeze-style anchor) that served as both tailpiece and bridge. The modern-day versions mount to studs in the same way as Tune-o-matic bridges and stop tailpieces. And, as with Tune-o-matics and stop tailpieces, there are locking versions available that rigidly fasten the bridge to its mounting studs.

I have this type of bridge on two of my guitars, and I love them. They offer excellent vibration transfer with reduced string tension for very comfortable playing with full tone and sustain. Having said that, I have also directly compared two PRS single-cutaway instruments, one with a wraparound bridge and the other a prototype for a new model with a separate Tune-o-matic-style bridge and separate stop tailpiece. There was a difference. Whether because of the extra string length between the bridge and stop tailpiece, because of the way the strings anchor into the stop tailpiece, or because of the increased down pressure resulting from the separate tailpiece, the tone of the prototype was thicker and chunkier, with longer sustain.

Tuning Machines

Can the type of tuning machine used on a guitar affect the tone produced? The strings are terminated at the nut, so the actual tonal impact of the tuners is inconsequential except in one regard: Some players and manufacturers feel that additional mass added to the headstock can even out a neck's response, helping to eliminate dead spots and other anomalies, as well as adding sustain. In fact, there was a device called a *Fathead*, originally manufactured by Groove Tubes, that simply comprised a thick sheet of brass that, when mounted to the back of a guitar's headstock, was intended to serve this very purpose.

In this regard, lightweight tuners may provide different response than heavy tuning machines, with locking tuners often being the heaviest of all. Personally, I have heavy tuners, locking tuners, and lightweight vintage-style tuners on my various guitars, and in most cases I have preferred the tone and resonance of guitars with lighter tuners, though the tradeoff can be tuning stability, especially if the guitar has a tremolo tailpiece. In my experience, those guitars with heavier tuners often seem to have less resonant necks than those with lightweight tuners, which translates to a less lively sound.

String Trees

The last piece of hardware on a guitar that affects the strings is the string tree—the small device found on the headstocks of most Strat- and Tele-style guitars. It is intended to increase the downward pressure of the string on the string nut. Does the string tree have any sort of tonal impact? Probably not, though if the guitar doesn't have adequate downward pressure on the nut without the tree, using one will certainly improve the tone! But as far as changing from a metal string tree to a graphite string tree to a metal roller string tree—expect no difference in tone.

Heavy Metal

Like everything else, the type of metal used to make a particular hardware component can have an impact on the tone a guitar produces.

▶ **Aluminum.** Aluminum is used to make very lightweight hardware, such as stop tailpieces. Most players find that switching to a lightweight tailpiece over, for example, a zinc tailpiece increases the clarity and resonance of the tone, with better openness and harmonics. This improvement sometimes may be at the expense of some low-end "chunk" or growl.

▶ **Brass.** A heavy metal that was very popular for bridges, tremolo blocks, nuts, tailpieces, and other hardware in the 1980s. A debate rages over the properties of brass. Some feel that brass reduces sustain and makes the tone dark. Others point to the traditional use of brass for other musical instruments, such as cymbals and horns. This camp feels that brass adds sustain, with thick midrange and warm top end. Based on my own experience with a Stratocaster equipped with an all-brass tremolo tailpiece, I concur with the latter opinion.

▶ **Chrome.** A thin layer of chrome is often electroplated onto guitar hardware to help protect against corrosion and sometimes to help make the surface harder. Although this could result in brighter tone, the difference created by the thin plating layer is too minor to consider.

▶ **Gold.** Gold is a very soft metal that in guitars is used for plating other metals, purely for appearance's sake. Normally, a soft metal would rob sustain and possibly tone, but the gold-plating layer is so thin that there is little or no effect on tone or sustain.

▶ **Nickel.** Like chrome, nickel is sometimes used to plate metal guitar hardware to help protect it from corrosion. The tonal difference is negligible. Appearance-wise, nickel will age, whereas chrome does not.

▶ **Steel.** Steel is the default material for making many guitar parts, though it is often plated with another metal, such as nickel, gold, or chrome. Steel offers a bright, round tone with good sustain.

▶ **Titanium.** An extremely hard metal that is used for guitar bridges, tailpieces, and occasionally string nuts. Titanium is as strong as steel, but it can be as much as 45 percent lighter. It offers very long sustain and extended clarity in the tone, with excellent transfer of vibrations.

▶ **Zinc.** Used for stop tailpieces and other guitar hardware, zinc results in a heavy piece of hardware. The tone includes a thick bottom end and lower midrange with a smooth and sometimes dark top end. Some manufacturers employed zinc as a substitute for aluminum, largely because it was cheaper. But therein lies the problem; zinc (also known as pot metal) can suffer from internal voids and other inconsistencies, which rob the material of solidity and can reduce tone. Having said that, some players have tried replacing zinc parts with aluminum parts and found that in the end, on their particular guitar, they preferred the sound of zinc.

Table 3.1   Hardware Tonal Factors

Tone Factor	Tonal Contribution
String nut material	Minor, only really affects open strings
Fret size/material	Subtle
Bridge/tailpiece type	Major
Bridge/tailpiece material	Moderate
Bridge piece/saddle material	Minor
Tuning machines	Subtle
String trees	None

Pickups

A N ELECTRIC GUITAR ISN'T GOING TO BE VERY, WELL, *electric*, if it does-n't have some way of producing and controlling an electrical signal! That's where pickups come in; they "pick up" the motion of the string or strings and convert that motion into an electrical signal—they're transducers that convert one form of energy (physical vibration of the strings) into another form of energy (electricity).

Basic electric guitar pickups are quite simple devices: A coil of wire and a magnet are really all it takes to sense the motion of a string. The metal string vibrates within a magnetic field, creating an electrical voltage within the coil. The ends of the coil connect to the guitar cable (with various tone and volume controls in between), which plugs into the input of the amplifier. The amplifier makes the signal strong enough to move a speaker, which creates sound waves in the air. The process of electricity produced in a coil of wire by a ferrous (iron-based) material moving in a magnetic field is called *inductance*.

But that simplicity belies the complexity of how the pickup components and their interaction affect the tone of the guitar's signal. Wire type and amount; coil height, width, and gauge; magnet type and strength—all these and many more can affect the tone that a pickup produces to one degree or another. That's why there are literally hundreds of pickups on the market, and why some players spend hours and hours and tons of money swapping out pickup after pickup, in search of the perfect coil of wire wrapped around the perfect magnet.

Changing any aspect of a pickup's construction can change the tone to one degree or another. Because of this, a tremendous amount of hearsay, myth, and legend has been fostered on the unsuspecting guitar-playing public. To wade through this mass of pickup lore and to sort out the tone fact from the tone fiction, let's take a look at the types of pickups and the various components that make up those pickups.

Types of Pickups

There are several different ways in which pickups can be categorized. At the highest level, there are two broad categories of pickups: passive and active. From there, pickups can be broken down by the number of coils they have, whether or not they are hum canceling, and so on.

Passive Pickups

The vast majority of guitar pickups are passive, meaning that they don't require an external power source, such as a battery, in order to function. From a functional standpoint, passive pickups consist of a coil or coils of wire and a magnet or magnets. The pickup functions as a simple inductor when a ferrous (iron-based) string vibrates in its magnetic field, generating an electrical signal at the frequency of the vibrating string, plus any harmonics the string vibration contains. The signal is small, but it's robust enough to make its way on its own through the guitar's volume and tone controls and switches, down the cable, and on to the first active stage in the chain, whether that is the input of a pedal or the input of an amplifier.

Active Pickups

Active pickups require a power source to operate, usually a 9-volt battery or, in some cases, two 9-volt batteries. There will be a preamplifier built into the pickup itself, or there may be a separate, external preamp mounted in the guitar. The preamp isolates the pickup, providing gain, tonal control, and often low-impedance output, which helps "condition" the signal for driving longer cables or a chain of effects without loss of high frequencies or noise/hum pickup. The preamp may also have an active equalizer (tone) circuit that can boost or cut treble, mid, and/or bass frequencies. (Passive guitars use passive tone controls, which can only cut frequencies.)

As for the active pickup itself, it consists of a coil or coils of wire and a magnet or magnets, just like a passive pickup, but the coils are usually wound for lower impedance. Much of the tone shaping and output is then derived from the preamp circuitry. Most active pickups are completely encased in resin or epoxy to protect the coil.

Although active pickups have developed a reputation as being high-output devices designed for high-gain hard rock and heavy metal, in fact, there are active pickups that are designed for more "traditional" sounds and styles as well. You'll see guitars with active pickups in the hands of everyone from James Hetfield and Kirk Hammett (Metallica), Zakk Wylde (Ozzy Osbourne and Black Label Society), Jim Root (Slipknot and Stone Sour), and Kerry King (Slayer) to Larry Carlton, Vince Gill, Steve Lukather (Toto), and David Gilmour (Pink Floyd).

Passive/Active Hybrids

It is also possible to use a "standard" passive pickup with an active preamp for tone shaping and equalization, for gain boosting, and for converting the signal to low impedance for better performance with long cables. This is more common with bass guitars and acoustic/electric guitars than it is with electric guitars. One advantage of having an active preamp along with passive pickups is that typically the preamp can be switched out of the circuit for "normal" passive operation and then the preamp can be turned on for a gain boost for solos or to push the front of the amp harder. And, if the preamp contains an EQ, it can be used to shape the tone in ways that can't be approached with a purely passive system.

The downsides are that any noise produced by the pickups will be amplified by the preamp. And, batteries have to be replaced as they wear out.

Single-Coil Pickups

Single-coil pickups, as you can probably surmise from the name, are made using a single coil of wire. They are the oldest type of pickup, as found on the original electric guitars, including the Rickenbacker "Frying Pan," Charlie Christian's Gibson ES-150, and Paul Bigsby's first solid-body guitars. Though many types of single-coils have been made, such as those from DeArmond, Danelectro "lipstick" pickups, and more, there are two primary kinds of single-coil pickups: "Fender style" and P-90, or "soapbar," style.

Fender Single-Coils

When we refer to "Fender-style" single-coils, we're generally talking about the thinner, Strat- and Tele-style pickups. Other types of Fender single-coils may have different dimensions—wider or taller—or slightly different magnet configurations, but the basic construction is the same. (Fender also used and uses P-90-style pickups, as described in a moment, on certain models.) The pickups are very simple, consisting of a coil of wire wound directly around six magnets, one for each string. On Stratocasters, plastic covers are used to protect the pickup coil. Telecaster neck pickups feature a metal cover, and Telecaster bridge pickups are usually uncovered.

These single-coil designs produce a bright, lively tone, with low to moderate output. They can be made with higher output, but the tradeoff is that the signature sparkling single-coil tone may be compromised. A traditional single-coil pickup does not have the ability to reject noise or hum from being picked up along with the vibration of the string—but many players are willing to put up with that noise and hum in order to have that bright, open tone. And, there are other solutions. For example, Lace Music Products' Lace Sensors utilize "Radiant Field Barriers," which surround the wire coil and protect it from hum and noise. Lace Sensors also use a weaker magnetic field, which is said to reduce the pull of the magnets on the strings (which can damp sustain and can pull harmonics out of tune). The field has wider dispersion, so a greater area of the string is sensed than with a standard single-coil. Fender has utilized Lace Sensors in some of their guitars; some players find that they produce an excellent single-coil tone with superior sustain and playing response—and, of course, no hum or noise. Others find they don't sound quite the same as traditional single-coil pickups.

Teles versus Strats

Traditional Telecasters and Stratocasters both feature single-coil pickups, but those pickups look quite different on the surface. Are they as different inside, or are the differences all cosmetic?

In fact, both guitars' pickups are made in the same way. But there are some differences that do affect the tone produced—and that, at least partially, explain the difference in sound between Teles and Strats.

All three Strat pickups (neck, middle, and bridge) feature plastic covers that don't have a whole lot of impact on the tone. The Telecaster neck pickup, however, has a metal cover that does affect the tone—the metal cover creates capacitance that eats up a bit of high-frequency information, making the pickup darker and warmer-sounding than a Stratocaster neck pickup. Plus, the metal cover can affect the magnetic field of the pickup and reduce the pickup's output.

The bridge pickups are where the differences really show up. There are a few reasons why Teles have more twang and spank than Strats:

▶ The bridge pickup on a Tele has a secret: There's a copper-plated steel plate mounted to the bottom of the pickup, something not found on Strat bridge pickups. This plate forces the magnetic field up through the pickup, making the tone brighter and contributing to that signature "twang." (Trivia: The copper plating on the Tele "elevator plate" makes it easier to solder the ground wire on the pickup and helps prevent the steel from rusting.)

▶ The bridge pickup angle on the two guitars is different. On a Strat, the bridge pickup is angled at 10 degrees off from perpendicular to the strings. On a Telecaster, the angle is 15 degrees off from perpendicular. This means that the Tele bridge pickup senses the string motion slightly closer to the bridge for the higher strings, making the tone brighter.

▶ The bridge pickup on a traditionally wired Stratocaster does not pass through the tone control, which affects its top end brightness. A Tele's bridge pickup does pass through the tone control—and even when the tone control is turned all the way up, it does still impact the brightness of the tone.

▶ A Tele's bridge pickup is mounted into a metal plate—the bridge plate—while a Strat's bridge pickup is suspended in a plastic pickguard. The metal surface of the Tele's bridge reshapes the magnetic field of the pickup, focusing it tightly upward toward the strings, increasing brightness and twang.

All of these things—with an additional major tone factor if the Strat in question has a vibrato bridge—combine to result in the sonic difference between a Strat bridge pickup and a Tele bridge pickup.

It is possible to mount a ferrous plate to the bottom of a Strat bridge pickup. Fralin, Callaham, and other manufacturers have plates that will work, and this will increase the brightness of the pickup. You could also custom-cut a Strat pickguard with the Tele bridge pickup angle. You could even go so far as to mount a Tele pickup into a Strat (which I have done). All of these things will get your Strat closer to a Tele, though never quite all the way there.

Conversely, you could mount Strat pickups into the middle and neck positions on a Telecaster (which I have also done), which will take the Tele a long way toward Strat-land—but again, never quite all the way there.

For extra flexibility or certain live-performance situations, these "hybrid" approaches may do the trick quite well. But for the purist, only a Tele sounds like a Tele, and only a Strat sounds like a Strat.

P-90/Soapbar

P-90 pickups—or "soapbars," as they are sometimes known—are also single-coil pickups. They were used on early Gibson hollow-body and solid-body guitars, as well as guitars from other manufacturers, and continue to be popular to this day. The design is slightly different from a Fender-style single-coil, though. Where the Fender has six rod magnets in the center of the coil, P-90s have two bar magnets under the coil with a metal spacer and six machine screws to conduct the magnetic field up to the strings. A P-90 typically has somewhat more output than a Strat- or Tele-style single-coil, with a thicker midrange and a punchier sound, but still with brighter, single-coil-style high end. A plastic or sometimes metal cover is used to protect the pickup coil. Like other single-coil pickups, P-90s have no ability to reject stray noise or hum from being picked up.

There are a couple of variations, but these really just relate to how the pickup mounts into the guitar. A regular P-90 mounts with screws that pass through the pickup coil and into the body of the guitar. Some P-90-style pickups have "eyelets" on their sides through which the mounting screws pass. And others, referred to as "dog-ear" P-90s, have tabs on the ends through which the mounting screws pass. This is simply a form-factor difference and does not affect the tone of the pickup.

Humbucking Pickups

As we've seen, there is one big problem with single-coil pickups: They pick up noise and hum along with the desired string vibrations. In certain situations, the hum can be so overpowering that it is difficult or nearly impossible to use a single-coil equipped guitar—particularly in critical studio-recording situations. Fortunately, Seth E. Lover was able to come up with a solution to this problem, a pickup that could "buck the hum" and that became known as the "humbucker."

The idea is brilliant in its simplicity: Two coils are connected together electrically out of phase and with reverse magnetic polarity. When a signal is induced in the magnetic field of the two coils by the string motion, it passes through without change. But hum and noise that are picked up from the air—the pickup coils basically serving as antennas—are cancelled out. Lover also added metal covers that further protected the coils from picking up airborne signals.

The "traditional" Gibson humbucker uses two coils of wire, with a bar magnet underneath and a metal spacer that conducts the magnetic field to the strings using fixed metal rods in one coil and adjustable machine screws in the other coil. The coil with the fixed rods or "pole pieces" has a slightly stronger magnetic field and therefore a bit more output and a slightly brighter tone. The adjustable machine screw pole pieces allow the output of the strings to be balanced for even response.

But there have been other types of humbuckers as well—"humbucker" simply refers to a pickup's ability to cancel noise and hum. It doesn't refer to a specific pickup model. Fender's humbucking pickups were also designed by Seth Lover. These were more similar to two Fender-style single-coils stuck together, as they featured magnetized pole piece rods (using CuNiFe, an alloy of copper, nickel, and iron, sometimes with added cobalt) instead of bar magnets under the coils.

Gretsch also made humbucking pickups, originally designed by Ray Butts for Chet Atkins (who later took them to Gretsch) that were known as "Filter'Trons." Atkins was unhappy with the DeArmond Dynasonic single-coils used in the Gretsch guitars he played, which had higher output and more low end than he wanted for his thumbpicking style. Atkins also felt the Dynasonic's heavy magnets inhibited guitar sustain—and he hated the hum the single-coils picked up. Butts had worked on transformers and knew that wiring two of them out of phase could cancel hum, which led him to the idea for a humbucking pickup.

Some historians believe that Butts' prototypes for these pickups may have pre-dated Seth Lover's humbucker designs for Gibson. Butts filed the patent for his humbucking design in 1954. Regardless of whether Butts or Lover was first, or who was granted what patent, a "gentleman's agreement" between Gibson's Ted McCarthy and Fred Gretsch allowed both companies to each manufacture their own versions of the humbucking pickup.

Vintage Filter'Trons are characterized by low resistance, low output, and a bright, twangy sound with "woody" midrange—somewhat between a single-coil and a Gibson-style humbucker. They use fairly weak alnico magnets (see the "Magnets" section later in this chapter) along with Fillister-head machine screws as pole pieces that are said to enhance string separation. Gretsch's newer "reissue" pickups use ceramic magnets, and many feel that they are brighter and harsher in tone than the original Filter'Trons.

Other Humbuckers

Gibson had a second version of their humbucker that was used in Firebirds, Les Paul Deluxes, and other models. These pickups were narrower than standard Gibson humbuckers and were referred to as "mini humbuckers." The difference was that the bobbin used wasn't as wide, so two coils would fit side by side in about the same space as a P-90 single-coil would occupy. Mini humbuckers have a brighter, slightly thinner sound than standard humbuckers.

The mini humbucker concept is taken to its extreme with the single-coil-sized humbuckers. These utilize two very narrow coils that are placed side by side, in the same amount of width as a standard single-coil. Yet they offer the tone and output of a humbucker—usually with brighter top end. These pickups are great for players of single-coil guitars who want a tone closer to a humbucker—whether a vintage style or a more modern, high-output model—without having to route out a bigger hole in their guitar or make other changes to the instrument.

Putting two coils side by side isn't the only way to create a humbucking pickup. Two coils can be stacked one on top of the other to create a hum-canceling pickup that is the same size as a single-coil and that produces a tone that is close to a non-hum-canceling single-coil. A "stacked" humbucker is a great way to reduce noise and hum while maintaining a single-coil-type tone—although purists feel that the tone is recognizably different from a standard single-coil's. But for situations where the look, feel, and tone of a single-coil must be maintained but hum must be controlled, a stacked humbucker is a good solution.

Other manufacturers, such as Kinman and Suhr, utilize passive "dummy" coils, which are used solely for hum cancellation; they do not sense the strings or contribute to the tone the pickup creates. Kinman's dummy coil is built into the pickup, while Suhr's is mounted to a replacement vibrato cover plate on the back of the guitar and wired into the circuit.

Lace Music Products has their Alumitones, which utilize several innovative new technologies to produce hum-canceling pickups with single-coil, P-90, and humbucker form factors. These pickups are based around aluminum structures that utilize secondary "micro-coils" containing 95 percent less copper wire than traditional designs to create a hybrid low-impedance/high-impedance pickup with low resistance—and very light weight—that can be voiced to create the specific tonal effects of single-coils, P-90s, and humbuckers. Alumitones are said to have a more "hi-fi" tonal quality, with thick bottom end and enhanced midrange.

PAF versus Patent Humbuckers

The original humbucking pickup was designed for Gibson by Seth Lover. The idea was to create a pickup that didn't pick up hum and buzz from nearby electrical devices—and it worked. A patent was filed for the humbucking pickup in June of 1955, and the company began making the pickups in 1956 (lap steels) and 1957 (Les Pauls), but the actual patent wasn't granted until July of 1959. In the interim, Gibson stuck a black decal with gold lettering on the backplate of their humbucking pickups that read "Patent Applied For." With the growing reputation of Gibson guitars from that era, the "patent applied for"—a.k.a "PAF"—humbuckers took on an aura and mystique of their own. Today, those early humbuckers command a pretty penny when they show up for sale, and guitars that contain them are worth much more than similar guitars that don't.

PAF pickups had around 5,000 turns of 42-gauge plain enameled wire and resistance ranging from 7.5k-ohms (7,500 ohms) to 9k-ohms (9,000 ohms). The bobbins used were black or white, sometimes one of each, resulting in a "zebra" pickup. (Though the color of the bobbins became a "thing" after Jeff Beck removed the covers from his PAFs, the color of the bobbin has no effect on tone.)

Alnico 2, 3, 4, or 5 magnets were used, depending on which type was randomly grabbed when the pickup was assembled, though alnico 4 was the most common type used. The different magnet types used explains why two PAF pickups can sound completely different from one another. One row of pole pieces was fixed iron rods, while the other was adjustable machine screws. The pickups were protected with metal covers—originally brushed stainless steel, later changed to nickel-plated brass. Neck and bridge PAF pickups were the same, though there were "jazz" PAFs made for Gibson's hollow-body archtops that had narrower string spacing.

So what about after the patent was granted in '59? Did the pickups change overnight, becoming instantly worth less from both monetary and tonal standpoints? Changes were made, though they didn't occur instantly—the first patent pickups were identical to their PAF predecessors. In 1961, alnico 5 magnets became standard. The magnets were also shortened from 2.5 inches to 2.25 inches. Shorter magnets don't have as much strength, but alnico 5 is a stronger magnet type, so the tonal difference from this change was minimal. By 1962, the resistance of the humbuckers had stabilized at 7.5k-ohms, though the individual coils could still be different (one 3.5k-ohms, one 4k-ohms, totaling 7.5k-ohms, for example)—another contributing factor in the tonal differences between various PAF pickups. In 1963, polyurethane-coated wire was substituted, and in the mid-'60s, the pickups began to be made using fully automated winding machines.

Wire and Coils

We've seen that the two major components in a very simple pickup are its magnet and its coil of wire. In most cases, the wire will be wound into a coil around a bobbin, which is a "form" that is usually rectangular in shape, though other shapes are used for different purposes. Bobbins have been made from bakelite, "vulcanized fiber" or compressed paper, and various types of synthetics and plastics, such as nylon, phenolic, and others.

In most pickups, including Gibson-style humbuckers, the bobbin consists of a center core with flanges at the top and the bottom; the wire is wound around the core part, while the flanges keep the winds or "turns" of wire from spilling off the bobbin. Some single-coils, such as those made by Fender and others, use two pieces of "flatwork" as the top and bottom flanges of the coil. The flatwork is separated by rods that serve as pole pieces. (We'll discuss pole pieces later in this chapter.) The wire is actually wound directly around the pole pieces.

In a few pickups, the wire is wound into a coil using a collapsing bobbin that is removed after the winding process is finished. This results in a so-called "air coil." Once the coil is finished, it is usually coated with varnish or wax to hold it together in the desired shape, and a bar or blade magnet is inserted into the hole in the center to create the pickup. The wire could also be wound right on a magnet. This is how the "lipstick" pickups from Danelectro were made. (Yes, the pickup covers on the originals were actually lipstick tubes.)

Could the type of bobbin material affect the tone the pickup produces? It's possible it could affect the inductance of the coil. But the likelihood of the differences between bobbins being audible is extremely small.

Wire and Windings

Even though wire is a major component in guitar pickups, there's not really all that much that's *special* about the wire used to wind pickups. It's just a thin strand of copper that's coated with a very thin layer of some sort of insulator, such as enamel or polyurethane. There can be variations though, resulting from the quality of copper used and how well the wire was manufactured. If the wire isn't of a consistent diameter, it will sound very subtly different in a pickup from wire that is super-consistent and made from purer materials.

The wire gauges used to wind pickups range from #36 to #46 (larger numbers indicate thinner wire), with most pickups using 42- or 43-gauge wire. The tolerances in wire manufacturing mean that a 42-gauge wire might range in diameter from 0.0024 inches to 0.0026 inches.

Could other metals besides basic copper be used to make pickups? Sure, at the time of this writing, Seymour Duncan had just introduced their Zephyr pickups, which use silver wire—said to produce more detail, better definition, denser midrange, smoother frequency response, and more—but any metal that is conductive but not magnetic could be used. However, with a few such exceptions, copper provides the best balance of cost versus performance.

The wire must be very thin so that a lot of it can be wound on a bobbin. A thicker wire (lower gauge) means that fewer turns and layers will fit on a given bobbin. Conversely, thinner wire (higher gauge) means more turns and layers will fit on a given bobbin. The more turns of wire around the bobbin, the more output the pickup will have, and the darker and thicker the tone will be (all other things being equal). Use fewer windings, and the tone will be brighter but the pickup will have less output. But it's not just the wire that has to be thin. If the insulating material used to coat the wire is too thick, fewer windings will fit on a bobbin, plus the wire won't be compacted as tightly, which can affect the tone and output and can also result in microphonic squeals and feedback at high gain or high volume. The insulation on pickup wire can range from 0.0002 to 0.0006 inches thick.

Though the standard is to wrap a single long wire around the bobbin to create a pickup's coil, there are lots of ways a pickup maker could play with the wire part of the formula to create a unique tone or to allow for a variety of tones from a single coil. For example, a length of thinner wire could be soldered to a length of thicker wire and then wound onto a bobbin. Or, two (or more) separate wires with different gauges could be wound onto a bobbin at once, side by side. The two wires could then be connected together in different ways or could be wired to a switch to allow for different combinations, each of which would have its own sound.

You could take this further by using more turns of one gauge of wire and fewer of the other, giving you intermixed lower and higher output coils on a single bobbin.

But for most guitarists, a single wire on a bobbin is sufficient to produce a desirable tone. And there are still plenty of ways the tone can be tailored without resorting to complex multi-wire winding schemes.

Hand Winding/Scatter Winding/Machine Winding

The earliest pickups were hand wound, or, as some refer to it, "scatter" wound. While it is possible to wrap wire around a bobbin purely by hand (if you have the time and the patience), in most cases, hand winding means that a machine is used to turn the bobbin, while the wire is fed and guided back and forth into layers on the coil by a human's fingers. So, while "hand winding" is not a 100 percent by-hand process, there still is a lot of human impact and influence on the final result. If the wire is held too tightly, it can stretch, which will result in the wire's characteristics (such as diameter) changing. If the diameter gets smaller due to stretching, more wire could be wound on the coil, meaning higher output. If the tension isn't consistent, the coil won't be evenly wound, and there may be air gaps or "sponginess" in the coil, which can lead to squealing and microphonic behavior. And, if the wire isn't evenly wrapped across each layer of the coil, there may be bulges and unevenness in the coil. An unevenly or "randomly" wound coil will have more capacitance, which acts as a filter for certain frequencies.

The early machines used for hand winding did have counters that kept track of the number of turns of wire on a coil, but they did not have an automatic shutoff that stopped the winding process when a particular number of turns was reached, so early pickups were often overwound. They were also often inconsistent in the DC resistance of the coil. These are two reasons why Gibson PAF humbuckers and vintage Fender single-coils can vary in their sound so much from one another.

Modern machine-wound pickups are much more consistent. The machine not only turns the bobbin, it guides the wire back and forth to create smooth, even layers and maintains the proper tension on the wire for tight layers without stretching the wire. The exact number of turns—and in some cases, the exact DC resistance—can be strictly controlled, which allows for a more consistent final product; one pickup of a particular model will have the same characteristics as another pickup of the same model.

This is clearly preferable from a manufacturing standpoint, and it certainly makes it easier for a player to choose a pickup and to know what characteristics it will have. But some players feel that there is a certain "character" to a scatter-wound pickup and that the inconsistencies result in a more desirable tone—some feel a scatter-wound pickup will have a richer, warmer tone, due to the increased capacitance and other factors that result from the "random" windings. The problem is that each scatter-wound pickup will sound slightly (or more than slightly) different depending on who made it, the skill and experience the person had, and so on. Modern manufacturers make more consistent hand-wound pickups, but there is still a variability to the final outcome—and that's the whole point.

Coil Height and Width

Seems simple; wind some wire around a bobbin, and you are good to go. But that bobbin and the resulting coil of wire can be tall and thin (like a Strat-style pickup or a Tele neck pickup), or they can be wider and shorter (like a Gibson P-90 or a Fender Jazzmaster). These different dimensions can result in the coil having fewer layers of wire, even though the length of the wire and the DC resistance are the same. For example, due to the width and height of the bobbin, a Fender Strat-style pickup will have more turns per layer than a Gibson P-90.

Rewinding for Tone

If you're not satisfied with the tone of your pickups, should you have them rewound? Unless the pickup is damaged or broken in some way, the results of rewinding are hard to predict, aside from the fact that you may get higher or lower output by putting on more or fewer turns of wire.

The overall tone a pickup produces is based on more than just the coil or coils of wire used; the entire thing functions as a system. The magnets, the coils, the pole pieces, the physical dimensions—all of these and more impact the tone. Changing just one thing—the coil of wire—may result in a positive change, and it may result in a negative change. The only way to find out is to try it—but in doing so, you may ruin the pickup. In most cases, you are better off just getting a new pickup with the sound you want and dropping that in your guitar.

In addition to these coil differences, each pickup has a particular magnetic "aperture," which is the width of the magnetic field the pickup produces and is shaped to sense the string vibration. A wider pickup has a wider magnetic field and vice versa.

So, how does this affect the tone? A wider pickup will tend to have a warmer sound (as always, all other things being equal), while a thinner pickup will tend to be brighter. Each turn on a wider pickup will have slightly more resistance, because the wire required for the longer dimension is slightly longer.

Resistance and Output

"Resistance" is the amount of opposition a given material puts up against the flow of electrical current. A short piece of wire will have very little resistance, but a long, very thin strand of wire will begin to show some resistance. When we're talking about a #42 or #43 strand of wire that's as long as the length of wire wrapped on a pickup bobbin—something like 5,000 or more turns—the resistance starts to jump up. For example, a typical Strat-style pickup might have a DC resistance of around 6k-ohms (6,000 ohms). The average Tele bridge pickup might be slightly hotter (around 6.5k-ohms), while a Broadcaster lead pickup might measure 7.5k-ohms. A Gibson P-90 single-coil might clock in around an average of 8.5k-ohms, while a Gibson PAF humbucker might have a resistance of that same 8.5k-ohms total (4.25k-ohms per coil), but of course the sound will be very different from a P-90 with the same resistance. A high-output pickup might come in as high as 16k-ohms or even higher.

There are factors that can influence the resistance of a coil in a pickup; temperature is one. When the temp is higher, resistance will be higher; cooler temps mean lower resistance—so yes, your guitar's tone actually could be very subtly different at a hot outdoor gig than in a cold basement rehearsal. Variations in the wire itself, such as inconsistent diameter and more, can affect the resistance and therefore the tone. The only way to get an accurate reading on the resistance is with the pickup outside the guitar's circuit; with the pickup wired into the guitar, the resistance measurement will be lower.

Though it's not a totally accurate indicator, a pickup's resistance will give a good idea of the output that it will have. In general terms, the lower the resistance, the lower the output of the pickup. The higher the resistance, the higher you can predict the output will be. But the resistance of a pickup affects more than just its "brute force" output level. All other things being equal, a hotter (higher output) pickup will be darker-sounding (less treble) with more midrange. The bottom end typically gets thicker as well, all of which can sometimes lead to muddiness when other aspects of the pickup aren't tailored to reduce the negative tonal effects of the high output.

The "ideal" amount of output for a pickup varies somewhat according to fashion and the other gear being used. For example, in the late 1970s and the 1980s, high-output pickups were the norm for hard rock and metal guitarists who were trying to push the front ends of their Marshall amps into heavier overdrive. In recent years, with amplifiers having plenty of gain even without being driven by high-output pickups, many players seem to be looking back toward the more open, less midrange-centric tone of lower- and moderate-output PAF-style humbuckers and vintage-style single-coils and P-90s.

Resonance

Due to the interaction of the pickup and its inductance with cables, potentiometers, and so on, every pickup will have a resonant peak that is a major determining factor in the tone of the pickup. Both the frequency of the resonance and the strength of the peak are important. Pickup resonant peaks typically show up somewhere between 2 kHz (2,000 Hz) and 5 kHz (5,000 Hz). This is the upper midrange and presence area of the frequency spectrum. A lower resonant peak (in the 2-kHz range) will result in a warmer, fuller-sounding pickup. As you move upward in frequency, the tone will get sharper and more present. Toward the 5-kHz range, the sound will begin to get brighter.

How much impact the resonant peak has on the tone depends on how strong that peak is. A weaker peak will have a smoother sound, while a stronger peak will be much more audible, even "spiky." The interesting thing is that although some manufacturers specify where the resonant peak might be for a certain pickup, the actual resonance that a pickup exhibits is based on *interaction* with the rest of the system, particularly the capacitance of the guitar cable. This means that if you use the pickup and the guitar in which it is mounted with a low-capacitance cable, the tone of the pickup will be different than if you use a high-capacitance cable with the same guitar and pickup.

Other components have an effect as well. A tone capacitor (which is in parallel with the pickup's inductance) will tend to lower the resonant frequency. The resistance of the tone and volume potentiometers can also affect the amplitude or strength of the resonance. The characteristics of the amplifier's input will also have an effect.

The lone coil in a single-coil pickup versus two coils interacting in a humbucking pickup could also make a big difference—so much that some players believe that the big difference in how a single-coil sounds versus a humbucker is due in large part to the much larger and higher resonant peak in a single-coil, along with the narrower aperture where the string is sensed by a single-coil. Single-coils have half the inductance of double-coil humbuckers, which substantially raises the resonant peak, but there might be some debate about whether this is really the defining difference between the sounds of the two types of pickups.

Potting

The wires in the average pickup coil are wound nice and tight, but there is still some possibility that those wires could vibrate under high-gain or high-volume situations. When that happens, the pickup emits a loud, obnoxious squeal of feedback, similar to what happens when a microphone is pointed into a PA speaker. The solution is to completely fill the gaps in the pickup coil with a substance such as wax or epoxy; this is called *potting.*

Originally, pickups were actually dipped into pots of liquid wax (thus the term *potting*), which solidified inside the pickup coils when it cooled off, making them stable and feedback resistant. Some manufacturers now use epoxy or bondable wire for this purpose. Bondable wire features an adhesive coating that makes the layers and winds of the wire on the coil stick together, essentially turning the coil into one solid object, though there can still be some gaps that allow for feedback. Epoxy is a more permanent solution than wax, but it may be thicker and harder to get into the interior of the coil. Some manufacturers use a vacuum to help pull the epoxy deeper into the coil.

But, despite these advances, many manufacturers still rely on wax, which does indeed do the job quite effectively. And, wax allows for the pickup to be disassembled and rewound later. A "permanent" solution such as epoxy or bondable wire does not allow for repair or rewinding. The downside to wax potting is that the hot wax could actually melt or soften a plastic bobbin in a pickup, causing it to deform. The heat of wax potting can also affect the magnetism of a magnet, particularly a weaker magnet.

Most pickups that are made these days are potted, and most players prefer a potted pickup for the feedback resistance it offers. However, a pickup doesn't *have* to potted, and there can be a tonal difference with a potted pickup. It seems that microphonics in a pickup can contribute subtly to the tone, making it slightly more open and lively. It's also more "vintage correct" to not pot a pickup. Pickup squeal didn't really become an issue until amp volume and gain levels increased. Some manufacturers, such as Gibson, Jason Lollar, and Seymour Duncan, still make certain models that are not potted.

Magnets

Magnetism is the fuel that drives the guitar fire. Think that a magnet is a magnet is a magnet? It is true that there is only one kind of pure magnetism, but the type of magnet, the size of the magnet, the formulation of the materials used to make the magnet, the strength of the magnet, and how that magnetism is deployed in the pickup can all affect the tone that the pickup generates. There are a variety of different magnet types that are used in guitar pickups.

Alnico

The earliest magnet type used for pickups—and still the most popular magnet variety—is alnico. The name "alnico" comes from a contraction of the three main metal types (besides iron) found in the magnet: aluminum, nickel, and cobalt. Alnico magnets were developed in the 1930s; they are temperature stable and relatively strong. They were designed to be permanent magnets for instruments and measuring devices, but those same characteristics that made them ideal for those applications also make them excellent choices for guitar pickups.

There are many formulations of alnico; the difference in each being the relative amounts of each type of metal in the magnet. The main types of alnico magnets used for pickups are alnico 2, 3, 4, 5, and 8. In general, the higher the number, the stronger the magnet, with one exception: alnico 3 is actually weaker than alnico 2. (See Table 4.1.)

In addition to the primary materials used to make the formulations of alnico, there will also be impurities in the mix, which can change the composition of the final magnet. In other words, two alnico 2 magnets can actually differ from one another due to impurities in the materials—even two magnets from the same

Table 4.1   The Formulations of Alnico

Magnet Type	Aluminum	Nickel	Cobalt	Copper	Iron and Other Trace Metals	Strength
Alnico 2	10%	19%	13%	3%	55%	40
Alnico 3	12%	25%	-	3%	60%	30
Alnico 4	12%	28%	5%	-	55%	52
Alnico 5	8%	14%	24%	3%	51%	48
Alnico 8	7%	15%	35%	4%	39%	100

manufacturer. This is also something that differs between vintage and modern pickups. It is nearly impossible to exactly duplicate the formulations that were used in the 1950s. And, if the formulation is different, the magnet will be different, it will be charged with a different level of magnetism, and the tone will be different.

Alnico, in general, is described as producing a sweet and musical tone when used in a pickup, but there are differences among the different formulations. These differences are highly subjective and can also vary between two magnets of the same type.

> ▷ Alnico 2—warm, round tone, with balanced frequency response.

> ▷ Alnico 3—more open than alnico 2, with brighter highs.

> ▷ Alnico 4—open and transparent, similar to alnico 5 in many applications.

> ▷ Alnico 5—less midrange, more highs and lows.

> ▷ Alnico 8—bright and powerful, with full bass.

By matching the magnet type with a specific DC resistance and a specific resonant peak, a pickup manufacturer can tailor the tone of a pickup to exactly what is desired.

Some players like to experiment with changing the magnets in their humbuckers. Swapping out an alnico 2 for an alnico 5 will definitely change the tone—whether that change is good or bad depends on many factors; the entire guitar acts as a system for creating tone, and the different components interact.

Ceramic

Around 1970, the price of cobalt, as used to make alnico magnets, began to increase. This led to manufacturers looking for less expensive replacements, with many settling on ceramic magnets. This has given rise to the impression that, because they're less expensive, ceramic magnets aren't as good as alnico. It's true that many budget pickups use ceramics, but this type of magnet is also used in mainstream and boutique pickups because of its characteristics.

Ceramic magnets, also known as *sintered ferrites*, are the strongest type of magnet used for guitar pickups, and a stronger magnet means more voltage output. They're made by creating a "slurry" of ceramic material and barium or strontium ferrous (iron) materials. The slurry is pressed or "sintered" into a raw shape and then fired in an oven (just like making a vase in a pottery class). When it cools, the ceramic is cut into its final shape and magnetized.

The tone of ceramic magnets is often described as hard edged, with bright top end and less midrange. For this reason, it is commonly used for hotter pickups with more coil winds—the brighter sound counteracts the tendency for overwound coils to be darker and midrange heavy and helps prevent muddiness.

Samarium Cobalt

Magnets using an alloy of samarium and cobalt were developed in the 1970s. The alloy, which typically contains 36 percent samarium and 64 percent cobalt, can be magnetized to create a very powerful magnet— one of the most powerful types of permanent magnet available. A line of SCN (*Samarium Cobalt Noiseless*) stacked-coil single-coil pickups, designed by Bill Lawrence, was introduced by Fender in 2004. These pickups were primarily used in Fender's American Deluxe family of instruments and were also offered as replacement pickups for Strat- and Tele-style guitars.

The Fender SCN pickups are highly resistant to picking up buzz and hum, which is a huge advantage for single-coil lovers who hate noise. As with everything, opinions vary on the tone of these pickups. Some players love them for their flat, even response. Others find that they lack the bright character expected from a single-coil pickup.

Cobalt

Early Gibson ES-150 guitars, commonly known as "Charlie Christian" guitars (although it was never a true "signature" model), featured unique single-coil pickups with blade pole pieces, wound with #38 wire. Early models (1936 to 1938) were wound to 2.4k-ohms resistance. This was later upped to 5.2k-ohms. These pickups also used a cobalt magnet, made with an alloy of 36 percent cobalt and 64 percent steel. Several companies make reproductions of this pickup, although most use alnico 5 magnets. There is a company in the UK (Charlie Christian Pickups) that claims to have sourced recycled vintage materials for more "authentic" reproductions. The magnets used in the originals are said to hold their strength for 200 years; given that they are now 70 years old, they have probably lost at least some of their strength, meaning that few, if any, people alive today have ever heard what these pickups (and their magnets) truly sounded like when new.

Magnet Strength

So what's the big deal with magnet strength? It's central to the output of a pickup: All other things being equal, a stronger magnet causes a pickup to put out more voltage than a weaker magnet. But there are other side effects as well. The iron in the guitar string is attracted to the magnet. With a more powerful magnetic field, this pull can actually damp the vibration of the string, which can lead to reduced sustain and out-of-tune harmonics. Stronger magnets also tend to have a brighter, louder, and sometimes harsher sound. Conversely, a less powerful magnet won't have as much voltage output, but it will generally sound warmer, more open, and less bright on the top end—and it may allow the string to vibrate longer, resulting in increased sustain.

Some builders tailor, or calibrate, the magnets they use to get a specific sound in a particular pickup model. The magnet may be fully charged to its maximum to be as powerful as possible, or it can be partially discharged for less magnetism. If magnetic pole pieces are used, they can be calibrated or charged to different levels to even out the output from each string.

Most builders accept as fact that magnets will lose some charge over time—and some manufacture "aged" pickups that incorporate magnets that have been discharged to a certain point to simulate this. Magnets can simply "age"—the metals used may change slightly. Pickup magnets can also lose power due to heat, physical shock, proximity to other magnetic fields, and exposure to other elements and incidents. Here are some things that many (or all) of us are guilty of doing that may affect our pickups' magnets:

▷ Have a habit of leaning your guitar against your amp? If the amp has a transformer in it, or large speaker magnets, you may be affecting the magnets in the pickups in your guitar.

▷ Ever tap your pickups with a screwdriver or other metal object to see whether they are functioning properly? The shock of the tapping and the magnetic interaction may have subtly changed the magnetism in the pickup.

▷ Dropping a pickup on a hard surface may alter its magnetism.

▷ If you work in a recording studio that uses analog tape, there's likely a demagnetizer in the room that is used on the tape heads. Don't bring this near your pickups!

▷ Anything with a coil in it—for example, some soldering guns—can create a magnetic field that can affect your pickups.

▷ Storing pickups together, particularly stacking them on top of one another, can affect the magnetism among them.

▷ Exposure to heat or temperature changes can affect magnetism.

In reality, it's not as if pickups and magnets are super-fragile things that are going to stop working if your guitar falls over in its case or if someone walks by carrying a speaker cabinet. But it doesn't hurt to be aware of the potential impact that things like those on the list above can have.

So, can you age your pickup magnets to change their sound? It's probably not a good idea to try—randomly tapping your pickup with a screwdriver just ain't going to do the trick! Rubbing your pickup with a magnet also won't do it, though it can realign the magnetism in ways that are less than desirable from a pickup standpoint. A better solution is to swap out the magnets for different magnets. But even there, you have to be careful not to ruin the pickup when you are taking out the old magnets and putting in the new ones. It's not a big deal with some pickups, but it is a delicate or even impossible task with others.

Pole Pieces

In many pickups, the magnets are located underneath the coils, at the bottom of the assembly. *Pole pieces* are used to direct the magnetic field up through the coils and to the strings. These pole pieces might be actual cast rod magnets, as in Strat-style single-coil pickups; they might be fixed steel rods or adjustable screws, as in Gibson-style humbuckers; or they might be steel bars or "blades," as in Bill Lawrence and some other pickups —a variety of shapes and magnetic materials have been used over the years. The shape, type, and material of the pole piece will all have an effect on the magnetic field the strings are exposed to, and therefore an effect on the tone produced as well as the string pull and pickup output.

Vintage versus New

Do old pickups sound better than new pickups? As is seemingly the case with everything vintage-guitar related, older is believed to better by many players, But before we casually dismiss the idea of "older is better," there are indeed some things that may be different between vintage pickups and modern pickups, even when the modern pickups claim to be "reissues" or replicas of the old units.

► The magnets may have been cast differently, to different sizes. Early Fender magnets, for example, were sand-cast with a rough surface. They averaged 0.197 inches in diameter. Later Fender magnets were standardized at 0.187 inches.

► The magnet type, alloy formulation, and strength may be different. Even if the exact same magnets and strengths are used, the older magnets may have "aged" or lost strength due to various reasons compared to the new ones.

► Vintage pickups were hand/scatter wound; most modern pickups are machine wound. With vintage pickups, the windings were counted using primitive devices; modern pickups are consistently wound using accurate counters to a specific number of turns or even to a specific resistance.

► Hand-/scatter-wound pickups tend to have "fatter" coils, because the layers were done by "eye" and are not as precise as machine-wound coils.

► The wire type, insulation, and gauge may be different. For example, early Strat pickups used 42-gauge Formvar, later 42-gauge enamel wire was used. This can result in different levels of inductance and capacitance.

► The quality of the wire, the magnets, and the other components may not be as high or as consistent with vintage pickups as it can be with modern pickups—or vice versa.

All of these factors and more can contribute to an old pickup sounding different from a newer pickup.

In most cases, there is one pole piece per string. But this gives rise to an interesting situation: The inner four strings (A, D, G, and B) each have their own pole piece and are surrounded by a pole piece for an adjacent string on each side. For example, the D string has its own pole piece and is surrounded by the pole pieces for the A and G strings. However, the two E strings have only their own pole piece and one adjacent pole piece. (The B for the high E and the A for the low E.) This means that these two strings are subject to a different overall magnetic field than the other strings. This can result in the two E strings having a slightly different tone or output than the other strings. As mentioned, some pickups solve this problem with bar magnets or blades; others increase the number of pole pieces. Carvin, for example, has pickups with 11 pole pieces per coil.

So, what happens if the pole pieces aren't there to direct the magnetic field? It is possible to use non-magnetic pole pieces in a pickup coil. For example, brass pole pieces could be used in one coil of a double-coil humbucker, effectively eliminating the magnetic field from one coil and turning the pickup into a single-coil, but still with the noise-canceling capability of a humbucker. Some manufacturers even make "dummy" coils that can be added to a single-coil-equipped guitar. When the dummy coil and one of the regular single-coils are used together, the result is humbucking-style cancellation of noise and hum.

Fender Single-Coil Pole Pieces

In Fender Strat- and Tele-style single-coil pickups, the pole pieces are also the actual magnets that drive the pickup's magnetic field—there is no separate magnet underneath the coil. The coils are wound right on the magnets, keeping the size of the coil more compact. Alnico rod-shaped magnets are used to make the pole pieces. The magnets are usually made by pouring the molten alnico into holes in sand (called *sand casting*). On vintage pickups, those rods were 0.197 inches in diameter. Modern rods are made slightly smaller, 0.187 inches in diameter. Alnico 2 and alnico 5 are two popular formulations for making single-coil pole piece rods.

Flat versus Staggered Pole Pieces

Fender vintage single-coil pickups often have their pole pieces staggered—the various pole pieces protrude different amounts from the flatwork on top of the pickup. This was done because in the early days of electric guitar, most sets of strings had a thick, wound G string, and the plain B string often had the loudest output. To balance the output of the six strings, the pole pieces were made longer or shorter, and therefore protruded more or less from the top of the pickup, making them more or less close to the strings.

Modern strings are much more balanced from a magnetic standpoint, so staggered pole pieces are not as necessary for balanced string-to-string output. Flat pole pieces also help to keep the output level more consistent as the strings are bent. As a string is bent, it moves from the magnetic field of its own pole piece and begins to enter the magnetic field of the adjacent string's pole piece. If that adjacent pole piece is raised or lowered, the bent string may get louder or softer as it moves. With flat pole pieces, the magnetic field from each pole piece is the same, so there is no volume increase or decrease when a string is bent.

Humbucking Pole Pieces

The two coils in a humbucking pickup usually have different types of pole pieces. Typically, one coil uses ferrous (iron) "slugs," which are rods that are fixed into the coil bobbin, and one coil uses pole pieces that are adjustable—basically machine screws that can be raised and lowered in and out of the coil bobbin to even out string-to-string output levels. The tops of the screws used for the adjustable pole pieces can be slotted, Philips style, hex-wrench style, rounded, flat—each type will create a slightly different magnetic field.

In many cases, the adjustable pole pieces will protrude from the bottom of the pickup. When this happens, there is a loss of magnetic field out of the bottom of the pickup. This creates an imbalance in magnetic field compared to the slug coil, where the pole pieces don't extend past the bottom of the coil. For example, original PAF humbucker adjustable pole pieces were 3/4-inch long machine screws, which stick out of the bottom of the pickup. Substituting 1/2-inch long screws will reduce the amount of magnetic field lost out of the bottom and extend the magnetic field out of the top of the pickup, toward the strings, where you want it. This will raise the output slightly and make the tone a bit brighter. Some players cut the extra length off the bottom of the pole piece screw, but unless you clean up the screw's threads after cutting it, you could damage the bobbin by raising or lowering the pole piece.

Pole Piece Spacing

Gibson- and Fender-style guitars use different string spacings at the bridge and the nut; therefore, the pole pieces on their pickups are spaced differently as well. On a Fender, the single-coil pole piece spacing is 53 millimeters (2.09 inches), measured center to center from the low E to high E string pole pieces. On a Gibson, the E to E center-to-center pole piece spacing is 50 millimeters (1.96 inches). Tonewise, this doesn't make much difference until you try to put a Gibson-spaced humbucker into a Fender-spaced guitar. When you do, the pole pieces don't line up exactly, and the E strings tend fall just outside the pole pieces.

Eddie Van Halen famously solved this problem by angling the bridge humbucking pickup in his original "Frankenstein" guitar so that the slug coil's pole piece ended up under the high E and the adjustable coil's pole piece ended up under the low E. But this solution does cause the magnetic field serving those strings to be less intense than if the strings were "properly" lined up with the pole pieces on both coils. Plus, the angled pickup sounds different from one that is perpendicular to the strings—no doubt part of the reason for the unique sound of Van Halen's guitar and of the myriad copies with similar angled-bridge humbuckers.

Manufacturers such as Seymour Duncan and DiMarzio have solved this problem with their "Trembucker" and "F-spaced" humbuckers, respectively. These models are regular-looking humbuckers, but their pole pieces are spaced the same as a Fender-style single-coil pickup. The pole pieces line up properly on all six strings, and the tone is more consistent with what you would expect from a humbucking pickup.

Slug Side toward Neck or toward Bridge?

There are two ways that a humbucking pickup can be oriented. The pickup can be turned so that the slug side is near the bridge or turned so the slug side is away from the bridge. The standard orientation is for the bridge pickup to be oriented so that its adjustable pole pieces are nearest to the bridge. The neck pickup is oriented so that its adjustable pole pieces are nearest to the neck. The slug side has a slightly stronger magnetic field, since some magnetism is lost out of the bottom of the adjustable pole pieces. In other words, when looking at the two pickups, the slug sides are toward the inside, and the adjustable pole pieces are to the outside.

But there's no law that says the pickups have to be oriented that way. Having the slug side nearer the bridge on the bridge pickup will result in a slightly brighter sound. Having the slug side away from the bridge on the neck pickup will result in a slightly darker sound and slightly more output.

Fleetwood Mac guitarist Peter Green's famous 1959 Les Paul Standard (later owned by the late, great Gary Moore) had its neck pickup reversed, which was part of the unique tone of that instrument. The Les Paul also has its neck pickup magnetically out of phase with the bridge pickup, creating a remarkable sound in combination with the bridge pickup. (See the sidebar "Peter Green's Les Paul" on the next page for more information on his Les Paul and its electronics.)

Peter Green's Les Paul

Looking to get the idiosyncratic sound of Peter Green's vintage Les Paul from your guitar? (Green replaced Eric Clapton in John Mayall's Bluesbreakers and then went on to be a founding member of Fleetwood Mac.) There were a few differences in the way his guitar pickups were set up—mostly due to what has been described as a "botched repair job."

The easy-to-manage change is that the neck pickup was flipped 180 degrees so that the adjustable pole pieces were on the bridge side, while the slug pole pieces were on the neck side.

A bit more difficult to manage is the out-of-phase orientation of the neck pickup. To achieve this, the bar magnet on the bottom of the pickup needs to be pulled out, flipped over, and slid back into place. There is a danger of ruining the pickup by pulling out the magnet; if you're not positive you know how to do it, take the pickup to a tech who can do the job for you.

Most difficult of all to replicate, the neck pickup was said to be rewound and "rebuilt" early on, which was when the pickup's magnet was reversed. Whether rewinding your Les Paul's neck pickup will give you the same tone is questionable. You could match the Green pickup's resistance, but you would likely still have a slightly different sound, due to the particular magnet in your pickup.

By itself, the flipped neck pickup sounded slightly different because the magnetically stronger slug coil was toward the fingerboard, resulting in slightly higher output and slightly darker tone—and it was apparently rewound. The bridge pickup was unchanged from the usual Les Paul–type positioning and tone. The big difference was when the two pickups were combined. The out-of-phase neck pickup created a thinner, honky, hollow sound when combined with the neck pickup.

Alternate Take

Guitar maker Jol Dantzig, co-founder of Hamer Guitars, had the opportunity to closely scrutinize the Peter Green Les Paul after it was purchased by the late Gary Moore. He disputes that the guitar was modified or changed during a repair. He states that the guitar appeared to be completely stock, without modifications to the pickups, and surmised that the neck pickup magnet was inserted incorrectly at the factory. He further states that a vintage '59 Les Paul owned by Joe Bonamassa has similar changes that appear to be factory-stock "mistakes."

Polarity

There are two ways that a single-coil pickup can be wound: clockwise and counterclockwise. Likewise, there are two ways in which its magnetic rods (pole pieces) can be oriented: magnetic north at the top of the coil or magnetic north at the bottom of the coil. When used on its own, neither the direction of the winding nor the orientation of magnetic north of a single-coil pickup make any difference. But when two single-coils are combined (as in the "in-between" positions on a five-way Stratocaster pickup selector switch), it makes a big difference. In this case, if one of the pickups is wound in the opposite direction and has its magnets reversed in polarity compared to the other pickup (called *reverse wound/reverse polarity*, or *RWRP*), then when the pickups are used together, the result will be hum-canceling. In effect, the two pickups become a wide-spaced humbucker.

Wiring Options

Though the coils of wire and magnets are the primary components that make up pickups, there are other things that can impact the sound the pickup produces. Chief among these are some different ways that the coils can be wired.

Coil Tap

While in most cases, a coil of wire in a pickup starts at its beginning and ends at its end, it is possible to break into the middle of the coil—to cut into the coil somewhere in the middle and tap off the signal at that point. Doing this reduces the total length of wire and number of turns, which in turn reduces the resistance, which in turn makes the sound brighter and lowers the output level. Using a coil tap, you could have a high-output single-coil pickup for a fat, powerful sound and then hit a switch that would tap into the coil at some middle point, cutting the output and creating more of a vintage single-coil type of sound. For further variation, a rotary switch could be used to access multiple taps in a single-coil, or a switch with two paths could be used to tap both coils in a humbucker simultaneously—though true coil tapping is usually done on single-coils. Humbuckers usually use coil splitting. (See the next section for more on coil splits.)

Coil Split

It's not unusual for a player who relies on humbucking pickups for a thick, full, powerful sound to also want access to single-coil sounds for the sparkle and chime they offer, and for the thinner rhythm tones they provide, which allow lead vocals or other instruments to cut through the mix. Since two pickups can't occupy the same location, this presents a problem.

The solution? Since there are two coils in the humbucker, why not hook up a switch that turns one of them off, essentially creating a single-coil pickup. Several things happen when you defeat one coil in a double-coil, humbucking pickup. First, the output drops in half (assuming the two coils are identical). The inductance is also halved, so the resonant frequency goes up by about 50 percent. The strings are now sensed over a much narrower physical area. And, unfortunately, you lose the hum-canceling function, so the pickup will now be susceptible to hum and other noise.

You can tailor the tone of a split humbucker a bit by choosing which coil is turned on; the stud or fixed pole piece coil will be a bit brighter with slightly more output than the adjustable pole piece coil. The two coils in a humbucker also physically sense slightly different physical positions on the string. The coil closer to the bridge will be just a bit thinner and brighter, and the one farther from the bridge will be very slightly fuller sounding.

Few players would claim that a coil-split humbucker sounds like a "real" single-coil; typically, a split humbucker sounds thinner and has less output than a true single-coil. With one exception: There are a few pickups on the market that use true single-coil pickups for either one or both of a humbucker's coils. In this case, when you split the humbucker, you actually are getting a true single-coil, and the pickup will deliver the "right" sound; the variable is how the pickup is placed. For example, the bridge pickup in a Stratocaster will be angled, but typically a bridge humbucker mounted in a Stratocaster won't be—so the split single-coil won't quite be sensing the string motion in the same way as a true single-coil would.

There is one more way to achieve a single-coil sound from a humbucker: Remove the adjustable pole pieces from the pickup. Doing this turns the coil without pole pieces into a dummy coil, getting close to a single-coil tone. Of course, this isn't something you can do between the verse and the chorus of a song during a performance onstage. But if you're in the studio, you need a single-coil-style sound, and you only have a humbucker guitar, just unscrew the adjustable pole pieces from the pickup (or pickups), and you'll get most of the way there.

Series/Parallel Coil Wiring

With a humbucking pickup, we have two coils of wire. How those two coils of wire are connected can make a huge difference in the tone the pickup produces. The "standard" method for connecting the coils is in series—the end of one coil is connected to the beginning of the second coil. This produces a thick, rich tone. Electrically, this makes sense; when two coils are connected in series, their resistance adds. So if two 4.4k-ohm coils are hooked up in series, the total resistance will be 8.8k-ohms.

The two coils could also be connected in parallel, with the beginnings of the two coils hooked together and the ends hooked together—think of it as wiring the two coils side by side instead of end to end. When you do this, the resistance is cut in half (if the coils are the same resistance), or the average of the two coils is cut in half. So, if each coil is 5k-ohms, the total in parallel will be 2.5k-ohms. If one coil is 5k-ohms and the other is 4k-ohms, the parallel resistance will be 2.25k-ohms. (The average of 5 and 4k-ohms is 4.5k-ohms; divided in half results in 2.25k-ohms.) In addition, the inductance is cut by 75 percent, which drastically affects the frequency of the resonant peak. The result is, when the coils in a humbucker are hooked up in parallel, the pickup is still humbucking, but the tone is quite different—similar to a single-coil, in fact. The treble is brighter, the output is lower, and there is less midrange and bass.

Pretty much any guitar with a humbucking pickup will have that pickup wired in series for the fattest, hottest output. However, some have switches for converting the pickup to parallel. If the guitar doesn't come with this capability, it's an easy modification that requires nothing more than access to the four conductors in the pickup plus a switch for changing the wiring.

In-Between Sounds

The original Fender Stratocaster guitars had three pickups—bridge, middle, and neck—and a three-way pickup selector switch; any single pickup could be turned on, but there was no way to combine more than one pickup at a time. Well, actually there was a way: by carefully balancing the selector switch in between positions 1 & 2 or 2 & 3 so that the bridge and middle pickups or the middle and neck pickups could be used together.

Fender eventually swapped out the three-way pickup selector switch for a five-way selector switch, with two added positions (2 and 4) that allowed the bridge and middle and middle and neck pickups to be combined. Guitarists have long referred to the hollow, "quacky" tones that these pickup combinations produce as "out of phase." But there's no "phase" involved. The three pickups in standard Strats are all wound in the same direction and all magnetized in the same way, so there is no "out of phase" cancellation going on. Even in guitars with reverse-wound/reverse-polarity middle pickups (which produce a humbucking, noise-canceling effect; see discussion earlier in this chapter), the tonal change when the pickups are combined isn't due to phase cancellation. If those positions were truly out of phase, the sound would be very thin and shrill and would have very low output.

So what's going on? Here's the deal: The pickups are connected in parallel and are in phase with one another. When two pickups with the same resistance are connected in parallel, the resistance is cut in half. If two Stratocaster single-coil pickups with a resistance of 6k-ohms are connected in parallel, the total resistance will be 3k-ohms, and the tone will be much brighter than either pickup by itself. If two pickups with different resistances are combined in parallel, the total will be half of the average resistance of the two pickups. So if a bridge humbucker with a resistance of 9k-ohms and a middle position single-coil with a resistance of 6k-ohms are combined in parallel, the overall resistance will be 3.75k-ohms. Once again, much brighter than either pickup by itself.

Pickup Covers

Pickups are available with bare coils (such as Telecaster bridge pickups), with plastic covers (such as Fender Stratocaster single-coils), and with various types of metal covers (such as Telecaster neck pickups and most Gibson humbuckers). There are three reasons why covers are used with pickups:

▷ To protect the fragile wire in the coils from damage. In particular, it isn't uncommon for the high E string on a guitar to get snagged under the edge of an uncovered bobbin, which can break the thin pickup wire. This is especially a problem if an uncovered pickup is raised up high out of a mounting ring or pickguard. A plastic (as used on Fenders) or a metal (as used on Gibsons) cover will work equally well to protect the pickup from physical damage.

▷ For cosmetic purposes—some players prefer the looks of an uncovered pickup, while others like the more "finished" appearance of a plastic or metal cover on a pickup.

▷ To reduce problems with hum and noise getting into the pickup. Seth Lover designed the original Gibson PAF with a nickel-silver cover, which, when combined with the humbucking action of the dual-coil pickup, created excellent protection from stray interference, hum, and noise.

The tradeoff is that the capacitance of the grounded metal cover interacting with the pickup and the metal cover changing the magnetic field can reduce the high frequencies, resulting in a bit darker or warmer sound and may reduce the pickup output by a small amount. So, some players follow in the footsteps of Jeff Beck and remove the metal covers from their humbuckers or substitute pickups without covers. Interestingly, according to Seymour Duncan, Jeff Beck removed the covers from his humbuckers because the covers would resonate and cause feedback in high-volume situations, not because they affected the tone of the PAFs in his Les Paul.

Pickup Calibration

When a guitar has more than one pickup, there's a small obstacle that must be circumvented. The string vibration gets wider as you move away from the bridge. Check it out for yourself. Pluck a string and notice how far the string moves near the bridge versus how far it moves near the neck. This difference translates to a difference in volume, where the pickup is concerned—the same note will sound louder when picked up near the neck versus when it is picked up near the bridge. (Actually, magnetic pickups are sensitive to the velocity of the string, not the displacement of the string–though the volume effect is the same. In other words, the speed of the string motion is more important than the amount of the string motion. In the same way, higher notes move less than lower notes, but this is cancelled out by a pickup's increased sensitivity at high frequencies.)

For this reason, neck pickups typically are calibrated with slightly less output than bridge pickups, particularly when the pickups are intended to work together as a set. For example, Seymour Duncan's PAF-style '59 model comes in two flavors: the bridge version, with 8.13k-ohms DC resistance; and the neck version, with 7.43k-ohms DC resistance. DiMarzio's True Velvet bridge single-coil has a DC resistance of 6.49k-ohms, while the neck and middle versions measure 6.21k-ohms. In some cases, the difference is even more substantial, to allow for a more clean, open, bright sound from the neck pickup versus the bridge pickup. The Duncan Full Shred bridge humbucker measures 14.6k-ohms, while the neck Full Shred measures 7.4k-ohms.

The resonant peak may also be calibrated, usually to help make the neck pickup a bit brighter and more open sounding compared to the bridge pickup, which senses a point where the string will be naturally thinner and brighter sounding. The Duncan '59 bridge pickup has a resonant peak of 6 kHz, while the neck has a peak of 6.8 kHz. The Full Shred bridge has a peak at 5.5 kHz, while the neck has its peak at 8 kHz.

But just because a pickup says that it is for the neck or bridge position doesn't mean that it has to be used there. In one particular guitar, one manufacturer uses a vintage-style P-90 in the neck position (with 8.22k-ohms DC resistance and a peak at 4.3 kHz), while a neck P-90 from a higher-output, more modern set is used for the bridge position (with 12k-ohms DC resistance and a peak at 4.5 kHz). And it works in that guitar model, with good balance between the two pickups. However, in nearly all cases, bridge pickups are used in the bridge position, middle pickups are used in the middle position, and neck pickups are used in the neck position.

Cryogenic Treatment

A few manufacturers have begun experimenting with cryogenic treatments for pickups—putting the pickups or their components into the deep freeze—literally. Other industries have experimented with supercooling metals to somehow change their structure over the past few decades. Some reports suggest an increase of 10 to 15 percent in conductivity after super-freezing pickups. If this is true, it is possible that the pickup could have more output without requiring more wire or turns on the coils, which would mean the pickup could maintain a cleaner, more open sound while still having more power. Manufacturers describe cryo-pickups as having better clarity, definition, and realism, among other adjectives.

As for player response, most seem to think that cryogenic treatment for pickups is a modern form of snake oil. It's difficult to do a truly scientific A/B comparison of two pickups, so we have to rely on subjective reports. And currently, most of the reports are coming from the manufacturers who make the pickups.

Could there be a tonal improvement with cryogenic treatment of pickups? Anything is possible, and it doesn't hurt to keep an open mind. But at this point, most players are waiting for some sort of objective proof before jumping on the cryogenic bandwagon and paying extra for cryogenic pickups.

Pickup Height and Tone

Adjusting a pickup's height properly relative to the guitar's strings is critical to maximizing tone—there is usually a "sweet spot" for the height of a particular pickup in a given guitar. Often players will adjust the pickup as close to the strings as possible to get the most output possible. But maximizing volume can sometimes be detrimental to the tone. The closer the pickup gets to the strings, the more the magnetism may interfere with the motion of the strings and affect the tone.

With single-coil pickups, the magnetism may even pull on the string. When this happens, the harmonics are also pulled slightly out of tune with the string's fundamental pitch. Some players like a small amount of this, feeling it adds richness to the tone. But if the pull is too strong, the upper notes on the string will begin to be audibly out of tune. This problem is commonly referred to as "Strat-itis," since it is most audible with Strat-style pickups, though the same thing can affect Tele-style single-coils and other pickups. The only solution is to lower the pickup away from the string to reduce the magnetic pull.

As a general rule of thumb, raising the pickups close to the strings will result in a hotter, more "compressed" tone with more attack, while lowering the pickups away from the strings will result in a warmer, more open tone with slightly less output. Most manufacturers have guidelines for where to start with pickup height:

> ▷ Gibson recommends starting with their humbuckers raised to within 1/16th of an inch from the bottom of the high and low E strings for the bridge pickup and 3/32nd of an inch from the bottom of the high and low E strings for the neck pickup, measured with each string fretted at the highest fret.

> ▷ For standard single-coils, Fender recommends setting the treble side of the pickup to 1/16th of an inch from the bottom of the high E string, while the bass side should be set to 5/64th of an inch from the bottom of the low E string, measured with each string fretted at the highest fret. According to Fender's specs, hotter pickups or those with stronger magnets may be set to 3/32nd of an inch from the bottom of the high E string and 1/8th of an inch from the bottom of the low E string.

> ▷ Seymour Duncan recommends fretting the strings at the highest fret and then raising the treble side of the bridge pickup to within 1/16th of an inch of the bottom of the high E string, and on the bass side to 1/8th of an inch of the bottom of the low E string. From there, the middle and neck pickups can be set to the same heights and then adjusted up or down to balance their volume against the volume of the bridge pickup.

From these recommended starting points, plug the guitar into your amp, play it, and then raise or lower the pickup by small amounts. There will likely be a point where you hear the sound come into focus, with the best tone. This is one of the easiest "mods" you can do to customize your tone to exactly where you want it. It usually works best to set the bridge pickup height first and then raise or lower the neck pickup until its tone comes into focus and its volume matches the bridge pickup. For both the bridge and neck pickups, the treble side of the pickup is usually set slightly higher than the bass side of the pickup.

What about the pole pieces? Even if they're adjustable, the intention usually isn't to use them to set the overall volume or proximity to the strings. Seymour Duncan, for example, recommends lowering the pole pieces until they are flush with the pickup bobbin and then raising the entire pickup up closer to the strings. The adjustable pole pieces are intended to let you balance the string-to-string volume across the pickup.

It is best if the pickup can be adjusted so that its top flatwork or top surface is parallel to the strings. In many cases, particularly with humbuckers, the pickup will lean one direction or the other compared to the string angle. To correct the angle of the pickup, a piece of foam or other material can be inserted into the pickup cavity, under one side of the pickup. In some cases, an angled bezel or surround can be used to mount the pickup, which may help correct its angle compared to the strings.

Matching the Best Pickups to a Guitar

Finding the best pickup or set of pickups for a particular guitar can be a serious challenge, first because there are so many options, and second because you never know exactly what a pickup will sound like in your instrument until you actually get it mounted in there and plug it in. You can predict, based on the characteristics and design of the pickup and the characteristics of the guitar: A bright pickup in a bright-sounding (acoustically) guitar will probably sound bright, for example. But to know all the final subtleties, there's no substitute for hearing the actual combination of wood, wire, and magnets.

Beyond matching a bright or dark pickup against the wood in your guitar, there's also the question of the pickup's output, which, as we've seen, can greatly affect the tone. Then there's the resonant frequency of the pickup and how that correlates to how the body and neck of the guitar resonate.

All of these factors also make it difficult to base any sort of pickup selection on what other players have experienced. How a pickup sounds in a friend's '75 Strat may be totally different from how it sounds in your '75 Strat—or it may be very similar. This makes it tough to take any more than general advice or basic direction from someone else's experience, whether in an online discussion forum or even when you're able to put your own ears on another guitar with a pickup like the one you are considering. Likewise, it is tough to draw much from the sound of a particular pickup in a favorite recording artist's guitar on an album—both for the reasons listed above and because it's impossible to know how much studio magic was worked to get that artist's recorded tone.

So, what to do? Well, despite the comments above, there is *some* value to talking to other players and to trying to hear as many pickups as you can. Play guitars with the pickups you are considering. Visit the manufacturers' websites; most of them have audio demos of their pickups. Get to know the sound of your guitar as well as possible, both acoustically and with its current pickups (if it has any).

Perhaps first and foremost, decide what sort of tone you want before you start experimenting with dropping pickups in your guitar. It's far easier to hit the target when you know what you are aiming for. At least figure out the basic characteristics you're seeking: humbucker versus single-coil, bright versus dark, high output versus low output, and so on. This will let you narrow down the options. From that point, you can continue to zero in based on others' experience, hearing the pickup in different guitars, and so on.

But, in the end, you have to get the pickup in your guitar to really be able to hear how the combination is going to sound. There's no getting around it; there's a certain amount of trial and error involved.

Table 4.2 Pickups Tonal Factors

Tone Factor	Tonal Contribution
Active versus passive	Minor to major
Single-coil versus P-90 versus Humbucker	Major
Design (stacked humbucker, mini humbucker, single-coil-sized humbucker, etc.)	Minor to major
Bobbin type	None to subtle
Wire gauge	Subtle
Hand/scatter winding versus machine winding	Subtle
Coil height and width	Subtle
Resistance	Minor to major
Resonant peak	Minor to major
Potting	Subtle
Magnet type and strength	Subtle to major
Pole piece spacing and staggering	Subtle to minor
Coil tap, coil split, series/parallel wiring	Major
Pickup covers	None to subtle
Cryogenic treatment	None to subtle
Pickup calibration	Subtle to minor
Pickup height	Subtle to minor

Guitar Electronics

I F THE WOOD AND THE HARDWARE THAT MAKE UP an electric guitar are its physical body, then its pickups are its heart, and the associated electronics are the mind of the beast, the elements that give it life. The electronics let us control the volume produced by the guitar, provide the means for selecting the various tones a guitar can produce, and allow for shaping those tones into the sounds that we desire. From the simplest single volume control screamer to a switch- and knob-laden active monster, a guitar's electronics let you dial in your tone and make subtle adjustments while you play to tweak it to create the voice you need for your musical expression.

Though manufacturers and builders design a guitar model's electronics to complement the natural vibrations the instruments produce, the electronics are one of the aspects of an electric guitar that we, as players, can easily modify. As long as you can figure out how to use a soldering iron, turn a few screws, and maybe loosen and tighten a couple of retaining nuts, you can do everything from changing out pickups to swapping volume and tone controls to completely rewiring a guitar's electronics. This lets you customize the instrument for exactly the tone or tones you want

But despite the fact that it is a relatively easy—and relatively inexpensive—matter to change out a guitar's electronics or to reconfigure a guitar's signal path, that doesn't diminish the importance of the electronics. A guitar's electronics can be a serious contributor to the tone of an instrument. The wood and steel provide the physical reso-nance, ringing, and sustain, but the pickups and electronics take that physical motion and bring it into the electrical signal realm. While the physical vibrations are the basis for the sound, much of the character of the guitar's tone, its tonal flexibility, and its responsiveness come from the electronics and how they interact with the rest of the signal chain.

Passive and Active Electronics

The vast majority of electric guitars use "passive" electronics, which means that the circuits don't require any power to operate. But this also means that with a passive circuit, there's no additional power available to drive the signal higher in any way. In other words, passive electronics can't boost, they can only cut, whether we're talking about volume or the frequencies affected by a tone control.

There are several nice things about passive circuits. First, they're inexpensive because there are no complex electronic components. Second, passive circuits don't require power, so you don't have to worry about batteries in the guitar—which can affect the sound of the circuit as they age and lose power and which also have to be changed—or figure out some way to route external electricity into the instrument. Third, there are no active components generating noise that might get amplified later. Guitars put out tiny electrical signals, and amps can have tremendous amounts of gain, so any background noise created in the guitar itself that you don't want to hear runs the risk of being amplified along with the notes you *do* want to hear. (Of course, passive components can still pick up hum and buzz from external sources.) The other nice thing is that passive circuits are by nature pretty simple, so anyone with even a little bit of skill with a screwdriver and a soldering iron can get in there and swap out components, fix problems, or even completely rewire the signal path to add new capabilities. There are really only a few types of components used in passive electric guitar circuits: volume and tone controls (potentiometers), various switches, capacitors, and maybe the odd resistor.

Active Electronics

Guitars with active electronics, by contrast, have a built-in signal preamp, which can provide several different functions. The price of this is that the guitar must have a power source, which is usually in the form of one or two 9-volt batteries, although a few guitars have been made that can utilize "phantom" power that is fed back to the guitar through its cable. Another aspect of active electronics is that unless the circuit is well-designed and uses good components, it can be noisy. I owned an active instrument from the late 1970s that produced an incredible amount of background hiss and noise, which was clearly audible even with a clean amplifier. (The state of the art is much improved today, though, and with high-quality modern circuits, noise usually isn't an issue.) And, active electronics are much more complex and are therefore difficult to modify unless you have specific electronics knowledge and training. (However, I was able to clip the wires and rip out the noisy active electronics from my '70s instrument without any trouble!)

Active electronics can provide several functions in an electric guitar:

▷ **Buffering.** As you'll see later in this chapter, many tonal issues can be caused by the interaction of the passive components in an electric guitar. The potentiometers, capacitors, pickups, and even the cable running to the amplifier all interact to affect the tone. With active electronics, however, the circuitry serves to isolate the pickups from negative interactions with the rest of the electronics.

▷ **Gain.** An onboard preamp can provide more output than any passive pickup could ever provide, without the tonal compromises that can result from pushing the limits of a passive design.

▷ **EQ.** Later on in this chapter, when we discuss tone controls, we'll see how limited passive tone controls really are. Active tone controls aren't subject to the same limitations and can provide far more flexibility than passive designs.

▷ **Noise control.** Active pickups and circuits can be designed to reject external hum and buzz pickup for much cleaner operation.

While all of these benefits are wonderful, most players still prefer the sound of passive electronics. Why? The usual response is that active electronics in guitars sound "sterile" or less "organic" than passive electronics. Part of this may stem from the fact that active pickups and electronics seem to be favored by players in the heavier, higher-gain musical styles. But while active electronics work well in that situation, it's certainly not the only style in which they are useful. Players such as Vince Gill, Larry Carlton, and David Gilmour have all used active electronics with very "organic" results.

Perhaps the "sterile" preconception comes from the conservative nature of guitarists. We like our amps tweed, blackface, or plexi, our pedals analog, and our pickups passive. (Though this has changed substantially as digital and modeled devices have improved and continue to improve.) One wonders, too, in a blind test, how many players or listeners could identify an active guitar versus a passive guitar.

Volume Controls

So, you've got the pickups on your guitar, and they're cranking out electrical signals—but for true expression and dynamics control, you've got to be able to adjust the volume and timbre of that signal. That's where the volume and tone controls come into play. It's also where we'll put potentiometers (components that provide continuously variable electrical resistance or variable voltage dividing, depending on how they are wired) to work in our guitar. The signal flows out of the pickup and into the potentiometer (or "pot") that we use for the volume control, which divides the overall flow of the signal and shunts some of it off to ground, reducing the level of the pickup's output signal.

And, there's a cool bonus to be had here: Because of the way in which passive components in the guitar interact, the higher the resistance of the potentiometer you choose for the volume control, the more the guitar's high frequencies come through, and conversely, with a lower resistance, the potentiometer will pull back the highs somewhat. Fender typically uses 250k-ohm potentiometers for their single-coil guitars, which tames the top end nicely, removing the harsh high overtones. Gibson, on the other hand, uses 500k-ohm potentiometers for their humbuckers to allow more sparkle and harmonics to get through. Most guitars use one of those two values for their volume pots, though some players and manufacturers like to use 300k-ohm pots with P-90s to let a bit more sparkle through to balance the tone on those slightly higher-output and thicker-sounding single-coil pickups. A 300k-ohm pot can also be a good compromise for guitars that have both humbucker and single-coil pickups installed. Some manufacturers even like to use 1meg-ohm potentiometers for humbucker-equipped guitars to allow for maximum brightness. Active guitar circuits usually use 25k-ohm pots, since the buffering in the active electronics make loading and loss of high frequencies a non-issue.

Tolerance

While you would think that a 500k-ohm pot would be a 500k-ohm pot, potentiometers can vary wildly between their specified resistance and their actual resistance. The only way to be sure of what you are getting is to use extremely tight tolerance pots (expensive) or to measure each one before you install it. I've seen pots in guitars vary from their stated resistance by as much as plus or minus 20 percent or even more! With 20 percent tolerance, this means that the "500k" pot you have in your humbucker-equipped guitar might actually measure as high as 600k (letting even more highs come through). Or, another "500k" pot might only measure 400k (making the sound darker). The only way to know for sure is to measure.

For example, if you've got a guitar with two pickups, each with its own (supposedly) 500k-ohm volume control, then one pickup might actually see a 600k volume pot while the other sees a 400k volume pot, and each will have an audibly different top-end tone because of this. If the guitar sounds okay stock, then all is fine. But if one pickup is dark while the other is bright, or if the guitar seems like its high end might be "off" from what you expect, the pots may be at least partially to blame. On the positive side, all of this means that you can somewhat tailor the tone of a guitar just by swapping out volume pots or by carefully matching the potentiometer value to the pickup to achieve the sparkle you want.

There is one exception to this: the "no-load" tone potentiometers that Fender has begun using recently. These pots are designed so that from "1" to "9" on the potentiometer, it functions as normal. At "10," or fully turned on, the pot has a detent that clicks it out of the circuit. The effect is the same as if the pickup were wired straight through the volume control to the output jack, with no effects from the tone potentiometer or capacitor in the circuit; no signal at all is shunted to ground through the tone control path. This allows all of the high end, harmonics, and signal from the pickup to flow unobstructed.

Treble Bleed

The "load" of a potentiometer isn't the only way that pots can affect a guitar's tone. Sometimes volume pots can make the sound increasingly darker as you turn them down; this is due to interaction between the volume pot and the guitar cable, which can act as a capacitor in the circuit. As the volume pot is turned down, the capacitance in the cable—and its effect of reducing the high end—can become more audible. Some players don't mind this and find that this slight change in tone helps solos pop out when the volume pot is cranked up and allows rhythm parts to sit back a bit when the pot is turned down. But if the treble loss is too noticeable, most players find it a negative.

One way to correct for this treble loss is to use a short cable, which has the limitation of restricting your movement around the stage. Another is to use a lower-capacitance cable, but this may also make the tone brighter when the volume is all the way up—plus low-capacitance cables are often more expensive. A more controllable solution is to solder a small capacitor, called a *treble bleed*, across the input and output terminals of the volume pot. The capacitor shunts the very high frequencies around the volume pot, keeping the treble intact. The guitar can be turned down and still retain all of its high-frequency sparkle.

A 0.001pf (picofarad) cap is a common value for treble bleed. Some manufacturers use a resistor soldered in parallel with a 0.002µF (microfarad) or a 0.0025µF capacitor to smooth the pot and treble bleed response. Others recommend a resistor in series with 0.001pf cap to control the amount of high frequencies that bleed across the volume pot. Usually the resistor value used is around half of the value of the volume pot. So, a 100k-ohm or 130k-ohm resistor might be used with a single-coil equipped guitar with a 250k volume pot. A 220k-ohm resistor might be used with a 500k-ohm volume knob on a humbucker-equipped guitar. In some cases, if the guitar has more than one volume control, different treble-bleed capacitor values are used for the neck and bridge pickup controls.

Depending on the pickups, the volume pot, and the capacitor and its value, the effect of the treble bleed cap can sometimes be too audible. This can result in the guitar actually sounding thinner as the guitar's volume is reduced. Some experimentation may be required: Adjusting the cap value (and resistor value, if one is used) can fine tune the response so that the sparkle is retained without the guitar sounding thin when the volume is reduced.

But a treble bleed circuit in a guitar doesn't work for everyone. Some players feel that even when the guitar's volume is all the way up, the "extra" top end that normally would be tamed by the load of the potentiometer gets passed through when there is a treble bleed cap installed, making the guitar sound too bright. It can work both ways. I have one Strat-style guitar with humbuckers where that extra bit of treble from the treble bleed works in the guitar's favor. But I have had two Telecasters that seemed just a bit too bright when the volume was all the way up. On one, when the treble bleed cap was clipped off of the volume pot, the top end seemed to settle right down to the proper point.

Pot Taper

The other aspect of potentiometer design that can affect a guitar's response is the pot's taper. There are two types of pots: linear taper and audio taper. Linear-taper pots reduce the level in an electronically and arithmetically smooth fashion; however, this generally doesn't sound correct to our ears. To human ears, linear pots often have most of their effect either at the top or the bottom of their range, with little effect in the rest of their range. If your guitar makes a big drop in volume as you turn down from "10" to "8," but there's little change after that, or if the volume or tone pot seems to have little effect until you turn down to "2" or "3" and then it abruptly shuts off, it could have a linear-taper pot. The problem is that with so much of the pot's effect taking place in such a limited amount of its turning range, it's difficult to set the level or tone where you want it.

The other type of pot, the audio-taper pot, changes level in a logarithmic manner, which is the same way in which our ears perceive changes in volume. (This is the same reason we use the logarithmic decibel scale to indicate volume levels.) Because of this, many players find that audio-taper pots sound as if they reduce the volume or tone smoothly from full on to full off. Most manufacturers use audio-taper pots in their guitars, though some substitute linear-taper pots for tone controls—having most of a tone control's effect in the bottom or top part of its range can make it useful for creating manual wah-wah effects, *a la* Danny Gatton or Roy Buchanan.

Tone Controls

The tone controls on most guitars with passive electronics are thought of as just adjustable treble-filter devices. A potentiometer (in most cases of the same value as the guitar's volume pot) routes a certain amount of the signal away from the main signal path—usually tapped off at the volume control—and sends it to ground. But the key is that a capacitor is inserted between the volume-control pot and the tone-control pot. The capacitor serves as a treble-frequency filter—only frequencies above a certain point will be routed through the tone pot and on to ground. This very simple "equalizer" can therefore be used to cut the high end, to make the tone darker. (Remember that we're talking about a passive tone control here. It can't boost the frequencies, it can only cut the level of certain frequencies.)

The smaller the capacitor value used for the tone capacitor, the higher the frequency the capacitor operates at, so the less effect it has on the upper midrange and lower treble. To put it another way, the bigger the tone capacitor value, the darker and bassier the tone will get when you turn down the control.

From a purely mathematical standpoint, an electrical engineer might tell you that a tone control/capacitor actually adjusts the resonance of the circuit, reducing the resonant frequency as the pot is turned down. But for non-engineers—like me—the treble-filter explanation is easier to follow...and the sonic effect is the same: The tone gets darker.

Tone Capacitor Values

Fender single-coil guitars generally use 0.047µF (microfarad) capacitors for their tone controls. Gibson uses 0.02µF capacitors on the tone controls for their humbucker-equipped guitars, although in some cases they use a 0.02µF cap on the bridge humbucker tone control and a 0.047µF on the neck humbucker tone control for more balanced response.

Making a quick run through the wiring diagrams on some pickup manufacturers' websites, Seymour Duncan specifies 0.047µF caps for humbuckers and Tele-style single-coils and 0.022µF for Strat-style single-coils. Jason Lollar sticks with the current Fender and Gibson standards. Lindy Fralin specifies a 0.1µF (as Fender used in the '50s) or a 0.05µF (as Fender used in the '60s) for Strat single-coils or humbuckers. If you want to experiment, it's a simple matter to swap out the tone capacitors in an electric guitar for different values to customize the response of the tone controls. You could even install a switch in the guitar that allowed you to select different capacitors for "tunable" tone control response.

Capacitor Voltage Rating

A capacitor has another spec besides its capacitance value. Capacitors are also rated for the amount of voltage they can store. Tube amplifiers, for example, often use capacitors rated for 500 volts. However, electric guitars are low-voltage devices. A voltage rating of half of a volt or so will be more than adequate to handle guitar signals. Some players feel that a cap with a high voltage rating will sound better than one with a low voltage rating—and there can be a difference between the construction of two caps of the same value but different voltage rating—but it's tough to find any blind test or measured evidence that the tone will change. Most experts feel that the tone capacitor will be operating so far below its voltage rating that the effect of that rating on tone is insignificant, if there is any at all. Note that, from a purely practical standpoint, there is one objective advantage to caps with lower voltage ratings: They're physically smaller, which makes them easier to install in the limited space inside a guitar's control cavity.

Mil Spec

Many electronic components, such as capacitors, are advertised as being "mil spec"—but what exactly does that mean? "Mil spec" refers to a standard that was established by the U.S. Department of Defense for the manufacturing quality and/or performance of a particular component or device. The idea is to set a "tolerance" range for the specification that falls well outside of the normal usage conditions so that the component or device won't fail in the field, under adverse or extreme conditions. At one time, there were more than 45,500 military specs listed! This has been reduced significantly, and, in fact, since 1994, the use of military specs without a waiver is prohibited. The use of ISO 9000, which is a civilian series of industry standards, is recommended instead.

Types of Capacitors

The smallest components in a guitar can affect its tone, and that applies to capacitors—which are among the smallest components. No one would claim that changing a capacitor to another type will radically affect how a guitar sounds, but some players do feel that different types of caps make an audible difference in the sound of the tone control or even of a treble bleed. There are many types of capacitors out there; specific types such as Sprague Orange Drops, Sprague "Bumblebees," "Black Beauties," and "Vitamin-Q" paper in oil are revered for their tonal qualities among certain players. There are also players who feel that there is a significant difference between, say, vintage ceramic caps and modern ceramic caps. (And there could be; caps do "age" more than many other components. This does explain the difference in sound with some vintage units, but it also makes the use of "NOS" caps somewhat questionable for obtaining vintage tone.)

The "type" of a capacitor refers to how it is made; especially the materials used:

▷ **Ceramic.** These are common caps, usually shaped like a disc with two signal leads coming off one side. Ceramic caps are used by many manufacturers, including Fender, because they are inexpensive. They can be inconsistent and are rarely made to tight value tolerances. Ceramic caps are said to be "harsh" or "crisp" sounding. Or they're said to sound "even," if not "natural."

▷ **Metal film.** Sometimes said to improve the clarity and openness of the top end of a guitar. Or, said to emphasize the guitar's mids. Or, said to have great dynamics.

▷ **Paper in oil/paper in wax.** Some profess these to be smoother in the high end, with wider range and "transparent" response. Others describe them as having "woody" and "warm" tone. Still others say "warm and creamy." Paper in oil caps were used by Fender in their original 1950s guitars, so they are revered for vintage tone. The "Vitamin-Q" paper-in-oil type have the advantage of being vacuum-sealed, meaning they won't age like other types of caps.

▷ **Polyester.** Said to provide "fat" tone. Or, said to be smooth on top and "transparent" sounding.

As you can tell from the sometimes conflicting descriptions above, if there are tonal differences between different types of capacitors, they're quite subjective. It's one of those things that, if you hear a difference, fine. But many players, under true blind test conditions, probably will find any tonal differences to be extremely subtle, if there are any at all. And, an engineer will likely tell you that there is no way that the type of capacitor used can influence the tone in any way. (It's been my experience, however, that even though things can't necessarily be measured or calculated mathematically doesn't mean that they don't cause audible differences —our ears are amazing instruments. My motto: Be objective and even skeptical, but let your ears decide.)

However, there may be one advantage to going for a high-end capacitor of whatever type you prefer: The tolerances are much tighter on many of these more-expensive caps, which means you know with much more accuracy what you're getting and what you're hearing.

Other Tone Controls

While passive pot-and-cap tone controls are by far the most commonly used type, there are other tone control types used on some guitars.

▷ **Varitone.** First used on the semi-hollow-body ES-345 in 1959, the Gibson Varitone circuit uses a six-position rotary switch. A network of 12 resistors and 10 capacitors is engaged using the switch, allowing six tonal possibilities, as shown in Table 5.1. Most Gibson guitars with Varitone circuits also feature standard volume and tone controls as well.

Table 5.1 Varitone Positions

Switch Position	Tone
1	Bypass, unaffected tone of guitar passes through.
2	–5 dB at 1,875 hertz; cut in "presence" part of the midrange of tone.
3	–6 dB at 1,090 hertz; cut in the midrange of the tone.
4	–7 dB at 650 hertz; cut in the "fullness" part of the midrange of the tone.
5	–10 dB at 350 hertz; cut in the lower midrange "punch" part of the tone.
6	–14 dB at 130 hertz; cut in the low frequencies. Brightest tone, similar to a single-coil.

▷ **TBX tone control.** Fender's TBX ("treble/bass expander") control was first introduced on the Eric Clapton signature Stratocaster. It's a passive control that uses a single "ganged" potentiometer, with 250k-ohm and 1meg-ohm sections. From "0" to "5" on the control's rotation a traditional tone control–style treble-filter circuit is engaged, making the sound darker and bassier as with a standard tone control. When the pot is set to the midpoint (center detent position) on its rotation, there is no effect on the guitar's tone. Turn the pot up above "5," and the sound gets progressively thinner and brighter.

▷ **Greasebucket tone control.** Fender's "Greasebucket" tone control is said to reduce the treble when turned down without making the sound muddy. A network of caps and resistors controls the bottom end, allowing the top end to be reduced without making the sound woofy or too bassy. Opinions on this are quite polarized. Some players find it effective and like it, especially for higher gain situations. Other players hate it and immediately remove it from their guitars.

▷ **Delta tone system.** Fender's Delta tone system for the Stratocaster has three components: a hotter bridge pickup for more output and midrange, a no-load tone control pot, and a rewired circuit featuring one tone control for the neck pickup and a shared tone control for the middle and bridge pickups. Proponents of this system say that the pickups sound louder, fuller, and brighter, no doubt due to the no-load pot removing the loading effects of the tone pots from the circuit.

▷ **Active tone controls.** There are several big advantages to active tone controls, which typically rely on a battery or two in the guitar for their power. First, since they are powered, active tone controls can boost as well as cut. This gives them more flexibility for shaping the sound. Second, because more extensive circuits can be used, active tone control systems can have more bands—bass, mid, and treble, for example—instead of the single treble-cut control found in most passive guitar electronics. Third, the tone controls can be "tuned" to specific frequencies, or you may even be able to adjust the tone control's frequency and bandwidth using knobs.

Active tone controls provide extensive tone-shaping power, especially when you factor in that they can boost as well as cut. This allows the guitar to drive effects and amps in a different way and to radically alter the "natural" tone of the guitar with extra bass, mids, or treble. The active mid boost found in Fender's Eric Clapton Strats is a good example—when cranked, it can give a single-coil a humbucker-like tone. When boosting a limited range of frequencies is taken to its extreme, you get the highly "tweaked" tones of Frank Zappa or the sound of a fixed wah pedal, *a la* Michael Schenker and others. However, heavily boosting a particular band of frequencies can also result in diminished clean headroom in the amp.

Switching

Some players can make it happen with a single pickup and a volume control, maybe with a tone control, maybe without. But for many of us, we enjoy the possibilities that at least two pickups can provide. There are many ways that guitar pickups, volume controls, and tone controls can be wired together, and it's certainly nice to be able to select among the various options for additional flexibility and more tonal options.

Most of the switching in guitars is simple and straightforward. Guitars with more than one pickup have switches for choosing between or among the different pickups and combinations. (See Table 5.2.)

If the guitar has extended features, such as coil tapping or coil splitting, there will be switches for these as well.

Table 5.2 Basic Guitar Pickup Switching

Guitar Model	Switch Type	Pickup Combinations
Telecaster	Three-way blade switch	Either pickup alone or both together
Vintage Stratocaster	Three-way blade switch	Any of the three pickups by itself
Modern Stratocaster	Five-way blade switch	Any of the three pickups by itself, bridge/middle pickups together, or middle/neck pickups together
Les Paul/SG	Three-way toggle switch	Either pickup alone or both together

Phase Switching

It's just common sense that pickups are always wired with their "hot" or "+" connection to the "+" connection on the rest of the signal path. But it doesn't always have to be that way, and which way things are wired makes a difference when the pickups are combined.

When two pickups are combined together electronically, they can be wired in polarity (the "hots" wired together and the grounds wired together), which results in a blend of the sounds of the two pickups, with certain frequencies likely to cancel out and reinforce one another to an extent. This results in the signature twangy, chimey sound of Telecasters when both pickups are on, and the brighter, chimey sound when both Les Paul pickups are on.

But the two pickups can also be wired with one pickup out of phase—that is, in reverse polarity ("+" goes to ground and ground goes to "hot"). This results in a thin, bright, hollow sound that provides an interesting tonal alternative. You won't hear much difference when the pickup is used by itself (though it may be noisier), but when the two pickups are combined, the out-of-phase tone will be obvious.

But few guitarists want their guitars wired out of phase all the time. A phase switch on the guitar allows you to flip one pickup out of phase whenever desired but still have access to the sound of both pickups in phase as well.

Series/Parallel Pickup Switching

In most cases, when two (or more) guitar pickups are turned on, they're wired in parallel. This means that the "+" or "hot" signal wires are connected together and the ground connections are wired together. Electronically, the pickups are "side by side"; they load each other, causing a loss of output and the loss of some low end. The end result is a combination of the tones of the two pickups, but with a brighter, thinner sound, as if the signal were passing through a high-pass filter.

The best examples of this are the second or fourth positions on a five-way Stratocaster switch, which combine the guitar's bridge and middle pickups or middle and neck pickups, respectively. The sound is brighter and thinner, with a distinct "quack" in the upper midrange. (These positions are often described as "out of phase," but this is a misnomer. The two pickups are still completely in phase, they're just combined in parallel.) There is a similar (though less intense) effect when the neck and bridge pickups on a Les Paul or Telecaster, which are also usually wired in parallel, are combined.

But that's not the only way that pickups can be wired. They can also be wired in series, with the "+" or "hot" of one pickup connected to the ground of the second pickup; in other words, one after another. In this case, the pickups do not load one another, so there is no loss of volume or low end. Two pickups in series are therefore usually louder and fatter sounding. Some Telecasters are now available with series pickup wiring; the result of the Tele neck and bridge pickups together is much fatter, louder, and punchier, with an almost humbucker-like quality.

In some cases, series wiring can be provided by the pickup selector—four-way blade switches are available for Telecasters that allow either pickup alone, both together in parallel, or both together in series. A separate switch could also be installed to work in conjunction with the pickup selector to provide series wiring, as is found in Fender's S-1 switching system.

Other Functions

Switches can, of course, be used for myriad other functions: coil tapping and coil splitting, to engage a preset tone filter, to bypass the volume control for instant solo boost, to turn a preamp on and off, as a master on/off switch (kill switch), and many other things.

Switch Types and Tone

There are several types of switches used in guitars: blade switches, toggle switches, mini toggle switches, push-on/push-off switches, and rotary switches. There are even potentiometers that feature switches built in. You pull the knob out to turn on the switch and push it back in to turn off the switch. Then there are pots with "push-push" switches built in. Push it once to turn the switch on, push it again to turn off the switch. The decision as to which type to use is generally one of preference and function; which type is most convenient and ergonomic and which will fit in the control cavity space that is available?

And, what about the tone of the different types of switches? Is there a difference? While any component can contribute to the tone, the impact of switches—assuming the switch is functioning properly, the solder joints are good, and nothing is oxidized or corroded—is likely far too insignificant to be noticed.

Shielding and Grounding

Making sure a guitar's electronics are well grounded is vital for two reasons: First, the instrument won't function without a ground connection. Second, good grounding is essential for keeping the instrument quiet. The circuit itself must be grounded within the guitar and connected to the ground conductor in the guitar cable, which connects to the ground in the rest of the signal path. There are two other ways in which grounding is handled in guitars, both of which are designed to minimize the external hum, buzz, and noise that the guitar picks up: string grounding and shielding.

String Grounding

Many instruments utilize string grounding, where a wire is run from the guitar's main grounding point (usually the back of one of the potentiometers) to the instrument's bridge. This effectively cuts any noise the guitar strings and other metal items may be picking up (those metal items can actually serve as an antenna for radio frequencies and other noise) and also any noise your body might be picking up. It's true, your body actually serves as an antenna for picking up noise—you can prove it by touching the "hot" part of a guitar cable that's plugged into an amp; you'll likely hear a loud buzz when you touch the cable. With a string ground, all those antennas—the guitar's strings and hardware, and your body—are grounded to the circuit. It works backward from the way most players assume it works. With a string ground, your body doesn't become the ground for the guitar. Rather, the guitar actually grounds your body and eliminates noise that your body is picking up. But however it works, it definitely works.

There is one danger, though: If there is a problem with the grounding or polarity of any of the electrical equipment in your rig or onstage, and you touch it while also touching your guitar's strings, you stand the risk of becoming part of a voltage path—meaning you could get shocked, and in a big way. It's wise to always check for voltage between your guitar and microphone and any other gear on stage before you pick it up and begin playing.

Shielding

A well-shielded guitar can be highly resistant to external noise pickup. Some instruments use shielded wire for connecting the components, which has a woven metal sleeve on the outside to screen out any noise that might be picked up. Others use metal foil, which is glued into the guitar's control cavities, and others use conductive paint that can be sprayed or brushed into the guitar cavities.

Some pickups are also shielded; some use metal covers that enclose the coils (such as many humbuckers and most Tele-style neck pickups), and others, such as EMG single-coil active pickups, are encased in a metal screen that serves as a shield.

All of this is for the purpose of creating a grounded barrier that will repel noise and hum that is carried through the air. The questions are, how much shielding is necessary, and are there tonal negatives to shielding?

Anyone who has played a Stratocaster with single-coils and vintage-style, cloth-covered wiring is well aware of how much noise an unshielded guitar can pick up. But most players find that heavy shielding isn't necessary under normal conditions. For example, Les Pauls often have humbucking pickups inside metal covers and may use unshielded wire, but they are not noisy under normal circumstances. Even a Strat or Tele can be used in most cases without too much trouble. Many players are simply willing to live with whatever noise their guitar might pick up.

But why not just completely shield the instrument and not worry about noise? For some players who just can't stand noise, or those who play with a lot of gain, that's certainly an option. (Another option is to use an external noise-reduction device or a noise gate, which shuts down the guitar signal when there are no notes present. Depending on the style of play and how things are set up, this can work fine. In other cases, though, a noise gate can chop off the ends of notes and cut desired sounds along with the noise.)

The problem—or perhaps, "danger"—is that shielding materials, if they're not grounded perfectly, can actually form a simple capacitor. And, as we saw earlier in this chapter, a capacitor can bleed treble frequencies to ground. This is the reason why some players find that their guitars sound darker if they have them heavily shielded. If everything is grounded properly, though, shielding should not affect a guitar's tone.

The Big Three Guitar Circuits

As with most other things we've discussed, the guitar circuits that many guitar models rely on have their roots firmly in the instruments of the '50s. A modern guitar might have an extra switched function or two, maybe an additional tone control type, or even active electronics, but the basic architecture can trace its lineage directly back to the Big Three circuits.

Telecaster

Leo Fender established the archetypal guitar circuit very early on. The single-pickup Esquire was first. Its three-position switch allowed:

▷ Pickup to volume control

▷ Pickup to volume control with tone control

▷ Pickup through heavy capacitor for thick bassy tone to volume control

When the Telecaster hit the scene with its added neck pickup, the switching and circuit had to change. The controls included master volume control, master tone control, and a three-way switch allowing either pickup alone or both pickups combined in parallel. Since then, this same type of circuit has been used by myriad guitar models from many manufacturers—multiple pickups, pickup switch, master volume control, and master tone control. For many situations, what more do you need?

Some modern Telecasters have expanded on this basic circuit with a four-position switch that also allows for selecting the two pickups combined but wired in series for a thick, fat, humbucker-like tone.

Stratocaster

Leo Fender set the standard again with the circuit for the Fender Stratocaster. With its three single-coil pickups and three controls, the Strat was a more complex beast than the Tele. Originally, the Strat wiring used a three-position switch that could select any of the three pickups by itself. The other controls included a master volume, a tone control for the neck pickup, and a tone control for the middle pickup. There was no tone control on the bridge pickup. It wasn't long before clever players realized they could carefully balance the switch between positions to get the neck and middle pickups together or the middle and neck pickups together, to get the infamous Strat "quack" tones. Fender eventually replaced the three-way switch with a five-way switch that allowed for those two "in-between" positions.

More recently, players such as Eric Johnson have begun rewiring their Strats with the second tone control moved from the middle pickup to the bridge pickup, or sometimes jumpered so that a single knob controls the tone for both the middle and bridge pickups. (The neck pickup tone control is left as is.) Fender now offers some stock models with this bridge or bridge/middle pickup tone control wiring.

Fender also recently expanded on the Strat's wiring with S-1 switching. This system uses a push-push switch in the master volume control, which, when combined with the five-way pickup selector, allows for certain series connections and pickup combinations not supported by just the regular five-way switch.

The basic Strat wiring—five-way switch, master volume, and tone controls—has appeared on all sorts of Super Strats and on many other guitar models with three pickups.

Les Paul

The Gibson Les Paul circuit can be found on tons of two-pickup guitars. Each pickup has its own volume and tone control, and a three-position toggle switch allows for selecting either pickup alone or the two pickups combined in parallel. Variations include pull switches on the tone and volume pots for functions such as coil splitting, series/parallel, and phase reverse.

There has been one change in Gibson's wiring for Les Pauls. In the 1950s, the tone control tapped the signal off the volume pot from the output lug of the pot. With "modern" wiring, the tone control taps the signal off the volume pot from the input lug of the pot. It might seem like a minor change, but there actually is a difference in the tone—the tone of the guitar typically gets brighter. The other thing that happens is that because of the interaction between the tone pot and the volume pot, the taper of the volume pot changes; some players prefer linear volume pots when using '50s wiring on a Les Paul.

Table 5.3   Guitar Electronics Tonal Factors

Tone Factor	Tonal Contribution
Passive versus active electronics	Moderate to major
Volume pot type and value	Minor
Treble bleed	Minor
Tone capacitor type	Subtle
Type of tone control circuit	Minor to major
Switching/signal path design	Major
Switch types	None
Shielding/grounding	None, if installed properly

Amplifiers

"The guitar is what you play, the amp is what you hear."

—Amp maker Ed Quidley, from an interview in *Vintage Guitar* magazine

A T THE BEGINNING OF CHAPTER 4, I stated the obvious: "An electric guitar isn't going to be very, well, electric, if it doesn't have some way of producing and controlling an electrical signal," referring to the vital role that pickups play in a guitar. And that's certainly true. But it doesn't stop there—the best pickups in the world aren't going to get you very far if you don't have an amplifier that can take their tiny signal and turn it into an electrical force that can drive a speaker to create cascading waves of tone.

No matter what type of amplifier you have, whether it's big or small, an amplifier has two primary jobs:

▷ First, to make the signal powerful enough to physically move a speaker cone back and forth.

▷ Second, to provide tone shaping for the signal. Amps do this "naturally" to some extent; most guitar amps are not made to transparently make the signal louder like a studio or PA system amplifier, they're designed to color the sound in a pleasing way—regardless of whether they have controls for adjusting that tone shaping.

Beyond these primary functions, an amplifier may or may not provide other capabilities, such as effects processing (which could be anything from built-in spring reverb to full-on, built-in digital multi-effects), routing to external effects, specialized outputs for feeding recording or PA systems without a microphone, and more.

Combo versus Head

There are two basic "form factors" for guitar amplifiers: combos and heads. An amp head is simply the amplifier circuits housed in an enclosure, with no built-in speakers—a separate speaker cabinet has to be connected to the head with a cable for it to produce sound. (We'll be digging into speakers and speaker cabinets in Chapters 8 and 9.) A combo amp is an amplifier built into an enclosure that also contains speakers—a one-stop, all-in-one solution.

If you have two versions of the same amp model, one a head and one a combo, then from a pure amp-circuit standpoint, there is usually no difference in performance or tone. The head version and the combo version of an amp circuit are identical (unless the manufacturer chooses to add or subtract features from one or the other for some reason). The difference is in the speaker or speakers and the different enclosures. With a combo, you usually have an open-back cabinet design with a particular speaker selected by the manufacturer. You can change out the speaker itself for something else if you want, but the cabinet design is fixed. (You may be able to plug in an "extension" speaker, which will give you more options.)

With a head, you can choose whether you want an open- or closed-back speaker cabinet, how big the cabinet is, the number of speakers in the cabinet, the type and size of the speakers used, and so on—you're free to match whatever cabinet you want with the amp head to achieve exactly the tonal characteristics you want.

There are a few tradeoffs:

> ▷ With a combo, you only have to move one unit; with a head, you have to move two (the head and a separate speaker cabinet).

> ▷ There may be a weight difference between the combined heft of a head and cab and the weight of a combo.

> ▷ Combos are often (but definitely not always) more compact, which can make packing them in a car easier.

> ▷ In the recording studio, you can sit in the control room with an amp head, while the speaker is placed somewhere else for sound isolation. With a combo, unless you want to run a very long guitar cable (which is often more destructive to the signal than running a long speaker cable), you have to be in the same room as the amp.

These are really only ergonomic/form factor differences, though. Tonally, the difference between a head and a combo comes down to the speakers and the cabinet; if you have the combo and head version of the same model amp, the circuit is usually the same in both cases. (There may be minor differences. One example: The second version of the Marshall Class 5 combo amp has a low-power mode, while the "identical" head version of that same amp has no low-power mode.)

Solid-State versus Tube versus Hybrid

Beyond the physical form factor of the amp, a second broad categorization of amps depends on the type of circuit used. There are three types: tube, solid-state, and hybrids of tube and solid-state.

Tube

When amplifiers were first created, tubes were the only solution for making an electrical signal bigger and stronger. Though technology has marched forward, many players still prefer tube amplifiers for the tonal response and shaping they provide for a signal—and for the "feel" and "touch" they have.

We'll be talking much more about tubes in the next chapter. But for now, the key is that tubes and the circuits that use them tend to emphasize and add even-order harmonics to the signal, which results in a sound that most people describe as warm, rich, and pleasing. As just mentioned, there is also a touch and feel aspect to this. Tubes and tube-based circuits often have a "softer," slightly compressed feel that "gives" more than other types of amp circuits. (Some of these pleasing effects may also come from the other components required to build a tube amp, such as transformers, not just the tubes themselves.)

Solid-State

When transistors were introduced, amp manufacturers immediately saw the benefits of the new technology: They were cheaper and lighter, they didn't require heavy transformers, and they didn't age or wear out the way tubes do. In those early days, transistor, or "solid-state" amps quickly gained a reputation for being a less than toneful solution—but solid-state amps were an affordable solution, especially if you didn't need a full-on stack. At the time, the plethora of smaller and medium-sized tube amps that we now enjoy just wasn't as readily available, at least in tube-driven form.

Those early transistor amps became known for having a harsher, "colder" tone than tube amps, and for not breaking up in a pleasing manner. One reason is because transistors tend to emphasize harsher odd-order harmonics, where tube amps emphasize even-order harmonics. Transistors also clip in a different manner than tubes, often with a "harder" feel or different compression characteristics than tubes provide. At the time, for those after "real" guitar tone, tubes were almost universally hailed as the best solution.

Manufacturers and amp designers didn't sit around assuming that situation was good enough, though. They experimented with new transistor circuits, different types of components, different ways to create and manage gain, and different ways to shape the sound, until solid-state amps became much more acceptable to players, especially for those looking for a lower-cost solution or for a more compact and lightweight solution. Jazz players, in particular, have been accepting of solid-state amps—most jazz players use a cleaner tone, want maximum headroom, are playing smaller rooms, and are in quieter solo or ensemble situations where they are often playing with unmiked acoustic drums, pianos, and basses. For all those situations, solid-state amps can be excellent solutions. And this led to the only really "iconic" solid-state amps ever produced: the Roland JC-120 Jazz Chorus (which, granted, doesn't come *close* to meeting the light weight requirement but does produce outstanding clean tones with tons of headroom) and the compact Polytone combos.

In the past decade or so, a new technology has greatly enhanced the status of some solid-state amps; that technology is modeling. With modeling, designers analyze the characteristics of an amp (or an effect or even a guitar), create a computer algorithm that can duplicate those characteristics, and then use that algorithm to process the guitar's sound. (For more on modeling, turn to Chapter 13, "Modeling and Software.") Depending on how detailed and accurate the original analysis was and how accurately the algorithm re-creates those characteristics, a modeling amp can sound incredibly close to the original amp it is trying to emulate. And, depending on the situation—in a full band mix, for example—it may be very difficult, if not impossible, to tell that you're not hearing the "real thing." Modeling amps have other benefits as well—light weight, preset storage and instant recall for your favorite sounds, tonal flexibility, good tone at low volume, and often built-in effects and other features not available on many tube or traditional solid-state amps. Want a new amp or need a different sound? Just switch to another algorithm or preset. For convenience, it's almost impossible to beat a modeling amp.

Still, most players are hard-core traditionalists—it's tubes or nothing! For those players, transistors and modeling will never do. Likewise, while the tone of a solid-state or modeling amp may be awesome, it may not quite be 100 percent the same as the real amp—and many players are purists; it's all or nothing. And, for those who only need the sound of a vintage combo or a dimed stack (and who can play that dimed stack without being shut down for volume transgressions), most or all of the benefits of modeling are negated. But for other players, modeling covers the tones they want, and the convenience and flexibility are tough to argue with.

Even if you're a diehard tubes-or-nothing player, a good, lightweight, highly portable solid-state or modeling amp can still be a useful thing to have around. I, and many other averred tone hounds, keep a small modeling combo amp with a few effects built in handy for practice at spouse-friendly volume levels, for learning songs, for low-volume rehearsals, for small "grab-it-and-go" gigs, and as a backup if my boutique tube amps go down or aren't appropriate for some reason.

Hybrid

As you'll see in the next part of this chapter, there are two large sections to a guitar amplifier: the preamp and the power amp. Some amplifiers take a hybrid approach, with a solid-state preamp and a tube power section, or vice versa—a tube preamp with a solid-state power section. Some new amps are even combining a modeling preamp section with a tube power section. (See the next section for more on preamps and power amps.)

Using this hybrid approach allows amp manufacturers to combine tube and solid-state in a way that makes sense to them for creating the sound they want for their amps. The first of this type of hybrid amps were the Music Man amps created by Leo Fender after his "non-compete" restrictions expired from when he sold Fender to CBS. The Music Man amps used solid-state preamps with tube power amps to create a "Fender-y" tone; they were adopted in the late '70s and early '80s by players such as Joe Perry of Aerosmith, Mark Knopfler, Albert Lee, and Eric Clapton, among others.

Other manufacturers also created hybrid amps with solid-state preamps and tube power sections, such as Marshall and Peavey. Manufacturers have also created amps with tube preamps and solid-state power amps, such as the Marshall Valvestates. Most recently, Reinhold Bogner (of Bogner amps) has pushed the envelope of hybrid amps with his designs for Line 6, which combine modeling technology with both 12AX7 preamp tubes and 6L6 power tubes. The DT50 series of Line 6 amps also blurs the lines by combining tube technology with onboard modeling and direct interfacing with external POD modeling processors—the tube power section of the amp can even electrically reconfigure itself to match whatever type of amp model is selected. (So you get a Class A tube power amp section when you choose a Vox, you get a Class AB tube power amp section when you choose a Fender, and so on.)

Some hybrid amps have been well-received—many Music Man amps are still in use today—while others were only successful as budget/entry-level amps. Some experts suggest that many players can't tell the difference between a solid-state preamp with a tube power amp versus an all-tube amp, while most feel that the difference between a tube preamp with a solid-state power amp and an all-tube amp is much more audible.

Preamp versus Power Amp

There are two major sections in virtually every guitar amplifier: the preamp and the power amp. The preamp takes in the small signal coming from the guitar or from pedals. It amplifies that signal up to a more robust level, which can then be processed with tone controls and sent on either to feed line-level effects or to feed the power amp section of the amp. The power amp section is where the heavy work gets done. It's where the signal from the preamp is juiced up until it's powerful enough to move a speaker.

Both sections of the amp are capable of contributing tonal qualities and distortion to the signal, as well as affecting the "feel" of playing the guitar. But there is a difference in the distortion tone and playing feel that each section contributes, especially with tube amplifiers. The preamp can be designed to contribute everything from pristine clean to light crunchiness to heavily compressed super-smooth sustain. The power amp can also be pushed into distortion—if you can crank the amp up loud enough. This results in a sweeter sound, with less compression and more articulation that many players feel is more "musical" sounding.

In most amplifiers, the preamp and the power sections are integrated into one unit—a head or a combo. Plug in your guitar, and the signal automatically passes through the preamp to the power amp and out to the speakers. But separate, stand-alone preamps and power amps are also available, usually in rackmount boxes. With this "modular" approach, you can match the preamp you want to the power amp you want. You aren't restricted to the preamp and the power section that a manufacturer matched together inside of a head or combo. You can also easily connect effects processors between the preamp's output and the power amp's input. Separate preamp/power amp systems were popular in the '80s, when many players were using big rack rigs and when a lot of players were using stereo setups, and they are still somewhat popular today. But the vast majority of players prefer an integrated amplifier that contains both sections in one enclosure.

Preamp

The primary gig of the preamp section of an amplifier—or of a standalone preamp, if one is being used instead of an integrated amp—is to make the guitar signal strong enough so that it can be passed along to the power amp. The preamp is also where most (or all) of the controllable tone shaping takes place on the signal and where any additional elements, such as reverb, vibrato, or sends/returns to external effects, take place.

Gain

Gain, in guitar amp terms, is the amount the signal level is boosted or can be boosted by a particular amp stage. In the early days—Fender Tweed, Brownface, and Blackface amps and their contemporaries—the idea (at least as far as the manufacturer was concerned) was to make the guitar's clean signal louder. There wasn't a ton of gain available in the preamp section; as the amp was turned up, the power section was driven harder and harder until it began to break up and distort. This limited the amount of distortion that could be produced and also required that the amp be turned up loud in order to get that rich, crunchy tone.

Players began using distortion boxes, fuzzes, treble boosters, and overdrives to hit the preamp section of the amp harder for more distortion and to be able to get that distortion at lower volume levels. (See Chapter 11, "Effects," for more on these types of effects.) Amp manufacturers responded with master volume controls, which allowed the preamp to be cranked up while keeping the signal level that was fed into the power section—and therefore the overall volume—low. Suddenly, players could get the distortion they craved at reasonable volume levels: a real breakthrough!

Players, of course, wanted more and more gain for a smoother, thicker, richer tone, more sustain, and more aggressive harmonic content. Manufacturers met that demand with higher and higher gain capabilities in the preamp. Other manufacturers offered high-output pickups as an alternative means to drive the preamp even harder.

Then, Randall Smith at Mesa/Boogie came up with the idea of cascading multiple preamp gain stages into one another. The first stage added gain; the second stage added even more gain, allowing for heavily distorted tones that could be achieved at low volume levels using the amps' master volume controls, which adjust the amount of signal being fed from the preamp into the power amp. Today, some amps, particularly those aimed at shredders and metal heads, have tremendous amounts of gain on tap in their preamps.

As far as gain is concerned, transistor and tube preamps work in the same way: The signal level is amplified. If it is amplified so much that the level exceeds the point where the circuit can accurately reproduce the signal, then distortion occurs. The "top" of the signal waveform is literally flattened out or clipped off. This "clipping" results in harmonics being added to the signal, creating tones ranging from gentle breakup (with light clipping) to screaming distortion (with heavy clipping). As the gain and distortion increase, the amount of compression in the signal—where the dynamic range or the difference between the lowest and highest dynamic levels the amp can reproduce is reduced or squashed—also increases. The more compression in the signal, the smoother it will be, and the more sustain the sound will have.

As always, there are tradeoffs. Light to moderate distortion can increase the presence of the tone, helping it punch through and be heard; there's an additional impact to a nice crunchy, broken-up tone that a clean sound doesn't have. But as the gain and distortion are increased, there can be side effects:

> ▷ Heavy distortion generally results in signal compression, which increases sustain but can diminish dynamics, presence, and articulation.

> ▷ Heavy distortion can change the perception of volume. Try it for yourself; if you have a sound level meter, play a clean sound and a heavily distorted sound at the same decibel level. Which sounds louder? Depending on the listener and the tones being used, the clean sound may be perceived as being louder, or the distorted signal may seem louder.

> ▷ Though it may seem counterintuitive, heavy distortion can make the sound of the guitar seem "smaller" and thinner. This may be a result of compression or of the emphasis on higher harmonics.

> ▷ Heavy distortion can make the sound muddy. Many players reduce bass to compensate for this, but then the sound can become thin and nasal or whiny.

> ▷ High gain will also boost any noise the guitar, effects, or amp are producing along with the guitar signal. Many players address this problem by using noise-reduction systems or noise gates with high gain amps.

Of course, there are benefits to high gain as well! Players love it for how easy it makes playing (especially legato playing), for the near infinite sustain it can provide, for the rich harmonic content it adds, and most of all, for the powerful, aggressive, *electric* sound that is produced.

Most amps have a single preamp gain control (often labeled simply "Gain") that is used to increase or decrease the amount of amplification being added to the signal. Amps with cascaded gain stages may have multiple gain controls that determine how much gain is added at each stage—and in some cases, these stages are voiced differently. For example, one gain stage may be brighter and more dynamic, while another is darker and more compressed; by balancing those gain stages, the tone and response can be adjusted along with the gain, before any EQ or tone controls are ever touched. (See the next section for more on EQ and tone controls.)

More complex amps may also add boost switches that add a predetermined amount of gain to the signal, and these may even be offered with a footswitch control, so that you can step on a switch to turn on the boost for a fatter, higher gain sound for a solo and then turn the boost back off when the solo is over to return to a cleaner rhythm guitar tone. These boost stages may even be of different types. Some Dumble amps (and the many Dumble clones on the market), for example, offer a choice of a solid-state or tube-first gain stage.

The thing that lets all this preamp gain work is the master volume control, which sets the signal level that is fed from the preamp section into the power amp section. By turning the master volume control down, you can crank up the preamp gain control to get as much distortion as you want, while still keeping the volume level that the power amp is putting through the speakers at a reasonable level. Without the master volume control, as you turned up the preamp gain, the volume would get higher and higher very quickly, making the amp too loud for many situations. (We'll talk more about master volume amps versus non-master-volume amps later in this chapter).

EQ and Tone Control

A preamp can do more than just generate distortion, of course. From the very earliest amps, tone controls have been part of the equation. Initially, these were simply a single control labeled "Tone" and were generally high frequency or treble controls; crank it up to make the sound brighter and more cutting, turn it down to make the sound darker and warmer.

The tone control circuit in a guitar amplifier is often referred to as a *tone stack*. The name comes from how the circuit appears on a schematic diagram, as if the components are stacked on top of one another. There are two types of tone controls in guitar amps: passive and active. Passive controls are only able to cut the level of frequencies—for example, a passive treble control can only turn down the highs. An active tone control, on the other hand, can both boost and cut the level of frequencies; this is more flexible but has the possibility of adding noise when a frequency band is boosted.

There are two uses for tone controls in an amp. The first is to adjust the sound resulting from the guitar passing through the amp to your liking—make it brighter, make it fatter, and so on. A subset of this is compensating for the inherent tone of your guitar (make a dark-sounding guitar brighter, for example) and other gear. Another subset is adjusting for the use of multiple guitars of different types; you can use the controls to make a humbucker-equipped guitar brighter so it doesn't sound too dark in comparison when you switch to a single-coil-equipped instrument.

The second application for tone controls is to compensate for the sound of the room you are playing in. Some rooms are so lined with carpeting and draperies that they seem to suck all the life out of the guitar (and it gets worse when such a room is filled with people, who soak up even more sound)—being able to adjust the tone to make up for this loss in the room is a nice tool to have.

EQ Bands

An amp may have a variety of tone controls, and each adjusts a particular band of frequencies. The more bands of EQ the amp has—in other words, the more different tone controls there are—the more the tone can be custom-tailored by the player—but also the more possibility there is for creating a bad tone or for increasing the complexity of operating the amp. Complexity isn't an issue in the studio or usually in rehearsal, but it can be a problem on stage, where you need to make adjustments quickly.

> ▷ As mentioned previously, early amps (and today's "retro" amps) often have a single treble control. This provides a surprising amount of tone-shaping power and can be fine as long as the bass and the midrange have been voiced by the manufacturer in a way that pleases you—and that works with your other gear. For example, the amount of bass in the amp may be fine when you use a guitar equipped with single-coil pickups but may be too much when using a guitar equipped with fat-sounding humbuckers.

▷ The next step in tonal shaping would be an amp with a second control for bass. In this case, the level of the midrange is generally preset, but you can give the effect of increasing the midrange by turning down the treble and bass (the midrange stays fixed but becomes louder in comparison to the highs and lows) or effectively decreasing the midrange by turning the highs and lows up (the midrange becomes quieter in comparison to the highs and lows).

▷ A third control for midrange gives the possibility for further adjusting or shaping the tone, while still leaving full control over the bass and treble using those respective controls. With a midrange control, where the control is placed in the frequency range or spectrum can dramatically affect the tones available from the amp. For example, a midrange control that is placed in the lower midrange will allow you to make the sound fuller or thinner but can't really be used to adjust the presence of the signal or to tame harshness. A midrange control that is placed higher in the frequency range will be great for adjusting the presence and articulation in the tone but won't be a lot of help in adding lower midrange fullness. For this reason, most midrange controls are fairly "broad," meaning they affect a wide range of frequencies when you turn them. This gives good shaping control but may not be specific enough to address a particular problem frequency or range of frequencies.

▷ Some amps add a fourth control, also in the mids; this gives you a control for bass, lower mids, upper mids, and treble, which can be a very flexible arrangement for dialing in the tone.

▷ A few amps have "parametric" or "sweepable" midrange controls, which, using either a switch or an extra knob, allow you to change the frequency where the midrange control is working. This adds even more flexibility and allows you to focus the action of a particular midrange control exactly where you want it in the frequency range.

The tradeoff for adding more EQ bands is that the amplifier becomes more complex and time consuming to operate and to dial in for the tone you want. You have to know what you're doing to dial in the desired tone (should you boost the highs or cut the mids to make the sound brighter?), you have to spend more time getting to know what the various tone controls do, and it simply takes longer to adjust more knobs than it does to turn a single treble control up or down.

Keep in mind that not all tone controls are created equal. Each manufacturer's tone stack will be voiced slightly differently. For example, the tone controls in a Marshall amp don't give the same aural effect as those in a Fender amp. The frequencies at which each tone control operates may be different. (For example, the mid control on a Marshall may be voiced higher than the mid control on a Fender amp.) And, the amount of boost and/or cut available from a control may differ between different manufacturers and even different amp models from the same manufacturer. There's a reason why many players simply start with all the controls on a Marshall full up, where the controls on a Fender often are set at bass = 3, midrange = 4, and treble = 6. (For those with Fender tube amps with no midrange control, there is a resistor inside the amp that "presets" the midrange level to the equivalent of 4 on an amp with a midrange control.)

Then there is the issue of interaction between the tone controls—the EQ bands may actually overlap a bit, meaning that turning up the treble control may also affect the level of some (or all) of the midrange frequencies.

Other Tone-Shaping Controls

An amplifier may be equipped with a number of additional controls (usually switches) you can use to shape the tone.

> **Bright switch.** Makes the tone more trebly and, well, brighter. Some players love bright switches for the extra sparkle and shimmer they can add, and other players find bright switches to sound brittle and harsh—it depends on your ears, how bright the amp is to begin with, and how bright the guitar is that's feeding the amp.

> **Deep switch.** Boosts the level of the bass frequencies. A deep switch can make the sound much fatter and add chunky "thump" on the bottom end (similar to what you might get with a big 4×12 cabinet), or it can make the sound boomy and muddy. The amount of gain, the amount of bass the amp and guitar naturally produce, and the type of speakers can all affect this.

> **Mid shift.** Changes the frequency where the midrange control operates.

> **Mid boost.** Increases the gain of the midrange frequencies.

> **Thick.** Midrange or lower midrange boost.

Tone Stack Bypass

Some amplifiers have a switch or switches that allow some portion or even all of the tone stack to be removed or bypassed from the preamp circuit. This generally results in more gain from the preamp if the tone controls are passive; remember, passive controls can only cut level, they can't increase it. Removing the tone stack lets the full signal through, resulting in more gain. For example, the 3 Monkeys Orangutan tube amp has a Lift switch that removes the bass control from the circuit. This has the dual effect of making the sound fatter and increasing the gain. The Vox Night Train is an amp where the tone stack can be completely removed from the circuit, to allow the maximum signal through with increased gain and sustain. Likewise, on Dumble Overdrive Special–style amps, engaging the mid boost bypasses the main tone stack (although if the amp has the HRM option, that remains active).

You could argue that playing an amp with no tone stack is a "purer" way to go, since all of the signal is getting through unimpeded. However, you are locked in to whatever tone shaping the manufacturer designed into the amp; there's no way to make any adjustments to the sound with no tone stack.

EQ Placement

A big variable with amplifier tone stacks is where they are located in the circuit. Is the tone stack before the gain stage that results in distortion or is it after? This makes a big difference in how the tone and amp response can be shaped. (There is less difference with tone stack placement with clean tones.) For example, having a bass control before the distortion allows much better control over muddiness and "flubbiness" than having it after, where the bass control will be more focused on general "shaping" of the low end of the overall tone. Likewise, having a treble or midrange control in front of the distortion results in a different sort of control and tone than having those controls after the distortion—it may also change the feel. Turning down the treble in front of distortion results in a muted attack. The effect is somewhat similar to turning down the tone control on the guitar itself, where turning down the treble after the distortion results in overall smoothing of the sound.

Built-In Reverb, Tremolo, and Vibrato

Many amplifiers, both combo- and head-style, feature built-in reverb. Although digital reverb is coming on strong, most amps still have spring reverb onboard. Reverb can fill out the sound, make it richer, make it smoother, and make it easier to play. Tremolo is common in some Blackface Fender-style amps, among other models from various manufacturers. This pulsating volume effect isn't used as prevalently as reverb, but it is a requirement for certain rootsy styles and swampy tonal effects. Vibrato, which is a pulsating pitch effect, is quite rare in guitar amps, though certain models, such as vintage models from Magnetone, did feature true vibrato effects built in. (There's much more discussion of reverb, tremolo, and vibrato in Chapter 11.)

Effects Loops

Although some players are 100 percent satisfied with the tone that comes from a guitar plugged straight into an amplifier, many other guitarists—perhaps most other guitarists—use at least one or two effects boxes. In most cases, it works fine to put those effects between the guitar's output and the amp's input. But there are some effects, such as delay, that often work better when they're placed after the gain has been added to the signal. If you run delay into the front of the amp, before the gain is added, it can be difficult to control the volume level of the echoes/repeats, plus the sound can sometimes get cluttered or muddy. Putting the delay after the gain stage allows it to work on the already distorted signal, for a cleaner effect and much better control over the level of the repeats.

That's where an effects loop comes in. An effects loop typically comes between the preamp and the power amp and allows the signal coming out of the preamp to be processed with effects and then returned into the amp to be mixed with the dry (un-effected) guitar signal.

Not all effects prefer to be placed in an effects loop. Some are simply happier in front of the amp. Here's how it breaks down. These effects generally perform better in front of the amp (between the guitar output and the amp input):

 ▷ Tuner

 ▷ Wah

 ▷ Compressor

 ▷ Boost

 ▷ Overdrive/distortion/fuzz

The following effects can work in front of the amp, but if your amp is generating distortion for you, they'll probably function better in the amp's effects loop:

 ▷ Delay/echo

 ▷ Reverb

 ▷ Stereo-izing effects (could be modulation effects such as chorus, could be delay)

What about modulation effects, such as chorus, tremolo, flanger, phase shifter, vibrato, Leslie effects, and others? It depends on what you want to hear. Placed in front of the amp, any modulation effects will be less intense and heavy. Placed in the effects loop, any modulation effects can work on the distortion generated by the amp and will create a much more intense effect—you may like this, you may not. The only way to know what you prefer is to try it both ways.

Pitch effects, such as octave dividers and harmony generators, may work better in front of the amp; in an effects loop, a distorted tone may sound unnatural when pitch shifted. However, it again depends on the effect that you are trying to create.

As for equalizers, the effect is different in front of the amp than it is in the loop (in a similar way to how amp tone stacks work differently when placed in front of and after gain stages). In front, the EQ can be used to craft how the distortion responds, cleaning up muddiness, making the midrange thicker, and taming hard attacks and harsh high end. Placed in the effects loop, an EQ can be used to shape the tone of clean and distorted tones, smoothing out the top end, removing problem frequencies, and more.

See Chapter 11 for much more about effects types and the best order in which to place your effects.

Series/Parallel Loops

There are two ways that an effects loop can be incorporated into the signal flow in an amp. The first way is in series. In this case, the effects loop basically breaks into the signal path and completely reroutes the entire signal through whatever external effects you have connected. Sometimes series effects loops are labeled as "preamp out/power amp in" jacks. Since the entire signal is passing through the effects that are connected, you'll need to use effects that have their own wet/dry controls for balancing the effects (wet) against the un-effected (dry) signal.

The second type of loop is a parallel effects loop. In this case, a portion of the signal is tapped off the main signal path to be sent out of the loop's output. Then, after passing through the effects, the signal returns to the effects loop's input, where it is mixed back in with the dry signal. In this case, the effects processors should be set for 100 percent wet operation, since the dry signal is still passing through the amp in parallel with the effects signal. You don't want to mix additional dry signal that has passed through the effects processor back in with the existing dry signal.

In either case, the loop may have its own level controls so that you can use either stompbox or rackmount effects in the loop. Most pedals operate at "instrument level," which is −20 dB. Rack effects tend to operate at either −10 dB or +4 dB (depending on the device). Unless the amp's effects loop can change its level, you may or may not be able to interface it correctly with the effects you want to use.

Channel Switching

The original guitar amps were single-channel devices. This worked fine for the music of the day, which didn't rely on both clean and high gain tones in the same song—and still works fine for situations where the amp gain is low enough that you can turn down your guitar's volume control to get a clean tone. Many players, though, want the option of being able to switch between a great clean tone and a great dirty tone, or to have two other different sounds easily accessible. The solution from manufacturers was the dual-channel amp. Initially, these were probably intended to let two players plug in simultaneously—consider the Blackface Fender amps with one straight-ahead channel and a second channel often equipped with vibrato/tremolo. On those early amps, there was no easy way to switch between the channels on the amps themselves; each channel had its own input jack(s), and an external A/B box had to be used to route the signal into those inputs. Even the first Mesa/Boogie amps, which had a clean channel and a dirty channel, required using an external box to switch from one channel to another.

The introduction of true channel-switching amps made life much easier for those seeking instant access to multiple sounds from the same amp. With a channel-switching amp, the player plugs into the amp and then can use a footswitch to route the signal through a clean channel or through a dirty channel—in some cases, amps have up to four footswitch-selectable channels, each with their own gain settings and sometimes their own EQ controls, for the ultimate in tonal variety from a single amp. More often, the two channels share the same set of tone controls, which isn't quite as versatile—whatever tone settings you have on your clean tone also have to apply to your dirty tone.

Some amps provide separate controls for each channel for other features of the amp, such as bright switches, reverb level, and even separate master volume controls. Some amps even allow the amp's effects loop (or loops) to be assigned to a particular channel or channels. The more controls there are dedicated to each channel, the more you can tailor and control the tone that channel produces.

Power Amp

Once your guitar's signal passes through the amp's preamp section, where it's shaped and enhanced to tonal perfection, it is time to crank it up so that it can drive a speaker—which brings us to the power section of the amplifier. This is where the signal is pumped up from a still relatively weak line-level to a beefy, brawny speaker-level signal. This takes a great deal of amplification. But with our signal buffed up by the preamp section, it's now ready for some serious bodybuilding. Whether you're using a tube or a transistor/solid-state amp, the function of the power section of the amp is the same: It takes the raw power coming out of the wall outlet and uses it to bolster the signal coming from the preamp.

There isn't a lot of player-controllable tone shaping that takes place in the power section, though any tubes, transformers, or other components in the signal path will add their own coloration to the signal. There is one notable exception on some amps: the presence control. Common on Marshall and Marshall-derived tube amps, presence is usually a rotary knob that affects the amount of negative feedback in a tube amp's power section and increases the amount of upper treble while reducing smoothness. A few amps also have a resonance control, which changes the damping factor of the amp (damping factor is the ability of the amp to control the attached speaker's motion) and mostly affects how "tight" the bass sounds.

Another place where we do have control is deciding where the drive is coming from in our signal. Are you pushing the signal hard in the preamp to create the tone and/or distortion you want with a master volume control as the governor on the whole thing, or are you running the signal through the preamp clean and then maxing out the feed to the power section to get maximum headroom and possibly some power amp distortion you want from there? Both approaches have their merit, but there is definitely a difference in the results. Driving the power section hard results in a different, less compressed, more articulate, thicker distortion than what you get when you overload the gain stages in the preamp section. As I mentioned earlier, the problem is that driving the power section of the amp hard comes at a price: high volume levels.

Master Volume versus Non-Master Volume

Until the 1970s, there was no such thing as a master volume control on an amplifier. This meant that to get distortion from an amp, you had to crank it up and deal with the volume level. Many amps are still made this way. You simply turn up the "volume" control (which is probably really a preamp gain control) until the amp reaches the volume level or the amount of distortion you want. Typically, you'll only get a noticeable volume increase over a portion of the volume control's rotation. Past a certain point, the amp will begin to break up—it will be unable to reproduce the guitar signal cleanly and will begin to clip. As you turn up the volume control, the amount of distortion increases, but the volume won't increase much, if at all.

If you've got a smaller amp, this may work just fine for you. For example, many players find that they can achieve the tone they want using smaller non-master volume amps in clubs and other venues without a problem. (One would have to assume 15-watt Vox-style amps and 18-watt Marshall-style amps have increased in popularity for this reason.) Other players find that even a smaller amp is way too loud for many situations. Part of the reason is the whole power versus volume issue, which we'll be talking about in Chapter 10. But it's also because the perception of volume changes depending on context. Played all alone in a small room, a 15-watt tube amp may seem super loud. But put that same 15-watt amp on a big stage next to a loud drummer, and it may not seem loud enough.

From a tonal standpoint, whether you use a master-volume amp or a non-master-volume amp comes down to how much gain you need (assuming you're using the amp to generate your distortion), where you want that gain to come from (preamp section or power section), how much clean headroom you need (see the sidebar "Headroom" later in this chapter), and how loud your situation will allow you to play.

Power Attenuators

But there is another solution to the volume control problem—one that still allows for power section distortion —and that solution is to use a power attenuator or another system that allows the output power of the amplifier to be controlled before it hits the speaker. A power attenuator connects between the speaker output of the amp and the speaker itself. Attenuators use heavy resistors and other circuitry to convert the power coming from the amp into heat, reducing the amount of power that actually makes it to the speaker.

Opinions vary on how "transparent" power attenuators are; some players find that with a power attenuator, their amp sounds the same, just quieter. Others find that an attenuator changes the tone, making it mushy, fizzy, or muddy, and may also change the feel, making the amp seem more compressed. In general, the complaints increase as the amount of attenuation increases. If you're using an attenuator to pull the power back by 3 dB, 6 dB, or 10 dB, the differences in feel and tone are less noticeable. But if you're trying to rein in a 100-watt Marshall so that you can play in your bedroom at 2 a.m. while the baby is sleeping in the next room, the heavy attenuation required will probably be at least somewhat audible and may change the playing feel.

There are two types of attenuators: resistive and reactive. Resistive attenuators use simple resistor networks to tame the volume. This is less expensive and simpler, but the results may not be as transparent. And, some experts fear that a simple resistive load may sooner or later result in damage to your amp or the components in the amp, such as the tubes and transformers. Some players have used resistive load attenuators for years with no damage to their amps, so the jury is still out—stick with your amp manufacturer's recommendations.

Increasingly, manufacturers are using the second type of approach to attenuator design, a reactive load. A reactive load is designed to respond (at least in the amp's eyes) like a speaker would. This is said to be safer for the amplifier and also to produce better, more transparent sonic results, especially at heavier levels of attenuation.

Power Scaling

Another approach for allowing an amp to be cranked up while still controlling volume is power scaling. Where most power attenuators are external boxes that connect between the amp and its speakers, power scaling is a technology that is normally found built into an amp. There are several different types in use from different manufacturers. The idea is to reduce the power that is being fed into the tubes, so that they must be pushed harder to achieve a certain volume level. These types of systems are characterized by their specs. Where a power attenuator will be rated for the number of decibels it can reduce the output, power scaling will be rated for how it reduces the wattage the amp puts out. For example, on the Tone King Metropolitan boutique tube amp, with the power control all the way up, the amp puts out 40 watts. Using the power control, you can drop this as low as 1/4 watt—which results in not just a serious drop in output power, but also a correspondingly serious drop in the volume level that the connected speaker or speakers put out.

Most players find that power scaling is a transparent way to reduce the volume level an amp puts out to a significantly low level. But, even with power scaling, you can only go so far (make the amp so quiet) before the tonal change and the change in feel of the amp to you as a player becomes noticeable.

Headroom

Clean headroom, or just *headroom*, is a term that gets thrown around a lot with amplifiers—and it can be a factor with either the preamp or the power amp. When discussing amps, headroom is the amount of volume or gain increase the amp can provide before the signal begins to break up. In other words, the way guitarists talk about it, headroom is the amount of clean, undistorted power the amplifier can produce. (Audio engineers and techs use the term slightly differently, to refer to the amount of gain that is available above the device's nominal level, before the onset of distortion.) Headroom is a function of the amp's available power, its efficiency, and the efficiency of its speakers.

Clean headroom depends on several things. In the amp itself, the gain of the preamp and the amount of power the amp can produce determine how much clean output the amp will have—an amp with lower gain 12AT7 preamp tubes will have more clean headroom than an amp with higher gain 12AX7 preamp tubes. And an amp that can put out 100 watts will have more clean headroom than an amp that can put out only 10 watts—the 100-watt amp will be able to produce clean tones much louder than the 10-watt amp.

Outside of the amp, the efficiency of the speakers and speaker cabinet can make a difference in clean headroom. And, the level of the signal feeding the amp will be a big factor—a low-output single-coil pickup won't drive an amp's front end nearly as hard as a super-hot "distortion" humbucking pickup, which could easily push the preamp into distortion.

How much clean headroom is enough? The answer depends on what kind of tone and response you want from your amp. If you never use squeaky-clean tones, always preferring to have some subtle breakup in the tone, then a low-headroom amp is what you want. If, on the other hand, you want very clean tones at extremely high volume, you're going to want a powerful amplifier feeding very efficient speakers.

Output Transformer

In a tube amp, you can't connect the output from the tubes directly to the speakers. You need to get the signal to the proper place in terms of connecting to a speaker—the tube output is high impedance and high voltage, while the speaker input is low impedance and low voltage. That's where the amp's output transformer comes in; it matches those two disparate things together.

A transformer consists of two or more coils of wire wrapped around a magnetic core. There's no connection between the coils; electrical current is induced in one coil from the other through the magnetic core. This makes transformers great for isolating circuits. By working with the coils, the designer can also set up different "taps," which can be routed to various places at difference voltages.

Some experts suggest that a tube amp's output transformer is one of the most critical components in determining the tone. The type of wire used for the coils may affect the tone, and transformers can color the tone and distort. The transformer design will also determine high- and low-frequency roll-off. And, a larger-output transformer will have better bass response, will offer more volume, and may have wider frequency response than a smaller transformer (all other things being equal).

Some players feel that changing the output transformer in an amp out for a higher- or lower-quality unit can make a huge difference in the sound of the amp and will even point to particular transformers as being good for certain styles of music or playing. Some players feel that hand-wound transformers are an improvement over machine-wound transformers. As with hand-wound pickups, this isn't always the case. A hand-wound transformer may be better than a machine-wound one, but it depends on the skill of the person making the transformer. In any case, a machine-wound transformer will be more consistent than a hand-wound transformer.

Unfortunately, changing out the output transformer is not as easy as swapping out tubes. It's a job best left to an expert, both from a practical standpoint and from a safety standpoint. Remember, there are high voltages inside an amp that can kill.

Power Transformer

The second, and usually largest, type of transformer found in amps is the power transformer—both solid-state and tube amplifiers require a power transformer. Its job is to determine how the voltage feeding from the wall outlet is converted so that it can be sent to the components of the amp. Tubes are high-voltage devices, so the transformer makes sure that they get the proper voltage they want to see.

Because of this, the power transformer and the power supply circuit can have a real impact on the "feel" of the amp; this is where "sag" occurs if the voltage drops when a loud note or attack is hit. In other words, if the power supplied doesn't keep up with the demand being made by the amp, the gain factor in the tubes will drop, resulting in a more compressed sound and a softer playing feel.

Rectifier

A rectifier in a tube amp has a simple job: It converts alternating current (AC, as comes out of the power outlet in the wall) into direct current (DC, as is used to run many of the components in the amplifier. DC is also what comes out of a common battery.) There are many types of rectifiers, but guitar amps tend to use either tube or solid-state rectifiers (which are basically strings of diodes). There is a difference. Solid-state rectifiers tend to produce a "harder" feel (they have a faster rise time and response than tubes), while vacuum tube rectifiers can "sag" a bit, resulting in a softer, more compressed feel. However, solid-state rectifiers are less expensive, provide more power, don't generate as much heat, and can be easy for a manufacturer to deal with.

Some amps will actually have more than one rectifier; they feature one rectifier per pair of output tubes—this is where the Mesa/Boogie Dual Rectifier and Triple Rectifier names come from, for example. The Dual Rectifier has four 6L6 power tubes and two 5U4 rectifier tubes, while the Triple Rectifier features six 6L6 power tubes and three 5U4 rectifier tubes. In other cases—including the Boogie Dual and Triple Rectifiers—an amp has more than one type of rectifier onboard—both tube and solid-state—and a switch for selecting which one is active. This can noticeably affect the tone, feel, response, and clean headroom in the amp.

Choke

A choke is an inductor that is used in the power supply of the amplifier. A choke is used to filter or smooth out "ripple" or variation in the DC current. Chokes tend to be used in more expensive amplifiers—less expensive amps often go with a straight resistor. In general, an amp with a choke will have less hum (all other things begin equal) and deeper bass response (again, all other things being equal). And, a larger choke (more inductance) will provide better bass than a smaller choke (less inductance). Some sources suggest that the quality of the choke can affect the amp's touch sensitivity and dynamics as well.

Hand-Wired versus PCB versus PTP

Does how an amp is put together make a difference in the tone it produces? Many players think so—in fact, some players refuse to purchase or use an amp that uses a construction method they believe will be detrimental to the tone. Yikes, what if you're using one that's made the wrong way? Is your guitar-playing life ruined forever?

Probably not—things aren't quite that dire. But is there any truth to this? Let's take a look at how amps are made and what effects each type of manufacturing can have on tone.

▶ **PTP.** With PTP, or "point-to-point" construction, the components in the amp are basically soldered directly to one another. This is how the earliest amps were built. It is a labor-intensive approach that requires electrical circuit and component knowledge, as well as good soldering and cable dress (routing) skills. Because of this, it is an expensive method for making an amp. There are advantages; when done properly, PTP amps are rugged and easy to troubleshoot and repair.

▶ **Turret board.** A "turret board" is a thin, non-conductive board. Holes are drilled in the board to correspond to the desired component layout. Then "turrets"—metal posts—are screwed into the holes, and the components are soldered to the turrets to create the circuit. For many years, turret-board construction was considered the most rugged and the best. It allowed the designer to lay out the circuit using the turret locations and then just about anyone could solder the components in place without needing to read a schematic or have electrical circuit knowledge. However, it is an expensive, labor-intensive method for building an amp, so it is rarely used today outside of small boutique operations.

▶ **Eyelet board.** An eyelet board is similar to a turret board, except that the components aren't soldered to turrets, they're soldered to terminal strips.

▶ **PCB.** PCB, or "printed circuit board," construction starts with a non-conductive board that is covered on one or both sides with copper cladding. The circuit is drawn out on the board and then the unnecessary cladding is removed using an acid bath or other method. What's left are "traces"—lines of copper on the board that serve as the "wires" for connecting components together. Holes are drilled in the board, the components are loaded in, and they are soldered to the traces. From a manufacturing standpoint, it's a fast, easy, consistent and repeatable, and inexpensive method for making an amp.

So which of these are "hand-wired"? After all, just visit any guitar forum, and you'll quickly surmise that the only good amp must be a hand-wired amp! In fact, any of these types of amps could be hand-wired to one degree or another—even a printed circuit board amp could feature hand-wired connections to components such as switches, pots, tube sockets, and more. But, most players use "hand-wired" to refer to point-to-point or turret/eyelet construction.

But, the big question remains: Which is best? Many players would point to PTP or turret/eyelet construction as best (although many wouldn't be sure why). When pressed, an "expert" will usually say that it's because PC board construction is hard to repair and is not as durable as the other methods. However, a well laid out PC board can be repaired, and with proper construction, a PC board can be quite durable—though perhaps not as durable as the other types under really rough conditions.

Because PCB amps are usually on the lower end of the price spectrum, sometimes durability is sacrificed for price. For example, the best PCB construction technique is to mount pots, switches, and tube sockets to the amp's metal chassis, where they are firmly supported, and then to run wires to the PC board as necessary. But this costs more money, so manufacturers looking to save a buck will use pots, switches, and sockets that mount directly to the PC board traces. And this is definitely not as durable as the other types of construction. It also makes the amps even harder to service.

But the big reason usually given for the belief that PCB is inferior is the idea that PC board construction suffers from increased capacitance between the traces, which can adversely affect the tone. In truth, any of the amp construction methods are subject to problems with capacitance between wires and component leads if they aren't laid out well and if the wires aren't properly dressed. A point-to-point amp that looks like a rat's nest of messy wires and components can have all sorts of capacitance and noise problems. Likewise, a poorly laid out PC board will indeed have increased capacitance. But a well laid out PC board won't have any more capacitance than a well laid out point-to-point or turret/eyelet design.

Here's the truth: The keys are proper layout and quality construction techniques. If the construction and layout are done to high standards, then a printed circuit board amp can sound just as good as a point-to-point amp.

The problem is that, as mentioned above, PCB construction is the least expensive method, so it tends to get used for lower-end, mass-produced amps, which are the least likely to have high-quality layout, wire dressing, and construction. In many of these amps, there are tradeoffs made concerning the price of the amp, the cost of making the amp, and the quality of the amp's construction. This can lead to layouts that aren't as good as they should be, traces that are suffering capacitance and tone loss, and other problems that lead to diminished tone and durability.

So, in the final analysis, here are the facts: When done properly, with high-quality and skilled construction and layout, there is no reason why any of the construction methods can't yield a great-sounding, durable amplifier—and there are high-end, boutique PC board amps that prove this. But in the real world, PC board amps often fall in the lower end of the price spectrum, and because of this, and because of the cost-cutting measures required to build them to meet a certain price point, their sound and durability aren't as good as amps made with other methods, leading to the "truisms" we've discussed here.

It's a classic case of *caveat emptor*—buyer beware. Look for good quality construction—regardless of the method used—and you'll get a good amp. But don't base your choice on myths and rumors. Base it on facts.

Table 6.1   Amplifier Tonal Factors

Tone Factor	Tonal Contribution
Head versus combo	None
Tube versus solid-state versus hybrid	Major
Preamp design	Major
Tone stack	Major
Effects loop	None to subtle
Channel switching	None
Master volume versus non-master volume	Major
Output transformer	Moderate
Power transformer	Subtle
Rectifier	Minor
Choke	Subtle
Construction method	None to moderate

Vacuum Tubes

THERE'S A LOT OF MYSTIQUE SURROUNDING VACUUM TUBES—especially considering that they're really pretty simple devices designed to perform basic electronic functions. There are just three main components in a tube: the cathode, the grid, and the plate. The cathode is heated up using a filament or "heater" voltage—this is why tube amps have to warm up before they can be used. Once the cathode is red hot, it starts to emit electrons; they boil right off of the cathode's surface. All of the air is sucked out of the tube when it's made (that's the "vacuum" part) so those loose electrons are free to fly where they will. The cloud of boiled-off electrons is attracted to the plate, where the electrons are absorbed and flow out of the tube as an electrical current that can be used to drive another component in the circuit, to drive a reverb tank, or to move a speaker back and forth.

The key to the whole thing is the tube's grid, which sits between the cathode and the plate. You can think of the grid as sort of like a window blind. Pull the blind and not much light gets in. Open the blind, and light pours in. The grid opens and closes in response to a signal—the guitar signal. The louder the guitar signal, the more the grid opens up, and the more electrons are allowed to pour from the cathode to the plate, creating a greatly amplified version of the original tiny guitar signal.

A tube with one grid is called a *triode*. (An example is the common 12AX7—actually, a 12AX7 is a *dual triode* that contains the equivalent of two complete, independent tubes in one glass bottle.) But a tube can have more than one grid, which can help to control the electron flow and various side effects. A tetrode adds a second grid. (A 6L6 is a special type, called a *beam tetrode*. Beam tetrodes are also known as *kink-less tetrodes*, giving us KT66, KT77, and other "KT" tubes.) And a pentode—such as an EL84 or EL34—has three grids.

Bias

Vacuum tube bias is a DC voltage that is applied to the tube's grid to control the flow of electrons from the cathode to the plate when no signal is present. Without the DC voltage applied to the grid, so many electrons would flow from the cathode to the plate that it would heat up to the point where the tube would melt. Bias works sort of like setting a car engine to the proper idle speed, as opposed to letting the engine run full blast all the time, even when the car isn't moving.

Preamp tubes don't need to be biased; they're part of self-biasing circuits. Power tubes, however, need to be biased. There are three potential bias "conditions" for the power tubes in an amplifier:

▷ **Bias too low.** The amp runs "cold"; the tubes will run cooler and will last longer; the amp will distort earlier, at lower levels, and may sound muddy. Capacitors and other parts may have reduced life or performance due to stresses from high voltages.

▷ **Proper bias setting.** Tube operation is optimized for tube life, power output, and amount of clean headroom. Proper bias is a compromise between tone, power, and tube life.

▷ **Bias too high.** The amp runs "hot," the tubes won't last as long, the amp will have more clean headroom (the amount of clean power the amp can put out before it begins distorting), and higher levels will be required to make the amp distort. Tubes and other components will need to be replaced more often, and some components or the amplifier itself may be damaged.

Some amps are set up for fixed bias, which you would think means that the bias setting is preset at the factory and can't be adjusted. However, in most cases, "fixed bias" means that the bias voltage is constant; it can (and usually should) be adjusted as necessary for different power tubes. In a few cases, such as Mesa/Boogies and some others, the bias really *is* fixed, meaning it can't be adjusted. With this type of fixed bias, when you replace the amp's power tubes, you'll want to follow the manufacturer's recommendation for the best tubes to use in the amp, so that they will be biased properly.

On amps that have adjustable "fixed" bias, the adjustment is usually accessible via trim pots inside the amp or sometimes via trim pots on the amp's back panel. In this case, you can dial in the bias to optimize it for the particular tubes you want to use and for the best tone. This isn't something you should fiddle with casually, however. If you don't know what you're doing you can mess things up; better to ask a qualified tech to set the bias properly. As tubes are used and begin to wear, their bias may also need to be adjusted to maintain consistent performance and tone over time. Recommendations range from checking the bias after 100 hours of play to checking it after 500 hours of play. (You're not going to hurt anything by double-checking the bias more often.)

The other type of biasing is "cathode" bias, where the tube itself supplies the bias voltage, based on the voltage flowing from the cathode to the plate. In a sense, the tube is continually biasing itself. In this case, different tubes will produce different bias voltages and could therefore sound or perform differently.

Amplifier Class

There are various classes or types of amplifier designs in use for guitar amps. The class of an amp affects its efficiency and its tone. Most players tend to think of American amps, such as Fenders, Boogies, and others, as being Class AB designs, while some British amps, such as Voxes, are pointed to as examples of Class A amps.

In fact, most manufacturers (whether British or American) have made amps that fall into each class; let's take a look at what these classes mean and how they affect tone.

Class A

In a Class A amplifier, the tubes have a positive bias voltage on the grid so they conduct the full amount of current all the time, whether idling or cranking out high volume. Because full current is always flowing, when a signal hits the amp, it is amplified nearly instantly and begins moving the speaker—this gives Class A amps a fast, "hard" feel. They tend to be inefficient designs that have very clean sounds. Most Class A amps are single-ended, meaning one tube (or transistor; there are also solid-state Class A designs) pushes all the signal through. This tends to limit the amount of power Class A amps are able to put out compared to other classes, though multiple tubes can be used in parallel to increase the power of a single-ended Class A amplifier.

Some of the amps we think of as Class A—such as Vox AC30s—are not true single-ended Class A designs. They're "push-pull" amps, using a pair or two pairs of out-of-phase tubes to amplify the signal, with bias set for less than full current flow, giving them characteristics of a Class AB amplifier. (See below for more on push-pull and Class AB.) These push-pull designs still have many of the characteristics of true Class A operation, such as fast response and clean sounds, but are more efficient and less expensive to make.

There are various characteristics common to Class A designs:

▷ Upper harmonics are emphasized, resulting in a brighter, "chimy" tone.

▷ The tubes are always running at full current, so they don't last as long as in other types of amps.

▷ Heavier-duty transformers are required for Class A than for other classes.

▷ A given wattage will tend to sound louder for Class A compared to the same wattage with other amplifier classes. For example, a 30-watt Vox AC30 may seem as loud as some 50-watt (or even larger) Class AB amplifiers.

▷ A Class A amp will sound more compressed but will have less headroom.

▷ Class A amps don't tend to transition into clipping (distortion) smoothly; there tends to be an abrupt shift from clean to dirty.

▷ With the emphasis on the upper harmonics, a Class A distorted tone may sound rawer or more ragged than with other classes.

▷ There typically is not as much bottom end in a Class A design as there is in a Class AB design.

Class B

The second type or class of amplifier is Class B, where a pair or pairs of tubes (or transistors, if the amp is a solid-state design) are used. One tube amplifies the positive half of the signal's waveform; it then turns off. The other tube in the pair then turns on and amplifies the negative half of the signal's waveform. This means that with a Class B design, when a tube isn't working on its half of the signal waveform, it is biased so that it basically shuts off. This is a much more efficient approach than Class A, and tubes last longer because they aren't on all the time, but it can result in more distortion (called *crossover* distortion, which results from the small amount of time it takes for the transition from the first tube in a pair to the second tube in the pair) and makes the amp less sensitive to the input signal as well as slower to respond. Not many tube guitar amps are "pure" Class B designs (some old Music Man amps, such as the HD120, were true Class B circuits), but some solid-state amps are Class B designs.

Class AB

This is the most common type of tube amplifier—Fenders, Marshalls, Mesa/Boogies, and many more use this type of design for amps with more than 15 or so watts of output. There is a negative bias voltage, so the tube idles at the bias voltage when no signal is present—the current isn't full on all the time as in a Class A design, just a small amount of bias is flowing. The amp is truly a hybrid; for part of the amplification process it operates in Class A (because a small amount of current is always flowing) and then moves into Class B for the remainder, where two tubes are required to fully amplify the positive and negative portions of the signal. Class AB is more efficient than Class A and requires a smaller power supply.

There are other characteristics of Class AB amplifiers:

▷ Class AB amps usually have tighter, more solid low end than Class A designs.

▷ There is less compression with a Class AB amp than with a Class A amp.

▷ Class AB amps tend to have increased headroom compared to Class A amps and a more open sound, with "sparkle" as opposed to "chime."

▷ Less powerful power supplies and less stout transformers are required for Class AB, with less stress on the transformer.

▷ Tubes in a Class AB amp are cycled on and off as they are needed, so they tend to have longer lives.

▷ Typically, there is a smooth transition from clean to dirty as the gain is increased.

▷ Most players notice a "softer" feel with Class AB amps compared to Class A amps, with some "give" in the pick attack.

Class D

There are other amplifier types as well, such as Class D, which is used for some solid-state designs. Class D is sometimes referred to as *digital* amplification, but there's nothing digital about it, though sometimes Class D amps have digital inputs. The amp works by switching transistors on and off to amplify the waveform. This makes it a very efficient class, with a clean tone, and extremely lightweight compared to other types of amps. How efficient? Class A amps are around 20 percent efficient, Class B and Class AB amps are around 50 percent efficient, and Class D amps can reach 90 or 95 percent efficiency. Many of the ultra-lightweight PA amplifiers as well as the lightweight, compact solid-state guitar and bass amps on the market are using Class D designs.

Negative Feedback

Some amplifiers are designed using negative feedback, which means that a small amount of the signal is fed back into the circuit. This does several things:

▷ Flattens the frequency response, so the tone is smoother.

▷ Extends frequency response, for more lows and more highs.

▷ Reduces crossover distortion for cleaner sound.

▷ Increases the damping factor. This means that the amplifier can more effectively control the motion of the speaker, providing tighter sound, especially in the low frequencies. Some players like this; others prefer the looser feel of a non-negative-feedback amplifier.

▷ Negative feedback can result in the transition from a clean sound to a dirty sound being more abrupt, rather than a smooth onset of distortion.

Sag

"Sag" is a characteristic of Class AB tube amplifiers, where the power supply momentarily can't provide enough voltage to accurately and instantaneously reproduce a transient (a large, swift "spike" in signal, such as a hard pick attack). This translates to a softer, more dynamic feel to the amp as well as some compression, which many players enjoy. It's also something that's often missing in "harder" amps, including some Class A tube designs and solid-state units. There are several places where sag can occur, such as in a tube rectifier, in transformers, and in the power supply's filter capacitors, which charge up to try to maintain constant voltage. If the capacitors can't keep up, the voltage drops, resulting in sag.

Preamp Tubes

When a guitar's signal enters into the input jack of an amplifier, it is at too low of a level to be able to drive the power tubes directly. So, the signal runs through the preamp section of the amp first, which raises its level up high enough that it can drive the power tubes. The preamp section and the tubes it contains amplify the guitar signal a great deal, so it is essential that the tubes that are used in the preamp are low noise and have sufficient gain factor (see later in this chapter for more on gain factor) to do the job. An amp may use one or several preamp tubes—12AX7 or equivalent dual-triode tubes are most common—to preamplify the signal. The earliest amps, which were designed to produce clean sounds, used just a few tubes. But with the advent of Mesa/Boogie, amp designers began cascading tube preamp stages into one another to increase the available gain, for more distortion and for more sustain.

The preamp tubes are where most of the tone in the amp is developed, but not all tubes in the preamp are used for gain and tone. Tubes are also used in the preamp section to drive spring reverbs and sometimes effects send/return loops. These dedicated function tubes tend to not contribute much to the gain or tone of the amp. The power tubes contribute to tone as well, especially when driven hard, but the preamp tubes will have the most impact on whether the sound is thick or thin, whether it is bright or dark, and the quality of the distortion (bright, fuzzy, thick, crunchy, rich, and so on). They also affect the dynamic response (how accurately the tubes follow volume changes and accents in your playing), the articulation (how well the tubes reproduce pick attack and transients), and the amount of compression in the tone.

Not only can tubes from different manufacturers sound different, the same model tubes from the same manufacturer can sound different from one another as well. Because of this, several tube resellers grade the tubes they import or receive for their quality and characteristics, which can be a big help in figuring out how a tube will sound. Many manufacturers—particularly small boutique manufacturers—have also experimented with using various tubes in their amplifiers and can be a good source of information on how different tubes will sound in their amps, as well as recommendations for the best tubes to try to achieve a particular tone with a given amp. For example, the maker of one of my amps used Electro-Harmonix 12AX7 preamps tubes for the clear, detailed tone they provide but was happy to suggest several warmer-sounding alternatives when I found the amp to be a bit too bright for my taste.

The preamp tube that is closest to the input jack (usually called "V1") will have the most impact on the tone, since it is the one that receives the raw, tiny guitar signal and gives that signal its first burst of gain increase. If you want to experiment with the impact of different tubes on your amp's tone, this is the one to change first.

The second preamp tube in the chain (V2)—assuming there is one—also impacts the tone, but to a lesser degree than the first tube in the signal path. Subsequent preamp tubes (V3 and so on)—assuming there are any in the circuit—have less and less impact on the tone, compared to V1. The last tube before the power tubes in a "push-pull" amp is the *phase inverter* or *phase splitter*, which actually feeds the signal into the power tubes. (See the next section for more on phase inverters.)

Keep in mind that just because an amplifier has multiple preamp tubes, that doesn't mean your signal is always passing through all of those tubes. For example, with some of Fender's amps with two channels, each with separate inputs and controls (such as a vintage Bassman), there are four preamp tubes. On a Bassman, two of those tubes are used for the Bass Instrument input channel, while the third is used for the Normal input channel. The fourth tube is the phase inverter that feeds the signal from both channels on to the power tubes. In this case, if you only use the Normal channel, changing the tubes in V1 or V2 won't make any difference— the signal from the Normal channel never even passes through those tubes.

In other cases, an amp may appear to have two channels—such as the Marshall 1959 Super Lead, which has Normal and Bright inputs. But with this amp, both "channels" pass through all three preamp tubes that the amp contains, albeit by slightly different paths, which result in the Normal and Bright signals sounding different.

Other amps use even more tubes—some for gain, some for other functions. In the Fender Super Reverb, for example, there are six preamp tubes. These tubes have the following functions:

> ▷ **V1.** Normal channel input gain.

> ▷ **V2.** Vibrato channel input gain.

> ▷ **V3.** Reverb driver; pushes the signal into the reverb tank.

> ▷ **V4.** Additional gain for the Vibrato channel and return gain for the signal coming back from the reverb tank.

> ▷ **V5.** Creates the vibrato effect.

> ▷ **V6.** Phase inverter that drives both channels to the power tubes.

In this case, some of the tubes will have impact on one of the channels, others on the other channel, and others won't really affect the tone at all. It's important to know what each tube does if you want to experiment with changing out tubes to improve tone or to change distortion characteristics.

It's also important to keep in mind that most preamp tubes (12AX7s, 12AT7s, and variants) are dual-triode tubes, which contain two halves, each of which can function on its own. This means that a single preamp tube could be performing two completely different functions at the same time. For example, in a complex amp, such as the Marshall JVM 410, there are five preamp tubes. In this amp, the four "halves" of V1 and V2 are switched in and out of the circuit for the different gain modes. Half of V3 is used for the tone controls, while the other half sends the signal to the effects loop. Half of V4 is used to bring the signal back from the effects loop; the other half is used to bring the signal back from the reverb. V5 is the phase inverter. In this case, changing V1 or V2 could impact the tone and gain of the amp. Changing V4 won't affect the tone much, but it may change or screw up the response of the effects loop or the reverb.

Phase Inverter

The phase inverter, also known as the *phase splitter*, is the last tube in the preamp signal path before the power tubes—it is the last gain stage in the preamp for a push-pull amplifier with multiple output tubes. Technically, the phase inverter splits the signal coming from the preamp into two signals and flips the phase of one of those signals by 180 degrees. In other words, the second signal is a mirror image of the original signal. The in-phase version of the signal feeds one power tube in a pair, while the out-of-phase version feeds the other power tube in a pair. Those two versions of the signal pass through the power tubes and then are added back together, giving even more power and also canceling some noise and undesirable distortion along the way.

It's not super-important to understand what a phase inverter tube does from a techy standpoint, but it is important to recognize that the phase inverter tube used can have an impact on the tone, feel, and distortion characteristics of the amp. In fact, some experts believe that the phase inverter is one of the most important tubes in an amp, from a tone and response standpoint. They feel that the phase inverter is what actually begins to distort as the amp is turned up louder—before or instead of the power tubes actually distorting.

Many Fender-style amps use 12AT7 tubes for their phase inverters. For more gain and for earlier breakup and distortion, a 12AX7 could be substituted. This may also change the tone, since 12AT7s can be thinner and brighter sounding than some 12AX7s.

Gain Factor

Gain factor is a measure of how much a preamp tube amplifies an input signal. (Power amp tubes also have a gain factor, but most amps are made to use only one specific type of power tube, so it really isn't a factor for choosing tubes.) The gain factor scale is relative, ranging from 0 to 100, with 100 being the most gain. A tube with a higher gain factor will make the signal louder and potentially more distorted, with reduced clean headroom. A tube with a lower gain factor will reduce the volume level or the distortion, while increasing the available clean headroom.

The gain factor in the preamp stage also affects how the signal hits the power amp section—a tube with a higher gain factor will hit the front end of the power amp harder, driving it to higher volume or into breakup more easily. Conversely, lower gain factor means that the power amp section has to work harder to achieve a given volume level. This can be a good thing if you prefer the sound of power amp distortion over preamp distortion.

Generally, you'll have better results replacing a tube with a higher gain factor with one that has a lower gain factor. If you replace a tube with one that has a higher gain factor, the rest of the amplifier may overload or not perform as well. Substituting tubes with different gain factors allows you to tailor the preamp distortion and clean headroom in your amp.

You can also use a lower gain-factor tube to reduce the volume level of a clean amplifier. For example, I had a pair of Fender Hod Rod Deluxe amplifiers that I used as a clean platform for creating stereo tones, using pedals for overdrive and distortion. But the amps were simply too loud for many of the situations I played in—by the time the volume knobs were barely cracked open, I was getting complaints. By substituting 12AT7 tubes as the first (V1) gain stage in the Hot Rods (replacing the stock 12AX7 tubes that came in the amps), I was able to noticeably lower the volume level of the amps, making them more usable for my needs. This also increased the clean headroom and reduced the amount of gain/distortion available in the overdrive channel, though neither of these facts mattered to me, because the clean channels were plenty loud and because I didn't use the overdrive channels at all.

As long as the pin outs and the plate voltages of the preamp tubes you want to use match those that you want to replace, you can freely substitute different tube types as you like. You can also use different types of compatible tubes at the same time in an amplifier. For example, a 12AT7 could be used in the first preamp gain stage (V1), while a 12AX7 is used in the second preamp gain stage (V2).

All of the tubes in Table 7.1 can be used interchangeably to tweak the gain and tone of your amplifier. However, different tube types and tubes from different manufacturers may have different tonal qualities than the tubes that came with your amplifier, and that it was designed and tuned to use. How much of a difference various tube types make will also depend on where the tube is located in the circuit. Changing the first gain stage tube in the preamp (V1) for another type will make the most difference, as a great deal of the gain and tone produced by the amp is created here. Changing the tube in the reverb driver will have little or no impact on anything but the reverb's gain and tone. Substituting other tubes in the circuit may have more or less effect on the gain and tone. And, keep in mind that some amp designers use half of a dual-triode tube for one purpose in the circuit, while the other half is used for another purpose. Changing a single tube may affect more than you expect.

Still, swapping out the tubes in your amp for other types with different gain factors and frequency curves is one of the easiest ways to experiment with customizing the gain structure and tone of your amplifier.

Table 7.1   Gain Factor and Preamp Tubes

Tube Type	Gain Factor
12AX7, ECC83, 7025, ECC803, E83CC, 6681	100
5751	70
12AT7, ECC81, 6201, 6679	60
12AY7, 6072	45
12AV7, 5965	41
12AU7, ECC82, 5963, 5814, 6189	19

Noise and Microphonics

A low-quality preamp tube or one that has been subjected to rough treatment may become noisy or "microphonic." A microphonic tube will make noise in response to shock or vibration. The earlier in the signal path a noisy tube is, the worse the situation will be. For example, in an amplifier with three preamp tubes, if the tube in the first gain stage or position of a preamp becomes microphonic and makes noise, that noise will be amplified by the tubes in the second and third gain stages of the preamp, resulting in that noise becoming quite audible. But if the tube in the third gain stage becomes microphonic, there are no preamp tubes after it in the signal path, so any noise it might make will be amplified significantly less and be far less audible.

Testing for a noisy tube is easy; put the suspected offender in the first position (usually farthest from the power tubes and nearest to the input jack), turn on the amp, and let it warm up. Tap on the tube with a pencil. (Tubes get hot, and there are dangerously high voltages in an amp, so be careful.) With a good tube, you may hear a light ping with each tap. With a microphonic tube, you'll hear rattling or other noises.

It's best not to have any microphonic or noisy tubes in your amplifier, but if you're forced to deal with one until you can get a replacement, try to put it in one of the later preamp positions where its signal (and any noise) won't be amplified as much.

When to Replace Tubes?

How long can you expect the tubes in your amp to last? The answer depends on how much and how hard you use your amp. And, also what the tube is doing in the amp—some tubes in the amp may be under more stress than other tubes. For example, the preamp tubes run with far less voltage than the power tubes, so in general the preamp tubes tend to last longer, especially if you run the amp at high volume a lot of the time.

There is no rule of thumb—different tubes in different amps under different amounts of play and volume will last different amounts of time. A tube may last for six months under super-heavy use, or it may last for many, many years with little or light use. The key is to notice when your amp is starting to sound and feel different. Other warning signs are changes in color in the tube—bluish or purple-ish colors are indicators that things may be failing.

With preamp tubes, watch for them becoming noisy or microphonic. If the tone begins to change, such as a loss of highs, loss of gain, or other tonal differences, it's probably time to change the preamp tubes. All of the preamp tubes do not need to be changed at once. The one in V1 may wear out first, while one used for a reverb send or other application may last longer.

With power amp tubes, the feel of the amp may change—it may get softer or less dynamic. The volume level may also drop, so that you have to turn up farther than usual to get the volume level you want. With power amp tubes that work as pairs, most experts recommend changing both tubes in the pair at the same time—or better yet, all of the power tubes at once.

The problem is that these changes tend to be gradual, over a long period of time (unless a tube decides to fail completely). Still, there will be a point where the amp just noticeably sounds and/or feels different enough to make it clear that it is time for a change.

What about using a tube tester to check out the tubes? It's probably not going to give you a good indication of the state of your amp's tubes. Most common tube testers can't do the job, particularly with power tubes, because they only use 150 volts or so, where guitar amp tubes can run 450 volts or even higher.

Power Tubes

The tubes that are used in the power amp section of the amplifier are, oddly enough, known as power tubes. While we think of EL84 and EL34, 6L6 and 6V6, 6550, and KT66 and KT88 tubes as power tubes, just about any tube can serve as a power tube. There are even amps that have used 12AX7 or other "preamp" tubes as their power tubes—and they can crank out a whopping watt or two, which is surprisingly loud and can be quite toneful.

But for the vast majority of amplifiers out there, power tubes are power tubes, and preamp tubes are preamp tubes.

The job of a power tube is really pretty simple: Take the guitar signal coming from the preamp tubes and crank it way up in level. How the power tube is biased and its plate voltage, along with other components and design factors, determine how much power (usually measured as maximum clean wattage) the tube puts out. For example, the same pair of tubes might max out at 40 watts in one amp or at 50 watts or even more in another amp.

Standing By

Want to start a spirited debate in the amp section of an online guitar forum? Post a question about what a standby switch is for, whether an amp needs one, or how one should be used. You'll quickly see posts touting conventional wisdom and a bit of misinformed rumor-mongering, all mixed in with posts from experts ("I took some electrical engineering classes in college, and I say..."), followed by lots of fun-to-read bickering.

There are several camps, with no consensus ever reached among them:

▶ **The "Why Does It Have It" camp.** This group will point to vintage amps that didn't have standby switches. If it worked back then, why do we need one on a more modern amp? A subset of this group divides things up to where tube amps with solid-state rectifiers need standby switches, while amps with tube rectifiers do not, since the rectifier tube warms slower than the power tubes and gradually feeds DC voltage to them. Others dispute this and state that some rectifier tubes put out full voltage immediately.

▶ **The "It's So the Tubes Can Warm Up" camp.** This group says that the function of the standby switch is to allow the tubes to warm up with a heater voltage before they are hit with high voltage. The idea is to turn the amp's power switch on while leaving the standby switch off. This is said to prevent cathode stripping, where the surface coating on the tube's cathode is damaged because it isn't warmed up before being hit with full voltage. Opposition to this group will state that there is no proof that cathode stripping occurs, especially at the voltages tubes run at, and that tubes don't have to warm up in this way before they are hit with voltages.

Others feel the tubes need to warm up before high voltage is applied to reduce stress on the tubes and to extend their useful lives. And, predictably, others dispute whether this makes any real difference in tube life at all.

▶ **The "It's a Standby Switch, Use It that Way" camp.** This group uses the standby switch to literally put the amp on standby during breaks; this keeps the tubes warm and ready to go, so you don't have to wait for the amp to get hot when you're ready to roll again. There could be some benefit to this versus turning off the power completely, since typically electronic components—any components, not just tubes—are put under the most stress when power is first applied. (Think about it, when do many electronic devices fail? Failure often occurs as you are turning them on.)

▶ **The "It's to Discharge the Power Caps" camp.** This group believes that the power switch should be turned off first, and the standby switch left on for a few minutes so that the power supply capacitors drain off their voltage. This is said to make it safe to work on the amp. Most techs will dispute this (or say that it depends on the design of the amp's power supply), and the rule remains: Make sure the amp is safe before you stick your hands in there—high amp voltages can kill you! But if you're not going to be poking around inside the amp, does it really matter whether or not you discharge the caps?

▶ **The "It Reduces Thermal Shock" camp.** This group thinks that the amp should be put on standby for a few minutes before turning off the power, so that the temperature of the tubes has a chance to drop a bit before the power is completely removed, at which point the temperature drops quickly as the tubes cool off.

Debates may rage, but why not play it safe? The obvious path is to follow your amp manufacturer's recommendations. But if you have more than one amp and receive conflicting recommendations, why not sort of take the best from all of the above? (You won't hurt anything, and who knows—you may extend the life of your tubes.)

▶ If the amp doesn't have a standby switch, don't worry about it!

▶ Turn on the amp and let it warm up with the standby switch off—turn on the standby after a few minutes, and you're ready to play.

▶ Turn off the standby switch when you take a break and turn it back on when you are ready to play.

▶ When you're done playing, you have your choice of a few options (choose the one that seems logical to you):

   1. Turn off the power switch first, leave the standby on for a few minutes, and then turn it off.

   2. If the amp makes a loud pop if you turn off the power switch first, turn off the standby first and then turn off the power switch.

   3. Turn off the standby for a few minutes so the tubes can cool a bit and then turn off the power switch.

Types of Power Tubes

There are several different types of power tubes in use, some famed for producing a British sound, and others for producing a more American sound. Most power tubes are *octal* designs, meaning they have eight pins that go into a socket in the amp chassis and connect the tube to the rest of the circuit. In many cases, assuming that voltages are compatible and that the bias can be adjusted properly—and that the amp's transformers can handle it—you can substitute one type of octal power tube for another. Some amps are even set up for this from the factory, allowing you to easily swap out 6L6 power tubes for EL34 power tubes and quickly change the amp's bias to match whichever tube you have installed. This allows you to tweak the output and tone of the power section of your amplifier.

▷ **6L6.** Also known as 5881 and 7027 tubes (in addition to other designations), these may be the most popular power tubes in larger "American" amps, such as bigger Fenders (Twins, for example), Mesa/Boogies, and more. Developed in the mid 1930s, early 6L6 tubes could crank out around 19 watts. Modern 6L6GCs can put out as much as 30 watts. 6L6 power tubes are generally described as having full spectrum; big, open, balanced, round tone, with good harmonic content (meaning rich sound); and good clarity, clean headroom, and punch. Tubes from different manufacturers definitely have different sounds, may also have different outputs (often 25 or 30 watts), and may operate at different plate voltages (400 volts or 500 volts).

▷ **6V6.** These tubes are popular in mid-powered American amps, such as Fender Deluxes and Princetons and others. The 6V6 is often thought of as the lower-powered little brother of the 6L6, with a some-what similar sound, though many 6V6s are described by players as warmer and creamier. Being lower powered, they have less clean headroom and break up at lower volumes. Other players describe 6V6s as having less and smoother midrange; sweeter, sparkling highs; and "piano-like" low end. In some cases, certain 6V6 tubes can be used in amps set up for 6L6 tubes, but if you try this, make sure that the 6V6s you use can handle the voltages without damage and without damaging the amp.

▷ **EL34.** Perhaps best known for their use in 50- and 100-watt Marshall amps, EL34s are renowned for their British sound and are often used for rock-oriented amps that thrive on producing distortion. EL34s may break up earlier than other tubes, such as 6L6s, and are often described as having a creamy, thick tone, with brighter top end and more distortion than 6L6s or KT66s. Some players find EL34s to have a softer feel and touch compared to other types.

▷ **EL84.** Like the EL34, the EL84 is considered a British-sounding tube. EL84s are used in many Vox and other similar amplifiers and have become increasingly popular as smaller (lower-wattage) amps have become more popular in recent years. This is a tube that is described as having sparkling, chimey top end, along with punchy high mids and a tight bottom end. Some players feel that EL84s can be harder sounding and less forgiving of technique and articulation flaws than other tubes. Other players love these same characteristics for the snappy articulation, fast response, crunchy breakup, and present sound that EL84-equipped amps produce.

▷ **KT66.** Similar to the 6L6 and developed by a competitor in response to that tube's introduction, the KT66 can be thought of as a cousin to the 6L6. The KT66 does use a different design and has some different features, along with larger physical size. These tubes sound thick and firm, with big lows and mids and open top end, but less clean headroom than a 6L6. Some KT66s can be directly substituted for 6L6s; in other cases, either the physical size or voltage requirements rule them out for certain amps. If you want to try KT66s in your amp, be aware that some tube manufacturers have been accused of placing 6L6 components inside a KT66-shaped and -sized bottle and calling the result a KT66. Be sure you are getting a real KT66.

▷ **6550/KT88.** Developed by Tung Sol in the mid 1950s, the 6550 was designed to be a higher-powered version of the 6L6. The 6550 can handle plate voltages as high as 600 volts. The KT88 was developed around the same time as the KT66 and is a similar tube, but it can handle upwards of 800 volts of plate voltage. These tubes tend toward very high clean headroom, low distortion, and high power. For this reason, they are more popular with hi-fi/audiophile applications or for high-powered bass amps than for guitar amps. However, amps such as the 200-watt Marshall Major, Orange Thunderverb, Blackstar 200-watt Series One, and various rackmount power amps have been released for guitarists in need of maximum clean headroom and wall-moving power.

There clearly are sonic differences among different types of power tubes, but the degree to which this fact is true must be considered in the context of the circuit in which the tubes are used. Contrast the saggy, raw sound of a Fender Tweed amp with the bright, sparkling tone of a Fender Blackface amp with the roaring crunch of a Fender Brownface amp—and realize that all three might use the exact same 6V6 power tubes. Likewise, an EL84 in a single-ended Class A amplifier is going to sound very different from the same tube in a Class AB push-pull amplifier.

It also depends on how you are running your amplifier. A certain tube can have a very different tonality with a clean sound than with a crunchy rhythm tone. And it might have a different tonality again when you wick it up to full power output, with lots of harmonics and distortion.

Safety Note

If you want to try different power tubes in your amp, be sure to check with the manufacturer and your tube supplier to ensure that you can safely do so, without damage to the amp or to yourself! For example, in some cases you can safely install certain 6L6 power tubes in specific 6V6 amplifiers and vice versa, but make sure you know what you are doing before you try such a swap.

Matching Power Tubes

From a technical standpoint, a push/pull amplifier performs at its best when its power tubes are matched. If the tubes are truly matched, then each tube is doing an equal amount of work.

Tubes are considered "matched" when they draw the same amount of bias current when idling. The tolerance for matching varies; some feel the two (or four tubes, if that's what's in the amp) need to draw within eight milliamps of one another, while others require that the tubes draw within four milliamps of one another. Beyond the bias current drawn by each tube, the transconductance or gain of the tubes should also be matched as closely as possible.

But not everyone prefers the power tubes in their amps to be matched, and some players will install mismatched tubes on purpose. If a pair of tubes is unmatched, one will work harder than the other and wear out faster. From a tonal standpoint, an amp with unmatched tubes will produce more distortion than one with matched tubes or will begin to distort at a lower level than one with matched tubes. You could even have an amp modded with separate bias controls for each tube; this would allow you to install a matched set of tubes and then adjust the bias for each one to either keep them matched or run them mismatched—though it may be easier to simply have several sets of tubes, matched and unmatched, that you can swap in and out of your amp.

So what about preamp tubes? Do they need to be matched? Preamp tubes generally don't need to be matched, as they don't work in pairs and they are self-biasing. Since preamp tubes contain two halves, you could match the two sides, but there really is no benefit to doing so, with one exception: Some techs believe that you'll get the best response from a push-pull amplifier if you use a phase inverter that has both sides of the dual-triode matched. However, it's difficult to find phase inverter tubes that have been "matched" in this way. Plus, other techs believe that imbalances in the two sides of a phase inverter tube can contribute to the "complexity" of the tone an amplifier creates, resulting in the positive and negative halves of the waveform being amplified slightly differently.

New, NOS, and Used Tubes

These days, there are three different varieties of tubes on the market: new (freshly manufactured), NOS (new old stock, which are tubes that were manufactured years or decades ago but were never used), and used (tubes that have been used for some purpose, possibly audio or possibly some other application in another industry, but may still have some life left in them).

At this writing, new tubes are being manufactured primarily in China and Russia. Companies have purchased the old, respected tube brand names (such as Mullard, Tung-Sol, and Genalex) and are making new tubes using those brands in those countries. The same factories are also making tubes for other "new" brands, such as Sovtek, who supplies many of the tubes used by amplifier manufacturers.

While the quality of new tubes has improved, some players believe that they will never equal the quality of "old" tubes—many believe that the "golden era" of tube manufacturing was in the 1940s through the 1960s. Pretty much everything electronic ran on tubes back then, so demand was high and manufacturers provided a variety of tubes to fill all needs. Most tubes were made in the United States, Canada, and Western Europe in those days, and the quality standards and consistency were extremely high. Fortunately, you can still get "vintage" tubes that are just like brand new—in fact, they *are* brand new. We're talking about NOS, or "new old stock" tubes. Tubes don't degrade over time. They generally are stable if they are stored well, so theoretically, an NOS tube should perform the same way today as it would have if it were installed in an amp 50 years ago, when it was freshly manufactured.

A lot of tubes were manufactured back in the day, and there are still stocks of NOS tubes that are available (depending on the specific tube model you're looking for—some are more readily available than others). The trick is to make sure you're getting a true NOS tube, and not an old used tube that is being passed off as new. Some things to look for with NOS tubes:

▶ The original box is in good condition.

▶ Any silk-screening or printing on the tube is clean and new looking (although on some tubes the printing will smear or rub off easily, so even new tubes may not have perfect lettering).

▶ There is no discoloration in the shiny silver "flashing" area of the tube. (Some military tubes were "burned in" as a quality test and may have some discoloration.)

▶ There are no bent pins.

▶ There are no scratches, scrapes, or marks on the tube base, which would indicate the tube has been inserted into a socket and clamped down.

▶ There is no white in the flashing. This doesn't necessarily suggest a used tube, but it does indicate a tube that has lost its vacuum.

▶ There is no darker coloration around the edge of the base, which indicates exposure to heat.

▶ There are no hairline cracks in the base.

If you do decide to give NOS tubes a try in your amplifier, many experts suggest "military" tubes, which are often called *JAN* (*Joint Army Navy*) tubes. Military tubes weren't made specifically for audio applications, but they have a few characteristics that make them superior for use in guitar amps: They were made to higher standards for heavy-duty applications or selected from special production runs. The noise standards were also higher—meaning a military-grade tube will typically be less noisy. And, military tubes were often "burned in" to ensure that they were in prime shape for critical applications. All of these are good things that can result in better tone when the tubes are used in a guitar amplifier.

For guitar amplifier use, some NOS tubes have emerged as the most desirable. For example, JAN Philips/Sylvania, JAN GE, RCA, Mullard, and Amperex are popular for 12AX7 preamp tubes, with Telefunkens being the most sought after and the most expensive. For 6V6s, many players look for JAN Philips, RCA, and Sylvania. JAN Philips, GE, Sylvania, and RCA grey plates are still affordable, while Tung-Sol and RCA black plates command higher prices but are said to have the best tone.

The biggest downside to NOS tubes is that they can be much more expensive than new tubes. The price of an NOS tube will reflect how scarce it is—and you can expect those prices to continue to rise as the supply of NOS tubes steadily dwindles.

As far as used tubes go, a good used tube could certainly have a lot of life left in it. However, it may not be up to spec, and because preamp tubes lose power as they are used, the gain factor could be reduced. Unless you know what you are getting, it's probably safest to stick with new or NOS tubes rather than chance it with used tubes.

Table 7.2 Vacuum Tube Tonal Factors

Tone Factor	Tonal Contribution
Power tube bias	Major
Amplifier class	Major
Single-ended versus push-pull	Major
Negative feedback	Subtle
Sag	Subtle
Preamp tube type	Moderate
Gain factor	Minor
Power tube type	Major
Matched power tubes	Subtle

Speakers

THE FINAL LINK IN THE GUITAR/AMP CHAIN OF TONE is the speaker and the speaker enclosure or cabinet (which we'll get to in the next chapter). The speaker is where the electrical signal coming from the amplifier is converted into sound waves. The type of speaker used and the type of cabinet in which it is mounted can have a huge impact on the tone that is produced. Fortunately, it is pretty easy to experiment with different speakers; swapping a raw speaker (also referred to as a *driver*) into or out of a cabinet or a combo amp is usually (though unfortunately, not always) a fairly simple matter. And, of course, it's a very simple matter to connect a new cabinet to an amp head or even to a combo amp that has an extension speaker output—all you need is a speaker cable.

It's becoming more and more common for players to swap out speakers in search of a different tone, to tame a sonic problem with an amp, or to find their own personal sound. There are tons of different speaker models available from many manufacturers, and each will have its own effect on the sound and playing feel produced—some experts feel that changing out the speaker can have a bigger impact on your tone than changing pickups or even changing your guitar to a different one! I'm not sure I'd go *that* far. But given how much impact a speaker can have, it's important to have a basic understanding of how they work, how the components used to make speakers contribute to their tone, and how different speaker characteristics affect the sound they produce.

Speaker 101

A speaker is a type of transducer, meaning that it is a device that converts one form of energy into another form of energy—in this case, we're converting an electrical signal generated by an amplifier into sound waves. It works like this: A large magnet is mounted onto a frame. A cone of paper or other material is suspended in the frame and connected to a coil of wire, called the *voice coil*, which is also suspended from the frame. When signal from an amplifier flows through the voice coil, the interaction between the voice coil (which has now become an electromagnet) and the speaker magnet causes the cone to move back and forth. Remember your high school science class? Like magnets repel, and opposite magnets attract. As the alternating current of the amp's signal flows through the voice coil, it attracts and repels the magnet, pushing and pulling against it. This happens very quickly; more than 80 times per second for the low E string and up to 6,000 times a second and even more for the highest frequencies the strings produce. Even more amazing, if you play a low E and the highest note on your guitar at the same time, the voice coil has to move in such a way as to re-create all of the frequencies that are sounding at once. And, if you play a six-note chord with distortion, the voice coil has to navigate all of the frequencies and harmonics that are present simultaneously.

Since the voice coil is suspended from the frame, the voice coil is free to move back and forth in response to this pushing and pulling. The speaker cone is attached to the voice coil and moves back and forth along with it, creating disturbances in the air called *compressions* (higher pressure, created when the cone moves out and pushes the air) and *rarefactions* (lower pressure, created when the cone moves in and "pulls" the air), which our ears perceive as sound waves.

Microphone or Speaker?

The process and technology of how a speaker works is the exact same as is used in a dynamic "moving-coil" microphone, such as a Shure SM57—just in reverse. In fact, you can take a regular old speaker, hook it up to a microphone preamp, and use it as a microphone.

But outside the realm of recording studio trivia, this has ramifications in our use as a speaker, too. When we are playing, the motion of the voice coil in the speaker's magnetic field creates a small amount of electrical signal in the coil, which tries to push back against the amplifier's output transformer and power tubes or output transistors. This is all part of the complex interaction between the amp and the speaker and is technically referred to as *motional impedance*. We'll talk more about this later in this chapter, in the section on impedance.

The speakers used for guitar amps are "full-range" designs, meaning that a single driver (speaker) can (and must) produce all of the frequencies necessary for the sound—no separate tweeter is used or required for the treble frequencies, and no separate woofer is used or required for the bass frequencies. Technically, though, guitar speakers are rarely true full-range drivers; guitars and amps don't produce much in the way of high frequencies or very low bass frequencies, so guitar speakers don't reach into those frequency ranges very far, and we probably wouldn't like the way it sounded if they did.

The speaker acts as a sort of filter, shaping the sound by rolling off the high frequencies and the low frequencies and generally focusing on the midrange frequencies. The highs on a guitar speaker often only reach up to 5,000 or 6,000 hertz; by comparison, human hearing can extend as high as 20,000 hertz. The lows on a guitar speaker usually start to roll off around 70 or 80 hertz; the low E on a standard-tuned guitar is around 82 hertz, and human hearing reaches down as low as 20 hertz, two octaves lower. This is why a CD or MP3 played through a guitar speaker sounds dark and muffled, without much deep bass or bottom end, and why a bass guitar played through a guitar amp sounds thin and midrange-y. And it's also why an acoustic guitar played through a regular guitar amp doesn't sound all that wonderful, with no sparkle or definition. A CD or acoustic guitar requires a transparent, wide-range speaker to sound its best—and that's not what electric guitar speakers generally are designed to be.

But those limitations are just fine as far as electric guitars are concerned. We want (and need) that shaping provided by the speaker for our guitars and amps. Without the speaker filtering the sound, particularly the highs, an electric guitar amp sounds thin, harsh, fizzy, and generally quite nasty—plug an amp or distortion box straight through a PA system or recording rig without a speaker, and you'll hear exactly what I mean!

Speaker Parts

Mechanically, a guitar speaker is a fairly simple device, utilizing just a few components in most cases. (From a vibration and sound-wave production standpoint, a speaker is incredibly complex. We'll get into various aspects of that later in this chapter.) But the impact of those components on the sound can be substantial. By carefully selecting and manipulating those components, a speaker designer can change the tone quite radically and can "voice" the speaker exactly as he wants it to sound.

The largest component in a speaker is its frame (also known as the *basket*), which has little or no impact on the tone the speaker produces. It's there to support all the other components and to ensure that they stay in their proper places. However, the frame is important for reasons beyond supporting all the other speaker components and making sure they stay in tight alignment. A speaker frame is usually made from steel, but some, predominantly higher-end, speakers use cast aluminum alloy for their frames' construction.

The metal in the frame serves as a heat sink for the speaker. Heat is a big nemesis of speakers; not only can heat increase the resistance of the voice coil, it can change the dimensions of the voice coil (which can affect its motion). And in extreme cases, heat could even demagnetize the speaker's magnet or deform parts of the speaker until it can't function properly—even a small amount of deformation of the voice coil will cause it to rub in the magnet's gap, creating noise or even total failure. The speaker frame conducts the heat that is generated away from the voice coil and magnet and dissipates it into the air, keeping the various components cool and performing well. Maybe that frame is pretty important to the tone after all!

But, as important as the frame is to the speaker's structure, longevity, and performance, there are other components that directly affect the tone the speaker makes far more than the frame does.

Magnet

The type of permanent magnet used in a speaker affects its tone and its response, as well as the playing feel. Most guitar speakers use either alnico or ceramic magnets. Alnico is made from an alloy of aluminum, nickel, and cobalt, with alnico 5 being used most commonly. (Alnico 5 is made from a blend of 8 percent aluminum, 14 percent nickel, and 24 percent cobalt, with the rest being iron mixed with a little copper and other trace metals.)

Alnico has an interesting characteristic in speakers: It is somewhat easy to temporarily demagnetize it. So when the speaker's voice coil magnetizes as signal flows through it, an alnico speaker magnet actually temporarily loses a bit of flux (magnetic power). This results in the speaker becoming less efficient as it is driven harder, creating an increasingly compressed tone and feel as the volume goes up.

Tonally, alnico magnets are said to have sweeter highs and smoother mids, with a "looser" sound on the bottom end. For years, alnico was the standard magnet in guitar speakers. But the rising price of cobalt (which mainly comes from Zaire in Africa) led manufacturers to look at other materials for magnets.

Ceramic magnets, which feature magnetic material mixed into a ceramic slurry, don't demagnetize or compress; they simply reach maximum movement in the voice coil and can't go any further. This can result in a harder sound and feel, though manufacturers have found ways to make ceramic have more "musical" response, and ceramic magnets are quite popular in situations where the player doesn't want speaker compression or the treble response of alnico. Because of their low cost, ceramic magnets are used in many speaker models.

Some guitar speaker magnets are also made from neodymium, which provides a high magnet strength to weight ratio—in other words, a neodymium magnet is much lighter in comparison to an equivalent ceramic or alnico magnet, yet it still produces a powerful magnetic field. (In still other words, it produces a large amount of magnetic flux per ounce.) This is great for making a lightweight "grab-it-and-go" combo amp, but this lighter weight becomes even more noticeable in cabinets loaded with more than one speaker; a 4×12 speaker cabinet can drop serious poundage when loaded with neodymium magnet speakers versus those with other types of magnets! Players describe speakers with neodymium magnets as clear and transparent, with tight, solid low end—"hi fi" is a term that comes up quite a bit.

So, in the real world, how much difference does the magnet type *really* make? It's almost impossible to do this, but if you could somehow get three identical speakers, each with one of the three magnet types, and with each of those magnets having the exact same magnetic flux, would you hear a big difference? Probably not, depending on the volume level—the alnico speaker would compress as the volume went up. That's not to say that speakers with different magnets don't sound different. But it may not be the magnet itself that is the major source of those differences. Many of the sonic characteristics attributed to the magnet type in all likelihood come from other parts of the speaker that are used based on the magnet type, how the magnet is implemented in the speaker, and other factors.

Which Side of the Pond?

You'll often hear the terms "British" sound and "American" sound applied to speakers, with some players setting the general dividing line at British speakers using ceramic magnets (such as Celestion Greenbacks), while American speakers are deemed to have alnico magnets (such as various Jensens). Of course, there's no such division; Celestion makes speakers with alnico magnets, and plenty of American companies make speakers with ceramic magnets.

You could say British speakers are those from Celestion and other British manufacturers that were used in Vox and Marshall amps, while American speakers come from JBL, Eminence, EV, and other American manufacturers and are used in Fender, Peavey, and other American amps. But it's not clear what this distinction gets you, since all of those speaker manufacturers make a variety of different-sounding models, regardless of whether they are American or British—plus Boogie uses "British" speakers in some amps and Fender now puts Celestions in some of their models.

Better just to examine each speaker on its own merits and not to worry overly much about which side of the pond the speaker comes from.

Magnet Size

There is a belief among some guitar players that size matters when it comes to magnets. In the old days, magnets were larger, so manufacturers seemed to have gone with bigger magnets just to keep the look going—and players were used to bigger magnets on the back of their speakers. But all other things being equal, it is magnet strength and how the magnetic field is focused that matter, not the size of the magnet.

Of course, the magnet and the voice coil have to work together, and a larger magnet can support a larger voice coil, which will be more efficient and will have better low-frequency response. But again, the physical size of the magnet isn't the issue here; it's the interaction with the voice coil.

Cone

The cone is the part of the speaker that actually causes compressions and rarefactions in the air, which our ears perceive as sound waves. (Well, it's the motion of the cone that causes those disturbances in the air, but run with me here.) The cone is suspended in the frame by the surround, which is flexible rubber, foam, or cloth. The cone is usually made from paper that has been dipped in acrylic and acetone to make it stiffer. Ideally, the cone is formed as one piece, using a "slurry" of paper that is shaped in a mold, although a single piece of stiffened paper rolled into a cone shape and then glued with a single seam is another approach. Other materials are also used, such as various plastics, hemp, and even aluminum. According to manufacturers who use these alternate materials, each one is better than paper in pretty much every way—more low end, smoother top end, extended high frequencies, better power handling (which in this case means that speaker breakup doesn't occur until higher power levels are reached), and more. Still most players continue to choose and use traditional paper-coned speakers.

What is important is the strength-to-weight ratio; the cone needs to be as light as possible but also as strong as possible given its weight. In this battle, paper is actually superior to most other materials, including metals. The cone must be very stiff so that it will accurately follow the intense, very fast motions of the voice coil, re-creating the signal waveforms.

Seems simple, but the vibrations required to create a broad range of frequencies simultaneously are very complex. At low frequencies, the cone tends to move in and out in one piece, like a piston. At higher frequencies, different sections of the cone vibrate separately; the motion and interaction among the vibrating sections are very complicated. Plus, the cone tends to want to keep moving in whatever direction it is currently going in (if it is moving out, it wants to keep moving out, and vice versa—plain old inertia, from good ol' Sir Isaac Newton), so it must be damped to control its motion.

The cone also slightly deforms and develops varying modes of distortion as it vibrates back and forth. The thicker the cone material, the less it will distort, and the more power it can handle. However, that cone distortion adds extra harmonic content to the sound produced, which can result in a richer and livelier tone. The thickness of the cone also affects the resonant frequency of the speaker, which can have an effect on the tone. (We'll look at speaker resonant frequencies later in this chapter.)

Surround

A speaker's surround is a ring of rubber, foam, fabric, or paper that is used to attach the cone to the basket. It suspends the cone inside the basket and is flexible enough to allow the cone to move back and forth in response to the voice coil's motion. The stiffness of the surround is a factor in the resonant frequency of the speaker; a "softer" or more flexible surround will lower the resonant frequency. The surround also plays a role in damping the motion of the cone and in returning the cone to its resting place when the signal stops.

Doping

Doping is a coating of glue-like material that is applied to the speaker's surround. It serves two purposes. First, it helps to strengthen the surround, which must be very tough and resilient to withstand the constant high-speed, back-and-forth motion of the speaker. Second, it damps some of the nastier high frequencies and helps to reduce or prevent "cone cry." (See the upcoming sidebar for more on cone cry.) Some players feel that an un-doped speaker has better top-end response; certain manufacturers will make an un-doped speaker as a custom item. The tradeoff is that the speaker probably won't last as long without the extra strength the doping provides. You can also order speakers with varying levels of doping from manufacturers such as Weber: light, medium, and heavy, to tailor the high-frequency response to your liking. In general, the lighter the doping, the brighter the sound. However, at high volumes and with high gain, lightly doped speakers can be harsh sounding, and there may be increased problems with cone cry and edge yowl.

Cone Cry

Also known as *edge yowl*, *ghost notes*, and *ghosting*, cone cry can result from two sources: The speaker cone itself may begin to resonate, producing a note of its own (usually referred to as *cone cry*). Another version of this phenomenon occurs when a speaker's surround begins to resonate and sends the frequency produced by that resonance back into the cone as an audible note. (Sometimes known as *edge yowl*, though it is hard to tell one from the other—the result is the same, even if the source is in a different location.) The problem is made worse by a thinner, lighter cone and by an un-doped or a lightly doped surround.

When either of these situations happens, the speaker is basically out of control and is outrunning any damping that may be in place to keep it stable. It has stopped working like a piston, driving straight in and out, and is rippling instead.

The problem is that the frequencies produced by cone cry are generally not harmonically related to the notes the guitarist is playing through the speaker and therefore sound dissonant. Fortunately, in most cases, cone cry is a subtle thing, though even small amounts of cone cry can drive some players crazy!

In some cases, what seems to be cone cry may just be the result of the harmonic interaction between two or more notes, particularly when distortion is involved. To hear this yourself, with a distorted sound, hold an E at the twelfth fret on the high E string. While the E is sounding, pick the note D on the fifteenth fret of the B string and bend it up to unison with the E. In many cases, you'll hear a "ghost" note clearly sounding below the two notes you are playing. In this case, you're probably not hearing true cone cry. Rather, you're likely hearing a subharmonic resulting from the two notes played combined with all the harmonic content coming from the distortion.

Can you cure cone cry or edge yowl? It's not an easy problem to fix. Heavier doping may help, and the problem may be reduced at different volume and gain levels. But if it becomes a real problem, the solution is usually to replace the offending speaker.

Voice Coil

The voice coil in a speaker is basically a coil of wire (one of several coils of wire we've encountered on our tone quest thus far). The voice coil resides at the "point" or apex of the speaker, in the center. It is the part of the speaker that actually connects to the amplifier's output and is the only part of the speaker through which the signal from the amp actually moves. When signal flows out of the amplifier, it enters the voice coil, temporarily turning it into an electromagnet that pushes and pulls against the speaker's permanent magnet.

Most voice coils are made from copper wire, though some use aluminum or other metals. (Aluminum is lighter, but copper can handle more power.) The wire is coated with a thin layer of insulating material to keep the layers or turns from shorting out against one another.

In a guitar speaker, each driver must produce all of the frequencies necessary, from the bass to the treble; there is no separate woofer or tweeter. This requires that a guitar speaker "motor" be as light as possible, in order to accurately reproduce the delicate higher frequencies. For this reason, guitar speaker voice coils tend to be relatively small, with fewer winds of wire. It's a tradeoff, though, as more wire and a bigger voice coil mean that the voice coil can work against the speaker magnet with more power and move the cone more forcefully. This increases sensitivity and frequency response and allows the speaker to handle more power from the amp, but it comes at the expense of efficiency.

Many speakers use traditional round wire, but this results in a lot of wasted space in the coil, as the round strands don't pack tightly together. To reduce this wasted space, some speakers use "ribbon" wire, which allows for much higher wind density. The ribbon is not laid flat on the former (see the next section for more on formers), as the wide ribbon would result in the voice coil being too long. Instead, it is stood on its edge against the former, with successive turns standing edgewise next to the earlier turns. This is called an *edge-wound* voice coil. An edge-wound voice coil has several advantages: It uses less space and is less susceptible to warping or deforming due to heat.

Former

The voice coil is wrapped around a *former*—basically, a hollow tube around which the wire is coiled. Paper is most commonly used for the former, though other materials are used, such as Nomex (a DuPont product often used for electrical insulation, with good heat resistance), Kapton (a DuPont polymide film product), various plastics, and aluminum. Some players feel that paper has the best sound, with Nomex a close second. They ascribe harshness to aluminum formers and a "plastic" tone to a plastic former.

However, many speaker experts state that there is no sonic difference between the different materials from which formers are made. What those materials can influence, though, is the weight of the former, which can affect the voice coil's response—remember, we want the voice coil as light as possible for the best high-frequency response.

Spider

The voice coil attaches to the base or apex of the speaker cone, but it also must be supported to maintain proper alignment with the speaker's magnet. This is the spider's job. The spider not only functions to hold the voice coil and the apex of the cone in place and in close alignment with the speaker magnet, but it also serves as a sort of spring that returns the voice coil to its normal resting position. It is usually made from corrugated material, often stiffened fabric.

Today's spiders most often are a corrugated disk of material, colored yellow or light brown. But the spiders used in early speakers were open, with "spokes" or legs connecting the voice coil to the frame—the appearance of those legs and the voice coil sitting in the center of them is the source of the term "spider."

Dust Cap

The dust cap—that dome-shaped circle of metal or impregnated cloth in the center of the cone—was originally intended to keep dust and other contaminants out of the inner workings of the speaker; the center of the speaker is hollow and would otherwise be full of potentially destructive debris. But, lo and behold, speaker designers found that the dust cap could actually have a noticeable impact on the response of the speaker, especially smoothing out peaks at certain frequencies, and even improving the high-frequency extension of the driver. A larger dust cap (as large as a 4-inch size is used) will tend to diffuse the high frequencies more than a smaller one (some are slightly over an inch in diameter, but a common size is 2-1/4 inches; other speakers use a 3-inch size) and may also reduce low frequencies by a slight amount. Plus, it was discovered that a dust cap made from aluminum can provide a bit of extra heat-sink action, helping to keep the voice coil cooled down.

Because the dust cap can affect the speaker's tone, it can also become the object of experimentation. Some players (there are seemingly always those who can't resist tinkering) will even remove the dust cap from a speaker by carefully cutting it free with a razor blade or by using acetone or another solvent to dissolve the glue holding it in place and then replace it with a different one to customize the speaker's tone to their liking.

As mentioned, most speakers use paper or felt dust caps, though a few use a sonically transparent gauze-like material; examples include the Celestion Vintage 30 and Greenback models. This is because the designers feel that the closed empty space resulting behind a solid dust cap can create a chamber that may resonate at certain frequencies, affecting the sound. A permeable gauze dust cap eliminates this problem.

Speaker Characteristics

Beyond the components that make up a speaker, there are various other characteristics of the speaker that go into determining the tone that it makes. Most of these can be controlled by the manufacturer by working with the components and materials that are used to make the speaker.

Size

The physical size of the speaker, given as the speaker diameter, is an important factor in the sound it produces. All other things being equal, a larger speaker can produce lower frequencies than a smaller speaker. (Of course, as we've seen throughout this book, all other things are never equal.) Conversely, smaller speakers are usually better able to reproduce high frequencies. That's why woofers are big and tweeters are small.

Most guitar amplifiers and speaker cabinets use 12-inch speakers, which provide a good compromise between the amount of low frequencies a standard-tuned guitar produces versus the high and mid frequencies that are also required. Ten-inch speakers are also common (Fender Princeton and Super Reverb, and many others), with very few guitar amps and cabinets using 15-inch speakers. (Fifteen-inch speakers are much more common in bass guitar applications.) Eight-inch and smaller speakers tend to be limited to use in small practice amps.

Here are a few general characteristics of the different speaker sizes (keeping in mind that there are many factors that affect the sound of a speaker and that we are talking about the raw speaker driver here, not the speaker working inside a cabinet):

▷ **8-inch.** Brighter top end, many have a surprising amount of bass, but will not rival a larger speaker in low end or volume. A smaller speaker will be lighter and may respond faster, with a tighter feel. An 8-inch speaker can be excellent for recording—consider Eric Clapton playing through an 8-inch-equipped Fender Champ for the *Layla* album.

▷ **10-inch.** A tighter feel than an equivalent 12-inch speaker, with taut midrange and bottom end. The highs may be brighter than a 12-inch. Cabinets with multiple 10-inch speakers, such as a 4×10 Bassman or Super, can provide a thick, rich, versatile tonal foundation to build from, without the heavy "thumpiness" that a 4×12 cabinet can have.

▷ **12-inch.** The standard for many players. A 12-inch speaker provides a good balance between full lows, good bass extension, thick mids, and bright highs. When combined, as in a 4×12 cabinet, the bass of the multiple speakers "couples," providing a solid bottom-end fullness and "thump" that many players, especially rock and metal players, thoroughly enjoy.

▷ **15-inch.** A 15-inch speaker can have more bass extension than a smaller speaker but may also have a surprising amount of high end. By nature heavier, a 15-inch speaker will respond more "slowly" than a smaller speaker—it takes a short amount of time for the larger speaker to actually begin moving in response to the amp's signal—and it also has more inertia and wants to keep moving in the same direction more than a smaller, lighter speaker. This means a 15-inch speaker has a less percussive attack, which can give it a "soft" feel and a warm tone. Many jazz players enjoy this. Fifteen-inch speakers are also common in pedal steel guitar amps.

Impedance

Technical definition: *Impedance* is the resistance to the flow of alternating current (AC). It is also defined as a mathematical combination of resistance (which doesn't change with frequency) and reactance (which does change dependent on frequency). Well, there you go, then—perfectly serviceable definitions that unfortunately mean little to those of us who are less technically inclined.

What does "impedance" mean to us in the real world? Basically, impedance is how hard it is for the signal to flow through the speaker, and it affects how much current the speaker will draw. Here's what you need to know: First, the speaker presents a "load" to the amplifier. Second, the amp's output components, including its power tubes and output transformer or its transistors (depending on whether the amp is tube or solid-state) are selected by the manufacturer, and the circuit is designed to provide maximum power to a specific load. Third, for maximum efficiency and minimum distortion, the load the speaker provides should match the load the amp wants to see.

Guitar speaker impedance is more accurately referred to as *nominal impedance*—"nominal" meaning "in name only." This is because the impedance of a speaker varies with frequency. An 8-ohm speaker may range from as low as 4 ohms at certain frequencies up to as high as 50 ohms for other frequencies. But that's okay; our amplifiers are looking for nominal impedance, so if the speaker says 8-ohm impedance, connect it to the amp's 8-ohm impedance speaker output, and all will be fine.

What happens if you connect a speaker to an amp without properly matching the impedance of the two together? Maybe nothing—some amps are fairly forgiving. But others are not—some Marshalls, for example, have a reputation for being extremely sensitive to impedance mismatches. And in that case, bad things can happen.

▷ **Too high.** In the case of tube amps, if the speaker has a higher impedance than the amplifier it is connected to—say, connecting a 16-ohm speaker to a 4-ohm amplifier output—you could damage the output tubes or the output transformer in the amp. In this case, the amp tries to deliver more and more voltage until something breaks.

The other thing that happens when the impedance is off in this manner is that the voltage coming back into the transformer from the motion of the speaker voice coil (remember "motional impedance" from the sidebar "Microphone or Speaker" earlier in this chapter?) gets stepped up radically by the transformer working in reverse and can cause huge voltage spikes into the tube sockets—as much as 1,500 volts or more. Needless to say, this can quickly destroy the tube sockets and the tubes. This voltage is called *flyback voltage*, and it can be tremendously destructive to an amplifier. The amp may not fail instantly—it's hard to predict how long it will last under these conditions, but it will probably fail eventually.

▷ **Too low.** If the speaker has a lower impedance than the amp wants to see, the amp could overheat and burn out, particularly with a solid-state amp—the amp tries to deliver more and more current, and eventually the output stage breaks.

Neither of these is what you want to happen! For maximum safe power transfer from the amp and speaker, match the output impedance of the amp to the input impedance of the speaker. Be especially careful when connecting an extension cabinet to a combo amp; make sure that the combination of the internal speaker and the external cabinet is safe for the amp to drive. It's also important to be aware of impedance when wiring up multiple speaker drivers to a single amp, as in a 2×12 combo or when rewiring a 4×12 cabinet.

Measuring Impedance

Because impedance is a combination of resistance and reactance, you can't get an accurate measure of it with a regular ohmmeter or multimeter from Radio Shack—you need special test equipment to measure impedance or AC resistance.

But what if you have a speaker or cabinet that's not labeled, and you need to figure out its impedance? Because guitar speakers typically come in one of three common impedances (4, 8, or 16 ohms), you can make a good guess at its impedance.

Here's how: Using an ohmmeter or multimeter, measure the resistance of the speaker. I know, I know, I just said that a regular ohmmeter or multimeter wouldn't work, and it's true one of those devices will not be able to exactly measure the impedance. But the measured resistance of the speaker does allow you to make your educated guess, using these guidelines:

► If the resistance is less than 4 ohms, the impedance is 4 ohms.

► If the resistance is less than 8 ohms but more than 4 ohms, it's an 8-ohm speaker.

► If the resistance is less than 16 ohms but more than 8 ohms, then the speaker's impedance is 16 ohms.

Depending on how you interconnect the speaker drivers in the cabinet, the resulting total impedance can be wildly different. (With four 16-ohm speakers, you could end up with a 4-ohm total impedance, a 16-ohm total impedance, or a 64-ohm total impedance—that's a fair span.) We'll look more at wiring schemes and impedance with multiple speaker drivers in the next chapter.

When in doubt, check with your amp's manufacturer. They designed the amp to work within certain impedance limitations and can advise you on what loads will be safe for the amp to drive.

Resonant Frequency

Every material has a frequency at which it resonates—a frequency where it begins to vibrate sympathetically in response to external vibrations or energy. When a material resonates, it generates a frequency. Think of blowing air across the opening of a bottle. When the air crosses the opening in just the right way, the column of air inside the bottle begins to resonate, creating an audible note. Speakers are no different; there is a specific frequency at which the cone, spider, and other components begin to resonate and to produce a frequency of their own.

This would seem to be a huge problem, since the resonance could add a peak at that particular frequency, meaning a certain note could jump out at a much louder volume than other notes.

In practice, it's really not a big deal. Guitar speakers are heavily damped to control their motion, and this tends to keep resonance under control as well. Plus, the resonant frequencies of speakers are usually quite low. The lowest note on a standard-tuned guitar is around 82 hertz, and the resonant frequencies for speakers are generally lower than that, in the 55- to 75-hertz range.

The resonant frequency determines the low-end cutoff frequency for the speaker, the point at which the speaker starts to roll off low frequencies. The resonant frequency is dependent on how heavy the cone is and therefore impacts the efficiency of the speaker. (You've probably already caught this, but with speakers, everything affects everything—it's a highly interactive system.)

Some generalities:

 ▷ A higher resonant frequency can mean stronger mids and possibly brighter top end, but at the expense of less very low bass.

 ▷ A lower resonant frequency can mean better low bass, thicker low mids, and better handling of detuned low notes, but at the expense of high treble frequencies and overall efficiency.

 ▷ To tame a combo amp with too much bass, try a speaker with a lower resonant frequency, such as 55 hertz.

 ▷ Because of effects of the trapped volume of air inside a sealed enclosure, installing a speaker into a closed-back cabinet can raise the resonant frequency of the speaker by as much as two and a half steps in musical terms. This means that a speaker with a resonant frequency of 80 hertz, which would normally emphasize the low E string, will be pushed up to a resonant frequency of 110 hertz, the frequency of the open A string. (See the next chapter for more on closed-back cabinets.)

Power Rating

Few things related to speakers are as confusing or ambiguous as power ratings. There are as many as five or more different types of power ratings for speakers. Two of these are of interest (or concern) for us. The first is RMS (*root mean square*) power, which is the power rating we generally get from the manufacturer. RMS is a rating of the continuous power that the speaker can handle. When a speaker is rated for 25 watts RMS, it means that the manufacturer says that the speaker can safely take a continuous signal (such as a steady test tone) at 25 watts for an extended period of time. The measurement is also done using the maximum clean volume available on the amp, so trying to match a 30-watt speaker to a 30-watt amp could still be problematic —the amp that puts out 30 watts of clean power could be putting out a lot more than 30 watts by the time you have it at full crank. Some experts recommend using a speaker cabinet rated at twice the wattage of your amplifier if you are going to really crank up the amp. Others recommend matching the cab to the amp wattage.

One other problem with RMS ratings is that guitar playing rarely consists of a continuous single tone, unless you're holding a note into feedback for a long period of time. And even then, RMS ratings are only of so much use, since the speaker will heat up and everything changes—with the rise in temperature, the voice-coil resistance goes up, and because of this, the power drawn from the amp drops. (This is one reason why, toward the end of a long gig when your amp and speaker are hot, your sound seems to get weaker and to lose attack —the technical term for this is *power compression*.)

The second type of power rating is peak power, which is the amount of power the speaker can handle for a transient or a brief spike or peak in power. The accepted way for manufacturers to specify peak power is to measure the amount of power the speaker can handle 20 percent of the time. (Whatever "20 percent of the time" means…)

A big problem is that there is no standard or governance over how manufacturers come up with their specs. Some rate them one way, while others use a totally different way or "spin" their specs to make the speaker look better on paper—they're going to try to make their speaker look as good as possible from a specs standpoint. And, specs are almost always incomplete, without information on how the spec was derived. (It's not just speaker manufacturers that do this; the same is true for pretty much everything in the world today.) So, the best we can really do is use power ratings as a rough guide.

One place where the power rating can be useful is in trying to get a handle on how much a given speaker will break up when driven hard, or at least whether it will break up early or late as the power increases. You can expect that a speaker rated at 25 watts is going to break up much more easily than a speaker rated at 60 watts, which should remain clean to higher power levels. (Technically, it's not the power that causes the speaker to break up; it's the thickness of the cone, which tends to relate to power handling. See the "Speaker Breakup" section later in this chapter for more on this.)

It's worth noting that power rating does not translate in any way to the volume the speaker can produce. In fact, in a shootout of 15 different speakers, *Guitar Player* magazine found that the one with the lowest power rating was actually the loudest of the bunch. This makes sense when you consider that to achieve a higher power rating, a manufacturer needs a larger voice coil, a larger magnet, and a heavier cone, among other things, all of which contribute to more power handling but at the expense of efficiency. A speaker designed for lower power handing can be made much lighter and will be more efficient, so it will often be louder for a given power level.

Efficiency

It's hard to believe, but most loudspeakers are only about 1 percent efficient—only about 1 percent of the electrical signal from the amp is actually converted into sound waves. The rest of the amp's output power is converted into heat in the voice coil and magnet and lost. There's no getting around it; 1 percent is a miserable figure! There aren't too many places in life where you could have a 1-percent success rate and still be considered to have done a good job.

Just imagine: If we could increase the efficiency of speakers, a tiny amplifier would produce a screaming-loud output level—we could run our Marshall stacks off of watch batteries. But, as the saying goes, "it is what it is," and for most of us, this abysmal performance is never an issue. The way amps and speakers are made and used, we get along with that 1-percent efficiency just fine.

Speaker efficiency depends on several factors, such as the impedance interaction between the amp and the speaker, the frequency of the signal, and how the speaker is interfacing with the air, which is one place where the speaker cabinet comes into play.

Sensitivity

Sensitivity is a measure of how well the speaker converts a signal from an amplifier into sound pressure. It is measured as the number of decibels of SPL (*sound pressure level*) that the speaker produces when fed one watt of power, measured from one meter away, often measured using a single frequency, such as 1 kHz (1,000 hertz). An example speaker sensitivity might be a rating of 97 dB @ 1 watt/1 meter. The higher the sensitivity, the louder the speaker will play for a given amount of power (all other things being equal). A few tips:

> ▷ If you're trying to make your amp as loud as possible, go for a speaker with the highest sensitivity you can find.

> ▷ If you're trying to keep the volume your amp puts out down, go for a speaker with the lowest sensitivity you can find.

> ▷ In a cabinet or combo with more than one speaker, it's generally best not to mix speakers with sensitivities that are too different from one another, as their volumes will not match very well—the more sensitive one will drown out the less sensitive one.

In Chapter 10, we'll look a lot more deeply into volume and power, but for now, when looking at sensitivity, note that a 3-dB change is a noticeable increase or drop in volume, but nowhere near double the volume—to double the volume as a result of sensitivity requires a 10-dB increase (say, from a sensitivity of 93 dB @ 1 watt/1 meter to a sensitivity of 103 dB @ 1 watt/1 meter).

Speaker Breakup

While not something quantifiable that ever gets spec'd out by a manufacturer for a speaker, breakup is very important to the tone the speaker produces. Breakup can be defined as interference of vibrations on the surface of the speaker with one another. Above 900 hertz or so, the speaker cone vibrates in sections, and the waves moving across those sections can meet and mess with one another. (Think of what happens when waves on the surface of a lake run into each other—the shape of the resulting waves changes.) This mostly happens in the midrange, and the extra harmonics generated by the breakup distortion can contribute a lot to the richness of the tone that is produced. It's commonly accepted that the power handling of a speaker determines at what point it begins to break up—a speaker rated for lower power handling should break up before a speaker rated for higher power handling. This isn't quite accurate. It's actually the thickness of the speaker cone that is the big factor in breakup, and a thicker cone typically comes with higher power handling.

What's the Difference?

At first glance, it seems as if speaker efficiency and sensitivity are the same thing. They're similar but not quite the same, and they tell us different things.

Efficiency is how much of the electrical input power to the speaker is actually converted to sound power. If you put in one watt of electrical signal, 1 percent (for example) of it is converted to sound power. If you put in 100 watts of electrical signal, 1 percent of that is converted to sound power. A more efficient speaker might convert 1.3 percent of the electrical signal power to sound power. This tells us that one speaker will be better at converting electrical signal to sound power than another, but it doesn't tell us how much volume we'll get out of the speaker for a given wattage, and it doesn't give us much basis for comparing speakers in real-world terms.

Sensitivity, on the other hand, gives us a measured figure for how much sound-power output we can expect from a given electrical signal input power. For example, say we put 1 watt of electrical signal into a speaker and measure the sound pressure level directly in front of the speaker, from 1 meter away, and we get 97 dB. Now we know that if we double the power to 2 watts, we should get 100 dB from 1 meter away. And if we double the power again, we should get 103 dB from 1 meter away, and so on. It's a more real-world-applicable spec that gives us a better idea of at least roughly how the speaker will perform.

It also allows us to compare two speakers. If one speaker puts out 94 dB @ 1 watt/1 meter, and another puts out 104 dB @ 1 watt/1 meter, we know the second speaker will be twice as loud as the first for any given wattage.

Regardless of where breakup comes from, you can certainly use it to your advantage in your tone. If you want maximum clarity and articulation, particularly when using distorted tones, then look for a speaker that doesn't break up until really pushed (which often means a higher power rating). If you want a brighter, more ragged top end (in a good way) or more richness at lower volume levels, then a speaker that breaks up earlier would be a good choice.

Classic Speakers

Over the years, certain models of speakers have been used over and over again for combo amps and speaker cabinets—so much so that they're considered standards in the industry. This is not to say that there aren't many other excellent speakers on the market or that other speakers, such as models made for vintage Fender and other amps by CTS, Oxford, and Utah, don't have their proponents. But these speakers have established themselves as benchmarks that are often used as touchstones for describing and achieving tones.

Celestion G12M "Greenback" & G12H 30

The G12M was Celestion's first speaker with a ceramic magnet. Its nickname—Greenback—comes from the green magnet cover that was used on it. (Other-colored covers were also used at various times.) Marshall put the 12-inch diameter Greenback on the map by using it in the early Bluesbreaker combos (beginning around 1966) as well as in their 4×12 speaker cabinets. These speakers originally had a 20-watt rating but changed to a 25-watt rating in 1968. Both of these relatively low ratings mean that Greenbacks break up quite easily. They have a fairly high sensitivity of 98 dB and a resonant frequency of 75 Hz. The Greenback provides good bottom end, with crisp, smooth highs and smooth mids. For many players, these speakers in a 4×12 define the sound of Marshall crunch. Despite the ceramic magnet, the G12M compresses a bit when driven hard, especially on the low end.

The current reissues are made in China, and opinions vary as to whether these are as good as the original British-made Greenbacks. For some, the originals are all that will make the grade. But many players find the new reissues get the tone once broken in. (Greenbacks desperately need to be broken in to tame out-of-the-box harshness.)

The G12H is similar to the G12M, but it's a heavier-duty speaker than the G12M, with articulate top end and more aggressive midrange, and with a 30-watt power rating that still allows for plenty of warm overdrive and rich speaker breakup. The G12H has a bigger and heavier magnet at 50 ounces (that's where the "H" comes from—"heavy") versus the 35 ouncer in the G12M ("M" for "medium-weight" magnet). It is slightly more sensitive and louder than the G12M, at 100 dB. It's a "flatter" speaker that some consider to have slightly less character than the G12M. Celestion currently makes two versions, one with a 75-hertz resonant frequency and one with a 55-hertz resonant frequency.

Jimi Hendrix is said to have largely switched over to 55-hertz G12H speakers later in his career for their bigger bottom end and stiffer cone—which also made this speaker well-suited to bass guitar.

Celestion Vintage 30

The Celestion Vintage 30 may be the most commonly used OEM (*original equipment manufacturer*) speaker on the market today—it appears in countless amps, from Fender to Marshall, Dr. Z to Egnator, Mesa/Boogie to Line 6, Bogner to Orange, and many, many more amps and cabs. Introduced in 1986 to meet the needs of the hair-metal shredders rocking modded Marshalls, the Vintage 30 has a power rating of 60 watts, a 50-ounce ceramic magnet (designed to get close to the response of an alnico magnet), and a resonant frequency of 75 hertz. If you want crunch, this speaker is all about providing it, whether in an open-back combo or in a closed 4×12 cab. Tight but full lows, thick mids, smooth top end, and a seriously noticeable peak in the upper mids define this speaker's sound.

Celestion Blue and Gold

Best known for their role voicing the classic tone of Vox AC30 amps, these alnico-based speakers offer the epitome of bell-like top end. Originally designed for radio applications, the G12 Bulldog "Blue" Celestion was adopted as the stock speaker for the AC30, where it provided punchy lows, attenuated but sweet midrange, and bright, chiming top end, with chewy compression and harmonics-laden breakup when pushed hard. Rated at just 15 watts of power handling (original early units were rated as low as 9 watts), with a 75-hertz resonant frequency, the Celestion Blue has a sensitivity rating of 100 dB—in the upper reaches of most guitar amp speakers, making it quite a loud speaker. At least until it goes into breakup, which it does quite early. The Blue is definitely a speaker that benefits from being broken in; the surround becomes more flexible, and the highs are toned down to a warmer, bell-like consistency.

Pre-Rola versus Rola

If you look into vintage Celestion speakers, you'll quickly encounter the terms "pre-Rola" and "Rola." Collectors and vintage aficionados feel that pre-Rola Celestions—speakers where the word "Rola" does not appear on the label—are superior to Rola Celestions, where the label reads "Rola Celestion Ltd." The reasoning behind this is that the pre-Rola labeled speakers used Pulsonic speaker cones, which were believed to be the best choice for Marshall amplifiers.

Here's the deal: Celestion was founded in 1924 but was purchased by the British Rola company after World War II, in 1947. Rola Celestion Ltd. continued to manufacture speakers as before, with just a few minor changes, such as the switch from paper to Nomex formers by 1973. They supplied Greenbacks—speakers with green magnet covers (and later gray, black, and cream covers)—to Marshall for use in their amplifiers and speaker cabinets. Greenbacks are famous for their use in Marshall Bluesbreaker amps as well as in "basket weave" Marshall 4×12 speaker cabinets, which feature distinctive basket-weave-patterned grille cloth.

Rola Celestion outgrew its facilities in Thames Ditton, Surrey, and in late 1968, production began to be moved to a new plant in Ipswich, Suffolk. The last of the production was moved by 1975.

In 1971, labels began to appear with the Rola name and the new Suffolk location on them. By 1973, all Celestions had the Rola label. Around this time, the cones began to be changed from Pulsonics to other types, sourced from an outside vendor. There is some overlap between the advent of the new labels and the last of the Pulsonic cones.

In 1992, Celestion was sold to Kinergetics Holdings, whose major shareholder was Gold Peak in Hong Kong.

So are the pre-Rola Celestions really the Holy Grail of speakers for Marshalls? Many collectors and experts feel they are better, and "pre-Rola" has become a buzzword that indicates the "best" production years for Celestions. However, there was substantial overlap between the pre-Rola and Rola days, so some Rolas are still basically the same speakers.

Pre-Rola Greenbacks are described as full sounding with clear but mellow top end. Some of this is no doubt due to the fact that the speakers are now 40 or more years old and are most likely very well broken in.

The Celestion Gold is designed to exhibit these "broken-in" characteristics right out of the box, with a bit more midrange richness compared to the Blue. It has a higher power rating, 50 watts, and does not break up quite as early as the Blue does. Consider it the "premium" version of the Blue, with a cleaner sound, though it will break up in similar fashion with an appropriate amount of signal from the amp.

Electro-Voice SRO and EVM12L

The alnico-magnet white "coffee-can" Electro-Voice SRO 12-inch speaker (so named for its huge magnet cover) is long discontinued but remains popular with many players. This speaker is a high-wattage model and will maintain a consistent tone until driven with a ton of power, despite its alnico magnet. It is described as having tight but full bottom end, thick midrange, and smooth, warm top end with excellent clarity.

The E-V SRO had a 48-ounce alnico magnet and was rated for 60 watts of continuous power handling, good for up to 300 watts of peak power. Sensitivity was an ultra-high 103 dB, making this speaker a volume-for-the-buck leader. These remain sought-after speakers by players who want a loud speaker with a clean sound, but with warmth and no harshness. Reconed units seem to survive being updated well and keep their tone well.

In later years, the SRO was switched to a ceramic magnet, and the model eventually morphed into the EVM12L. If you want really clean tones, the EVM12L is an excellent choice; it's almost impossible to drive this speaker hard enough to cause it to break up. It offers a full sound with good brightness. Some players feel its "cleanliness" leads it to sound sterile. Others find it is ideal for accurately reproducing the output from the amplifier and for its super-consistent tone at all volume levels. Players as disparate as Larry Carlton, who uses one in a ported 1×12 cabinet with his Dumble Overdrive Special amp, and Zakk Wylde, who loads up Marshall 4×12 cabinets with EVM12Ls and drives them with Marshall JCM800 amps, enjoy the tone and output of this speaker.

The EVM12L is rated for 300 watts of long-term power handling. It has a resonant frequency of 55 hertz and a sensitivity rating of 100 dB. One caveat: It also weighs more than 19 pounds. For many years, I used an EVM12L speaker in a 1×12 Mesa/Boogie Mark IIB combo amp. From personal experience, I can share that this is one heavy speaker—make sure your back is up to the task and that your amp's baffle board is nice and stout. I can't imagine having to deal with moving Zakk's 4×12 cabs loaded with these weighty beasts!

JBL D120F and E120

JBL speakers, particularly the D120F, became very popular in Fender amps—a dream rig for many players in the '70s was a Fender Twin with two D120Fs installed. The "D" indicates the speaker has a metal dome/dust cap. The "F" stands for "Fender," who was the biggest D120F customer and who also handled distribution to music stores for the JBL guitar amp speakers. However, the speakers were not designed for Fender, nor were they designed for Dick Dale (as he has stated). The D120F guitar speaker was nearly identical to the D131, a full-range 12-inch home stereo speaker with an alnico magnet. The biggest difference was that the D120F had a wider magnet/voice coil gap that allowed for easier mounting to a guitar amp baffle board—when the speakers were installed, they often screwed down too tightly, causing the frame to warp and the voice coil to rub. The wider gap solved this problem. The D120F also had a slightly more durable surround. The surround on the D131 tended to dry out and crack.

In the early days of the Allman Brothers, Duane Allman and Dickey Betts were said to use JBL D120F speakers with their Marshall amps. The D120F has a clean, uncolored sound and maintains that tone until it goes into breakup when driven hard. These speakers were rated for 100 watts of continuous power (which, according to some sources familiar with JBL's ratings, puts the RMS rating at 50 watts; other sources say the RMS rating was 100 watts). Harvey Gerst, the man who developed these speakers, has stated that he arrived at the power ratings by playing guitar through the speakers at increasing wattages until they blew up and then backing the rating off by a few watts for safety. (Not very scientific, but definitely a practical approach!) These are also speakers with high sensitivities, which makes them quite loud.

Later, these speakers were renamed the K120, and later still the E120, and other things were changed along the way. The E-series speakers used ceramic magnets and had massive power ratings, up to 300 watts. The E series also used a cloth surround versus the pleated paper surround in the D120F. This speaker has a reputation as being super clean and bright, with less breakup and less compression than the D120F. The D120F is usually described as warmer, with fuller midrange. Jerry Garcia of the Grateful Dead used D120Fs in his amps in the early days, replacing them first with K120s and then with E120s, which he used until the end of his career.

These are heavy speakers (around 14 pounds each), and installing them in a Twin or a multi-speaker cabinet results in a weighty, hard-to-move monster!

Jensen P12 and C12

Jensen made guitar speakers from the 1940s through the 1960s. The company offered two series of speakers, the P series and the C series, which were used in Fender amplifiers and also in amps from Gibson, Ampeg, and more. Examples include the P10R, the C10Q, the P12K, and so on. The model name of each speaker included quite a bit of information about it. The first letter indicates the type of magnet: The "P" series use an alnico magnet, while the "C" series use a ceramic magnet. The number in the model name indicates the size of the speaker—8-inch, 10-inch, 12-inch, and 15-inch. The letter following the number indicates the power rating and voice coil size:

Table 8.1 Jensen Speaker Codes

	Voice Coil	Reissue Power Rating	Vintage Power Rating (alnico)	Vintage Power Rating (ceramic)
R	1 inch	25 watts	12 watts	15 watts
Q	1.25 inch	35 watts	15 watts	20 watts
N	1.5 inch	50 watts	18 watts	25 watts
K	2 inch	100 watts	N/A	N/A

With their low power handling, vintage Jensen speakers break up easily. They provide a round midrange and bright but warm top end. The alnico models compress in a nice way, while the ceramics maintain a slightly more "stable" tone. For many players, the sound of a Jensen speaker is tightly linked to that of vintage Fender amps, from Tweed to Blackface.

In the late 1990s, an Italian company acquired the rights to the Jensen name and began manufacturing reissues of the original vintage Jensen speakers, which are once again used in Fender and other amplifiers. The reissues are fairly faithful to the originals. They do need to be broken in well to reduce harshness and to tame the extra brightness and edginess on the top end.

Speaker Break In

Few players or manufacturers would claim that a speaker sounds its best fresh off the manufacturing line. Out of the box, a speaker will tend to sound and feel "stiff," with a hard-edged tone and excess brightness. It may be tight in the bass and mids as well.

As the speaker is used, the surround and spider loosen up, and the cone softens very slightly. Plus, with certain types of magnets (especially alnico), the magnet will lose a tiny amount of strength over the first year or so after it is made, after which it settles down and remains stable for decades.

All of this is to say, once the speaker "breaks in," its tone will change, almost always for the better. It will soften and smooth out, particularly in the upper mids and highs, and the lows will loosen up a bit.

Most experts will tell you the best way to break in a speaker is to play it long, loud, and often. How long it takes for a speaker to break in depends on the speaker and how you use it, but estimates can range from 20, to 50, to even more hours of serious use.

You can accelerate this process. Some manufacturers, such as Weber and others, will break in a speaker before it is shipped. You can also break in a speaker yourself. Simply run a signal through it. Eddie Van Halen is rumored to lock his new speakers in a room with a guitar feeding back through them. Another approach is to hook up a CD, iPod, or other sound source; set it to loop a song; and play it through the speaker for a few days at a good loud volume level—close it in the basement or a closet, cover it with blankets, lay the cabinet face down, set up the speaker and go on vacation, do whatever it takes to not drive yourself crazy listening to the same song over and over! You could also run a good pounding drum loop (with some nice hi-hat and crash-cymbal action) through it for a couple of days.

The advantage to using a piece of music versus a steady-state signal or feedback is that you are sending a constantly changing full-range signal through the speaker, subjecting it to a variety of frequency combinations, including very low and very high frequencies, at varying dynamic levels.

However you do it, breaking in your speakers is going to happen—the only difference between letting it happen naturally by playing guitar through it and accelerating the process by running some other signal through it is the time required, particularly if you don't play at high volume levels.

Table 8.2 Speaker Tonal Factors

Tone Factor	Tonal Contribution
Frame material	None
Magnet type	Minor to major
Magnet size	None to minor
Cone thickness	Subtle to moderate
Doping	Subtle to minor
Former type	None to subtle
Dust cap size	Subtle to minor
Speaker diameter	Major
Impedance	None
Resonant frequency	Minor to moderate
Power rating	None
Early versus late breakup	Moderate to major
Efficiency	None
Sensitivity	None

9

Cabinets and Enclosures

IN CHAPTER 8, WE WERE TALKING SOLELY about the speaker driver itself—the actual cone-and-magnet device that creates the sound waves when a signal is fed to it from an amplifier. But there's more to the picture than just the driver. Speaker drivers generally aren't intended to be used in free space; they're designed to be mounted into a cabinet or enclosure of some sort, which is built to strengthen the tone, shape the sound, increase the projection, bolster the efficiency, and enhance the performance of the driver.

The enclosure that the speaker or speakers live in can be part of the same box that also holds the electronics for the amplifier, in which case it is known as a *combo* amp. Or, the speakers can be mounted in a separate enclosure from the amp's electronics, in which case it is known as a *speaker cabinet*, or *cab* for short. In either case, the enclosure has specific purposes: It is intended to protect and house the speaker, of course, but it is also required to interface the speaker with the air.

With hi-fi speaker enclosures and studio monitor enclosures, the idea is to make the cabinet as dead and neutral as possible, to remove it from the sonic equation. With guitar cabinets, we don't go quite that far. Many players enjoy a cabinet that adds some character to the sound, thus the debates over plywood versus MDF versus pine for construction, finger jointing versus butt joints for manufacture, and other cabinet design features. The cabinet's vibration must be controlled but not completely deadened. Often there is a certain volume level where the cabinet "activates" (my term) and begins to add a nice resonance to the tone—I believe this is one of the reasons why players like to crank the volume, to get that extra contribution from the cabinet.

The interesting thing about guitar cabinets is, as with speakers intended for guitar, they're not really made to sound *good* or accurate in pure audio terms. In cabinet designs aimed at pristine sound, such as studio monitors, the ideal is for what goes in to equal what goes out, just louder. The speaker and cabinet should not color the sound in any way. As opposed to this approach, a guitar cabinet is made to, in audiophile terms, sound inaccurate—but in a very specific, controlled way. You don't want too much in the way of low end below 80 hertz (the frequency of the low E string), or the guitar will sound boomy. You don't want much above 5,000 or 6,000 hertz, or the guitar will sound fizzy and harsh. Plus, we're not striving to remove speaker and cabinet distortion from the signal. ("Distortion" here being defined as coloration and changes to the input signal, not necessarily as fuzz or overdrive.) Even a clean electric guitar tone has a certain distortion component to it; it's part of what we expect to hear from the instrument. Without some distortion (whether it is audible as breakup or not), an electric guitar sounds thin, sterile, and lifeless. Plug your guitar straight into your home stereo and listen—not many players would call that anemic, ragged, shrieky sound an enjoyable tone.

As you saw in the previous chapter, the speaker is the main mechanism for this sonic shaping. But the cabinet is a platform for and extension of that speaker, bringing it to life and spreading its goodness throughout the room, all the while reinforcing those desirable qualities and minimizing the undesirable qualities.

The difference is that a guitar cabinet is a producer and creator of sound, whereas a hi-fi speaker or studio monitor is a reproducer. You want a reproducer to get out of the way and reproduce the sound as cleanly and accurately as possible. You want a creator of sound to color it, to shape it, to add character, and to contribute to the tone that is produced—to make the sound as "musical" as it can be.

Types of Speaker Enclosures

There are two main types of boxes into which speakers can be mounted, whether they are combos or separate cabs: open back and closed back. The difference is that one type has an open back, while the other is sealed with a closed back. Simple enough and pretty obvious, right? But that simple difference between the two types results in major differences in the sounds the enclosures produce.

A speaker driver produces sound from both the front and the back of its cone. The two types of cabinets deal with the energy from the rear of the cone in different ways. An open-back cabinet lets the sound from the back of the speaker emerge from the rear of the amp. This increases the dispersion of the speaker cabinet, giving you more coverage in the room. The bottom end on an open-backed cabinet tends to be looser, with more openness in the mids and highs; a broader "focus" is perhaps a good term.

A closed-back cabinet is also referred to as an *acoustic suspension* design. The cabinet is sealed, and the speaker is able to use the air trapped inside the cabinet as a sort of spring against which it can work. This adds low-end "thump" to the sound compared to an open design; however, it reduces the efficiency of the amp—a closed-back cabinet will not be as loud as an open-back cabinet with the same speaker and amplifier. Closed-back enclosures also tend to have much tighter dispersion patterns than open-back enclosures. Think of a flashlight beam emerging from the front of the amp. This is good for controlling where the sound is going, but it can also mean that your stage volume is deafening the audience members directly in front of you while those a few feet off to the side can't hear you at all.

The resonant frequency of the speaker inside the enclosure also makes a difference when you compare the two types of cabs. With an open-back cabinet, the speaker can generate a ton of energy at that resonant frequency, which gets dispersed into the room. With a closed-back cabinet, the trapped air in the cabinet modifies that resonant frequency, raising it slightly—which can put the resonance into the range of the lower guitar strings and give them more punch—and preventing the speaker from resonating as freely.

Combo amps are almost always open-back designs, though there are a few manufacturers, such as 3rd Power, that make closed-back combo amps. (Actually, the 3rd Power amps, along with amps from some other manufacturers, have a removable panel and can be operated either closed back or open back.) One big reason combos are usually open is to allow air to freely flow into the enclosure to keep the amp's electronics cool.

Another option is one of the newer "3/4-backed" or "3/4-closed" designs, such as those from Mesa/Boogie, which have backs that are mostly closed but still with a good-sized opening. This type of cabinet combines aspects of both the closed-back and open-back sounds—tighter bottom end than an open back, but more open-sounding and with broader dispersion than a closed back.

Table 9.1   Open-Back versus Closed-Back Enclosures Sonic Characteristics (All Other Things Being Equal)

	Open-Back Enclosure	Close-Back Enclosure
Bass	Softer, less focused	Tighter, deeper, bigger
Treble	Chimy and open	Smoother and darker
Midrange	Round and open	More focused, punchy
Volume	Louder	Quieter
Dispersion	Broad, from both front and back	Tight and beamy
Efficiency	Higher	Lower
Resonant frequency	Speaker can resonate freely at this frequency and put out more low-end energy.	Sealed air inside the cabinet controls amount of speaker resonance and raises resonant frequency slightly.

Speakers and Cabinets

Not every speaker driver is ideal for installation in every cabinet. Some speakers work well in open-back cabinets, while others work well in sealed or closed-back cabinets. In most cases, the difference comes down to how heavily the speaker is damped, although the speaker's resonant frequency also plays a part.

If a speaker is well-damped, then installing it in a sealed cabinet, where the enclosed air acts as a spring on the speaker and increases damping, may result in a compressed, flat, dead-sounding speaker. The same speaker may, however, be perfect in an open-backed cabinet, where there is no additional damping from the air in the cab.

If, on the other hand, a speaker has less damping of its own and is freer to move, then it may benefit from the additional damping a sealed enclosure provides.

Ports

One way to increase the low-frequency performance of a sealed or closed-back guitar speaker cabinet is to add a port. A port is a slot or hole in the front or rear of the cabinet. The port allows the sound waves and air motion from the back of the speaker to be combined with the sound waves coming from the front of the speaker. The port's size is specifically calculated to resonate at a frequency that is below the speaker's resonant frequency. This way, when the speaker's bass response begins to drop off below the resonant frequency, the sound waves from the rear of the speaker cause the port to resonate, adding in more low-frequency energy.

There are a few problems associated with porting: A port only resonates at one frequency, so it is of less help at other frequencies. There can also be noise associated with the air rushing through the port (technically known as *port viscosity*). This noise can be reduced by using multiple ports to spread the moving air stream out and to reduce turbulence and noise. Miking a ported cabinet can also be somewhat more challenging, since you must avoid placing the mic in the air column coming from the port, and without miking the port, you may not get the full bottom end of the cab as it is heard in the room.

These problems don't stop designers from creating cabinets with ports, though. They're especially common in closed-back 1×12 cabinet designs and in some 2×12 cab designs. The advantage is that a compact ported cabinet can generate a surprising amount of bass resulting in a sound that is bigger than you would expect.

Seems ideal, and for many players a ported cab is an excellent solution. But for heavier styles, where tight, thumping bottom end is required, it may not serve as well as a larger, completely sealed cabinet. And, where the player doesn't want or need the additional bass reinforcement, a port serves no purpose.

Enclosure Size

The dimensions of a speaker enclosure and the amount of air volume it encloses have some effect on the tone produced, but perhaps not as much as many players assume. In fact, it's likely that many of the classic speaker cabinets, such as Fenders, were designed without any real consideration for the enclosure's impact on the tone—Leo was simply using the wood that was available and trying to keep manufacturing costs down. And, Jim Marshall has been known to state that when he designed the classic 4×12 Marshall speaker cabinet, he simply used the smallest dimensions he could come up with that comfortably held the four speakers.

Of course, some builders do try to tune the size of their cabinets for a certain acoustic result and may even try to match the enclosure's dimensions to the specs of the speakers being used to attain the best results possible. But that approach is surprisingly rare.

In general:

▷ With an open-back cabinet, a larger enclosure means a more open sound, more bass response (especially if the baffle ends up being larger in size), and a less boxy midrange.

▷ With a closed-back cabinet, a larger enclosure can increase bass response but will also make the bass response looser, with less punch. The midrange will also be less boxy.

Woods

Does the material a cabinet is made from affect its tone? Yes, although other factors, such as the cabinet type, size, construction, and speaker selection, probably have a bigger impact. The original Fender cabinets were mostly made from pine, probably because Leo Fender found that wood to be readily available in the right-sized planks, and it was inexpensive. The cabinets were assembled using finger-jointed (interlocking) corners where the side, top, and bottom boards met. The pine provided a resonant, warm sound from the cabinet. Around the time of the change to Blackface amps (1963 or so), Fenders switched over to using birch plywood, which is now the accepted "standard" for a classic cabinet wood. The plywood cabinets are more rigid and resonate less, contributing to the brighter, tighter tones of Blackface amps compared to Tweed amps. Fender also went to MDF baffles, which were extremely dense and rigid. (See the next section for more on baffles.)

Typically, cab makers use between 1/2-inch and 3/4-inch sheets for building enclosures. The thicker the wood used, the heavier and the more rigid the cabinet will be, and the less it will contribute "color" to the tone, although a heavier, more rigid cabinet may have more bottom end.

Most modern amps use birch plywood, though on the lower end you may find MDF or particleboard cabs, which are even denser and resonate even less. Some builders going for a "vintage" or retro vibe use pine. With plywood, the better cabs use void-free sheets. Voids are those spaces where knots are removed from the wood and the holes left behind are replaced with an inset piece of replacement wood. Voids can rattle and buzz when the amp is driven hard.

Some builders also use hardwoods of various types for their enclosures. The harder the wood, the brighter sounding the cabinet will be, although the effect can be subtle. Hardwood cabinets are also often left uncovered, with a stain finish instead of a Tolex or vinyl covering. This can contribute a tiny amount of additional brightness to the tone.

Baffle

The baffle is the front of the speaker cabinet, the piece of wood into which the speakers are actually mounted. Aside from holding up the speakers, the baffle serves another purpose: It separates the front of the speaker from the back of the speaker. This is important because the sound coming from the back of the speaker is out of phase with the sound coming from the front of the speaker. When the speaker moves forward, a compression is created in the air. Simultaneously, the air behind the speaker is being pulled forward, creating a rarefaction. These two are completely out of polarity with one another, and if they combine, they will cancel one another, with the result being silence. This is especially a problem with low frequencies, which are long enough sound waves to bend right around the speaker baffle.

To counter this, the baffle has to be big enough to stop the sound waves behind the speaker from mixing with the sound waves in front of the speaker. As far as the thickness of the baffle, there are two camps: One believes that the baffle should be heavy and rigid and should not move when the speakers move. This provides maximum separation from the front to the back and also does not allow the baffle board to resonate and add to (or subtract from) the tone. This camp prefers a heavy, 3/4-inch baffle, made from a dense material, usually plywood or MDF, that does not resonate at guitar frequencies.

The other camp believes that the baffle is an integral part of the tone and should resonate freely when the speakers are pushing air. This camp uses thinner baffles (1/2-inch or sometimes even thinner) made from more resonant solid wood, such as pine or from high-grade, void-free birch plywood. The thinner baffle lets some of the rear sound through, which can then cancel frequencies in the sound coming from the front.

It also resonates, adding its own coloration into the sound being produced. And, since it is allowed to move, it interacts with the movements of the speakers, changing their response along the way.

Tweed Fender amps take the idea of baffle resonance to the extreme with their "floating" baffles. With a Fender floating baffle, the baffle is screwed to cleats on the top and bottom of the cabinet but is not secured on the sides. Some amp makers going for a similar effect attach the sides of the baffle and leave the top and bottom free; the result is the same. The grille cloth may also be wrapped around the edges of the baffle, between the cleats and the baffle, and may provide extra isolation and freedom for the baffle to resonate. This approach to mounting the baffle allows it to vibrate freely. It definitely contributes to the tone produced, with a less tight bottom end, honkier midrange, and creamier overdrive tone.

Somewhere around the beginning of the Fender Blackface era, the company switched to baffles made from MDF. And, around 1972, Fender began gluing in the baffles, attaching them on all four sides. Most other companies, including Marshall and Vox, used fixed baffles throughout their history.

For most players, the desirability of a floating baffle or of a more resonant baffle comes down to musical style and the amount of gain used. For a more vintage tone, a pine cabinet with a 1/2-inch floating baffle will contribute richness, midrange, and in some cases, almost a sense of reverb to the sound—it's a "looser" sound, for lack of a better descriptor. Many blues players, roots rockers, and traditional country players enjoy this. But for a higher gain, more classic rock or modern tone, with tighter bottom end, better bass response, and more efficiency, a thicker fixed baffle in a rigid plywood or MDF cabinet largely removes cabinet resonance from the equation; in this case, the cabinet provides a tight, articulate platform upon which the speakers can do their job.

Front-Loaded versus Rear-Loaded Cabinets

Talk about a tweaky debate! There are players who will argue the merits of attaching the speaker driver to the front of the baffle (with the speaker projecting through the hole in the baffle) versus attaching the speaker driver to the rear of the baffle (with the speaker hanging off the back of the baffle). (Note: The terms *front-loaded cabinet* and *rear-loaded cabinet* are used to refer to different types of cabinets in the live sound reinforcement/PA world.)

Can that 1/2-inch or 3/4-inch difference really change the tone? Some players think so. And, believe it or not, there is a *very* small possibility that there could be a *very* subtle sonic difference. The difference could result from the cone of the speaker being recessed away from the actual column of air that it is working on, decoupling it from resonances at the "mouth" of the speaker.

Despite that somewhat plausible possibility, it's doubtful the tonal effect will be of any significance.

Cabinet Coverings

Is there a difference in tone between tweed, Tolex, textured vinyl, leather, and other coverings on a combo amp or a speaker cabinet? I've never encountered anyone who claimed to be able to hear the differences among various amp and speaker cabinet coverings. But potentially, the addition of a limp material on the outside of the amp could damp its resonance a bit—at least one builder claims that even the glue used to attach the covering to a cabinet can affect the tone. It is tough to assess the reality of a claim like this; you'd need several identical cabinets, each with a different covering and/or glue, that you could immediately switch among from a single amp to do a true comparison.

Players including Eddie Van Halen have been known to strip the covering off of their Marshall cabinets. Part of this may just be to get the look of the semi-trashed cab exterior, but some of those players also claim that there is a difference in the resonance of the cabinet. It's doubtful whether there is a huge tonal difference with a stripped or covered cab, especially when we're talking about a fairly rigid and non-resonant 4×12-style cab. Still, the removal of that damping material on the outside of the cab might allow it to breathe a bit more. And, with a lighter, pine cabinet with a floating baffle, it might make a bigger difference. But you do lose the protection the covering offers. The tiny bit of potential difference in the tone probably doesn't justify tearing off the covering, unless you really like that look.

Grille Cloth

Ideally, the grille (not "grill"; that's the thing you cook your burgers on) cloth covering the front of the speaker cabinet should be acoustically transparent. The grille is just there to protect the speaker from damage while letting all the sound pass through unimpeded. But in reality, anything you place in proximity to a driver will influence the sound that driver makes to one degree or another. And in the case of grille cloth, that influence is to absorb and disperse a tiny bit of the very top-end frequencies. Some grille clothes are even designed to filter the sound—to remove just a bit of the very high frequencies in order to tame shrillness.

Multi-Speaker Cabinets

Almost from the beginning, amp manufacturers have experimented with mounting more than one speaker driver into a combo or a speaker cabinet to get more volume, more low end, and more projection and coverage.

When you combine more than one speaker in a cabinet, interesting things happen to the tone. In the low frequencies, assuming the speakers are in proper polarity (see next section), the drivers will piston out together, and their low frequencies will couple and reinforce each other. This is one reason why cabs and combos with two or more speakers tend to have a bigger bottom end, thicker lower midrange, and more deep bass.

In the midrange and highs, the speakers tend to "phase" against each other, causing some cancellations and reinforcements at certain frequencies. This can give the sound more richness and punch and may also smooth out some peaky frequencies—though it could also make some peaky frequencies even more peaky. Some players hear this interaction as extra "depth" in the sound or even a stereo chorusing or phase-shifter type of effect.

Polarity

Polarity, or phase, in a multi-speaker enclosure refers to how the voice coil/cone moves in response to the signal. Specifically, you want all the speakers to move in the same direction at the same time. When the signal pushes one speaker out, you want all the speakers to move out, not some to move out and some in, which tends to create cancellations in the tone and can diminish the attack and impact of the sound. Usually, this means that a positive voltage applied to the positive speaker terminal will result in the speaker moving out. But not all speakers work this way; in some cases, a positive voltage at the positive terminal makes the speaker move in.

With a single speaker, polarity doesn't really mean anything. However, some purists subscribe to "absolute polarity," meaning that the speaker should move out with a positive voltage at the positive speaker terminal.

If you can't tell which terminal is positive, just hook a nine-volt battery up to the two speaker terminals. If the speaker moves out, then whichever terminal is connected to the battery's positive pole is the positive terminal and vice versa.

Straight versus Slant

Traditionally, 4×12 speaker cabinets—and a few 2×12 cabinets—come in two forms or types: straight front, with all of the speakers aligned on the same vertical plane, and slant front, where the top two speakers are angled back slightly while the bottom two are vertical. The idea is that the slanted cab will improve dispersion of the sound, for better stage coverage, and also make it easier for the player to hear himself or herself. The slant format also causes a slight reduction in the internal cabinet volume and changes how the top speakers interact with the bottom speakers —so yes, there could be a subtle tonal difference between a slant and a straight cab. It depends on the cab and the tone, but slant cabs are often described as brighter, sometimes with more midrange, while straight cabs are deemed fuller sounding, with deeper bass and smoother highs.

Part of this difference could be that with an angled cabinet, the upper speakers are aimed more at the player's ears, while a straight cab aims all four speakers at the player's knees. Before making a decision as to whether you prefer the slant or straight version of a cabinet, be sure that you are listening to both cabinets on axis, from the same perspective and angle.

Power Rating

When you combine more than one speaker, the total power rating equals the sum of all the individual speakers' power ratings. So, if you connect two 30-watt speakers together, you get a total power rating of 60 watts. This is true even if the speakers have different power ratings. For example, connecting a 25-watt speaker with a 30-watt speaker results in a total power rating of 55 watts. And, this is true no matter how you wire the speakers together. Series or parallel (see the "Impedance" section, next in this chapter), the power ratings still add.

Impedance

One big concern with multiple drivers in a single cabinet is wiring them so that they present the proper load or impedance to the amplifier. With a single driver, it's easy—there's just the impedance of the one speaker to consider. But when you add a second driver, or a third, or a fourth, things can get more complicated. There are three ways you can wire up multiple speakers in a cabinet, and each results in a different total impedance for the cab.

Parallel

In this case, the positive terminals of the two (or more) speakers are connected to the positive terminal on the cabinet's jack. The negative terminals on the two (or more) speakers are likewise connected to the negative terminal on the cabinet's jack. It's sort of like you've split the speakers off from the single jack.

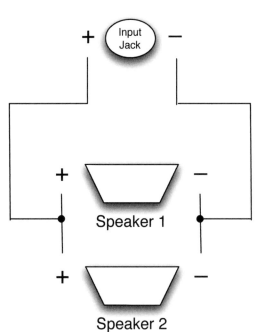

Figure 9.1
Connecting two speakers in parallel.

Additional speakers connect in the same way. Assuming the speakers each have the same impedance, you can find the total impedance for the cabinet by simply dividing the impedance of one speaker by the total number of speakers. So, for two 8-ohm speakers:

8 ohms (the impedance of one speaker) / 2 (the number of speakers) = 4 ohms

If you have four 8-ohm speakers:

8 ohms / 4 (the number of speakers) = 2 ohms

If you have three 16-ohm speakers:

16 ohms / 3 = 5.33 ohms

Easy enough. If you have speakers with different impedances, it's a bit more complex—we'll need some algebra chops. In this case, the formula is:

1/R1 + 1/R2 = 1/R total

If you have a 4-ohm and an 8-ohm speaker:

1/4 + 1/8 = 1 divided by 3/8 (1/4 or 2/8 + 1/8), or 2.667 ohms total impedance

Fortunately, for the math challenged, we usually use speakers with the same impedance inside a cab!

So, what happens in the real world when you connect speakers in parallel?

▷ The cabinet's total impedance drops below that of the speaker with the least impedance. (See math examples above.)

▷ The speakers draw more current from the amp, split to the various speakers depending on their individual impedance. If all the speakers have the same impedance, they each get an equal share of the power.

▷ Compared to a single speaker and all other things being equal, the volume goes up by 3 dB for two speakers, 6 dB for four speakers.

▷ As described earlier in this chapter, the power handling becomes equal to the power handling of all the speakers added together.

Series

With series wiring, the speakers are connected in daisy-chain fashion in a loop, starting with the positive terminal on the first speaker connected to the speaker jack's positive terminal. Then the negative terminal on the first speaker connects to the positive terminal on the second speaker, the negative on the second connects to the positive on the third, and so on. The negative from the last speaker connects to the negative on the speaker jack. The amp has a single path for feeding signal into the speakers.

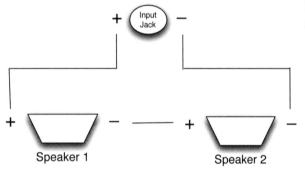

Figure 9.2
Connecting two speakers in series.

Additional speakers connect in the same way. You can find the total impedance for the cabinet and all its speakers by simply adding the impedance of the speakers. So, for two 8-ohm speakers:

8 ohms (the impedance of 1st speaker) + 8 ohms (the impedance of 2nd speaker) = 16 ohms

If you have four 8-ohm speakers:

8 ohms + 8 ohms + 8 ohms + 8 ohms = 32 ohms

If you have three 16-ohm speakers:

16 ohms + 16 ohms + 16 ohms = 48 ohms

If you have speakers with different impedances, it still works—just add to get the total.

4 ohms (1st speaker) + 16 ohms (2nd speaker) = 20 ohms total

What happens in the real world when you connect speakers in series?

▷ The cabinet's total impedance becomes the sum of the impedances of all the speakers in the cab.

▷ The speakers draw less current from the amp because the load is higher.

▷ The volume goes down compared to parallel wiring of the same speakers because the resistance (impedance) to the signal flow is higher.

▷ Just as with parallel wiring, the power handling for series wiring is equal to the power handling of all the speakers added together.

Series/Parallel

As you can see, with multiple speakers connected inside a cabinet, if you hook them up in parallel, you get a low impedance, sometimes too low for the amp to enjoy. But if you connect the same speakers in series, you get a very high impedance, which can also be a problem. For this reason, 4×12 cabinets, for example, often use series/parallel wiring, which is a blend of the two methods. The speakers are hooked up in parallel in pairs. Then the two pairs are connected in series.

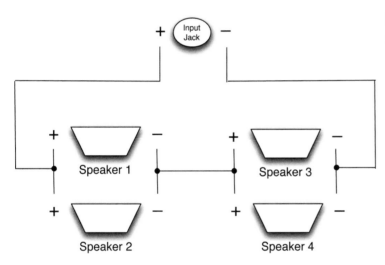

Figure 9.3
Connecting four speakers in series/parallel.

If the speakers each have the same impedance, you can find the total impedance for the cabinet by finding the parallel impedance for each pair and then adding the impedance for the pairs together to get the total. So, for four 16-ohm speakers in series/parallel:

16 ohms / 2 (first pair) + 16 ohms / 2 (second pair) = 16 ohms

Some 4×12 cabinets containing four 16-ohm speakers have a switch that allows the speakers to be changed from series/parallel to parallel, allowing the impedance to be switched from 16 ohms (series/parallel) to 4 ohms (parallel).

But, after all of that, does how a cabinet is wired affect its tone? When you leave aside the volume differences between series and parallel cabinets, the answer is no. All other things being equal (there's our favorite phrase again), the speaker doesn't care how it is connected to the amp. However, cabinet wiring is important from the standpoint of ensuring that the speakers are properly interfaced with the amp, at the ideal impedance, in order that maximum power and tone get through the chain to your ears.

Stereo Wiring

Two or four speakers in a cabinet can be wired for mono use, with one jack that feeds signal to all the speakers at once. Or the cabinet can be wired with two jacks or a switching jack, which allow the speakers to be split and accessed separately for stereo use. Having both speakers for a stereo rig in one cabinet is a convenient thing, as you only need to move one cabinet instead of two. However, with both sides of the stereo field coming from a single enclosure, you don't get a lot of spread between left and right.

Mixing Drivers

In general, when you buy a combo or speaker cabinet with more than one speaker in it, all of the speakers will be of the same type and model. This doesn't have to be the case, of course. It's been fairly common practice for players to mix two types of speakers in a 4×12 cabinet, for example. In recent years, this has become more widespread. A number of 2×12 combos and cabinets now feature two different drivers, such as a Celestion Greenback with a G12H 30 or a Greenback with a Vintage 30. The idea is to combine two speakers with different sounds to create a different composite sound, taking advantage of the characteristics of each speaker to build a new tone.

There are a couple of caveats, though. First, make sure that the speakers you combine have similar sensitivities. Otherwise, the speaker that is more sensitive will be louder than the one that is less sensitive. Second, the combination of the two speakers will be more difficult to capture with a microphone when recording or for live use through a PA system. You'll probably need to have a separate microphone on each individual speaker to ensure that you are capturing the entire picture.

But mixing drivers isn't just limited to, say, two different 12-inch speakers in a cabinet. You could also mix drivers of different sizes in the same cabinet—why not plug in a 10-inch and a 12-inch driver? This is less common than mixing speakers of the same size, but it does allow you to further tailor the response of the cabinet. The problem is that not many cabinets come stock with a baffle cut for two different size speakers, so you'll need to make or have someone make you one and figure out how to install it in your enclosure. And, you'll need to make sure the sensitivities of the two speakers are well matched so the speakers put out similar volume levels.

Isolation Cabs

Want the sound of a screaming loud amp, but you can't turn it up without offending your spouse, family, or neighbors? Tired of visits from your friendly law-enforcement officials for noise violations? You could use a digital modeler to get your tone. Or, if you want to continue using a real speaker, then perhaps an isolation cabinet (iso cab) is the way to go.

An iso cab seals the speaker inside a closed box. Usually a microphone is mounted inside the box so that you can run the signal out to a PA or studio recording system—you could also run the microphone out into a headphone amp so you could listen or practice in private.

You just hook the speaker out from your regular amp into the iso cab's speaker input and play. Your amp still sees a speaker, so it is happy and performs as you would expect it to. And you get all the coloration and breakup from an actual speaker. But since the speaker is closed off from the world, you don't get the massive volume. You may still hear some noise coming out of the iso cab, but it will be so quiet that it will likely even pass the spouse-watching-TV-in-the-next-room test.

Seems ideal! The negative is that most iso cabs are too small to really give the speaker the volume of air it needs to sound its best. The output from these cabs tends to be mid heavy and sort of boxy sounding—both of which can sometimes be cured with careful equalization and the addition of some room ambience-style reverb.

I've used iso boxes in the recording studio with good success, and I know players who use them live on stage in place of a regular speaker cab, which certainly cures volume complaints from the rest of the band and the sound man. Iso cabs are also popular for praise-and-worship bands—there aren't too many churches where you can wind up a 100-watt Marshall through a stack of 4×12s! But with an iso cab, you can still wind up that Marshall amp head, while keeping the volume from crushing the congregation. As in-ear monitors—which prevent you from hearing much sound from instruments on stage—become more common, you'll likely see these sorts of volume-control solutions become more popular.

Table 9.2   Cabinet and Enclosures Tonal Factors

Tone Factor	Tonal Contribution
Enclosure type	Major
Speaker matched to enclosure	Moderate
Porting	Moderate
Enclosure size	Subtle to minor
Wood/materials	Subtle to minor
Baffle type	Subtle to minor
Front-loading versus rear-loading	None
Cabinet covering	None
Grille cloth	Subtle
Straight versus slant cab	Subtle
Multiple speakers	Moderate
Polarity	None with a single speaker, subtle with multiple speakers
Cabinet power rating	None
Cabinet impedance	None
Parallel versus serial speaker wiring	None
Mixing drivers	Moderate

Volume

GUITAR PLAYERS HAVE A BAD REPUTATION for being too loud—"If it's too loud, yer too old, dood!" Maybe so, but ever heard the old joke: "How do you get a guitar player to turn down? Put a piece of sheet music in front of him." That's a dig not only at the limited sight-reading skills of many guitarists, but also at our tendency to play at inappropriate volume levels in many situations.

There are several reasons why guitar players constantly struggle with volume issues. One is the gear we've traditionally used—non-master volume amplifiers, for example. Another is the piercing and/or aggressive tone many of us use, which may seem louder than it actually is. Perhaps another is conscious or unconscious rock-star posing or emulation. (There's no denying that there is something cool about a row of Marshall stacks behind a guitarist onstage…but in a 100-seat club?)

And there's precedent for needing lots of power. In the early days, PA and monitor systems weren't up to the task, so guitar players used louder and louder amps onstage just to be heard—after all, amplifiers were developed so that the guitar could be heard over a big band. As shows and concerts got bigger and crowds got louder, the need for more power onstage followed, perhaps reaching its pinnacle in the late 1970s with artists such as Ted Nugent claiming to use six 100-watt Fender Twins through Dual Showman 2×15-inch cabinets (with a hollow-body Gibson Byrdland, no less), Ritchie Blackmore playing through 200-watt Marshall Majors, and other artists playing at truly awe-inspiring onstage volume levels. Bravado aside, there's no question that the volume on stage can and does get way over the top.

Times have changed, however. Today's PAs are capable of stunning fidelity at any volume level from whisper quiet to stadium filling; you literally don't even need an amp onstage in order to be heard. (Whether the tone is what you want without an amp is another question entirely.) Some artists still subscribe to the "rows of Marshall stacks turned up to 11" approach, but a surprising number of today's touring artists aren't even using speaker cabinets on stage anymore; they use load boxes that take a direct feed from the amplifier and route it to the PA. With in-ear monitor technology being widely used, some stages are completely silent except for the acoustic drums. Silent stages are also becoming the norm in worship/praise band situations, where volume control is essential.

So does it make sense anymore to have a 100-watt stack? Why do some companies still make 200-watt tube amps? Is there a tonal reason to use a big amplifier? Jeff Beck has been known to play concerts with a couple of very small Fender Pro Junior combo amps (15 watts, one 10-inch speaker). If he can play large venues with those, shouldn't you be able to get by with a 1-watt combo with one 8-inch speaker?

If you grew up with your parents constantly telling you to turn it down (God bless all parents of burgeoning guitar players. I can't imagine listening to a beginner at screaming-loud volume levels for hours a day), then you know their answer would be a resounding "Yes!" But for a player, the relationship between volume, tone, and playing is a complex one with many facets. Let's take a look at volume from an objective standpoint.

Power and Volume

There's an odd relationship between amp power and the actual volume produced. While you'd think that a 50-watt amp would be twice as loud as a 25-watt amp, it doesn't work out that way in the real world. Likewise, a 100-watt amp isn't 10 times as loud as a 10-watt amp, nor is a 10-watt amp 10 times as loud as a 1-watt amp. The whole thing has to do with how decibels work and our ears' perception of volume. We don't have to get into the math (too many pesky logarithms to deal with), but it is worth understanding a bit about how power changes translate to volume changes.

It's impossible to predict how loud an amp will be for a given wattage. We can't say, "You have a 10-watt amp, so at full volume, it will produce 76 dB of SPL (*sound pressure level*, or volume)." There are so many factors that influence how much volume an amp puts out: the input signal feeding it (from the guitar or effects), the efficiency of the speakers (how well they convert wattage from the amp into decibels of sound pressure), the cabinet type and how it throws sound, and more. Beyond these "physical" things, there is a whole array of "perception" and "context" things to consider.

▷ A brighter or harsher tone may seem louder to our ears than a smoother, darker tone.

▷ A distorted tone may seem louder than a clean tone (or vice versa).

▷ In a silent room, an amp may seem very loud. The same amp in a noisy room or next to a drum kit may not seem loud at all.

▷ An amp at ear level, two feet away, will seem louder than an amp on the floor, two feet away.

▷ An amp in a small room may seem louder than the same amp in a large room.

There are tons more, too—all factors that affect how you are hearing the sound of the amp. So it's difficult to talk about the absolute, measurable volume level of an amplifier based on its power. What we can talk about are relative volume changes and how the power of the amp affects them.

There are a couple of important things to discuss before we actually look at a chart of volume change versus power change. One is the phrase "all other things being equal." When we talk about volume changes, there are so many things that can affect our perception; changing more than the one we are focused on here—the amount of power—changes the perception and possibly the actual measurement. For example, if you go from 10 watts to 20 watts *with all other things being equal*, you'll get a certain volume increase. But if you go from 10 watts to 20 watts, and also change from one speaker to a different speaker, the volume change results may be different. Tricky, tricky…but all part of the volume game.

The other thing to talk about is what a decibel is: not the scientific discussion—you can look that up if you're interested—but a real-world sort of explanation. Think of it this way: A decibel is the smallest change in volume most people can hear without any sort of reference to compare to. The trained ear can do better than that, and with a reference, some "golden ear" studio recording engineers can hear a change as small as 0.1 of a decibel.

Now, check out Table 10.1.

Table 10.1   Power versus dB versus Volume

Power Change	Decibel Change	Volume Change
2×	3 dB	Noticeably louder
4×	6 dB	Large increase in volume
10×	10 dB	Twice as loud
1/2	–3 dB	Noticeably quieter
1/4	–6 dB	Large drop in volume
1/10	–10 dB	Half as loud

The volume changes resulting from a given power change may surprise you. We often say (or think), "Wow, that's twice as loud as it was before." In actuality, very few people can accurately gauge when one sound is twice as loud as another without an SPL meter to guide them. Our ears and our perception just don't work that way, and, as mentioned, there are so many factors involved outside of just the power/volume change itself.

But the fun doesn't stop there. All of those entries for volume, power, and decibel changes in Table 10.1 are relative. Here's what that means: A change from 10 watts to 20 watts is doubling the power and results in a 3-dB increase—a noticeable volume change. But a change from 20 watts to 40 watts is also doubling the power and results in a 3-dB increase and a noticeable volume change. Going from 40 watts to 80 watts? Three dB and a noticeable volume change. (In all these examples, "all other things being equal.")

Want to complicate things even more? Other changes can also result in a 3-dB change. Here are a few examples. (Remember the golden rule—"all other things being equal.")

▷ Going from a single 12-inch speaker to two 12-inch speakers adds 3 dB.

▷ Going from one 4×12 cabinet to two stacked 4×12 cabinets of the same type adds 3 dB.

▷ Doubling distance also results in a 3-dB change, so moving from one foot away from an amp to two feet away from an amp drops the volume by 3 dB.

▷ Moving from five feet from an amp to 10 feet from an amp drops 3 dB.

All noticeable changes in volume level, but none of them are anywhere near twice or half as loud.

Watts and Volume

In the real world, it's surprising how loud a 1-watt amplifier can be. And, yes, a 100-watt amp is substantially louder than a 1-watt amplifier. But the interesting thing is that most of the time, that 100-watt amp isn't putting out anywhere near 100 watts. The average wattage output most of the time that you're playing a 100-watt amp is probably just a few watts, even if you have the amp cranked.

So why use that 100-watt amp? Why not use a smaller one? The big reason is for maximum headroom and dynamics. (See the "Headroom" sidebar in Chapter 6.) Even if the amp is using only a few watts most of the time, all that power in reserve allows for powerful, clean dynamic changes, strong pick attack, seriously thumping low end (which requires a lot of power), and more. That 1-watt amp may seem loud, but you're probably close to maxing out its headroom almost all of the time. But all of this is influenced by the sensitivity and efficiency of your speaker(s) as well. Consider this: You connect your 1-watt amplifier to a speaker with a sensitivity of 100 dB with 1 watt, measured at 1 meter. From 1 meter away, it produces 100 dB of sound pressure level.

▷ Double the power to 2 watts; the output increases to 103 dB.

▷ Double the power again to 4 watts; the output increases to 106 dB.

▷ Double again to 8 watts; output increases to 109 dB.

▷ At 16 watts, we get 112 dB.

▷ At 32 watts, 115 dB.

▷ 64 watts gives us 118 dB.

▷ 128 watts pushes 121 dB.

Now, these are all measured at one meter (around 39 inches) from the speaker—those levels fall off by 3 dB each time you double distance. Still, this shows that with a moderately efficient speaker, you can still create a very high sound pressure level. 115 dB from around 30 watts is nothing to sneeze at! This is why speaker efficiency and sensitivity are so important to the volume produced. And why a small amp can still produce a big, loud tone!

Volume and Tone

There's another aspect of volume to consider: how it relates to tone. Once again, this is a perception thing. The response of the human ear changes as the volume gets louder. This is why home stereo systems have "loudness" controls; that loudness button boosts the lows and the highs to compensate for the fact that our ears don't hear low and high frequencies as well at softer volume levels. As the volume goes up, the loudness button's effect diminishes because our ears hear differently. At around 85-dB volume level, our ears are about flat, meaning they hear lows, mids, and highs equally well. This is one reason why in recording studios, many engineers like to work at 80–85 dB in the studio monitors.

As the volume gets louder, our perception of highs and lows gets better, but eventually we reach a point where the volume overloads our ears and may even begin to cause damage—when your ears ring after a loud noise, you've exceeded your ears' threshold. Stay above that threshold for too long, and the damage—and the ringing—may become permanent. (Loud volumes can literally kill the little cilia—tiny hair-like cells in your ears that sense sound waves—and they don't come back.) There's also a "threshold shift" that occurs with high volume where your ears become deadened to high frequencies—standing next to a drummer bashing on cymbals can do this very quickly. How many times during a loud gig have you reached back to turn the treble on your amp higher? By the end of the gig, your amp may be so bright that you're killing your listeners, yet you can't hear those highs yourself (scary).

But, assuming you're below the point of damaging your hearing, there are reasons amps sound better at higher volumes. Our ears perceive differently at higher levels, the amp is working hard and contributing distortion and coloration from the power section, the speakers may be working hard and contributing distortion and coloration, and the actual speaker cabinet may even begin to resonate at certain frequencies. I have a tube amp with built-in power scaling that sounds very different at 8 on the power knob than it does at 10—somewhere in between 8 and 10, you can hear the speaker cabinet come to life and begin to resonate, adding fullness and depth to the sound.

Two other points: At a certain volume level, the guitar begins to interact with the amplifier in a different way as well. We're not just talking about feedback, where the sound waves coming from the amp cause the strings of the guitar to vibrate, but a different sort of connection where the amp and the guitar come together and resonate. This changes the feel of the instrument and also increases the sustain. Of course, you can go too far—a guitar played through a *really* loud amp becomes a wild, untamed beast that can get away from you and unleash piercing squeals, sheets of feedback, and uncontrollable noise.

Last, there is a visceral aspect to all of this—a physical impact that you get from transients and notes played at an elevated volume level. When you can really *feel* the sound, the guitar suddenly seems to come to life and sound more musical. Some of these points may seem arcane, and opponents of volume excursions may write them off as simply justifications for playing loud, but there's no denying, for most players it is great fun to play through a loud amp!

A Bit of Preaching

As you've seen in this chapter, there are sometimes real reasons why playing louder may result in better tone than playing quietly. But hopefully you won't think this gives you a free pass to play as loud as you want all the time. You're still responsible for playing at a volume level that's appropriate to the situation and the venue, that blends and matches with the rest of the band, and that is safe for you, your bandmates, and your listeners. You're also responsible for making sure that the volume at which you play onstage still allows the sound person to get a good blend out front for the audience to enjoy. It is great to be a rock 'n roll rebel and stubbornly insist on playing at full volume onstage, but if that volume level comes at the expense of good sound out front for the crowd, what have you really accomplished? All of these are reasons why many players have found themselves moving toward smaller amps and more controlled volume levels.

One last bit of preaching: Invest in good hearing protection and use it anytime the volume gets loud—and not just when you're playing. Lawnmowers, power saws and other power tools, sirens, driving on the highway with the window down, industrial machinery, and of course, loud concerts —there are tons of sources of loud noise in the modern world. Most people also don't realize just how loud the earbuds on their MP3 players are cranking—it doesn't take long to blow out your ears when they're sealed tight with a miniature speaker.

What good is great tone if your ears are too messed up to enjoy it? Just ask Pete Townshend, Myles Kennedy, Jeff Beck, Paul Gilbert, Ted Nugent, and many other musicians who suffer from tinnitus (constant ringing in the ears) or deafness from exposure to too-loud volume levels.

Volume-Control Strategies

There are many different things you can do to manage your volume. Here are a few; one or more may work for you.

▷ **Aim your amp at your ears, not at your knees.** Hard to believe, but many guitar players have never heard what their amp really sounds like—and they might be appalled if they did! When a combo amp is set on the floor facing forward, the bulk of the sound blows past your knees and ankles; no ears there! What you hear at your ears is very different from the real sound, which is often much brighter and louder. Try tilting the amp back so that it aims at your ears.

▷ **Raise the amp up, closer to your ears.** If tilting the amp back won't work, consider raising it to ear level. "But it will tear my head off...." Well, *yeah*, that's the point. Turn it down and adjust the treble so it sounds good and is at the proper volume level.

▷ **Power attenuators.** These devices absorb some of the amp's power before it hits the speakers, reducing the volume level. Refer to Chapter 6 for more on attenuators.

▷ **Power scaling.** Various technologies are available to reduce the power coming out of tubes, so the amp thinks it's running full out, but it isn't cranking out as much wattage as usual. Refer to Chapter 6 for more on power scaling.

▷ **Speaker isolation boxes.** If you put your speakers inside a sealed box, their volume will be dramatically reduced. Most isolation boxes have built-in microphones so you can record or send the signal straight into the PA without any volume from the amp. Refer to Chapter 9 for more on isolation cabinets.

▷ **Move your cabinets offstage.** Try taking the speakers and moving them offstage, into an unused room or closet, then mike them up. This lets you have the feel of playing through your speakers but keeps the volume away from the crowd.

▷ **Aim your speakers backward or cross-stage.** Most guitar cabinets have a beaming effect; the sound sprays out of them in sort of a beam like a flashlight. This means that they're loudest directly in front, with the volume dropping off to the side. Try pointing the speakers cross-stage instead of to the front, or even aim them toward the back of the stage. (Aiming backward won't help with an open-backed combo amp.) This won't reduce the stage volume, but it will reduce the volume being sent into the audience.

▷ **Use a shield around the speakers.** Players such as Joe Bonamassa place a clear plastic shield around their speaker cabinets. This helps to contain the sound so that it isn't blasting directly into the audience and into drum microphones. It won't completely control the onstage volume level, but it will help to reduce the amount of guitar volume, especially right in front of the amp.

▷ **Use a smaller, lower-power amplifier.** This allows you to turn up the amp to take advantage of power amp distortion and cabinet resonance, but it keeps the volume at manageable levels. Keep in mind the "relative volume changes" chart—half the power is a noticeable change, 1/10th the power is half the volume.

▷ **Switch to less-efficient speakers.** If the speakers don't do an efficient job of converting the power coming from the amp into sound waves, the volume level will be reduced. The trick is to find less-efficient speakers that have the same sound as your regular speakers.

▷ **Use a load box.** This has become common practice for many touring artists. The amplifier speaker output feeds into a load box, which absorbs the power and applies speaker tone simulation. The output from the load box feeds straight into the PA or recording system. This eliminates the need for live speakers as well as for a microphone on your cabinet and can really clean up the sound both on stage and through the PA. Some players have a hard time adjusting; others find that it works and sounds just fine.

▷ **Use a modeler.** Today's amp and effects modelers can produce very authentic sound and allow you to connect your guitar directly to a PA or recording system without the need for an amplifier. The key is to find a modeler that produces the tones that you want. As above, some players have a hard time finding one they like; others have no problem getting their sound from a modeler. (See Chapter 13, "Modeling and Software," for more on modeling.)

Effects

MANY PLAYERS CAN GET THE TONES THEY WANT and need by taking the purest (or, depending on your viewpoint, the "purist") route: an electric guitar plugged straight into an amp, with only a cable to color the sound. And, that's great if it works for you. But there are other options for getting different tones, for adding unique sonic possibilities, or for taking guitar performance in completely new directions. We're talking, of course, about the myriad effects processors that are available out there.

The designers of the original electric guitars and amps could never have foreseen where guitar tones would go—for them, creating the cleanest sound was the goal. All they wanted was to make the sound of the guitar louder, not change it or enhance it in any way. But that all changed when electric guitars actually got into the hands of players. Since the days of Les Paul himself, guitar players have searched for new and different tones and new means of sonic expression. Once players discovered that pushing their amps past clean tones and into overdrive could make them sound even better, the search for new sounds began. The guitar and amp became not the end system, but the platform upon which tone was built.

To allow for the creation of innovative electric guitar sounds, it was necessary to find or make electronic processing resources to modify the basic guitar tone. The first such processors were the built-in tremolo and spring reverb effects found in amplifiers such as the Blackface Fenders of the early 1960s. By the mid and late '60s, the first external pedals—stompboxes—began to appear, such as fuzz boxes, wah-wah pedals, and more.

Fast-forward 40 years or so. Today we are blessed (or perhaps cursed—for those of us obsessed with the never-ending quest for exactly the right pedals for our tone) with a market completely saturated with pedals from hundreds of manufacturers, with no end in sight to the new pedals or the new manufacturers coming on the scene.

Though there are hundreds and hundreds of effects boxes on the market, in a broad sense they can be broken up into a few large categories.

Gain

The first guitar amps were designed to produce clean tones—why would you possibly *want* to add distortion to a signal? But the real-world situation brought changes. The original amps weren't very powerful and weren't very loud, at least by today's standards. It was a matter of keeping up; players cranked their amps as loud as possible to be heard in raucous blues and country clubs, and the burgeoning rock bands maxed out their amps to keep up with the volume demands of their gigs. Those early amps, pushed to (and past) their limits, screamed with glorious tube breakup. Soon players began seeking out that sound. Some guitarists (such as Dave Davies of the Kinks) sliced their speakers with razor blades, and abused them in other warranty-threatening ways to get the sweet harmonics-laden sound and sustain they craved. But clearly this wasn't a great solution for most players—once you've sliced up your speakers, it's kinda hard to go back to a clean sound!

It took manufacturers a couple of decades to respond with master volume controls, higher-gain preamps, and other features in their amps that were designed to produce distortion sounds in a more controllable manner. In the meantime, players discovered the joys of pedals that could create distortion—in particular, fuzz boxes and boosts. Since then, many pedals intended to either create distortion or to push amps into distortion have appeared. In the last decade, the "gain" category has exploded with an unprecedented onslaught of overdrives and distortions, designed both to create amp-like tones as well as other fuzz and distortion textures and tones.

All of these pedals function in the same way. They boost or amplify the level (gain) of the guitar signal until it begins to clip—meaning that the signal reaches a higher level than the electronic circuit can cleanly pass. The "waveform," or tonal characteristic of the signal, is altered; it begins to compress, and harmonics are added. Depending on the design of the circuit, the result may be raw breakup, smooth distortion, harsh rasp, bumble-bee buzzing, light fuzziness, or a variety of other textures.

There are several subcategories of gain pedals, including overdrives, fuzzes/distortions, and boosts.

Overdrive

Push an amp—whether tube or solid state—past the limit of where it can cleanly reproduce a signal, and it will begin to break up, or distort. The problem was, back in the day, it wasn't easy to get that warm, richly distorted "overdriven" sound without winding up the amp to obscene volume levels. And, on many amps, it wasn't easy to switch from a clean sound to a distorted sound or to match the volume level of the clean sound to the dirty sound. One solution came in the form of overdrive pedals, which can provide two functions: They can boost the guitar's signal enough to push the front end of the amp into distortion ("overdrive" the amp's input), or they can generate enough gain within themselves to cause the signal to overdrive before it is sent out of the pedal and into the amplifier.

Most overdrives are fairly low-gain devices. They're not intended to get into heavy distortion territory. (There are exceptions, of course.) They can be made with solid-state circuits, usually using diodes to provide the internal clipping, or, less commonly, with tube circuits. Functionally, there isn't any difference between the two types—both overdrive the signal. There can be a tonal difference, of course, though many solid-state overdrives achieve a convincing tube-like tone. There can sometimes be a slight "touch" difference, with tubes being somewhat softer—meaning more compressed—than some solid-state designs.

Overdrives can also be made using digital and modeling designs. Digital and modeling devices convert the analog guitar signal into a stream of computer data. This data can then be manipulated using mathematical algorithms to create the effect of clipping distortion or to emulate the sound of a specific analog or tube overdrive. Opinions vary on how well digital overdrives work and how closely modeled versions emulate the originals—some players feel they sound sterile compared to analog units. Most players still prefer analog overdrives, though digital and modeling offer serious advantages: stability, storage of presets, consistency, and controllability. Many digital multieffects processors also include digital or modeled overdrive as part of their arsenal of effects.

There are two further broad classifications of overdrive/distortions, at least in the minds of players who use them: overdrives that color the sound and those that don't. Ibanez Tube Screamers are a prototypical example of the first (and the progenitor of hundreds of clones and descendants). These pedals have a definite mid "hump" in the tone and a characteristic cut in the low frequencies. The second type are designed for a "transparent" overdrive, without the mid boost or low cut.

Another design characteristic of overdrives is the amount of compression in the signal. Some pedals are more open, with wider dynamics. Others are compressed sounding, meaning that the dynamics are more limited, and that for a given gain setting, the available range from the quietest tones to the loudest tones is narrower. While this might sound like a negative, a compressed overdrive can provide a smoother sound with more sustain.

Fuzz

A fuzz box creates a tone by boosting the signal within itself until the signal distorts. Hmmmm, sorta sounds like the same thing as an overdrive. In fact, the two categories are quite similar in function, if not in result or technology. Most fuzzes push the signal way beyond what an overdrive will typically do and often have a far more compressed output as well. Though technically, most of the difference is one of degree, the outcome can be very different. This is because of the way in which the distortion is created. With overdrives, diodes are usually used to provide the distortion. Fuzzes, on the other hand, generally use germanium or silicon transistors. Most fuzzes are actually quite simple circuits—the original Fuzz Face (see the "Dallas Arbiter Fuzz Face" section in Chapter 16), for example, used less than a dozen electronic components.

With a fuzz or distortion, the result usually isn't amp-like; the sound is, well, *fuzzier* and more *electric* in nature. The range of tones can run from light fizz to raspy breakup to hornet-like buzz. Typically, fuzzes offer tons of sustain, loads of additional harmonic content, and a brighter, rawer sound.

Fuzz was one of the original pedal effects in the '60s. The first recorded example of a fuzz box is credited to the Ventures with "2,000 Pound Bee" in 1962. The Ventures had heard an earlier recording that featured distortion from a recording console preamp and asked pedal-steel player/electronics maven Red Rhodes to build them a device that would give them the same type of sound, which they then used for their recording.

Maestro is usually credited with introducing the first commercially available fuzz box, the Fuzz Tone FZ-1, in the early '60s. This was the pedal that created the famous fuzz sound used by Keith Richards for "Satisfaction" by the Rolling Stones. Many other fuzz boxes followed, and the lore of the fuzz box has grown very deep. Fuzz lovers will, for example, debate endlessly about the merits of silicon versus germanium transistors. Here's roughly how it breaks down.

Germanium

▷ Smooth, thick tone.

▷ Sensitive to temperature variations. The pedal will sound different at higher or lower temperatures.

▷ Very wide tolerances in component values, resulting in two "identical" pedals sounding quite different from one another.

▷ Sensitive to battery type. Alkaline batteries cause a darker sound; non-alkaline typically result in a brighter tone.

▷ Sensitive to power. If batteries are used, as the battery ages the tone may change.

▷ Often react negatively (screaming oscillation or loss of level and bass) if any buffered (non-true bypass) pedals are inserted between the guitar and the fuzz. (See sidebar, "True Bypass versus Buffers" later in this chapter.)

Silicon

▷ Fuzzier, brighter tone.

▷ Can sound harsh compared to germanium.

▷ Not subject to the inconsistencies of germanium.

▷ Not sensitive to temperature changes.

▷ Not as sensitive to different types of batteries as germanium.

All this would seem to indicate that silicon would make for a better fuzz box, and many players (including Jimi Hendrix and Eric Johnson) would concur. Still, many other players are willing to deal with the foibles of germanium to achieve that "authentic" thick, rich tone with warm top end.

There are other ways to create fuzz besides just silicon and germanium transistors, such as digitally and by using modeling. As with overdrive, digital fuzz has its proponents and its detractors, its benefits, and its short-comings.

Clean Boost

There are times when you want to increase the level of an electric guitar without adding any extra distortion or coloration to the signal. That's where clean boosts come in. Clean boosts can be thought of as "transparent" preamplifiers that can be used to make a guitar's output level louder. There are several reasons why you might want to kick up the level of a guitar signal with a clean boost:

▷ To match the level of a guitar with low-output pickups to a hotter-output guitar so that it's easier to switch between them onstage.

▷ To increase the amount of distortion by placing the boost in front of an overdrive or a semi-distorted amp.

▷ To make an overdrive's sound louder without making it more distorted by placing the boost after the overdrive in the signal chain.

▷ To boost the guitar signal so that it overdrives the input of a tube amplifier.

▷ As a volume boost for playing solos with a clean guitar signal.

There are also some "clean" boosts that, well, aren't so clean—in the sense of tonal coloration, not in the sense of distortion. For example, players such as Eddie Van Halen, Ritchie Blackmore, and others were known for playing through old tape echoes. While the echo aspect of the box was important, the coloration and boost that the preamp in the echo provided was as much of a factor in their choice. Recently, several manufacturers have released stompboxes that contain similar preamp circuitry to what was in vintage Echoplexes and that re-create the tonal goodness and the level boost of the original.

Treble Booster

In the early '60s, some U.K. players, including such notables as Tony Iommi (Black Sabbath), Brian May (Queen), and Rory Gallagher, found that the amps of the day (mostly Vox AC30s and Marshall Bluesbreakers) were too dark sounding—that there wasn't enough "cut" to make the guitar audible in the midst of a loud band. These players turned to treble boosters, such as the Dallas Rangemaster and Vox Treble Booster, for a brighter sound and for more gain. Just like fuzz boxes, some treble booster circuits were based around germanium transistors, while others were based on silicon transistors.

Treble boosters weren't just a '60s phenomenon. They continued to be used later—to this day—as well. In the early '70s, for example, David Gilmour of Pink Floyd used a Coloursound Power Boost for driving his Marshall rhythm tone and for a boost in front of his Fuzz Face for leads.

Treble boosters do two things to a guitar's signal: They cut the low end and raise the overall level. The end result is that the midrange and highs get louder, while the bottom end tightens up. The front end of the amp overdrives for more distortion, and the tone gets brighter and cuts better.

Stacking Gain Pedals

Many players feel that a gain pedal, such as an overdrive, sounds best when run into an amp that is either on the verge of breaking up or that is lightly distorted itself. This seems to result in a thicker, meatier tone. To simulate this, or to get an even thicker tone, some players will "stack" two overdrives—cascade them together, with the output from the first overdrive feeding the input on the second overdrive. One prominent proponent of this technique was Stevie Ray Vaughan, who was known to cascade two Ibanez Tube Screamers together.

The tonal effect of running one overdrive into another is not the same as turning the gain higher on a single overdrive. Overdrive pedals react differently to a distorted input signal than they do to a clean input signal. The sound is generally thicker, with more harmonics and more sustain. Plus, you can tailor the tone and distortion levels of the two overdrives in different ways to optimize the three total overdrive sounds that are available (each pedal alone, both pedals combined—plus a fourth sound, with both pedals off). Just a few examples:

▷ Set the second overdrive for a crunchy rhythm tone and then set the first overdrive as a semi-clean boost to push the second overdrive into thicker, sustaining distortion.

▷ Set the second overdrive for light distortion, and set the first overdrive for thick distortion to simulate the effect of an overdrive feeding a slightly broken-up amp.

▷ Set the second overdrive for a distorted tone and then use the first to push it even harder into heavy distortion.

▷ Set both overdrives for light distortion, for a very dynamic, crunchy sound that you can control with your pick attack.

The range of possibilities is wide, especially when you factor in that many overdrives have tone controls that can be adjusted as well. Feeding a bright overdrive tone into a dark overdrive tone will sound different from the opposite setup. Manufacturers have even begun making "dual" pedals that have two overdrives in a single case, which makes stacking convenient and space efficient.

But, you don't have to stick with two overdrives. You could stack an overdrive and a distortion/fuzz. In this case, most players put the fuzz first, in front of the overdrive, though there is no rule that says you must do so. This type of "stack" will let you switch from a crunchy overdriven rhythm to a saturated, fat lead tone when you step on the fuzz. As with dual overdrives, manufacturers now make pedals that contain both an overdrive and a fuzz in one chassis.

Another example of "stacking" is to cascade an overdrive and a boost. In this case, the final result will depend on the order of the effect. Putting the boost in front of the overdrive will push the overdrive into more distortion. You could, for example, use the overdrive alone for a crunchy rhythm tone and then step on the boost to kick up the distortion and to add sustain for leads.

If you reverse the order, with the boost after the overdrive, when you step on the boost, the overdrive sound will get louder, but it will not get more distorted. This is nice when you want to increase the volume level for a solo, but you don't necessarily want to add more dirt to the tone.

Choosing the Best Dirt

With all of the myriad overdrives, distortions, fuzzes, and boosts on the market, how in the heck are you supposed to choose the best one for your rig? It really can be difficult, as your entire rig interacts. Some amps work well with overdrives; others get mushy or congested sounding. A treble boost drives some amps into sweet distortion, but it makes other amps sound thin and harsh. The same types of things go on at the other end of the signal chain, where the guitar feeds into the distortion box or boost. Some overdrives work well with single-coils but don't sound so great with humbuckers and vice versa. This continues on to the rest of your signal chain. Certain pedals work together well, others not so well.

For these reasons and more, many players end up with several different types of dirt boxes in their arsenals, and some even have multiple overdrives, fuzzes, and boosts living on their pedalboard at the same time, both for the purposes of stacking and for the different tonal options and compatibilities they provide.

Many manufacturers now have audio demos on their websites, and there are video demos of many models on the web. But ultimately, the only way to know for sure is to try as many dirt pedals as you can, with your guitars and your amps, to see which work the best.

Modulation

Whoosh, swoosh, and warble—these are the hallmarks of modulation. In technical terms, "modulation" is simply change. But we've extended that definition in guitar effects terms to mean some sort of cyclical, repeating change. These types of effects mess with (modulate) the volume, pitch, tone, or timing of the guitar's signal to create effects that add richness, depth, and movement to the tone. There are a number of different modulation effects types.

Leslie/Rotating Speaker

The original modulation effect was the Leslie speaker, created by Don Leslie around 1941. It was developed for use with Hammond electric organs. The organ signal is sent into the speaker cabinet, which has a built-in 40-watt tube amplifier and has a high-frequency horn mounted so that it can rotate horizontally. There is also a bass speaker, which is surrounded by a cylinder that rotates around the speaker; the cylinder is slotted so that sound can escape as the cylinder spins. Rather than having a front panel, like a traditional speaker, Leslie speakers have slots or louvers in the cabinet to let sound escape. There are three speed settings for the speaker rotation: fast, slow, and stop. When switched between speed settings, the speaker rotation ramps up or down in velocity slowly.

The result is a rich sound with a lot of motion. In addition to the pulsating bass, the high-frequency horn takes advantage of the Doppler effect—where sound from an object coming toward you rises in pitch, while sound from an object moving away from you drops in pitch. (Think of the pitch of the engine sound from a fast-moving car or motorcycle as it comes toward you, passes you, and then moves away from you.) As the horn spins toward you, the pitch goes up slightly; as it rotates away from you, the pitch drops slightly. This results in a rich "chorus" effect.

The problem is that a real Leslie speaker is a large piece of equipment in a heavy wooden cabinet, clocking in at more than 100 pounds. Hauling it around is no small task. In addition, a Leslie is a complex mechanical device, stable when put in the studio and not moved about. But take it on the road, and reliability may be an issue.

While the Leslie is *de rigueur* for Hammond organ players, that hasn't stopped guitarists from making the sound of a Leslie part of their signature tone—for one example, think Peter Frampton on *Frampton Comes Alive*. Other examples of Leslies or other rotary speakers in use by guitar players include Eric Clapton on Cream's "Badge" and Stevie Ray Vaughan on "Cold Shot."

Today you can still purchase new Leslie speakers (the company was owned by CBS—the same crew that bought Fender—from 1965 to 1980, when it was purchased by the Hammond Organ company), including some models that have been optimized for use with electric guitar; there is one current model with a built-in amp and another that is configured for use with your regular guitar amp. Or, there are numerous Leslie simulator effects on the market, ranging from analog effects to digital modeling processors. Few people who have heard a Leslie in action would tell you that a simulator can achieve the same bold, room-filling presence that the real thing can crank out, though the latest simulators can come very close. Plus, the tradeoff for using a real Leslie is that they don't fit very well on a pedalboard—or in most cars!

Tremolo

Despite the name that Leo Fender gave to the bridge on his Stratocaster (the Synchronized Tremolo), a true tremolo effect doesn't have anything to do with pitch. In classical terms, tremolo is defined as a rolling, repeated note technique (*i.e.,* tremolo picking on guitar; tremolo is a slightly different technique on other instruments, such as marimba, where the mallets are rolled on a key) or the effect of repeating pulsating variation in volume. Tremolo was first introduced on electric organs and then began to be included on Fender guitar amps. (The Tremolux, introduced in 1955, was the first Fender amp with built-in tremolo.)

Electronically, there are two methods used for creating tremolo effects. The first method, signal modulation, is by far the most common. An oscillator produces a low-frequency wave that is used to control slight variations in volume. The actual volume changes are created using an "opto isolator"—a combination of a light source and a light-sensitive resistor.

The second method for creating tremolo is bias modulation, where the bias voltage fed into the amp's power tubes is dropped and increased. As the bias voltage is turned down, the tube output and, correspondingly, the amp's volume drops. This method is generally not used with amps over 40 watts or so in power.

With the signal modulation method, the gain of the preamp is affected, changing any distortion that is being created there. With the bias modulation method, any power tube distortion will vary, and the tone may change as well.

The speed of the volume pulsing can be controlled, from slow to very fast, and the depth, or amount of volume variation, can also often be controlled. At low depths, the effect creates a light pulsing volume change. At higher depths, the effect starts to sound "swampy," with heavier pulsation. At the highest depths, the effect is of rhythmically chopping the sound, with the volume sharply turning on and off. The shape of the waveform used to control the tremolo also affects the sound created. A sine wave provides a smoothly pulsing sound; a triangle wave has sharp corners. As the waveform moves toward a square wave shape, the volume switches on and off sharply.

Today, some amps still have built-in tremolo. But many players rely on tremolo pedals to create the effect. Some of these pedals even provide tap tempo/speed control for setting the speed of the effect by stepping on a footswitch; this allows the player to easily synchronize the tremolo effect to the tempo of the song. (See the section later in this chapter on delays for more on tap tempo.)

There can be one negative to using tremolo: The overall volume of the guitar will often seem to drop when the tremolo is engaged. To counter this, some tremolo pedals have an output volume control to allow for balancing the volume when the effect is on versus when it is off.

Vibrato

Many players (and gear manufacturers) confuse what vibrato and tremolo are. As we've just discussed, in guitar effects terms, tremolo is a pulsing variation in volume. Vibrato, on the other hand is a pitch-based effect. There's finger vibrato, as practiced by every guitar player out there; there are vibrato bridges—from Bigsby to Fender to Floyd Rose—and there is the electronic vibrato effect, as produced by amplifiers and some effects boxes.

In truth, very few amps actually have true vibrato circuits—mainly just old Magnatone vintage units from the '50s. Most amps with "vibrato" actually have tremolo circuits. But, in further truth, electronic vibrato and electronic tremolo can sound remarkably similar. Vibrato, especially at lower depth settings, is perhaps a bit richer sounding, and at higher depths, the difference between the two becomes obvious (wider pitch variations versus intense volume pulsing).

Though straight vibrato effects boxes are available (often combined with tremolo or chorus), when most players think of vibrato effects they think of the much-vaunted Uni-Vibe (see the "Univox Uni-Vibe" section in Chapter 16). Though the Uni-Vibe was actually a phase shifter (see the "Phase Shifter" section later in this chapter), it had a switch for producing vibrato-style effects. And, the Uni-Vibe effects, which were aimed to reproduce the sound of a Leslie-style rotating speaker, had an aspect of slight pitch shifting to them.

Chorus

Chorus as an effect may have reached its popularity zenith in the 1980s, but the effect remains widely used today. The original analog chorus effects worked using a short delay; the delayed signal is mixed back in with the dry signal. The delay time is modulated longer and shorter in a cyclical fashion. As the delay is increased and decreased, the pitch changes very slightly. (Try it yourself; play through a delay and sweep the delay time. You'll hear the pitch go up and down. The effect is, of course, much more subtle in a chorus.) The combined dry and wet signals simulate the sound of multiple instruments or voices playing or singing a part at the same time.

In newer designs, especially digital choruses, the delayed signal may also be detuned slightly (just a few cents sharp or flat), creating even more thickening and motion in the sound, or in some cases, a sound similar to a 12-string guitar. With this added detuning, chorus can range from a subtle shimmer to watery washiness to richness and thickening, with or without motion in the sound. Most choruses are "single voice" designs and use one delay to create the effect. But the richness of the chorus effect can be increased if multiple delays are used, called a *multiple-voice* chorus. In a multiple-voice chorus, the delays may all be modulated in sync with one another, or each may be modulated separately for an even more complex and rich effect.

The first chorus effects box was the much sought-after BOSS CE-1 (see the "BOSS CE-1 Chorus Ensemble" section in Chapter 16), which produces the same effect that was contained in the Roland JC-series Jazz Chorus amplifiers (see the "Roland Jazz Chorus" section in Chapter 15). In the Jazz Chorus amp, which had two completely separate amps and speakers, one side was processed by the effect, while the other was dry. When the sound from the two speakers combined in the air, the chorus effect enhanced the tone with a lush, shimmering richness. The CE-1 duplicated this effect. Since then, BOSS has made many descendants of the CE-1, and other manufacturers have created their own versions of the chorus effect.

Chorus is most often used with clean sounds for added depth and richness. As with other modulation effects, when used with gainier sounds, the chorus effect either gets more intense (if the chorus is after the distortion) or gets somewhat washed out (if the chorus is before the distortion).

One of the first artist names that comes to mind when discussing chorus effects is Andy Summers of the Police, though he has asserted that, at least originally, his "chorus" tones were produced by a modified flanger, not a true chorus. Since then, countless guitarists have used the effect both in the studio and on stage.

Flanger

The original "flange" effect was created in the recording studio. The same audio was played back from two reel-to-reel tape decks simultaneously, in synchronization. The recording engineer would place a hand on the reel of one tape deck, slowing it down slightly and taking it very slightly out of sync with the other tape deck. With this technique, the combination of the original signal and the slightly delayed signal creates cancellations or "notches" in the tone; if the delay time is varied by applying more or less pressure to the tape on either deck, the notches move up and down in frequency, and a swooshing/whooshing/sweeping sound results. At higher intensities, the sound is somewhat reminiscent of a jet airplane landing.

In effects boxes, flanging is produced in similar fashion to chorus: A delayed signal is blended back in with the dry signal, and the delay time is modulated (slowed down and sped up in cyclical fashion). The cancellations when the delayed signal is mixed with the dry signal result in a series of peaks and notches progressing upward in frequency from a base frequency that is determined by the delay time.

Sounds very similar to chorus, right? A delayed signal mixed with a dry signal. There are two big differences between chorus and flange. First, with flange, the delay times are shorter—in the range of a few milliseconds versus 20 to 50 milliseconds. Second, with a flanger, it's usually possible to feed some of the signal back through the input to be processed again, intensifying the effect and, at high settings, adding a sweeping resonance to the tone.

Examples of flanging date back as early as the 1940s on Bing Crosby and Les Paul recordings, but the effect became much more prominent in the 1960s on recordings by the Beatles and perhaps the prototypical example, "Bold as Love" by Jimi Hendrix, which may have been the first stereo example of the effect. Myriad examples have followed.

Phase Shifter

A phase shifter (a.k.a. *phaser*) produces an effect somewhat similar to a flanger, though the electronics behind the effect are quite different. With a phase shifter, the signal is split into two paths (in the same way a chorus or flanger works). One path goes through dry (unprocessed). The other goes through an all-pass filter, which lets all the frequencies through but delays the signal very slightly, changing the phase versus the dry signal. The phase changes vary depending on the frequency, resulting in a series of notches and peaks in the tonal response. The phaser's depth control adjusts how much of the filtered signal is mixed in and determines how deep the notches are. Modulation sweeps the notches up and down. The number of "stages" in a phase shifter equates to the number of all-pass filters the sound runs through and correlates to the number of notches that are produced. Each filter produces one notch or peak, so a two-stage phaser has one notch and one peak, a four-stage phaser has two peaks and two notches, and so on. As with flangers, some of the signal can be fed back to the input and back through the process to intensify the effect—the peaks get higher and the notches get deeper, resulting in a more resonant sound.

Phase shifting can be used to create a swooshing, sweeping effect, as with Brian May's tone on Queen's "Sheer Heart Attack." Or, it can be used more subtly to create a slight treble boost with motion to bring a tone to life. Many of Eddie Van Halen's early leads featured a phase shifter used in this way. The effect is also commonly used on electric piano; check out Billy Joel's "Just the Way You Are" for a prime example.

Ring Modulator

A ring modulator is a very different kind of effect from the other modulation effects we've discussed thus far. A ring modulator works by modulating (in this case multiplying) one signal (the *carrier*, which is the guitar's signal) with another signal (the *modulator*), which is produced inside the effects box. In fact, the principle is the same as is used for broadcasting AM radio. (The "AM" stands for amplitude modulation.) The end result is an entirely new output signal that contains sum and difference tones, which are harmonically unrelated to the original signal—the sounds can range from bell-like tones to total distortion-like wackiness to mechanical, robot-like sounds. Ring modulation is often described as jagged, atonal, metallic, dissonant, chaotic, and random. The effect is sometimes used to create "robot voices" in sci-fi movies.

By no means the most common of guitar effects, there are ring modulators on the market for those who want to take their guitar's sound outside the realm of normal possibility. To make them a bit less alien, most guitar ring modulation effects include a mix control so that a certain amount of the ring-modulated sound can be blended in with the original guitar tone.

Jeff Beck has been known to use a ring modulator ("Two Rivers" off of *Guitar Shop*), and David Gilmour is said to have used one for certain parts on the Pink Floyd *Wish You Were Here* album. But perhaps the most mainstream example of ring modulator is Tony Iommi's lead break on Black Sabbath's "Paranoid," with Incubus' "Megalomaniac" being a more modern example. Other ring modulator users include Tool, Devo, Sonic Youth, and more.

Stereo versus Mono

To add even more spaciousness to a modulation effect, it can be run in stereo through two separate amplifiers. The original stereo effects, such as the Roland Jazz Chorus amp's onboard chorus, ran the "wet" or effected signal through one amp and the dry, un-effected signal through a separate output to a second amplifier. Later effects sometimes ran different versions of the effected signal out of both outputs or flipped the phase of one output for even more spaciousness. For the best stereo effects, two identical amps, with identical settings and volume levels, are ideal. But you can also get nice effects using two different amplifiers or amp settings.

Filter/EQ

In addition to effects that add to the original signal, such as the gain and modulation effects we've already examined—where something new is added to the signal—there are effects that work on the guitar's existing tone, either reshaping it or turning it into something completely new.

Equalizers

EQ, or *equalization*, is a fancy term for tone control or adjustment. Though guitar amps usually have built-in tone controls, and of course, most guitars have their own tone controls, there are times when there may be need to either enhance or reshape the tone with additional equalization.

In some cases, the equalizer is wired into the signal path and left on all the time—it becomes part of the overall tone. In other cases, the EQ is designed to switch in and out of the signal path, sometimes in pedal format or sometimes using a footswitch to control a tabletop or rackmount unit. You might want to bring EQ in and out, for example, to boost the midrange during a solo for more cut or for more fullness. Or, to scoop out the mids for a brighter, more shimmering tone in a clean passage, or to cut all the highs and lows for a midrangy "telephone" effect. You could also boost certain frequencies and cut others to either perfect a tone or to create a new, different tone. And you could set the EQ so that a humbucking pickup sounds more like a single-coil or vice-versa.

There are two types of equalizers: parametric and graphic. With a parametric EQ, there are just a few bands, but you can set the frequency each band operates on as well as how much each band is boost or cut. In some cases, you can also adjust the width of the frequency band. This allows you to go in and either pull out a frequency to fix a problem or boost a particular frequency to create a "peaky" sort of sound—Frank Zappa used parametric EQ in this way to get some of his highly tweaked tones.

A graphic EQ has a separate slider control for each frequency. This makes a graphic EQ very easy to use. Just push up or pull down the slider that affects the frequency you want. When you're done, the arrangement of the sliders creates a rough visual ("graphic") curve of the overall frequency response. Because the frequency of each slider is fixed, graphic EQs are generally better for shaping the overall sound than for pinpoint surgical adjustments—that's where a parametric EQ shines.

Wah Wah

"Voodoo Chile (Slight Return)." "Tales of Brave Ulysses." "White Room." "Whole Lotta Love." "Theme from *Shaft*." These are all prime examples of a wah-wah pedal in action. A wah pedal is basically a manually (foot) controlled filter. The filter is set for a boost over a certain narrow range of frequencies.

When the treadle (foot pedal) is rocked with the foot, the filter sweeps from low frequencies to high frequencies, creating a vocal-like "wah" tonal effect along the way.

Though there were previous pedals that were basically foot-controlled tone controls custom-made for players such as Chet Atkins, the first real wah pedal to hit the market was from Vox, in the late 1960s, quickly followed by a U.S. version, called the "Crybaby" wah. (See the "Thomas Organ Company Crybaby" section in Chapter 16 for more on Vox and Crybaby wah pedals.)

Inductors and Pots

A big part of the sound of a given wah pedal is the type of inductor used to create the effect. The first wah-wah pedals used Italian Fasel inductors or British halo inductors. The next generation of pedals saw the appearance of TDK 5103 cube inductors. These and other inductors were used by manufacturers, often because they were less expensive than the earlier Fasels. Over the years, various halo, TDK, and Fasel inductors with several different casing colors were used to make wahs, each with a slightly different tonality—though some experts feel that all of the "vintage" inductors used in early wahs (except for the TDK) basically sound the same.

The potentiometer used in the wah can also affect its tone. The originals used ICAR pots, which are long out of production. Other pots used by manufacturers included ERTs, Clarostats, Centralabs, and more. Some experts believe that the pots don't actually affect the tone of the wah, but rather change the *taper* of the pot, or how quickly and smoothly it changes from zero to full on (and therefore how quickly and smoothly it sweeps the filter setting in the pedal from bassy to trebly). Likewise, some experts purport that whether the pedal is set up so that the full range of the pot can be used when the pedal is moved affects the throw and shape of the wah effect more than the actual tone of the pot used affects anything.

Recently, Geoffrey Teese at RMC claims to have been able to closely duplicate the original vintage inductors and pots, resulting in eerily close reproductions of the early vintage Vox wahs. Of course, not everyone prefers an accurate vintage tone; some want more highs, more lows, thinner or fatter midrange, or whatever. The wide array of models on the market allows players to choose exactly the tonal wah color they want or to get a pedal that features enough controls to customize the tone to any liking.

Today, wahs are made by a wide range of manufacturers. Jim Dunlop owns the Crybaby name and makes a number of Crybaby wah models. Vox has reissued their classic wahs as well as come out with new models. Then there are the "boutique" manufacturers, such as Fulltone, RMC (Real McCoy Custom), Budda, and many more, who each have their own take on the wah pedal. Some include extra options, such as switchable volume boosts, controls for adjusting the "voicing" of the wahs, and even multiple inductors, which can be switched in and out to change the sound of the wah.

Another feature added by many manufacturers of current wah pedals is true bypass switching. Older wahs featured bypass switching circuits that were well known for "tone suck"—especially the loss of high end.

The pedals used SPDT (*single-pole, double-throw*) switches, resulting in only the output from the circuit being bypassed; the input to the wah circuit was still connected to the signal path and impacting the "bypassed" sound. These circuits also interacted (in a bad, screeching, squealing sort of way) with some stompboxes, such as Fuzz Faces. Because of this, for many years, it was conventional wisdom to place your wah as the first pedal in your effects chain. With modern wahs (post mid-'90s), this isn't as much of an issue, though many players still prefer to have their wah first in the chain, fed directly from the guitar.

Some manufacturers, such as Dunlop, have even developed "switchless" wahs, where the effect is activated by simply stepping on the pedal and deactivated by taking your foot off the pedal, as opposed to the traditional switching scheme, where the wah treadle (the moving "gas pedal" part) must be firmly pushed fully forward to engage a switch at the "toe" of the pedal to turn on the effect, and firmly pushed fully forward again to switch off the effect.

The honor of the first wah-wah pedal recording goes to Del Casher, who was commissioned to make a demo for the then-new Vox wah in December of 1967. However, myriad guitarists have used it since: From Eric Clapton (a Vox Clyde McCoy on "Tales of Brave Ulysses" and "White Room") and Jimi Hendrix (another Vox Clyde McCoy user) in the 1960s through to Zakk Wylde (with his own signature Dunlop Crybaby model) and Kirk Hammett (also with his own signature Dunlop Crybaby) today, the wah-wah has been a popular effect in rock music. But it has also been used prominently in other styles, such as funk and soul (Isaac Hayes' "Theme from *Shaft*" is a prototypical example) and blues.

Because of its expressive quality, the wah-wah pedal manages to sound unique in just about any player's hands. In some cases, the pedal isn't even used to create vocal-like tones—as far back as early Frank Zappa and Jimmy Page with Led Zeppelin, players were "parking" the pedal in a fixed position, using it as a "filter" for a midrange or high-frequency boost. Some players, such as Michael Schenker (the Scorpions, UFO, and the Michael Schenker Group), build their entire sound around a wah-wah pedal fixed at a particular frequency.

Envelope Filter/Auto-Wah

What if you can't stand on one foot, play guitar, and work a wah pedal with the other foot all at the same time? Should you be denied wah effects? Okay, maybe that wasn't the original impetus behind the development of the auto-wah effect for guitarists—but it is an obscure benefit for some balance-challenged players.

Instead of having its filter controlled using a footpedal as in a regular wah pedal, an auto-wah uses an electronic circuit to automatically sweep the filter under control of an envelope follower. The envelope follower looks at the guitarist's playing and creates a voltage based on the guitar signal. That voltage is then used to sweep the filter, creating a "wah" effect. Depending on the guitarist's playing style and how the pedal is set up, this can result in effects ranging from a "wah" on every note or chord to a choppy, continuously varying filter effect often used for funk rhythm parts. A few auto-wahs contain oscillators that can be used to modulate their filters for rhythmic filtering effects.

The first auto-wah was developed by Aaron Newman and Mike Beigel at Musitronics (a.k.a Mu-Tron). Called the Mu-Tron III, the device was based on the envelope-controlled filters in analog synthesizers at the time but could be used by any electronic instrument. Other manufacturers followed with their own envelope filters/auto-wahs, such as MXR, BOSS, and Electro-Harmonix.

True Bypass versus Buffers

Several times already in this chapter, the issue of "true bypass" versus "non true bypass" has reared its ugly head. Here's the deal: When you step on a pedal to turn it on and off, you're not really "turning off" or "turning on" the effect in an electrical power switch sort of fashion. What you're doing is re-routing the guitar signal so that you do or don't hear the effect.

In the early days, some designers thought it was sufficient to simply disconnect the output from the effect from the guitar signal feeding the next pedal or the amp input. This stopped the sound of the effect, but since the input of the effect was still connected to the guitar, its circuitry sucked out some of the guitar's tone—not good.

As a solution to this, some manufacturers began adding circuits called *buffers* to their pedals and used electronic switching to disconnect the signal from the effect. This had some benefits:

▶ Mechanical switching can pop when it is turned on or off. Electronic switching is silent.

▶ The buffer conditions the signal so it can drive multiple effects or longer cable runs.

▶ Treble response is maintained.

The downside (according to some players) is that the preamplification/buffering circuitry may change the sound of the guitar, even when the effect is bypassed. And, the tonal changes may compound if multiple buffered pedals are used in a row.

As an alternative, manufacturers began using "hardwire" or "true" bypass. With this scheme a multi-pole switch is used that disconnects the guitar signal from both the input and the output of the effect at the same time. When the effect is off, the signal routes straight from the pedal's input jack to the output jack, as if they were connected directly by a straight wire. This has some advantages:

▶ The tone-sucking effects of the pedal's circuit are eliminated.

▶ There is no tonal change from a buffer.

But, there are couple of potential downsides:

▶ There may be a pop in the signal when the effect is switched on and off.

▶ Long cable runs or multiple true-bypass effects in a chain may result in signal degradation.

These days, the original single-sided signal switching has fallen by the wayside; true bypass and buffered designs rule the day. And, some pedals have recently come out where a buffer may be switched in and out of the circuit at the player's whim, giving the option of either type of operation.

But which is better, buffering or true bypass? The answer depends. Purists will probably always go for all true-bypass pedals. But many players find that, with modern electronic designs, buffers don't change the tone an appreciable amount or that the benefits of a buffered signal are worth any slight tonal change. I even have one buffered pedal where I think the buffer adds a nice tonal enhancement to the signal even when the pedal is bypassed versus not running through the pedal.

Ultimately, especially for players who use more than a few pedals, the best solution may be a mix of true bypass and buffered pedals, or true bypass pedals used in association with a separate, high-quality external buffer amp.

Delay/Echo

The sound emerging from a guitar amp is dry—what you hear is the amplified electronic signal through a speaker. There's no resonance or space around the sound. The problem is made worse if the room the guitar and amp are heard in doesn't have much ambience to contribute to the sound.

To expand the sense of space around the guitar sound, many players enjoy adding artificial ambience, either reverb (see next section) or delay, also known as *echo*. Delay or echo boxes create a discrete repeat of a sound after a set length of time. Some of the signal can also be routed internally back through the delay to create a series of repeats that fade away in volume level. The effect is similar to standing on the edge of the Grand Canyon, shouting a word, and hearing that word come back to you like a boomerang after a certain period of time.

In guitar terms, delays can create a variety of effects, including the following:

▷ Short, tight slapback echo, as is commonly heard in '50s rock, rockabilly, and some country styles.

▷ Doubling or ADT (*automatic double tracking*) uses a very short delay to create the fat-sounding effect of two guitars playing the same musical line.

▷ Longer delays are used to spice up leads and arpeggiated clean sounds.

▷ Very long delays are used for leads and for special cascading sound effects.

▷ Washes of delay—sometimes even from more than one delay—are used to create long sustaining sheets of ambient sound.

▷ Delays can also be set to create rhythmic effects for creating patterns in time with a song's tempo—triplet delays, dotted-eighth-note delays, and more are used to produce musical effects and to produce chordal and single-note patterns that a human player couldn't physically manage.

Tape Echo

The earliest type of delay/echo effect was the tape echo, with examples including the venerable Echoplex (see the "Maestro Echoplex" section in Chapter 16), the Roland Space Echo (see the "Roland RE-201 Space Echo" section in Chapter 16), and others. A tape echo works by making an actual recording to tape using the same type of magnetic record head and recording tape as regular tape recorders use. A playback head, spaced some distance farther along the tape path, picks up the recorded sound and sends it to the output. The distance between the record head and the playback head and the speed of the tape determine the amount of time that elapses between the original sound and the playback of the sound from the tape, creating the echo effect. On Echoplexes, the playback head was physically movable, allowing the player to set the delay time by sliding the head back and forth. On Roland Space Echoes, there were multiple playback heads. By switching among different combinations of those playback heads, delay times and rhythmic delays could be set up. To create multiple echo repeats, some of the repeated signal was tapped off and routed back to the record head, where it was re-recorded to tape and played back again by the playback head(s).

But there are flies in the ointment:

▷ the playback head captures not only the recorded sound but also a certain amount of hiss from the tape. With a single repeat, the hiss isn't a big deal. But with multiple echoes requiring that the delayed sound be re-recorded and re-read off the tape, the hiss quickly accumulates, until it is clearly audible.

▷ If there is any variation in the tape speed, those variations will show up as "warbling" in the pitch—which can sound great for thickening up the sound (sort of like chorus) or may just sound like a strange pitch warbling.

▷ There's also a certain amount of frequency loss with each "generation" as a sound is re-recorded and re-played back. This affects the high end, treble frequencies the most, meaning that the sound gets darker and darker with each repeat. Many players like this, because it makes the echoes sit comfortably behind the dry signal, without competing with it. But this frequency loss is always there; you can't turn it off if you want a pristine repeat of a note or lick.

▷ The maximum delay time is also limited. The playback head can only be physically moved or placed so far from the record head, or the unit becomes oversized and unwieldy. You could slow the tape down to increase the delay time, but the sound quality quickly suffers at lower tape speeds.

Some players are willing to live with all those negatives of tape echoes (and the constant maintenance that they require) to enjoy the specific sound that those units can create. There's a warmth, a richness, a vibe to tape echoes that analog delays and standard digital delays can't match—some of the new modeling delays come really close, though, even re-creating things such as pitch fluctuations. Others find that tape delays are too much hassle and that the flexibility of analog or digital delays wins out from both a usability standpoint and a tonal standpoint.

Analog Delay

Tape echoes are great, but they can be cantankerous. Among other things, they are mechanical, so life on the road can be hard, and on most, the tape runs continuously, so it wears quickly. Plus, they're big, bulky beasts. They sound great—as mentioned earlier in this chapter, even just passing a guitar's signal through an Echoplex can make it sound better, even when no delay is added. They were state-of-the-art technology for their time, but it's hard to classify tape echoes as truly practical for most guitar players.

For these reasons and more, manufacturers began seeking to make non-mechanical delays that were more compact, more durable, more practical, and more affordable. The result was the analog delay. Analog delays work by passing the input signal through a series of capacitors. Each capacitor delays the signal by a very, very small amount of time. Therefore, thousands of caps in a row must be used to create an audible delay. Using thousands of discrete (separate) capacitors would be difficult—the amount of space required for them and the cost would make it prohibitive. So integrated circuit chips, called *bucket brigade* chips, each containing thousands of capacitors, are used, combined with a digital "timer" chip to control the delay.

One of the earliest bucket brigade chips was the Reticon SAD 1024, which contained two groups of 512 capacitors. Panasonic later came out with the MN3205, which had around 4,000 capacitors. This chip was used by many early analog delays. Panasonic eventually discontinued it, around the time that digital delays began appearing. Recently, Chinese chip manufacturers began making bucket brigade chips again, and there has been a resurgence in the manufacturing of analog delay pedals.

Many players enjoy analog delays because they feel the analog design adds warmth and helps the delayed sound sit correctly in relation to the dry or unaffected signal. This warmth is actually the result of the small amount of degradation the signal suffers as it passes through each capacitor in the bucket brigade chip; a small amount of noise may also be added at the same time. To combat these effects, some analog delays feature EQ to restore the delayed sound's tone. Some analog delays also use companding—a process that compresses the level of the signal on input, before the noise is added by the pedal. The signal is expanded on output, which restores the proper level of the desired signal while simultaneously reducing the level of any noise that was added by the bucket brigade circuit.

There are some drawbacks to analog delays, especially when compared to digital delays: It's tough to accurately set the delay time on an analog delay, as there is no delay time readout. Few analog delays feature tap tempo control, which allows you to set the delay time on the fly by repeatedly pressing a switch or footswitch. Maximum delay times are limited; beyond a certain point, the degradation the delayed signal suffers is too audible for the delay to really be usable. For this reason it's rare to find a true analog delay with a delay time longer 300 or 400 milliseconds, though a few newer models will do up to 800 milliseconds. Some hybrid delays have also appeared, which combine analog and digital circuitry for longer delay times without extreme degradation.

But for all those drawbacks, analog delays remain very popular for their warm delay tone and their organic sound quality. And, one workaround from manufacturers is using digital technology to control an analog delay. This allows more precise, repeatable settings and more stable operation.

Digital Delay

The most modern type of delay is the digital delay. Digital delays are also the type that is most capable of creating a pristine-sounding echo repeat, without any coloration. With a digital delay, the sound that is repeated has the same (or extremely close to the same) fidelity and quality as the original sound. The sound quality is mostly defined by the quality of the analog-to-digital converters that change the guitar's analog voltage signal into digital data and the digital-to-analog converters that change the digital signal back into a voltage the rest of the signal chain can use. With today's high-resolution converters, the sound quality of most digital delays is virtually identical to the raw guitar sound.

Digital delays work in very different fashion from analog delays. In fact, they're more similar to tape delays in concept than they are to analog delays. A digital delay works by "sampling" or recording an analog signal as digital data and then storing that data in memory. The signal is held in the memory for a certain period of time and then played back as many times as is required to create the repeats desired. Because of the way in which they function, digital delays are capable of extremely long delay times, with no degradation of the sonic integrity of the repeats.

As with all digital devices, this process can be tightly controlled down to a fraction of a millisecond for the delay time, and down to the exact number of repeats desired. The sound can even be reversed to play back backward and altered in other ways. It's digital data, not an analog voltage, so these types of processing don't result in reduced audio quality or other artifacts. Some digital delays offer built-in filtering and tone controls so that the repeats can be made darker to simulate an analog or tape delay. Presets can be stored so that favorite sounds can be instantly recalled, and specific effects can be used whenever desired.

Modeling delays take the digital delay concept to the next level. The delay functions just like a regular digital delay, but additional processing algorithms are included that can re-create the sound and functions of tape delays and analog delays. This allows tremendous flexibility and tone-shaping power—use a tape echo–type effect on the verse, an analog-type delay on the chorus, and a digital-type delay for a special effect at the end of the song—all from one modeling delay processor.

Normally, there's a big chasm between players who use analog effects and those who use digital effects, but in the case of delays, the gulf isn't as large. Early digital delays had a reputation for being somewhat sterile sounding, but as analog-to-digital and digital-to-analog converters improved, this reputation faded. Today, some players still prefer analog delay effects, but many also find that the sound and flexibility provided by digital units can't be beat. There are many players who use both types for what each does well.

Modulated Delays

Some analog and digital delays allow the repeats to be modulated slightly—very subtly pitch shifted. When those modulated repeats are mixed back with the dry signal and with other repeats, the various different pitches rubbing against one another creates a chorus-type effect that can add greatly to the lushness of an echo effect, particularly where washes of sound are desired. In fact, when properly set up, a delay with modulation capabilities can create chorus and flange effects as well as modulated delay and straight delay effects.

Stereo versus Mono Delays

The inputs and outputs for delays, whether tape, analog, or digital, can be configured in several ways, including:

▷ The dry signal and the repeats are sent out of the same output for monophonic use with a single guitar amp.

▷ The dry signal is sent to one output while the repeats are sent to another output. Each output can be connected to a separate guitar amplifier, for a spacious effect that preserves the punch and clarity of the dry signal, enhanced with the echoes coming from a different physical location, played through a different amplifier and speaker.

▷ The dry signal is sent to two outputs, with different repeats sent to the two outputs in alternating fashion. The two outputs are connected to two separate amplifiers. This type of "ping-pong" setup results in the dry signal seemingly coming out in the middle, "between" the two amps, while the repeats bounce from amp to amp and side to side in the stereo field.

Stereo delay effects can greatly enhance the "width" of the guitar's sound, while also adding depth to the sound. But it's not just the outputs that can be configured in stereo. Some delays feature two discrete inputs as well. In some cases, the dry signals coming in those inputs are mixed to mono inside the box before it is processed for delay effects. In other cases, the signal coming in each input is processed separately with its own delay effects. This results in two discrete outputs that are not as tightly "correlated" together. This is called *true stereo* operation and is especially valuable if there is another stereo effect, such as a stereo chorus, feeding the inputs of the delay. True stereo operation allows the stereo field created by the stereo chorus to be preserved while also adding separate echo effects on each side.

Tap Tempo

While the tempo for a delay can almost always be set using a control knob or other method from the front panel of the effect, some delays offer another method: tap tempo. With tap tempo, the delay time is entered by either pressing a button or by stepping on a footswitch at the rate desired. This is a much easier method for matching a delay time to the tempo of the song and for being able to quickly change the delay time between songs or even between sections of songs.

Reverb

While delay and echo effects can greatly enhance the depth of a signal, ambience can add substantial enhancement as well. By "ambience," we're talking about reverb—the wash of sound that remains in a room after the dry sound stops. Think of a gymnasium or auditorium; clap your hands, and you hear the wash of sound that rings on the room for some period of time. That same ambience when applied to a guitar signal can bring the tone to life, increase its apparent size, help smooth out the highs, and let the notes ring together subtly for richer overall sound.

Spring Reverb

Reverb effects were among the first effects added to guitar amplifiers back in the 1960s. However, reverb effects were around long before that. In the 1930s, Laurens Hammond was looking for a way to simulate the sound of an organ playing in a huge church or hall. His solution was to send the sound from his electric Hammond organs into several springs. The sound traveled down the spring and returned, where it was picked up and added to the dry signal. The original reverb units were four feet tall, which wasn't a big deal given the size of a Hammond organ and its accompanying Tone Cabinet speakers. Later, in the late '50s, Hammond engineers managed to shrink the spring reverb down to slightly larger than a one-foot square—still too large for a guitar amp. In 1960, a Hammond engineer named Alan Young developed the Type 4 spring reverb, which was much more compact—and it was quickly adopted by Leo Fender for the Fender Twin Reverb amplifier. Over the years, the Type 4 was manufactured by various divisions in the Hammond company, eventually becoming known as the Accutronics reverb. It is still in production today.

In most spring reverb tanks used in guitar amplifiers, there are two or three spring "lines," each of which is made using two springs that are linked together. The springs have different numbers of coils, so each one provides a slightly different "ambience"; this results in a richer, deeper sound. The springs provide the delay and reverb-like ring; the length of the springs can therefore affect the tone created in subtle ways.

In a guitar amplifier, a tube or solid-state component is required to drive the reverb, or to send a signal into it. The key is, the signal actually needs to be fairly powerful to mechanically drive those springs into motion. Interestingly, amp designers such as Leo Fender chose to use preamp tubes to provide that drive. You'd think that a power tube would be a better choice. But, a 12AU7 preamp tube can actually provide around one watt of power per half in a push-pull configuration. (Recently, amp manufacturers such as Vox and others have put this fact to work in the tiny "micro amps," such as the Vox Lil' Night Train, which uses a 12AU7 as its power tube to provide two watts.)

Fender ended up using a 12AT7 preamp tube as the reverb driver in his amps because it produces about the same gain and current as the 12AU7 but has a narrower frequency response—given that the sound is being routed through a spring, the frequency response really doesn't matter. Plus, the 12AT7 has plenty of frequency response to cover the frequency range of the electric guitar. Further, most reverb tanks require the use of a high-pass filter to remove low frequencies that would muddy the reverb sound. In the stand-alone Fender '63 Reverb unit, a 6K6 power tube is used to drive the springs—basically, the Reverb is a Champ amplifier driving a reverb tank instead of a speaker. Later, as 6K6 tubes became hard to get, 6V6 tubes were substituted.

At the other end of the tank, a "recovery" circuit is required to bring the effected signal back into the amp at sufficient level and quality. This circuit is critical to the sound of the reverb, since what's coming off of the spring and its pickup can get noisy. Generally, a potentiometer is provided to allow the reverb sound to be mixed in with the dry sound, so that the balance or mix between the two can be adjusted. A second parameter, "dwell," may also be adjustable with a pot; this controls the gain of the reverb. Some reverbs also provide a tone control for adjusting the EQ of the reverb signal before it is blended with the dry signal.

There are some "prices" associated with using spring reverb. They're sensitive to impact—smack an amp with a spring reverb in it, and you'll hear the violent crash and bang of the springs hitting one another. Too much drive to the circuit can result in messy overdrive (usually only in units with a dwell or drive controls). Plus, you really can't adjust the reverb time or characteristics without changing the tank or the springs in the tank. And, too much vibration onstage can result in the springs beginning to ring even when there's no guitar signal feeding them.

But that doesn't stop most players from relying on spring reverb. A Fender amp with built-in reverb is an iconic sound. But, spring reverb hasn't just established itself as a must-have sound in Fender amps. Most other amp manufacturers offer their own take on spring reverb as well.

Digital Reverb

Unlike delay or echo, there really isn't an analog equivalent for reverb. There is, however a digital equivalent. Though there are digital reverb pedals, the rack version of this effect is far more prevalent. And, some newer amplifiers are featuring built-in digital reverb as well. Digital reverb works by re-creating two parts of the overall reverb: the early reflections, which are more sparse, comprising the short echo-like portion of the reverb heard immediately after the original sound occurs (representing sound waves reflecting off walls, floors, and other nearby surfaces), and the reverb tail, which is the long wash of ambience that typically rings on in the room after the sound source has stopped.

A digital reverb may use presets that represent certain types of reverb sounds—concert halls, churches, small rooms, and so on—or may represent artificial reverbs, such as the large plate reverbs used in recording studios or the spring reverbs in amplifiers. Pedal reverbs typically don't offer many parameters for tailoring the effect, while a rack reverb may offer way more parameters than you would ever want to have to mess with.

Digital reverbs have the advantages of flexibility (a spring reverb really only has one sound, while a digital reverb can emulate many different sounds), adjustability, the ability to save and recall presets for your favorite sounds, clean and pure sound quality, and more—including immunity to impact and stage vibration. You can often use tone controls in the reverb to tailor the sound so that it "sits" well with the original guitar tone—to cut the bass or cut the highs to customize the reverb sound to your liking.

Pitch

The standard-tuned electric guitar is capable of creating some 144 pitches, depending on the number of frets the instrument has. Of course, some of those pitches are duplicates, but there are still 45 to 48 discreet pitches to work with—enough for creating a fair amount of music in the past six-plus decades! But, being musicians, we want more options, more possibilities, more sounds, and manufacturers have delivered, giving us access to extremely useful pitch-processing effects.

Octave Divider

Known variously as *octavers*, *octave dividers*, and *octave doublers*, this type of effect transposes the guitar's pitch by an octave, either up or down (or both). In basic terms, the effect is very simple; just cut the signal's frequency in half, and the pitch drops by an octave. Double the frequency, and the pitch goes up by an octave.

But a vibrating string is actually quite a complex thing. It creates both its main pitch (called the *fundamental*) and also a slew of harmonics, which are at multiples of the fundamental frequency. You isolate those harmonics whenever you play a "natural" harmonic at the guitar's 12th fret, 7th fret, 5th fret, or other locations.

The problem is that when you halve or double the frequency of the fundamental to create an octave down or up effect, you also halve or double the frequency of those harmonics. With voices, this results in unnatural-sounding Jolly Green Giant and Mickey Mouse effects. With guitar, the result is a changed tonality in the transposed notes, which may not sound entirely natural.

That hasn't stopped guitarists from putting the effect to work. Perhaps one of the best-known examples of an octave effect in action is "Purple Haze" by Jimi Hendrix, but there are myriad others. And, today, those "artifacts" of transposing the pitch can be made to be less of an issue—digital technology allows the pitch to be shifted without such a radical change in tone. The note or notes created by the pitch shifter can now sound just as natural as the original, unaffected guitar note. But in this case, most players don't want the ideal, natural sound. That whistling or growling octave effect is exactly right, especially when combined with a nice fuzz.

Pitch Shifter

Also known as a *transposer* or sometimes referred to as a *Harmonizer* (though this is a trademarked term owned by Eventide), another type of pitch effect can generate notes that are related to the guitar's note—the effect might create a fourth, a fifth, a third, or some other harmony note. There are two ways this can be done: Early effects that generated harmonies created notes at parallel intervals to the original guitar note. So, if the effect was set for a major third above the guitar note, it would play a note a major third above the guitar note, even if a major third wasn't the "correct" note in the context of a given key or scale. For example, in the key of C, a major third up from the note C would be the note E. All well and good. But, if the guitar plays the note D, the effect will create an F# note as the major third harmony. But F# isn't the correct note in the key of C—it should be an F in order to stay in key. This doesn't mean that parallel pitch shifting isn't useful; you just have to be careful of how you're using it and which notes you're playing against which chords.

Today, effects devices are much smarter and can create harmony notes that are "correct" within the harmony of a given diatonic scale. So, if you choose to have the device create a harmony a third above the guitar note, the effect will intelligently choose whether that third should be major or minor based on the note the guitar is playing and the key of the song. For example, in the key of C, if the guitar plays a C note, the harmony should be an E note (a major third). But if the guitar plays a D note, the harmony should be an F (a minor third)—and the pitch shift effect is smart enough to know this and to play the correct note.

Today there are also pitch shift effects that can simulate detuning the guitar or using a capo—they can instantly transpose the pitch being played to match the way it would sound if the entire guitar were tuned down or up by a half step, whole step, or even more.

Doubling/Chorus Effects

Pitch shift effects can be used for more than creating intervals above or below the note the guitar is playing. A common use is to split the signal in two and slightly pitch up or down (detune) one signal and blend it in with the dry signal. Minimal pitch shift is required—4 to 8 cents. The result is a chorus-like effect. An even thicker effect can be created by splitting the signal into three, pitching up one, pitching down one, and then blending them with the dry signal. To create a wide stereo effect, the pitched-up signal can go to one amp while the pitched-down signal can feed another. Or, use three amps: pitched up to one amp, dry signal to one amp, and pitched down signal to the third.

Pitch Bend

Among the most recent effects are the pitch bend pedals, a new category that uses digital technology to smoothly bend the guitar's pitch up and down, as you might using a tremolo arm on a guitar. First out of the gate with this type of effect was DigiTech with their Whammy pedals, and others have followed. These pedals can be used for everything from subtle detuning to multi-octave dive bombs and supersonic shrieks to expressive pitch bends, all by rocking a pedal with your foot.

Mono versus Polyphonic

Until quite recently, octave and pitch transposing effects were monophonic—they could only operate on one pitch (or string) at a time. This meant you could use them for playing riffs or leads, but not for chords or for passages where two or more notes were played or sounded simultaneously. If you did play more than one note at a time through a pitch effect, the effect would "glitch" or make an ugly noise.

Recently, however, this has changed. Certain pitch effects, such as digital capos and pitch bend (whammy) effects can now deal with polyphonic material (more than one note at once), and we can expect this trend to continue. We can also expect new doors to open and new sounds to appear as polyphonic pitch shifting becomes more developed and capable.

Other Effects

Beyond the main categories of effects described earlier in this chapter, there are other types as well, which provide specific functions. Let's take a look at some of these.

Compressors

Some players consider compressors to be a type of gain pedal, and to be exactly correct, they do operate on the gain of the signal, and you can use them to boost the gain of the signal. But even though compressors are capable of increasing gain, that's not their main function in most cases—compressors are all about dynamics control.

Compressors are very common tools in the recording studio, where they are used on individual instrument and vocal tracks as well as on the master stereo mix. A compressor is used to reduce the dynamic range of a signal. It does this by setting a threshold and turning down the highest peaks that pass this threshold. The signals are turned down based on a ratio; a 2:1 ratio means that a 2-decibel change on the input results in a 1-decibel change at the output. A 4:1 ratio means that a 4-decibel change on the input results in a 1-decibel change on output. Another parameter, attack time, determines how long it takes before the compressor starts to clamp down on the signal. Once these peaks are pulled down, the overall signal can be made louder without danger of overload or distortion. This means that the quieter parts of the signal get louder, and overall signal is smoothed out.

There's a benefit to this besides just dynamics control. As you've just seen, when a compressor is applied to a guitar signal, the loudest peaks are reduced in level. Pick attacks (which tend to be loud peaks) are turned down or pulled back. The softer parts of the note—such as the sustaining portion after the pick attack—are turned up. This increases the apparent sustain of the instrument without requiring the use of distortion. For this reason, compressors are very popular for clean tones and playing styles. But compressors can also be used with distorted signals to increase sustain and smooth out the tone, while evening out dynamics.

A compressor may use either solid-state electronics or an opto-electronic (light-based) approach to do its job. Some compressors are very simple affairs, with a knob for the amount of compression and a knob for the output gain. Others provide control over threshold, ratio, attack time, and more. More knobs means more control and flexibility, but they also make setting up the compressor more difficult than simply twisting one or two controls until it sounds good.

If you're a country player, then a compressor is just about a requirement (an MXR Dyna Comp being the standard; see the "MXR Dyna Comp" section in Chapter 16)—especially if you're chicken pickin' with a Tele. But compressors are useful for far more than just country twang; they're great for adding sustain to clean and dirty solos, for making chords chime and ring, for preventing distortion on clean parts, and for making hard-struck clean chords pop.

The tradeoff is that since a compressor makes the soft parts louder, it also brings up any background noise that might be hiding in the guitar signal. Some players (me, for one) also find that compressors can be "grabby"— that the feel of playing the guitar changes in an annoying way if the compressor squashes the pick attack too much. For this reason, some manufacturers have begun adding blend or mix controls to their compressors, so that some of the dry, unprocessed signal can be added back in with the compressed signal. This allows the signal to be heavily compressed for good sustain and dynamics control, but still to feel natural and to retain a strong attack and sparkly top end.

Noise Gate/Noise Reduction

It's a strict, parallel relationship: Up the gain, the background noise goes up. But add a few pedals into the scenario or use single-coil pickups, and you have a recipe for a constant wash of hiss and buzz. In most cases, the noise will be masked when you're playing and only become audible (and annoying) in the silences between parts. What if you could have an automatic third hand that would instantly turn down the volume, eliminating the noise, as soon as there is a silence between notes?

That's exactly what a noise gate does. It works as an automatic volume control that silences noise as soon the guitar signal stops. A noise gate works in some ways like a compressor. There's a threshold, but unlike a compressor, when the signal drops below the threshold (when the guitar playing stops), the noise gate closes, eliminating any background noise. The problem is that the gate can't discriminate between noise between notes and when the sustain portion of a long note has dropped below the threshold level. If the gate isn't set properly, the quiet ends of sustaining notes could get chopped off, or the gate may "chatter"—rapidly open and close because it can't decide whether the signal is above or below the threshold. But well set up, a noise gate can bring a noisy rig under control and even be used to create super-tight rhythm parts *a la* Dimebag and other high-gain metal maniacs.

Volume Pedal

Virtually every electric guitar has a volume knob. The problem is that one hand is fretting, one hand is picking —and that leaves no hands to twist the volume knob. Some players become adept at running the volume knob with their little finger while picking, but for real freedom, a volume pedal is the answer. It's handy for general volume control duties, although most players can free up enough time to run the guitar's volume knob for that. It's also great as a noise control device—when you stop playing, step on the volume pedal to kill the noise. A volume pedal is also handy for smooth, violin-like volume swells. Once again, you can do all those things with the guitar's volume knob, but a volume pedal makes it easier for many players. Some volume pedals also provide extra functions, such as a gain boost or alternate routing that sends the signal to a tuner when the pedal is stepped back. As long as you can stand on one foot while you play, using the other foot on the pedal, you're good to go!

The most basic volume pedal design is simply a potentiometer mounted in a treadle-style foot pedal enclosure. A string, chain, or band connects the pot's shaft to the pedal; as the pedal is pressed, the pot shaft turns, raising the volume. As the pedal is rocked back, the pot shaft turns the other way, reducing the volume. Other pedals use optical circuits in place of the potentiometer. These have the advantage of no pot to wear out, get scratchy, or get noisy. There's no tone suck/loss of high end, as there can be with a mechanical potentiometer. Plus the taper of the volume change can be controlled. The key is finding a volume pedal that doesn't change your tone. As mentioned, some suck tone, but others also produce a slight drop in gain compared to the straight guitar cable, even when they are turned fully up.

Opinions vary as to where the volume pedal should be in signal path. Some players like it at the beginning, so that it responds just like the guitar's volume knob would. Others place it after gain pedals, so that it can be turned down to control background noise. Others place it before delay and reverb effects so that the echoes or ambience will keep ringing when the volume is pulled back, and so that the echoes or ambience can be used to smooth out and extend the sound when the pedal is used for volume swells. (This is where the string is picked with the volume pedal off and then the pedal is rocked forward to swell the sound in. The effect is similar to a violin or other bowed instrument or a synthesizer.) Others place the volume pedal after all the other effects as a final level control for the entire rig. And, it's not out of the question to have multiple volume pedals performing different duties at various points in the signal path.

Buffer

Running through a lot of pedals or running long cable lengths can suck a great deal of the life out of a guitar's relatively weak electrical signal. Some pedals have buffers or buffer amp stages built in to help combat this. (See the "True Bypass versus Buffers" sidebar earlier in this chapter.) But some players and technicians prefer to use a separate, super-high-quality buffer amp instead. Usually the buffer is the first thing the guitar hits; it can condition the signal in a few ways. It may simply boost the level; it may convert the signal to low impedance to help it withstand long cable runs or to bolster it in other ways. Ideally, a buffer won't change the tone of the guitar, but it's almost impossible for the signal not to be affected in at least some small way. However, a good buffer can add a slight pleasant coloration that can enhance the guitar signal as well as condition it against various sources of tone suck.

Multi-Effects Processors

Individual pedals are not the only way to go when it comes to effects, especially if you're using a number of different stompboxes. You could also choose to use a multi-effects unit, which combines numerous effects into one enclosure, either rack-based or in a floorboard. The first such units were analog; they were simply a single box holding multiple analog pedal circuits, which could be switched in and out of the signal path using switches or footswitches. Today, multi-effects usually feature digital effects and/or modeled digital effects, or, in a few cases, some analog effects (usually overdrives) along with digital effects.

It's not unusual for a digital multi-effects box to provide 50, 70, 100, or even more different effects types. Usually, a number of those effects can be used simultaneously to create a complex signal path. The effects chain, routing, settings, and other parameters can all be saved and recalled instantly, allowing the user to switch between sounds as required. Some multi-effects boxes include loops (send and return access points) for wiring in external effects, so you can still use your favorite analog overdrive or fuzz if you want to.

So what are the advantages and disadvantages of using a multi-effects box instead of individual pedals? Let's begin with some of the disadvantages:

▷ Because all the effects come from one manufacturer, some players feel that the effects within a multi-effects box are more generic or uniform sounding. With separate effects, you can pick and choose exactly the pedal you want for each effect, choosing the specific character and tone you want from each. (This "negative" may be less valid when the multi-effects box in question features models of specific analog effects.)

▷ If a multi-effects box breaks down, the whole thing is dead. With separate stompboxes, if a pedal breaks down, you can simply remove it from the chain and still finish the gig using the remaining pedals.

▷ Many multi-effects boxes are not as easy to program and configure as separate effects, where you can simply reach down and turn a knob. Once you get past the initial learning curve, it gets easier and faster, but few multi-effects are ever as fast and easy to use as separate effects pedals. (Some multi-effects can connect to computers and use editing software to make programming much easier.)

▷ If you aren't satisfied with a particular effect in a multi-effects box, the only solutions are to either live with the less-than-happening effect or to use a separate effect along with the multi-effects box,which defeats the purpose for many players. This is most common with overdrives and distortions, where many players still prefer analog types over digital types.

▷ Individual effects tend to hold their value better than multi-effects boxes, because digital technology advances so quickly that older units become outdated quickly. This doesn't mean that they're any less useful than they were when you bought them, but they won't be worth as much money on the used market as separate pedals would.

Contrast these negatives to the advantages of using a multi-effects box:

▷ With a multi-effects box, you don't have to connect all the separate pedals together with individual cables. Because each cable is a potential bad connection and a source of potential signal degradation, one cable in from the guitar and one cable out to the amp is a very clean solution.

▷ Multi-effects boxes are generally more portable than an array of separate pedals or even a pedalboard. They're ideal for a "grab-it-and-go" situation.

▷ Only one power cable is required, versus the various battery and power supply requirements of separate pedals.

▷ With a multi-effects box, there is one analog-to-digital conversion going into the box and one digital-to-analog conversion on the way out of the box. If you're using individual digital stompboxes, each one will have its own A-to-D and D-to-A conversions, potentially degrading the sound.

▷ If separate pedals have buffers in them, each one may affect the tone. With a multi-effects box, there is only one buffer or one true bypass switch to affect the tone.

▷ A multi-effects box can offer many more effects types than even a huge pedalboard or rack effects system.

▷ Many multi-effects offer built-in expression pedals for wah, volume, pitch bend, and parameter control, or jacks for connecting external expression pedals. Not many individual pedals provide expression control capabilities.

▷ A multi-effects box may offer effects chains and even effects types that are difficult or impossible to achieve using separate effects.

▷ Multi-effects provide storage of presets for easy recall of your favorite sounds. Each song in your set list can have its own specific, custom-programmed sounds.

▷ Many multi-effects boxes allow you to change the order of effects around to whatever you like. It's difficult to instantly change the order of effects and then instantly change them to another arrangement when you're using separate stompboxes connected by cables.

▷ Many multi-effects boxes offer flexible input and output connections so that some effects can be placed in front of the amp while others are used in the effects loop of the amp.

▷ Most multi-effects boxes support stereo operation.

▷ Many multi-effects devices provide built-in looping capabilities for songwriting and performance use.

▷ Some multi-effects units have a stereo input for an MP3 or CD player for learning and practicing along with songs.

▷ Some multi-effects boxes have headphone jacks for private practice.

▷ Some multi-effects units can be used as audio interfaces for direct recording guitars and other signals into computer-based studio systems.

▷ Many multi-effects units feature amp and speaker cabinet emulations for direct feed into PA systems and for laying down tracks without microphones in the studio.

▷ Some multi-effects units provide sophisticated switching and control capabilities for amplifiers and other devices.

▷ No matter how you make the comparison—unless you're only using one or two pedals—multi-effects are generally much less expensive than separate pedals.

From the pros and cons lists, it looks as if the advantages outweigh the disadvantages when it comes to multi-effects boxes. And, for many players and many situations, they are a great solution. But despite this, most players still come down on the side of individual pedals purely for their character and sound quality, ease of use, and, let's be frank, cool factor. But even those players who are dyed-in-the-wool stompbox lovers often find that a multi-effects unit is useful for direct recording, for grab-it-and-go sessions and gigs, as a backup for a stompbox-based stage rig, for practice, and for learning songs.

Pedal Order and Signal Routing

Getting an array of pedals wired up and in the best order can be a time-consuming process, but there are some rules of thumb that can help with minimizing the trial-and-error approach it generally takes. Before you proceed, please note the use of the word "best" rather than the perhaps expected word "correct" in that last sentence.

The reason for this word substitution is that there is no "correct" order for pedals. You can place your pedals in any order you desire; there really is no danger of damaging a pedal or amp by putting a stompbox in one place in the signal chain versus another. That said, here are some basic guidelines for pedal order:

▷ Most players put their tuner first, especially if the tuner has a buffer in it for conditioning the signal before it hits the rest of the signal chain. However, certain pedals, such as some vintage wahs and fuzzes, may react negatively to a buffer. In this case, the tuner can be placed later in the chain.

▷ Compressors generally go early in the chain, for establishing sustain and controlling dynamics before the signal hits the other pedals, especially overdrives. Placing a compressor after an overdrive or fuzz may result in a thin, flat tone.

▷ Most players run wah pedals—especially vintage-style units—early or first in the chain. However, some players enjoy having the wah after gain pedals for the more intense effect this can provide.

▷ Typically, gain pedals go next in the chain—overdrives, fuzzes, boosts. This provides the remaining pedals with the most harmonic content and the richest signal upon which to operate.

▷ Modulation pedals—chorus, flange, phaser, tremolo, vibrato—are usually placed after gain pedals. However, Uni-Vibe-style pedals are often placed pre-gain, and tremolo pedals are also sometimes used pre-gain.

▷ Most players run delays last in the chain, so that the entire signal, with all the other effects, can be delayed and repeated.

▷ If there is a reverb pedal, it probably will be placed after the delays.

A few others:

▷ Noise gates can be placed after the gain pedals (which produce the most noise) or at the end of the chain. However, placing a gate after delays or reverb may result in quieter repeats or ambience being chopped off.

▷ Equalizers can go anywhere in the chain. Before the gain pedals, they allow the guitar tone to be shaped pre-distortion and to influence how the guitar signal "hits" the overdrive or fuzz. After the gain pedals, they allow the overall distorted sound to be shaped.

▷ As discussed earlier in this chapter, boosts can go either before or after the gain pedals. Before, they increase distortion; after, they boost the output level feeding the other pedals and the amp.

▷ Pitch shifters can go pre-gain or post-gain; there definitely is a sonic difference between pitch shifting a clean guitar signal and then distorting it versus pitch shifting an already-distorted signal—shifting all of the extra harmonic content in the distorted signal can result in a thin and shrieky sound.

▷ An amp/speaker simulator that takes the place of a "real" amp is usually last in the order just as an amp would be, although it may be placed earlier in the chain if you would prefer to use some of the effects on the "amped" signal.

Now that you've made it through all those time-tested guidelines, remember that they're just that—guidelines. Feel free to deviate from these guidelines in any way you choose. As mentioned earlier, there's no danger of blowing anything up by changing the order of your pedals, so try them in any order that might occur to you. Sometimes changing the order of a couple of pedals won't have much effect at all, but in other cases, swapping two pedals around can change everything. That's the beauty of it; your signal path can be completely individual to you and can be customized to result in exactly the variety of tones that you want and need.

Power Supplies

Pedals don't run on air; it takes electrical current to wake them up, get them out of bed, and get them on the job. Most pedals will run on a standard 9-volt battery (in some cases a couple of batteries), and many will alternatively run on a power supply (commonly referred to as a *wall wart*), which converts 110-volt alternating current (AC) to 9-volt direct current (DC). A few pedals require 9 volts AC, some need 12 volts DC, and a few must have 18 volts DC to be happy.

Batteries are the most variable of the sources of power, and in some pedals they definitely can affect the tone. Years ago, Eric Johnson made a comment about being able to hear the difference between various types of batteries, and he was soundly mocked for his claim. Since then, he's been vindicated—which goes to show, when we're talking about questions of tone, great ears rule the day, not commonly accepted "fact."

Now, we'll temper this validation of EJ's ears by saying that you probably won't hear a difference between fresh batteries in a brand-new digital delay. But it is entirely possible that different types of batteries and batteries of different strengths will be audible in certain vintage analog fuzz boxes and other effects.

So, it would seem that simply choosing the right kind of batteries would be the end of it. But the sound of certain pedals can degrade as the output of a battery falls off (as it ages or goes dead). So, for many players, an AC power supply is the best solution—it's certainly more convenient to just plug in a power supply than to have to open a pedal and change its battery, especially if the pedal is mounted to a pedalboard or in a rack.

But AC power supplies can sometimes increase hum and noise. For this reason, an isolated power supply is usually cleanest, where each pedal gets its own voltage feed, separate from the others. Some power supplies even provide voltage "sag" adjustment to simulate the effect (and tone) of a dying battery, without the hassle of using a real battery. And some power supplies can also output different voltages simultaneously, so you can power your 9-volt DC, 12-volt DC, and 18-volt DC pedals all from one box.

For one or a few pedals that are set on the floor, batteries may be fine. But for a pedalboard or rack where the pedals are permanently or semi-permanently mounted, a power supply is the clear choice.

Effects Loops

If your amp has an effects loop, then you have more options for placing your pedals. In this case, the pedal types are usually separated into two broad categories: those that go before the amp, feeding the amp's input, and those that perform best in the effects loop. Here's how it usually breaks down:

▷ Tuner, wah, compressor, and gain/boost typically are set up to feed into the amp's input.

▷ Modulation, delay, and reverb generally go in the loop.

As for other effects, the routing depends on how the amp is being used; if the amp is used only as a clean platform and all distortion and overdrive will come from pedals, then noise gates and equalizers can run in front of the amp. If the amp will be used to generate distortion, in addition to or in place of gain pedals, then noise gates and EQs can go in the loop.

As we discussed earlier, where to use effects in your signal path is completely up to you. There is no law that requires that a delay be placed in your amp's effects loop; it could be the first pedal you go through. Likewise, if you want a dirt pedal in your amp's effects loop, try it there—it may give you exactly the sound you want.

4-wire Rigs

Some multieffects are designed to work either in front of the amp or in an effects loop—rack effects, in particular are often happiest in the amp's effects loop. A recent development is multi-effects that are capable of "4-wire" setups. In this case, the multi-effects has its own send/return loop, which can be used either for bringing an external stompbox into the signal path or for effectively splitting the multi-effect in two, with some effects running into the front of the amp and others inserted into the effects loop. Here's how it works:

  ▷ First wire: The guitar feeds into the input of the multi-effects.

  ▷ Second wire: The "send" connection on the multi-effects feeds into the input of the amplifier.

  ▷ Third wire: The send connection from the amp's effects loop feeds into the return connection on the multi-effects.

  ▷ Fourth wire: The output from the multi-effects feeds into the return connection on the amp's effects loop.

In this case, tuner, compressor, and gain/boost effects from the multi-effects can be used to feed into the guitar amp, while the modulation, delay, and reverb effects can be used in the amp's effects loop. A single multi-effects processor can be used to provide all of these effects, making for a compact but still highly flexible and powerful rig.

Stereo Rigs

When running effects to create a stereo sound, you can use a stereo effect, such as a chorus, delay, or reverb plugged into the front of two amplifiers. Usually, two identical amps are used, though different amps can also be used for more tonal disparity between the two sides. For many situations, a better solution is to use two amps with effects loops. The send from the "main" amp's effects loop feeds the stereo effects. Its left and right outputs are then routed to the loop returns on the two amps. In this case, the second amp is really only being used for its power amp and speaker.

Wet/Dry Rigs

Some players don't like running effects such as delay, chorus, and reverb into the same amp as their dry signal. They feel that the effects diminish the presence of the signal and take away from the clarity and punch of the sound. In this case, a second amp can be used just for the effects, while the main amp remains dry. Usually, the effects loop send from the main dry amp is routed to the chorus/delay/reverb, with the output from the effects feeding into the effects return on the second amp.

Wet/Dry/Wet Rigs

Taking things a step further, some players add a third amp, so that the center, main amp is used for the dry signal. The send from that amp is routed to a stereo effects processor and then that stereo output is sent to a second (left) and third (right) amp, which produce the wet effects signals only.

Loop Switchers

Using more than a few pedals can result in a change to your tone—especially if those pedals have less than stellar buffers in them. For this reason, players with multiple pedals often turn to loop switchers. A loop switcher has a send/return loop into which a pedal is inserted. The send/return loop can be turned on and off using a footswitch or remote control. When the loop is turned off, the pedal is completely bypassed, passing straight from the loop switcher input to its output. When the loop is turned on, the signal is routed out, through the pedal, back into the loop switcher, and then on to the rest of the signal path. So, when the loop is switched off (bypassed), any signal loss or noise from the pedal is completely removed from the signal path when the pedal isn't in use.

A loop switcher might have a single loop, or it might have many loops. It might be a floorboard device that mounts to a pedalboard, or it might be a rackmount device that can be controlled through MIDI or some other protocol. There are some significant advantages to using a loop switcher:

> ▷ As described earlier, a loop switcher can bypass any noise or tone suck created by a pedal, resulting in the quietest, cleanest possible sound.

> ▷ Multiple pedals can be inserted into a single send/return loop, allowing them to all be turned on and off *en masse*, with one button push. So you could, for example, put an overdrive pedal and a delay pedal set up for a particular lead tone in a loop and then instantly switch both pedals on with one footswitch stomp that activates the loop, instead of the usual two stomps required to turn on both pedals.

> ▷ Some loop switchers with multiple loops have memory and preset capabilities that allow combinations of send/return loops to be turned on and off with one footswitch press, so you can completely change the signal path. You could, for example, create three presets: a clean sound with a compressor, a chorus, and a reverb; a dirty, modulated rhythm sound with an overdrive and phase shifter; and a heavy lead sound with a compressor, fuzz, EQ, and delay. Each could be assigned to a footswitch and instantly recalled.

> ▷ If something goes wrong with a pedal mounted on a regular pedalboard, you'll have to stop playing, pull cables, and route around it to get it out of the signal path. If something goes wrong with a pedal in a loop switcher, just turn off its loop, and the pedal is completely bypassed.

> ▷ With a loop switcher, when no pedals are in the path, the wiring is as short as it can be for maximum tonal purity. On a regular pedalboard, even when pedals are turned off, the signal is still going through extra lengths of wire between the various pedals.

Having said all that, some players still prefer the simplicity of just wiring one pedal into another. But the longer and more complex an effects chain gets, and the more you have to "dance" to quickly turn multiple pedals on and off for various tones, the more attractive a loop switcher begins to look. And, even if a programmable multi-loop switcher isn't the answer, many players still find a single loop switcher—or a couple of them—to be useful for cleaning up the signal path.

Pedalboards versus Racks

If you only have one or two pedals, then placing them on the floor may be just fine. Carry them to the gig in a duffle bag, set them down, wire them up, and start playing. But if more than a few pedals are involved, some sort of system for mounting and wiring them becomes much more convenient. Yes, you can continue to throw them in a bag and to duct tape them to the stage at each gig, but it's a lot easier and cleaner—and less hazardous to the pedals—to figure something else out.

The two solutions that present themselves are a pedalboard and a rack system. The decision is really an ergonomic one; there's little tonal difference between having an array of pedals on a piece of plywood or a fancy commercial-made pedalboard in front of you or having the same array of pedals fastened into drawers or on shelves in a rack back by the amp. The only real tonal effects that might arise could result from having to run long lengths of cables to and from the pedalboard versus using the short cables that would be required to reach from a rack to your amp.

Table 11.1   Effects Tonal Factors

Tone Factor	Tonal Contribution
Effects types used	Major
Analog versus digital versus modeled effects	Subtle to major
Single effects versus multi-effects	Subtle to major
Pedal/effects order	Subtle to major
Mono versus stereo	Major
Stereo versus wet/dry or wet/dry/wet	Minor to major
Pedal-to-pedal wiring versus loop switcher	Subtle to major
Pedalboard versus rack	Subtle

The Little Things

WE'VE ALL HEARD THE CLICHÉS: "THE LITTLE THINGS MATTER," "The devil is in the details," and any number of variations on the theme. The point is the same, regardless of the words used: You can't stop with the big stuff. To really be a success in whatever you're doing, you've got to take care of the little things, too. As applied to your ongoing quest for guitar tone, there are a number of things you need to be aware of. The impact of these items may not be as radical as getting a new amp—or even changing the settings on your amp. And changing the little things may not change everything about your sound the way a new guitar can. In fact, the little things may not even make as much difference as changing out a tailpiece or changing a pickup can. But that doesn't mean that changing something small doesn't affect the overall sound. The effects of the little things may be subtle, but add them all together, and you have a much more noticeable tonal effect than you might think.

Picks

Perhaps the smallest of the little things we deal with as guitarists is our pick (a.k.a. *plectrum*). What could be less consequential? It's just a small, thin slice of plastic! How much can what you use to put the string into motion really matter to the overall sound?

You might be surprised. Depending on other variables (such as the amount of gain or distortion you use, as well as your basic tone), the pick you use can definitely impact the sound of your guitar. There are a ton of variations on the basic plectrum and different types to choose from: various materials, shapes, edges, surfaces, thicknesses—and at a range of prices. Ordinary, garden-variety plastic picks may cost just a few pennies, but if you feel so moved, you can spend as much as $4,000 on a single pick—made from an ancient meteorite, no less. Gold picks, silver picks, brass picks, stone picks, wood picks, wire picks, nylon picks, Delrin picks, tortoiseshell picks, rubber picks, felt picks, a peso as a pick, a sixpence as a pick, straight picks, curved picks, twisted picks, textured picks, smooth picks, pointy picks, round picks—there's even a quarterly online magazine for pick collectors (www.pickcollecting.com).

Shape

Guitar picks are available in a variety of shapes, including the following general shapes, with a near-infinite array of shapes that fall in between these main types:

▷ **Regular.** The "standard" pick is shaped like an isosceles triangle, with two sides of equal length, a shorter third side, two rounded corners of the same angle, and a third corner with a smaller angle and often with a sharper point.

▷ **Teardrop.** Generally, a smaller overall pick shape than the regular pick shape, with a larger, rounded end and a smaller, more pointed end.

▷ **Jazz.** The "jazz" pick shape is sort of a variation on the teardrop shape, with sharper corners, what some might consider more of a diamond shape. The jazz shape is favored by many high-velocity shredders and fusion players.

▷ **Triangle.** This is a larger pick with three equal sides and three equal corner angles. The sides may be straight with sharp and defined triangle corners, or the sides may be slightly curved with more rounded, smoother corners.

▷ **Sharkfin.** Literally a "shark fin" shape, which offers several different corner angles and points, so the player can choose which will work best for a particular articulation and application.

▷ **Round.** A circular or near-circular pick. One advantage is that there is no specific direction the pick should be held—it's all the same angle and shape!

The shape of a pick affects the tone it produces subtly, if at all. Any tonal effect results from the amount of pick material that contacts the string. A wider pick, with more area contacting the string, will sound darker and perhaps fuller than a pick with a pointy end, where only a small amount of pick material comes into contact with the string.

Pick Materials

The material a pick is made from can affect the tone it produces. A harder, stiffer material will typically have a brighter attack and overall sound, while a softer material will sound warmer and rounder, with less high end on the attack portion of each note. There are a lot of different options for pick material, from the conventional to the radical.

▷ **Faux tortoiseshell.** If real tortoiseshell is the Holy Grail of pick materials (see the upcoming "The Holy Grail?" sidebar), then the search for a turtle-friendly replacement has been the pick world's equivalent of the quest for the Holy Grail! Over the years, several different materials have emerged in response to this quest, with some of the current favorites being Tortex, which is used by Dunlop, and Tortis, which is used by the Red Bear Trading Co.

▷ **Delrin.** A plastic developed by DuPont. Delrin is used by Dunlop to make Tortex and Delrex picks because it has a texture that is similar to tortoiseshell.

▷ **Nylon.** A popular material for making picks, particularly extra-thin and thin picks. Because the nylon surface is extremely smooth and glossy, nylon picks often feature a textured grip area. Thin and extra-thin nylon picks may lose flexibility after some months of use.

▷ **Celluloid.** This synthetic is made from nitrocellulose and camphor. It originally had many uses, primarily as a substitute for manufacturing items previously made from expensive animal products, such as ivory, horn, and tortoiseshell. Celluloid's big drawbacks are that it is fragile and extremely flammable. Today, the two big uses for celluloid are table-tennis balls and guitar picks.

▷ **Acetal.** A class of plastics that offer excellent rigidity and durability, as well as a matte finish that is easy to grip with sweaty hands.

▷ **Ultem.** An extremely stiff and durable plastic that produces a crisp, bright-sounding pick said to have a sound somewhat like tortoiseshell.

▷ **Polycarbonate.** Also known as *Lexan*, polycarbonate is the same plastic used to make water bottles, bicycle parts, and other objects that may be subjected to impacts and hard use. Polycarbonate picks are very smooth, which generally requires some sort of depression or other grip. They are durable and offer a bright tone.

Dunlop makes a line of gel polycarbonate picks, which are translucent and come in a range of colors. Their tone and response are similar to standard polycarbonate.

▷ **Wood.** Various woods are used to make picks, including rosewood and ebony, as well as lignum vitae, which is said to be among the hardest and densest of hardwoods. Wooden picks produce a rich, round tone with controlled top end. However, wooden picks can't be made as thin as plastic or metal picks, generally do not flex at all, and may wear more quickly than other materials.

▷ **Stone.** Want the super-hardest, smoothest, and densest of picks? Perhaps stone will fit the bill for you. Agate, amber, jade, and other stones are used to manufacture picks, which certainly can make for a beautiful plectrum! As with wooden picks, it is hard to find a stone pick that is thin—most tend toward the thick side. They also (needless to say) don't flex much.

▷ **Metal.** Brass and steel picks are preferred by some players for several reasons, including durability and bright, lively tone. However, the feel of a metal pick striking a metal string bothers some players, as does the very bright tone and strong pick attack produced. A metal pick can also do serious damage to a guitar's finish!

Another "class" of metal picks is used by players such as Brian May and Billy Gibbons—coins. Gibbons used a Mexican peso that had been filed into somewhat of a standard pick shape, while May uses a silver sixpence. The serrated edges of these coins produce a unique attack with different harmonics than a more standard pick.

▷ **Wire.** There are two types of picks that use wire. The first uses a plastic grip area that is connected to a length of wire that is bent to create the shape of a pick. The wire is used to strike the string. Copper and copper-beryllium wire can be used, which have the advantage of being very hard and of not being magnetic—so they aren't attracted to the guitar's pickups. Steel can also be used, which offers a bright tone, but steel is magnetic. The second type of pick is manufactured by Jellifish. It features a "comb" of wires, which are used to brush across the guitar's strings, creating something of a 12-string guitar effect.

▷ **Rubber.** Steel-string acoustic and nylon-string classical guitar players sometimes use rubber picks, which simulate the sound of bare fingers on the strings, without the hard attack of picks made from other material. Rubber picks are easy to hold, but they do take some getting used to, and they don't wear extremely well.

▷ **Felt.** Bass players and ukulele players sometimes use felt picks to simulate the sound of fingers on strings. They're not commonly used on electric guitar but could be put to work to create a soft tone with a mellow attack.

▷ **Other materials.** Water buffalo and ram's horn, camel bone, coconut shell, glass, mother of pearl, ivory, quartz, and more can all be used to make picks. The feel of the pick will depend on the texture of the material's surface, while the sound will depend on the density, weight, and composition of the material. The harder and smoother the material, the brighter the tone will be. The softer the material, the rounder and warmer the tone will be.

The Holy Grail?

For many guitar players, real tortoiseshell has become almost legendary as the best of all materials from which to make a plectrum. Those who use or have used tortoiseshell swear by the tone, feel, and durability of these picks. However, tortoiseshell has been illegal to use for manufacturing items for many years. The material used to make tortoiseshell picks—and a wide range of other items, including picture frames; jewelry boxes; tea sets; hair ornaments, brushes, and combs; sunglasses; and more; dating as far back as the ancient Greeks and Romans—came from a specific type of sea turtle, the hawksbill turtle.

Tortoiseshell is made from the thin "scutes" or scales that cover the bone plates of the carapace (the top portion) of the turtle's shell. The thin scales are molded together to create thicker sheets using heat that partially liquefies the material. The resulting "tortoiseshell" can be easily worked using heat, pressure, and lathe techniques.

Unfortunately, the hawksbill turtle, which lives in tropical coral reefs around the world, has become critically endangered due to overtrading in shells and other parts. In fact, some experts point to the limited availability of tortoiseshell as a factor in the development of celluloid (which can be made to look similar to tortoiseshell) in the early twentieth century.

In 1973, the capture and killing of hawksbill turtles for their meat (which is a popular food in many parts of the world) and skins, as well as trade in tortoiseshell, was banned as part of the CITES (*Convention on International Trade in Endangered Species*) agreement, though there are a number of countries that still allow the legal harvest of hawksbill turtles.

Being in possession of tortoiseshell items is not illegal (unless the material was obtained illegally). However, sale or trade of any tortoiseshell item made after June 1, 1947, is illegal. Even reworking an item made after that date is illegal. (Sorry, no making a pick from your great-grandmother's antique hairbrush.) Selling or reworking an item made before 1947 requires an Article 10 certificate —and you'll have to prove the tortoiseshell's age and how you acquired it to get one. In most cases, this proof will be impossible to provide satisfactorily, and the material or item will be confiscated. And, for example, in the UK, you could face up to five years in prison and/or an *unlimited* fine—best to stay with faux tortoiseshell picks!

Thickness

Picks are available in a broad range of thicknesses, ranging from thin to super-thick. Manufacturers define the "gauge" of their picks in various ways, but as a vague guideline, thicknesses fall into these ranges:

▷ Extra-light/thin—less than 0.40mm

▷ Light/thin—0.50 to 0.60mm

▷ Medium—0.70 to 0.80mm

▷ Heavy/thick—0.85 to 1.20mm

▷ Extra-heavy/thick—1.5 to 2.0mm

▷ Super-heavy/thick—2.5 to 5.0 mm or more

Opinions vary on how the thickness of a pick affects tone. One manufacturer's marketing campaign says, "The bigger the pick, the bigger the tone." Yet, you also have players including Eddie Van Halen (at least based on the pick he gave me at a recent music industry trade show) who use very thin, highly flexible picks. There are some general characteristics that players seem to apply to different pick thicknesses.

Thinner picks:

▷ The thinner the pick, the more flexible it is.

▷ More percussive sound.

▷ Brighter sound.

▷ Slower response, as the pick takes time to bend back after plucking the string.

▷ Good for strumming.

Thicker picks:

▷ The thicker the pick, the less flexible it is. Past medium gauge or so, the pick will bend very little, if at all.

▷ Faster response.

▷ Fatter, darker tone.

▷ More controlled tone with heavy distortion.

▷ More control over volume and attack.

▷ Good for lead/single-note work.

These statements are, of course, all subjective and certainly open to debate—and are also subject to other variables, such as the material the pick is made from and how the player holds it. Like many things having to do with guitar tone, it's easy to find a player to support every viewpoint on the effects of pick thickness on the sound produced. However, what almost all players *will* agree on is that there *is* a difference in tone and, of course, feel when you go from a thin pick to a thick pick.

Texture

There are two places where "texture" is used on guitar picks: on the upper part to aid in gripping or hanging onto the pick and on the actual pick surface that contacts the string. In the first case, there will be no effect on tone. But if the surface of the pick that hits the string is rough, it will definitely change how the string is set into motion and the sound of the initial attack. With players such as Billy Gibbons (with his peso coins and their serrated edges) and Brian May (who uses sixpence coins with similarly serrated edges), this effect is taken to its extreme. But "regular" picks also vary in their texture, from completely smooth and glass-like to rough and scratchy or to shapes that have built-in serrations on the edges, such as those found on some shark fin–shaped picks. A rough-textured pick may pull back your speed or force you to slightly modify your technique—it won't slide off the string as easily—but you may find the tonal result to be worth it.

The effect of pick texture on tone can range from a scratchier attack, with less impact or focus to it, to an emphasis on harmonic content and a brighter overall tone. You can experiment with this yourself by taking a piece of rough sandpaper to a smooth pick to remove its glossy finish or even by using a sharp object to add scratches to a pick. Or, you could always go to your piggy bank and pull out a quarter, which will have a rough, serrated edge. Be careful, though—a serrated coin can wreak havoc on your guitar's poor strings!

Case Study: Does It Really Matter?

How you attack the guitar with your picking hand is an often-overlooked aspect of playing. Occasionally, you'll come across someone like Eric Johnson; I remember reading a magazine interview with him years ago where he talked about how he very specifically controlled his pick attack to achieve his much-vaunted "violin" tone. And classical guitarists are extremely conscious of how their fingers/nails strike and pluck the string, where on the string the attack occurs, what type of stroke is used, and so on. With electric guitar, shredders and fusion players tend to be conscious of alternate picking, and punkers and hard rockers will focus on down strokes for driving rhythms, but beyond that, in many cases, it seems that, "Grab any handy pick and move it back and forth across the strings," is about as far as the consideration for the lowly pick goes.

But there may be a lot more to it than that. For many years, I had been using these picks called *HIO Speedpicks*, which are now made by Dunlop. They're standard-shaped nylon picks, but with a twist—literally! The sharp end of the pick has a twist of a few degrees; the idea behind this is, when you hold the pick and the guitar in playing position, the side of the pick contacts the string straight on—flat or parallel to the string, and not at an angle, as often happens with a regular flat pick. (Check it out for yourself; it's likely that your picks wear unevenly—more on one side than the other—with the wear pattern indicating that the pick doesn't contact the string flat on.) I used the Speedpicks because I liked the way they felt, the twist made it easy to hold the pick, and they lasted well. But I had never really thought about whether they were affecting the tone.

Then, at a Paul Reed Smith Guitars event, I was given a bunch of standard-style picks imprinted with the PRS logo. When I tried them at home, I realized there was a difference in the tone compared to my usual Speedpicks. The PRS picks, which had the standard pick shape and were made from nylon, didn't hit the strings flat on (given how I hold the pick and how I hold the guitar); the tone was rounder, with more low end. The Speedpicks, on the other hand, had a tight, focused, dynamic, hi-fi sound. I also found I played slightly differently with each pick, based on the sound produced and on the way the string and pick interacted. My interest was sparked.

A few months later, I attended the annual NAMM (*National Association of Music Merchants*) music industry trade show in Anaheim, California, and came home with a pocketful of picks that I gathered from the booths of a bunch of manufacturers. I ended up returning with a nice, random assortment of materials, sizes, shapes, and textures. I set about trying all the various picks I had scored: thin, medium, and thick picks, faux tortoiseshell, nylon, acrylic, metal, even stone and wood picks, with shapes ranging from circular to triangular to teardrop, in tiny to huge sizes. From a playing/technique standpoint, some worked well for me, some less so. Some seemed to be better for rhythm playing; others were uncomfortable for strumming but worked great for leads.

Here's the conclusion that I came to: It may seem like the smallest of things, but the pick you use really can affect your tone, and it can also affect your technique and how you play. So, here's your assignment for the week: Spend a couple of bucks and get yourself the biggest pile of assorted picks you can find—different sizes, shapes, thicknesses, and materials. Set up your rig for a nice clean sound using your usual pick. Now work your way through the pile. Give each one a real try, preferably playing the same licks and rhythms as identically as possible with each one. What do you hear? How is the feel different? Switch to an overdriven sound. Do a bit more playing with each pick. Is the sound different? Does your technique change?

If you're like me, you'll quickly narrow the selection down to three or four likely candidates that stand out above the others for sound and comfort. I predict that over the next few days or weeks, you'll naturally gravitate toward the one that sounds best and that feels right. I ended up with three picks: a normal-shaped nylon pick, the aforementioned Speedpicks for when I want that focused sound (especially for leads), and, to my surprise, the very thin EVH-brand pick that Eddie Van Halen uses—surprising, because I haven't enjoyed using light, flexible picks in the past. But for certain parts, I find it's perfect.

Now, I'm not taking three picks with me to gigs and switching off which I'm using on the fly for different parts. I'll use the standard nylon one I liked best for live gigs and for most other things that I do. But in the studio, you can bet I won't hesitate to reach for one of the others for a particular part or passage.

Are we talking about trivial minutiae here? Some probably think so—but as a musician trying to push my art forward and trying to achieve the best tone possible for each situation, these details are absolutely vital to me. The little things may not each make a big difference, but add them all together, and suddenly you're talking about a major change.

Strings

The string is the source. It's the root. It's the fountainhead. It's the wellspring. Okay, maybe that's all a bit melodramatic—they're just wires, right?

Maybe, maybe not!

Melodramatic as it may seem, the string really is where the instrument's vibrations originate, and we certainly must consider the impact of different types of strings on a guitar's tone. What the string is made of and how it's constructed are two big factors, but there are other things to consider as well, such as the gauge of the string, the string action or height, and more.

It should be completely simple. Just buy a pack of strings, slap them on your axe, tune up, and start wailing. But it's more complicated than that, starting with which strings you use. There are literally hundreds of choices on the market these days! Different types and constructions, different materials, different gauges, coated, uncoated, handmade, precision machine-wound, dozens of manufacturers—walk into any music store, visit any music retailer website, or open any catalog, and you'll see a seemingly endless list of options for something as seemingly simple as a set of guitar strings.

Let's explore some of those options and their tonal impact.

String Type

How a string is made, or its "type," will have a big impact on the tone it produces—at least when we're talking about the wound strings. For the "plain" or unwound strings, there is only one type: a single wire of smooth metal that is manufactured to a certain thickness/diameter or gauge.

The lower three strings (in some cases also the third, G string), however, are made in a different fashion. A round or hexagonal core wire is wound or wrapped with thinner wire to produce the desired outside diameter or gauge. The reason wound strings are used is because solid strings thick enough to produce the low frequencies required would be too stiff to play comfortably. By using a thinner core wound with additional wire, the rigidity and tension of the string can be managed while enough mass is available to produce low notes.

Round core wire is said to provide more contact for the windings and a softer, more flexible feel. Some players also feel that round-core wound strings sustain longer. Hex-core (six-sided) wire is said to provide a tighter connection between the core and the windings, with the six points of the core gripping the windings and preventing them from slipping. Today, most manufacturers use hex cores.

There are many extremely subtle factors that go into wound string construction; one example is the core-to-winding ratio. When creating a given string gauge, a thicker core with thinner windings will be stiffer, while a thinner core with heavier windings will be more flexible and easier to play. Adamas uses what they call *composite gauging*, where the core and the winding are the same gauge wire. This is said to produce greater volume and more precise tone.

Other wound string factors can include the winding direction, the wire tension, and more. But probably most significant from a tonal standpoint is the type of wire used for the winding; this is where truly perceivable tonal differences realistically begin to appear among various strings.

> **Round-wound.** Using polished round wire for the winding will result in the brightest tone. The disadvantage is that fingers sliding across the strings can result in squeaks and string noise. But, on the other hand, sliding the edge of a pick down a wound string produces a very cool noise.

> **Flat-wound.** Jazz players often prefer flat-wound strings, where the core wire is wrapped with a flat metal "ribbon" to create the desired gauge. Flat-wound strings have a warm, round tone, with darker top end compared to round-wounds. One advantage that flat-wounds have is that, because of their smooth surface—not only is the winding flat, but flat-wound strings are often polished for an even smoother feel—they don't produce squeaks or string noise when fingers slide across them.

> **Half-wound/ground-wound.** For tone and feel partway between round-wound and flat-wound, there are half-wound strings, sometimes known as *ground-wound* strings. These are created in one of three ways:

- One is to wrap the core with a winding that isn't quite circular but instead has a flattened top and bottom. In some cases, the flattened winding is created by compressing or squashing the winding wire slightly out of round; this is known as compression winding.

- A second method is to wrap the core with a half-round or semicircular wire, with the flat side out. This results in a string that looks and feels similar to a flat-wound but that has the same interaction between the core and windings as a round-wound string would.

- The third type isn't quite "half" round; in this case, a round-wound string is burnished or polished enough to remove the rounded tops from the winds, slightly flattening the string's surface. This is the brightest-sounding type of ground-wound string. There may be some finger squeaks and string noise, but not nearly as much as with a round-wound string.

Alloys and Metals

All electric guitar strings are made from a magnetic metal or magnetic alloy of one sort or another; that's how a guitar's pickups are able to "sense" the motion of the string and convert it into electricity. (Yes, it is possible that an "electric" guitar might solely use piezo pickups and therefore not require magnetic pickups, but in practice nearly all electric guitars use magnetic pickups.) The type of metal a string is made out of will have a big impact on its "electrified" tone. Some metals and alloys produce a fuller, darker tone, while others produce a very bright tone. In general, the harder the metal, the brighter the tone.

> ▷ **Plain strings and wound string cores.** Virtually all plain (unwound) electric guitar strings as well as the cores of virtually all wound strings are made from tin-plated Swedish steel, which has excellent magnetic properties.

> ▷ **Nickel.** Nickel is a fairly soft metal, so it will have a warmer, thicker tone. It will also cause less fret wear, though the strings will wear more when they contact the frets.

> ▷ **Nickel-plated steel.** The majority of wound electric guitar strings feature nickel-plated steel winding wires. Nickel-plated steel provides a balanced tone, with good brightness and durability; the thin nickel "cushion" helps reduce fret wear compared to plain steel.

> ▷ **Stainless steel.** Stainless steel is a hard metal and will produce a bright, lively tone. It will also wear the guitar's frets the most.

> ▷ **Chrome-plated steel.** Sometimes used for flat-wound string windings, chrome plating offers a hard, oxidation-resistant surface for the string. Some players enjoy the smoother feel (even smoother than other flat-wound strings) and slightly brighter sound (still much darker than a round-wound string), while others find the chrome plating makes the strings feel stiffer than comparable strings of other alloys, at least until the chrome strings are played in.

> ▷ **Gold-plated steel.** Since gold is quite a soft metal, it provides a warm, round complement to the steel, with a smooth feel. The gold plating is said to protect the steel from corrosion and to extend string life, and many players find that gold-plated strings feel nicely "broken in" right out of the box, with extended tonal life and longer sustain. Needless to say, the 24-carat gold plating makes these strings significantly more expensive than regular strings. Brian May from Queen has a signature set of gold-plated strings from Optima and is said to rely on them exclusively.

> ▷ **Titanium.** Manufacturers such as Ernie Ball have introduced strings made from titanium, a metal with the strength of steel but at a much lighter weight. It is said to prevent string breakage, to reduce string slippage, and to stay in tune longer than a similar steel-based string.

One last thing to consider as far as metal and alloy go: With strings, you just might get what you pay for. That's not to say you need to buy the most expensive strings to get great tone. Rather, rumors circulate that very cheap imported strings may not be made from the same quality alloy or metal as those made by domestic string manufacturers. This is a difficult one to address, as there's no way for an end user to know what the true metals being used are; still, if a string set seems too cheap, there's a chance what *seems* to be true may just *be* true. Ultimately, the only way to tell is to buy the strings, install them, and see what happens to the tone and playability of the guitar. For my money, I prefer to stay with known reputable manufacturers (though there is no guarantee where they are having their strings manufactured or what is being used to make them).

Cryogenic Strings

A number of manufacturers are offering so-called *cryogenic* strings. What's the deal; does putting the strings in the freezer really have an effect on the strings and their tone?

For one thing, we're not talking about sticking the strings in a Frigidaire—the cold we're talking about goes way past ice cubes and frozen pizza. Cryogenic strings are actually cooled down to −318 or −320 degrees Fahrenheit using liquid nitrogen and kept at that temperature for up to 15 hours. Then they are warmed back up to room temperature over another period of 15 hours or so. This process is called *tempering* the strings, and it does have a metallurgical basis in fact. The effects of tempering include refined grain structures in the metal, reduction in stresses in the metal, reduction in austenite (a crystallized form of iron or iron alloy that results from heating), and increased elasticity, pitch stability, and durability. The idea is that the string will stay in tune better and will retain its tone longer after visiting the deep freeze.

Fresh out of the pack, a set of cryogenic strings may be a bit brighter than the equivalent strings that haven't been super chilled. However, as the strings are played, the difference will become more apparent: Many players find that the cryo strings last longer, retain a brighter, "newer" sound for a longer time, and keep their tune better.

Coated Strings

Since the invention of the first instrument string, players and manufacturers have been on a quest for longer-lasting strings—strings that would retain their brightness and intonation for an extended length of time. Cryogenic strings have certainly been a step in the right direction, at least as far as longer-lasting brightness. (See the previous section.)

But cryogenics can't address two of the biggest enemies of guitar strings: oxidation from humidity in the air and the finger crud (that's the scientific term) that naturally builds up between the windings during the course of playing. The biggest advance toward oxidation-resistant strings has been coatings applied to the wound strings. Elixir launched the first coated strings with their Polyweb fiber coating, and manufacturers including GHS, DR, Black Diamond, D'Addario, Cleartone, Ernie Ball, Aurora, and more have followed suit with their own coated strings, using materials including enamel and others to protect the wound strings.

The ongoing search has been for the thinnest possible coating—one that would impact the tone and feel of the string the least, compared to a similar uncoated string. Two examples of ultra-thin coatings are Elixir's Nanoweb and DR's K3 coatings.

Some players find coated strings to feel too different from uncoated strings and also find them to have a duller sound than uncoated strings. Others enjoy the smoother feel of the coated wound strings and are willing to trade off a slight loss of brightness at the very beginning against longer bright tone—few would dispute that coated strings do maintain a consistent tone for longer than uncoated. Most coated-string manufacturers claim a usable string life of three to five times that of uncoated strings.

String Gauge

String diameter is measured in thousandths of an inch; the diameter of a string is referred to as its *gauge*. Sets of guitar strings are referenced by the diameter of the high E string. In other words, a player might say that he or she prefers "nines" or "tens," referring to sets where the high E is .009 inch or .010 inch. Strings are also referred to as *light, heavy, medium*, and so on, with most manufacturers subscribing to fairly standard delineations (though the names each manufacturer uses vary):

▷ Super Light—.008" to .038"

▷ Extra Light—.009" to .042"

▷ Light—.010" to .046"

▷ Regular/Medium—.011" to .050"

▷ Heavy—.012" to .052"

▷ Extra Heavy—.013" to .056"

Manufacturers may also package custom gauges together, such as "light top/heavy bottom," where lighter unwound strings are combined with heavier wound strings.

It stands to reason that the bigger the string, the bigger the tone. And many players would agree that this has been their experience. But exceptions abound—no one would ever accuse ZZ Top's Billy Gibbons of having a thin sound, yet, by all reports, he relies on some of the skinniest strings available—.007s or .008s. Then there are those, including David Grissom, Joe Bonamassa, and others, who go for .011s—and even those mighty-fingered souls who go for .12s or .013s, such as Stevie Ray Vaughan—and trust those heavy wires to be the source of their thick tone. Jazz players typically run .013 sets on their archtops for a very thick, clean tone—but it must be remembered that there is little string bending in most traditional jazz.

The reality probably falls somewhere smack in the middle of the "bigger is better" ideology: All things being equal, a thicker string will sound bigger than a thinner string. So there may be some difference between the tone of .009s and .010s, but it may not be a huge difference. To state the obvious: The greater the difference in the size of the strings, the more likely there will be a greater tonal difference. So there may be a difference between .009s and .010s, but there will be a bigger difference between .009s and .011s or between .008s and .012s.

The tradeoff, of course, is that heavier strings are harder for some players to manage. And very heavy strings may challenge the stability of less-than-robust guitars.

String Action and Tone

How a guitar is set up will affect how the strings vibrate. Set the string action too low or with improper relief, and the strings can buzz and rattle against the frets. This will obscure the tone and reduce sustain. Shorter-scale guitars in particular, such as Les Pauls, seem to get "plinky" when the strings are set too low, killing sustain and tone. Higher action results in "purer" tone, with longer sustain. The tradeoff is that higher action is more difficult to play, and at higher settings it may affect intonation.

Low action is easier to play, especially for certain styles and for those players with a lighter touch. Still, with low action, the vibrational arc of the strings is limited by the proximity to the frets. Also, even those with a light touch when practicing can ramp up how hard they play when they hit the stage or when going for maximum dynamic impact.

Many players take the approach of setting up their guitar with the lowest possible action without buzzing, for ease of playing. But for maximum tone, it might be worth trying the opposite: Set the strings as high as possible without impacting playability—being sure to allow a bit of time to adapt to the new string height before making a final decision. The less the strings are buzzing and rattling on the strings, the longer they will sustain and the better the tone will be.

Note that when raising the action of a guitar, it may also be necessary to correct the intonation settings at the bridge and to adjust the pickup height(s) accordingly (although leaving the pickups set lower can sometimes open up the tone and may reduce magnetic drag on the strings).

Cables

Want to start a furor online? Just open up a forum topic discussing the comparative sound of guitar cables and then stand back and watch the fireworks fly. Some players don't hear a difference when changing cables; others feel that different cables can sound vastly different.

Personally, I fall on the side of those who feel that cables can indeed sound very different. There are two reasons for my opinion. The first dates to my tenure as the senior technical editor at *Keyboard* magazine. (What's a guitar player doing working at *Keyboard*? That's a long story....) I was given the assignment to test various cables, from super-cheap RadioShack specials to high-end boutique cables. First, we conducted a listening test with a panel of editors. Then I abused the cables—drove over them with a car, slammed them in a pickup tailgate, coiled/uncoiled/coiled them numerous times, and so on. Here's what we found: When the cables were brand-new, fresh out of the package, we couldn't reliably discern a difference. But once the cables had been "broken in" with a little abuse, we *could* hear a difference. Now, the other thing to note here is that these listening tests were done with line-level signals, which are more robust than guitar-level signals. You can only expect that the effects would be more dramatic with the low-level guitar signals.

Second, there are electronic variables at work, even in something as simple as a guitar cable. The problem is that when connecting different cables between a certain guitar and amp you may hear differences, but connect the same cables between a different guitar and amp, and you may *not* hear differences. Makes it sort of difficult to make a definitive statement, yes?

Three factors can affect how much of a difference you will hear among various guitar cables: Most guitarists are aware that there is capacitance in a guitar cable, which basically acts in the same way that a tone control does in a guitar—it sucks out high end. The more capacitance, the less high end gets through. But few guitarists recognize how much impact the output impedance of the guitar and the input impedance of the amplifier can make (assuming a regular passive guitar pickup and not an active pickup, and that there's nothing between the amp and the guitar but the cable).

If the amp's input impedance is low, it can load down a pickup and make it sound dull, as well as suck up output level from the pickup. This can also affect how effective a guitar's tone control is; if the amp is loading the pickups, it will also reduce how well the tone control functions. High amp input impedance reduces loading and improves the function of the tone control, but it does increase the effects of cable capacitance and may lead to more noise and RF (*radio frequency*) pickup. Likewise, high guitar output impedance increases the effects of cable capacitance—and most passive guitar pickups are high impedance. Table 12.1 shows the way it all breaks down.

In the first two instances in Table 12.1, you won't hear much difference if you switch among various cables. You wouldn't want to subject your tone to the third instance at all, so it doesn't matter what cable you use. In the fourth instance—which, fortunately for us, is the standard passive guitar pickup to tube amp that most of us enjoy—you may hear differences between cables, depending on the cables and their capacitance.

In the real world, these are some of the things that can determine how much a cable will affect your tone:

▷ **Cable capacitance.** Every shielded cable, by nature, has a certain amount of capacitance, which makes it act as a high-frequency tone filter. Some manufacturers will publish a spec for the amount of capacitance (in picofarads, or pF) per foot for their cable, especially if you are buying raw or bulk cable and soldering up your own guitar cords.

Table 12.1   Guitar Impedance, Amp Impedance, and Cable Capacitance

Guitar Impedance	Amp Impedance	Sonic Effects
Low	Low	Cable capacitance will not have much effect—various cables won't change the sound much. Guitar tone controls may not have much effect.
Low	High	With guitar volume all the way up, same as above. As guitar volume is turned down, cable capacitance will have more effect, and the tone will get darker.
High	Low	The amp will substantially load the guitar's pickups, reducing level and killing tone.
High	High	The amp will not load the pickups, allowing maximum level and high end to get through. However, cable capacitance can have a major effect on the tone.

▷ **Cable length.** It only makes sense that if every cable has a certain amount of capacitance, that the longer a given cable is, the higher its total capacitance will be.

▷ **Coil cable versus straight cable.** Coil cables may look retro and cool, but they tend to have higher capacitance than straight cables.

▷ **Heavy-duty versus lightweight cable.** In many cases (but not all, by any means), heavy-duty cables have higher capacitance.

Given these facts, what can you do to maximize signal integrity? For the best signal integrity, a high-quality buffer amp will isolate the guitar pickups from the amp, solving the problem (though many buffers also color the tone). If you don't want to use a buffer, then using a straight cable, keeping it as short as possible, and choosing a cable with the lowest possible capacitance will all help to ensure that the most level and high end will get through from the guitar pickups to the amplifier.

But wait! Beyond all of the highly compelling objective facts we've looked at, there's something else to consider—the *subjective* side of things. You may not *like* the sound of your guitar and amp combination when all of the high frequencies are getting passed through. In fact, you may prefer the tone of a higher-capacitance cable because it attenuates or pulls back the brightness slightly. In fact, most of the vintage tones that we all grew up loving in concert and on records were the result of a high pickup impedance feeding a high amplifier impedance through a coiled cord that probably had quite high capacitance. The amp wasn't loading the pickups, but the cable was probably sponging up some of the highs and rounding out the tone.

Given the above—that maximum transfer of high end through a cable may not be ideal for some players' ears—it makes sense to evaluate the cable that you're using for your guitar. You may find that you enjoy the clarity and brightness that an expensive, low-capacitance boutique cable provides, or you may find that you prefer the darker tone that a coiled or high-capacitance cable serves up. You may even find that you like a more a balanced-sounding cable, but that you need a longer-length cable to get exactly the tone you want. We're getting pretty tweaky here, but many players can hear the difference, particularly if the guitar and amp being used are up to the task of making the difference audible. Take a look at some of the online photos and videos of Eric Johnson's pedalboard and amp rig. Think that all those coils of extra cable length are there because he can't find a shorter cable?

Wireless

One of the negatives of playing electric guitar is that you're always tethered—there's always a cable tying you to your rig onstage. Always, that is, unless you're using a wireless system. Many players find the draw of the freedom that wireless systems provide to be irresistible. Nothing to tie you down as you freely roam around and cavort about the stage…

But all freedom has a price, and with wireless systems, the price was often compromised tone. Players complained of artifacts from the companders (compressor/expanders) that were used to reduce noise. They also complained of lost highs or boosted highs or thin tones.

Fortunately, technology marches on, and wireless technology has come forward light years from where it was before. In particular, digital technology has made a big difference in how wireless systems perform. It's no longer necessary to use companders to control noise, and, when using a good-quality system, tonal changes have largely been eliminated.

One of the other big "gotchas" with wireless systems has long been that the interaction between the guitar and amplifier was removed, resulting in a "disconnected" feel for some players. (Check out the earlier section on cables, impedance, and capacitance for some of the reasons that might be behind this.) But even this has been addressed by new technologies. For example, Radial Engineering's Dragster can supply amp-input-like characteristics that make playing through a wireless much more natural feeling. And the new Line 6 wireless systems even feature cable simulation, where you can dial in the "length" of cable you want to play through.

But even with those technologies, many players still prefer cables, both for the feel and for the sound. And though manufacturers keep claiming that their new wireless units sound "just like a cable," not all players are convinced. It comes down to three questions: Can you hear a difference? Can you feel a difference when playing? And if the answer to either of the preceding questions is "yes," is the tradeoff worth it for the untethered mobility that wireless can offer?

Table 12.2   The Little Things Tonal Factors

Tone Factor	Tonal Contribution
Pick size and shape	None to speak of or very subtle
Pick thickness, texture, and material	Subtle to minor
String type	Subtle to minor
String gauge	Subtle to minor
String action	Subtle to minor
Cable capacitance	Subtle to minor
Guitar/amp/cable interaction	Subtle to minor
Cable versus wireless	Subtle to minor

Modeling and Software

STRANGE AS IT MAY SEEM WITH ALL THE ANTI-ESTABLISHMENT rebellion and proclaimed independence and free thinking of rock 'n roll and other musical styles, guitar players are a highly conservative bunch—at least when it comes to gear. Yes, there are the innovators among us, but with very few notable exceptions; even the innovators rely on many of the same tried-and-true tools that the rest of us have been using for decades. Has there really been serious change in the form or function of the electric guitar since the late 1940s or early 1950s? To look at the selection in most music stores and at the axes being played on concert stages, you probably wouldn't think so. The standards of the day remain Fender Teles and Strats and Gibson Les Pauls and ES-335s, or one of the numerous variations or "tributes" from other manufacturers or boutique builders. In fact, take a look at the guitar wall in any retail store, page through a gear catalog, or jump onto a guitar website. Many of the instruments you find there will be reissues of models from the 1950s and early 1960s, the so-called Golden Era of the electric guitar.

Where there *has* been innovation, it has often come in the form of evolution rather than revolution, or as variations on the established themes. For example, some builders use synthetic body or neck materials, but the basic form is still the same (and most players will still prefer a good ol' wooden instrument anyway). Amps and effects? The story is no different there. It's Marshall- and Fender-style amps all day long (and to be completely accurate, the early Marshalls were based on Fender amps), with the occasional cascaded gain Mesa/Boogie for variety. (And even the innovative cascaded gain preamp of the Boogies was based on modified Fender circuits.)

There's no denying it; we like our guitar tones traditional. We'll progressively add more gain for certain styles, scoop the mids, or add some chorus or delay, but ultimately, most of today's guitar tones harken directly back to Jimi Hendrix, the Beatles, Chuck Berry, Charlie Christian, Wes Montgomery, the triumvirate of Kings (B.B., Freddie, and Albert), and other mid-century groundbreakers. And not only are the tones directly descended from those artists, but we're still using the same technology to get there, mostly vacuum tubes. (And everyone knows new old stock vacuum tubes are better than modern tubes, right?) This isn't an indictment; what works is what works, and there's no doubt that certain combinations work very well for specific styles of music.

Given this fixation on the tried and true and the lack of interest among many guitar players to put their trust in new technologies or to break new tonal ground, imagine the plight facing manufacturers who first introduced digital modeling technology to the guitar world! To give them credit, the innovators in the digital modeling world, such as Roland and Line 6, followed by computer-based software modeling proponents, such as IK Multimedia and Native Instruments, have stood strong on the road despite the apathy of many tone hounds. But it's paid off big for those companies. Guitarists have begun to recognize the potential of modeling-based rigs and to see the benefits of going digital, such as smaller-sized rigs, lighter-weight gear, more tonal flexibility, more detailed control, preset storage and recall, manageable stage and studio volume, easy system integration —without microphones—in the studio and onstage, and more. Plus, in blind "taste tests," it's gotten to the point where, in a mix, it's very tough—and often impossible—to tell a modeled sound from a "real" sound.

Though there are still holdouts, most guitarists have come to appreciate the benefits of modeling—if not for their complete rig, then for certain parts of it, such as effects processors. Players in cover bands who strive to exactly copy all the different tones in the songs they play, in particular, have a lot to gain from modeled processors. Many guitarists in worship and praise bands, where volume control is often a major issue, have also turned to modelers. And, because many modeled processors and amps are quite affordable, they have become very popular with beginners as well. Interestingly, there has also been a move among higher-end guitarist toward advanced modelers, such as the Fractal Audio Axe-FX, especially for live stage use, whether just for effects or for complete effects and amp simulation.

What It Is

Modeling is a digital/software technology that uses DSP (*digital signal processing*) and mathematical algorithms and formulas to re-create and emulate certain conditions and processes. It can be used for everything from predicting the weather to simulating dangerous scientific experiments to simulating the sound of a guitar amplifier. For example, an algorithm might calculate the response of a particular vacuum tube, which can then be combined with other algorithms to create an emulation of the complete sound of a specific amplifier model. When a digitized guitar signal is passed through those algorithms running on a computer or dedicated DSP chips, the output signal will more or less resemble the sound of that same guitar run through that amplifier—less if the algorithms aren't very good or if they aren't detailed enough, more if the algorithms accurately represent the response of the amplifier.

There are many things for the programmers to take into account, and few of them are static. In a "real" amp, things change as the volume and gain are turned up, as the speaker and cabinet begin to resonate, as the tubes are pushed into harmonic distortion, as the power supply sags under heavy transient action, and so on. It's a complex business, and all of that detail has to be balanced against what is required of the available DSP power, whether it comes from an integrated circuit chip in a dedicated standalone box or from the processor in a Mac or Windows PC running a piece of computer software. There's only so much DSP power available in any system, and the software code necessary to create the model must "fit" within those confines.

Early models were, shall we say, less than convincing to some listeners and players, though the advent of the technology was exciting stuff! Modern models are extremely detailed and getting better all the time, and even tone-obsessed artists have begun adopting them for the studio and the stage. It's tough to beat the price, convenience, and versatility. The converters required to change the analog guitar voltage to a digital signal that can be processed by the modeler have also improved greatly, allowing all the dynamics and detail the guitar is putting out to be accurately used to drive the algorithms.

There are three different types of modeling hardware processors and software modelers in use today: guitars, effects, and amps.

Guitars

Once the output voltage from a guitar pickup is converted to a digital signal, the data making up that signal—it really is just data at that point, a stream of ones and zeroes—can be manipulated easily. Usually a piezo pickup mounted to the bridge or a special magnetic pickup mounted near the bridge is used to provide the uncolored "base" signal. Algorithms are used to perform calculations on that digital signal and to change the captured tone from the pickup into other tones. For example, the modeled characteristics of a humbucker could be applied to the raw signal, or modeled single-coil characteristics or modeled P-90 characteristics could be applied to it. Then the desired modeled body resonances and vibration characteristics can be applied to the signal. The result is that the output from the guitar's piezo pickup can be made to sound like a Les Paul, a Stratocaster, a Tele, even a 12-string or an acoustic guitar or banjo. Or, other types of algorithms could be applied to create synthesizer-type sounds.

Effects

Algorithms can also be used to emulate the response of various effects, from vintage distortion boxes to tape echoes. These types of modeled effects might be built into another piece of equipment, in a computer-based software processor or plug-in, or in a standalone stompbox. The beauty is that the modeler can emulate all of the good or "signature" aspects of an effect, such as the warmth added by a tape echo, the harmonic distortion produced by a vintage fuzz box containing transistors that are no longer available, or even the tonal effects of worn-out or aged components.

The manufacturer analyzes the response and operation of the original effect and sometimes even all of the original components in the device and then creates mathematical representations of those components, the control parameters, and the tonal capabilities, responses, and imperfections. These mathematical models are then coded into the stompbox circuits or computer software program.

Modeling stompboxes—particularly delays—have become standard issue for many guitarists, but there are also rackmount and floor-based multi-effects units. The beauty of a modeling multi-effect is that it can change its personality instantly, from a warm, liquid analog chorus model to a crystal-clear digital delay with a single button press, then switch to a vintage fuzz with another button press. Some multi-effects modelers have more than 100 different modeled effects inside, from vintage to modern, from conventional to whacked out. And all those modeled effects choices can be chained together to create a massive effects rig with a number of effects operating at once, all within one compact, easy-to-manage unit. The convenience, control, flexibility, and tone-building power are almost impossible to beat. Basically, you have way more effects at your fingertips (or toes) than you could ever mount on even the largest pedalboard—and even if you could mount that many effects on a pedalboard, it would be unmanageable, to say nothing of it certainly being a tone sucker. Besides that, the cost of even the most expensive modeled multi-effects is a fraction of what it would cost to purchase a similar array of individual boxes—and it's a heck of a lot easier to move a single multi-effects box to a gig than to move a huge crate containing more than 100 pedals! And, many modeling multi-effects let you configure the effects in any order you want or need. Want the wah pedal before the fuzz? No problem. Rather have it after the fuzz? Also no problem. Try that with a pedalboard without using a sophisticated (and expensive) switching system.

Finally, many modeled multi-effects devices also include built-in amp and speaker modeling, so you can run them straight into a PA system or studio mixer. This makes them great for live performances with a minimal rig (and no microphone hassles) and convenient for making studio recordings without having to crank up an amp to loud volume levels.

Amps

An amplifier is a complex system comprising an input section that places a certain load on the guitar and affects its output and tone, a preamp for bringing the tiny output from the guitar pickup up to a more usable level or even driving it into distortion, an EQ stack that shapes the tone, a power amplifier that raises the preamp output to a level capable of driving a speaker, a power supply that makes the whole thing go, tubes or transistors that comprise the various amplification stages, the speaker assembly, the speaker cabinet, the output transformer, and more. Modeling of all those different parts of the system must take into account not only how each individual section functions but also how they all interact and influence one another.

Careful analysis and mathematical calculations can take all of this into account. The one exception, where modeled amps are concerned, seems to be the input stage. The initial input stage—the first components the signal hits when the guitar cable plugs into the amp—affects the tone of the guitar, but more importantly, where modeling is concerned, it affects the *feel* of the guitar as you play it through the modeled amp. And if the feel isn't right, the model will never *sound* convincing—there's a direct connection there that must be established. For this reason, the analog circuitry used to drive the device doing the modeling has to be right. For modeled amps and hardware boxes, the manufacturer can build in whatever analog circuitry is necessary to get the loading of the guitar correct. But with computer-based software modelers, the manufacturer usually has no control over what box the guitarist will use to connect the guitar to the computer and how its input stage performs. Where the audio interface doesn't provide an optimal connection for the guitar, there are manufacturers, such as Paul Reed Smith/Waves and MOTU, who make interface boxes that connect between the guitar and the modeler and that establish an amp-like input load.

Form Factor

There are two basic forms that a modeling device can take: either a dedicated, standalone hardware box or a piece of software (which might either run standalone or as a plug-in within another piece of software). There are benefits to each type.

Hardware

The biggest benefit of a standalone, hardware modeling device is familiarity. If, for example, you're a manufacturer designing a standalone modeling delay pedal, it can be made to appear exactly like a conventional analog or digital delay. The same shape, same control set, same functionality. The only difference might be the addition of an extra knob or two (say, for selecting the model type or for controlling a simulated characteristic of the original box) and maybe (or maybe not) an LED readout. From the guitarist's standpoint, just plug the guitar into one side, connect the output to the amplifier, and use it like any other stompbox. Now, deep inside, a modeled effects box is technically nothing like an analog delay and really not even anything like a conventional digital delay. But all of those deeper aspects are hidden away; to the user, a modeling box is as plug-and-play easy as an analog box. The same is true whether you're modeling a vintage delay or you're creating a standalone modeling amplifier—all that "tech" stuff can be hidden away inside, while on the surface you're presented with the usual array of control knobs and features (with, as mentioned earlier, the addition of an extra knob or two to handle the modeling functions.)

The second big benefit of a standalone piece of hardware is that it's portable. You don't need a computer to run it; just grab it and take it to the gig, rehearsal room, or studio, plug it in, and start making music.

Software

It's true that even with a laptop computer, modeling software isn't quite as portable or as plug-and-play easy as a standalone box. In truth, that's the big weakness—maybe "limitation" is a better word—of software-based modelers: You need a computer to run them. While some guitarists are comfortable taking a laptop and audio interface on stage and to rehearsals, others aren't. Plus, unless you bring along your own powered speakers, you have to depend on plugging the output from the computer into the PA system. For guitarists who are accustomed to being responsible for their own tone from strings to speakers, turning over that control—not just out front for the audience, but also for the sound you hear on stage back through the monitors—may seem like a risky proposition.

Beyond those physical issues with using computer-based software modeling for stage or rehearsal, there's another problem that can rear its ugly head: latency. Latency affects any digital audio system or device, though some deal with it better than others. Here's the deal: It takes a certain amount of time for a digital device to convert an analog audio voltage (such as a guitar signal) into a stream of ones and zeros. Then it takes a certain amount of time for the digital device to process the signal. And, once the digital signal has passed through device, it takes a certain amount of time to convert it back to an analog voltage that can be amplified and used to drive a speaker. Now, with modern digital gear, these three time requirements can be dropped down to very small amounts. Roundtrip, all the way through a computer-based system and back out, we're seeing latencies as low as a few milliseconds.

To put latency into perspective, a millisecond is about the amount of time it takes for sound to travel one foot through the air. So, for example, a latency of three milliseconds is equivalent to standing about three feet farther away from your amp. This is much improved over just a few years ago, when latencies were two or three times longer—there was an audible delay between when you plucked a string and when the sound came out of the speaker. In many cases, the tradeoff for low latency is increased demand on the computer, which may mean that the modeling software can do less than it could at higher latency settings.

Still, a latency of even a few milliseconds seems to bother some players. The delay isn't audible at that time length, but there seems to be a feel difference—a physical disconnect between the guitar and the end sound coming from the computer.

But there are big advantages to software. For one thing, the user interface—the actual screen appearance of the program and how you interact with it—can allow for unique control possibilities as well as access to an array of parameters that can provide in-depth control not available in a standalone box, or even access to extended parameters that can take the model to places far beyond where the original box could go. Software is also significantly more configurable than hardware; the signal path can be made completely malleable and can be twisted, split, combined, and reordered with just a few mouse clicks. Want six chorus pedals in a row? Done. Want six chorus pedals in parallel? Done! (Well, maybe—it depends on the software you are using.) Whether you have a taste for the conventional or a yearning to explore new tonal vistas, high-powered modeling software will arguably give you the widest array of possibilities of any type of gear.

More advantages? Software can be updated with new features and upgraded with new amp and effects models, bugs can be fixed, and performance can be optimized, all with the release of a simple, downloadable new version. Likewise, as computer hardware increases in speed and power and RAM drops in price, the software can be updated to efficiently use that increased DSP power and memory space. Plus, the software can be integrated with other software applications, such as DAW (*digital audio workstation*) software, to extend its capabilities. And, several manufacturers have come out with dedicated foot controllers/guitar-friendly audio interfaces that make operating computer-based modeling software seem much more natural—similar to running a multi-effects floorboard or an analog pedalboard.

The Sound

So, modeling offers a variety of benefits and a few tradeoff compromises, whether you're using a hardware box or a piece of software running on a computer. The big question is, does a modeler deliver the sound that guitarists want, and does it re-create the feel of the real thing? Opinions definitely vary. Some players feel that digitally modeled effects and amps sound sterile, that they don't have the "life" of a "real" piece of gear. Others find them to feel stiff, as if the guitar is disconnected from the modeled effect or amp. Other players have no problem plugging into a modeled box and getting exactly the sound and feel they want. There are several factors that can go into this:

▷ **Preconceived notions.** Many players find it hard to let go of the idea that they're playing through and hearing a computer simulation, whether from a dedicated box or from an actual computer. Their ears and fingers can't get past the preformed assessments that their minds have made. If you want to objectively try out a modeler, the only real way to do it is "blind." Have someone else plug you in, without knowing what you're hearing or playing through. Is it an amp or is it a modeler? What clues you in either direction? Do the differences really matter?

▷ **The speaker system.** Some modeling devices are intended to be used with regular guitar amps or at least guitar-style cabinets; others are intended for full-range speaker systems, such as PAs or studio monitors. Some can be switched for use through an amp or use through a full-range system. Matching the output settings to the sound system can make a huge difference.

▷ **The sound you want.** Modelers can certainly do the sound of a '50s Tweed tube amp on the verge of breakup, but for many players (including me), this isn't where they're the strongest or the most convincing. In many cases, modelers are better at more modern sounds, more distorted sounds, and more effected sounds.

▷ **The context.** Are you hearing the guitar sound in isolation or is it in a mix? This can work both ways; what sounds like a thick, present sound in isolation may get lost in a mix. Conversely, a sound that seems artificial when heard by itself may sound totally "real" in a mix.

▷ **Who's hearing it.** Guitarists can be a picky bunch—and rightfully so. The sound of a player's instrument is what it's all about. Still, in the grand scheme of things, the little things we hear as players will be completely inaudible to almost everyone else. Even other guitarists—until (or unless) you tell them—will in most cases never know the difference.

These perceptions, preconceived notions, factors, and contexts have to be weighed against the other advantages and disadvantages of modelers. Like any other piece of gear or category of gear, it comes down to what you want and need. Modelers are perfect for some players. Other players can't stand them. Interestingly, few players fall in the middle—modeling may be the most polarizing tonal tool in the guitarist's arsenal. Still, with advances in technology—and declines in the availability and quality of things such as vacuum tubes—you can only expect that modeling will get better and better and will become more and more a major force in the guitar tone world.

Modeling Software in the Studio

Our primal tendency as guitarists is just to plug in and wail—whether we're using a tube amp or modeling software running on a computer. But, in the studio—if we step back a little bit—there are other ways that we can use guitar amp/effects modeling, especially modeling software running within a digital audio workstation, such as Steinberg Cubase, Cakewalk SONAR, Avid Pro Tools, Apple Logic, Ableton Live, or MOTU Digital Performer. Here are just a few possibilities:

▶ Plug in and use the modeling software in place of your amp, recording the output straight to a track. (Okay, that one's obvious.)

▶ Record your amplifier with a microphone. Use the effects portion of your modeling software to provide any reverb, delay, chorus, or other effects you might want. The effects in modeling software are optimized for working with guitar tones—they're often ideal for processing the sound of a real amp recorded with a microphone as well as for processing the software's own modeled amp sounds.

▶ Here's one that allows you to use your regular guitar amp, but you don't have to mike up a speaker. If your amp has a direct line out, record it straight into your computer (without using a mic on the speaker). Or, if your amp doesn't have a line out, use a load box to reduce the speaker-level output to a line-level output your computer can digest. (Caution: *Never* plug a speaker output straight into anything but a load box or a speaker—the high speaker level will destroy any other components.) The direct sound of the line-level recording of your amp without a speaker or mic will probably sound pretty awful—thin, harsh, and fizzy. But, your modeling software has built-in speaker simulation. Turn off the software's amp and effects and just use the speaker simulation to process the direct amp sound. *Voila*—you've got the sound of an amp through a speaker cabinet, without having to mess with a microphone.

▶ Record the guitar signal dry, using a direct box. Now you can insert your modeling software on the track after the fact (during mixdown) and change the sound to any amp or effects you want. You're free to select exactly the sound you want, without having to commit to a specific sound while recording.

▶ Record your guitar signal dry, using a direct box. Now copy that track to one or more additional tracks. Apply a different amp/effects sound to each track (say, Fender with reverb on one track, Marshall with chorus on another, dry Vox on another). Blend those different tones together to create a massive, layered final tone.

▶ Apply your guitar amp/effects modeler to other tracks in your recording, such as drums, bass, keyboards, or even vocals. You'd be surprised how much energy just a little (really, just a *little*) amp distortion can add to a vocal or other sound.

▶ Let your imagination run wild! The beauty of software is that you can experiment to your heart's content without ruining your original recording. Just be sure to save a backup copy before you begin your experiments, so you can get back to where you began if things aren't working out.

Iconic Guitars

THOUGH EVERY MUSIC STORE ON THE PLANET seems to be stocked with piles of different guitar models from many different manufacturers, a few models stand out as time-tested icons—guitar models that have been in production for many years, have been used as the basis for many other guitar models from other manufacturers, and have emerged as standards that guitarists point to as progenitors of particular tones. Of interest is that the majority of these models are the same ones that have been around since the dawn of the electric guitar—and are the original ones that were designed by Leo Fender and Ted McCarty/Gibson, with a few by other innovators of the early electric guitar.

Let's begin by examining the "Big 3," the electric guitar models that are probably the most immediately recognized by guitar players—and even by the non-guitar-playing public! More guitar models by more manufacturers have been created based on these three original guitar models than perhaps all other guitar models combined: the Gibson Les Paul Standard and the Fender Telecaster and Stratocaster.

Fender Telecaster

Let's start at the beginning, with the first production electric guitar to come out of the gates, and more than six decades later, still one of the great examples of iconic tone. This is a prime example that just goes to show, new and complicated doesn't always rule—when it comes to tone, well matured (like a fine wine or vintage single malt) and elegantly simple can definitely be the ticket!

In the guitar world, it doesn't get much more elegantly simple (or more well matured) than the Fender Telecaster: a few hunks of wood, two straight-ahead single-coil pickups, a switch and two control knobs, bent metal for the bridge plate, a few other bits and pieces of hardware—bolt it all together, and you have the formula for the world's first production solid-body electric guitar. Part of this simplicity and bolt-together modularity was due to Leo Fender's interests in affordable functionality and mass production and his desire for players to have the ability to quickly replace a broken or defective part by simply slapping on a new one—based on inspiration he took from how the Ford Model T was manufactured and serviced.

Yet, despite its simplicity and beautiful, no-nonsense functionality, the Telecaster is responsible for one of the world's iconic guitar tones: There's no mistaking that twang and bite, and there's no other guitar that quite delivers the same sound. Though nearly universally accepted as the prototypical country axe, the Tele has also found a home in the hands of well-known fusion players (Mike Stern), metal shredders (John 5), blues masters (Albert Collins), jazzers (Bill Frisell), rockers (Keith Richards and Bruce Springsteen), punkers (Joe Strummer), alt-rockers (Frank Black), and countless more, who have all made one version or another of the Telecaster a part of their personal tone.

While it is clearly the sum of the parts that make the Telecaster what it is, there are several keys to the Tele's iconic tone: the bolt-on neck design; the large metal bridge plate, which also houses the bridge pickup; the bridge pickup design, with a heavy metal base plate attached to the underside of the pickup; and the metal-enclosed neck pickup.

The result, with the bridge pickup, is a bright, clear sound, with plenty of upper midrange twang and lots of punchy bite that cuts right through even the densest mixes. With the neck pickup, the sound is less bright than, say, a Stratocaster; full, with warm roundness. Combine the two pickups for a chimey, twangy tone with attenuated midrange.

The Telecaster was first introduced as the Broadcaster in 1949, with the single-pickup Esquire released in 1950. (Trivia: Less than 50 of these guitars were made, and most ended up being replaced under warranty due to warped necks—there was no truss rod in the original release.) The dual-pickup version followed later that year, originally named the Broadcaster but quickly renamed the Telecaster after Gretsch claimed the Broadcaster name violated their trademark on the Broadkaster line of drums. (The guitars released between the Broadcaster and the official advent of the Telecaster are known as "Nocasters," since they have no model name on the headstock.) The Telecaster has been in continuous production since, with very little variation in the basic model, though many different models based on the original have come and gone through the decades.

A few changes have occurred though the years, such as the replacement of the original three bridge pieces (two strings per bridge piece) with six bridge pieces (one string per bridge piece), moving the truss rod adjustment from the heel of the neck (which required removing the neck from the body to make adjustments) to the end of the fingerboard behind the nut, and replacing the stamped bridge plate with bent-up sides with a flat bridge plate, though many of these changes have been reversed in various reissue and custom-shop models.

Table 14.1   Fender Telecaster Characteristics

Body	Alder, ash, or pine (very earliest vintage units).
Neck	Bolt on. Maple.
Scale length	25-1/2 inches.
Fingerboard	Maple or rosewood.
Fingerboard radius	7-1/4 inches (vintage). 9-1/2 inches (modern).
Frets	21 nickel-silver (vintage and modern). 22 nickel-silver (certain modern models).
Bridge pickup	Single-coil with no cover. Heavy metal base plate on bottom of pickup.
Neck pickup	Single-coil in metal cover.
Bridge	Bent or stamped metal bridge plate. Three bridge pieces (vintage). Six bridge pieces (modern). Most Teles come with "ashtray" metal bridge covers, which most players promptly remove and lose.
Tailpiece	Through-body stringing; metal ferrules in back of body to anchor strings. A few models were offered with Bigsby tailpieces.
Tuners	Six mini tuners on one side of headstock.
Finish	Nitrocellulose lacquer (vintage and certain modern models). Polyurethane or polyester (most modern models).
Electronics/controls	3-position pickup switch selects either bridge or neck pickup alone or both pickups together (modern wiring). Master volume. Master tone. Very early vintage guitars used a 3-position pickup switch that selected the bridge with the neck pickup blended in using the "tone" knob, the neck pickup alone, or the neck pickup through a heavy tone capacitor for a dark, bassy tone.
Variations	There have been many variations, reissues, Custom Shop, and signature models of the Telecaster released over the years, such as: Esquire—single bridge pickup, no neck pickup. Telecaster Thinline—semi-hollow body, neck and bridge humbuckers with separate volume and tone controls for each pickup. Telecaster Custom—neck humbucker. Telecaster Deluxe—neck and bridge humbuckers with separate volume and tone controls for each pickup.

Tele Tonemeisters

Andy Summers	Steve Morse	Steve Cropper	James Burton
Albert Lee	John 5	Keith Richards	Albert Collins
Brad Paisley	Roy Buchanan	Mike Stern	Danny Gatton
Bill Frisell	Joe Strummer	Frank Black	Vince Gill
Mike Campbell	Jerry Donahue	Ted Greene	Merle Haggard
Keith Urban	Robyn Hitchcock	Chrissie Hynde	Bruce Springsteen
Brent Mason	Steve Howe	Roy Nichols	Buck Owens
John Jorgenson	Pete Anderson	Don Rich	Robbie Robertson
Jimmy Page	Johnny Hiland	Will Ray	Arlen Roth
Clarence White	Marty Stuart	Pete Townshend	Redd Volkaert
Ray Flacke	Muddy Waters	Prince	Richie Kotzen
Scotty Anderson	G.E. Smith	Syd Barrett	Tom Morello
Waylon Jennings	Jimmy Bryant	George Harrison	Ed Bickert
Francis Rossie	Rick Parfitt	Jerry Reed	

Gibson Les Paul Standard

What could be more "rock star" than strapping on a Les Paul Standard, slinging it low, and jacking it into a Marshall stack on the verge of tube meltdown? Based on the solid-body electric guitar construction experiments of the legendary Les Paul, and brought to fruition by the always forward-thinking Ted McCarty at Gibson, the Les Paul, in one or another of its many incarnations, has been seen and heard in the hands of countless guitarists. Of those many Les Paul incarnations, from student to luxury models, arguably the most iconic one is the Les Paul Standard, a solid-body with a thick mahogany back and carved maple cap or top, a mahogany neck, and a rosewood fingerboard. Two humbucking pickups at the bridge and the neck positions capture the tone; in vintage models, these were the much sought-after PAF (*patent applied for*) pickups originally designed by Seth Lover. Various other pickups have also been used through the years. Today, '57 Classics (along the lines of the PAF) or Burstbuckers (unpotted PAF-style) are used.

It would be a tremendous task to catalog all of the Les Paul–based models and their variations—one that would require a large book of its own—so we'll confine our focus here to the Les Paul Standard. Let's take a look at how this model has evolved over the years, beginning with its immediate ancestor, the original Les Paul Model.

▷ **1952.** The Les Paul Model is introduced with a "goldtop" finish. No serial numbers. Two P-90 single-coil pickups. Floating trapeze bridge/tailpiece with strings wrapped *under* the bridge due to the shallow neck angle. Mahogany body. Two- or three-piece maple top. Mahogany neck. Mother-of-pearl inlay. Brazilian rosewood fingerboard. Early models had no neck binding. "Barrel" control knobs.

▷ **1953.** First serial numbers appear on the Les Paul Model. One-piece wraparound bridge/tailpiece. First appearance of Rhythm/Treble plate around pickup selector switch. Neck angle increased to three degrees to accommodate new bridge. Slightly shorter barrel control knobs.

▷ **1954.** Les Paul Model: Neck angle increased to four degrees to allow more downward adjustment of the guitar's bridge height.

▷ **1955.** Les Paul Model: Wraparound bridge/mounting studs changed slightly. Bridge pickup moved toward neck by 1/8 inch. First ABR-1 Tune-o-matic bridges with separate stop tailpieces appear in the fall of 1955, along with "bonnet" control knobs.

▷ **1956.** Les Paul Model: Tone capacitors changed to Sprague "Bumblebee" models.

▷ **1957.** Les Paul Model: Introduction of PAF humbucking pickups, which were designed for Gibson in 1955 by Seth Lover.

▷ **1958.** Les Paul Standard replaces Les Paul Model. By mid-1958, finish changed from goldtop to cherry red sunburst. Two-piece center-seamed maple top. Back of guitar changed from brown to cherry red. Figuring on maple tops ranges from plain to "flamey."

▷ **1959.** Wider frets. Jack plate changed to square-cornered shape.

▷ **1960.** Due to lack of demand, single-cutaway Les Paul models discontinued. Replaced by the double-cutaway Les Paul SG Standard and other double-cutaway variations.

▷ **1963.** Model name changed to SG Standard, ending the "Golden Era" of the Les Paul.

▷ **1968.** The single-cutaway Les Paul Standard returns with a 1956 goldtop reissue. Indian rosewood fingerboard. Long neck tenon. Sprague "Black Beauty" tone capacitors. Chrome plating replaces nickel plating on hardware. "Reflector top" control knobs.

▷ **1969.** Gibson purchased by Norlin. Wider peghead. By mid-1969, multiple-piece maple tops. Short neck tenon. Laminated "pancake" back made from multiple slabs of mahogany with a layer of maple on top. Volute added to reinforce the neck-to-headstock joint to prevent the headstock from cracking or breaking off.

▷ **1971–1975.** Most Les Pauls are made by special order only, many with mini-humbuckers and designated as Les Paul Deluxe models.

▷ **1976.** Three-piece maple neck with a five-piece headstock.

▷ **1978.** Solid mahogany body returns.

▷ **1981.** Neck volute removed.

▷ **1986.** Henry Juskiewiscz, Gary Zebrowski, and David Berryman purchase Gibson from Norlin. Return of the one-piece mahogany neck.

Les Paul Standards are characterized by their "chunky" bottom end, thick midrange tone, rich singing sustain, and warm top end. The sound is very different from the traditional bright, thinner Fender single-coil tone, often separating players into Fender versus Gibson camps—and leading many players to want to have both in their tonal arsenal!

The Les Paul Standards of 1958, 1959, and 1960 are regarded as "Holy Grails" in the vintage guitar world, both because of perceived differences in the guitars themselves (lighter, more resonant woods, PAF pickups, Brazilian rosewood fingerboards, and so on) and because of the artists who made genre-defining music on those guitars, such as Eric Clapton, Mike Bloomfield, Peter Green, and more. Opinions vary on whether this perception of the quality of late '50s Les Pauls is truly because the guitars and woods were better then, is because the woods and pickup magnets have aged over the years, or is due to simple nostalgia and belief that older and vintage is better than new.

The Norlin Years

Much has been made of the decline in quality of Gibson guitars, including Les Pauls, during the "Norlin years" (late 1968 or early 1969 to 1986). Some players separate the Norlin years into two eras: from 1969 to 1977 and from 1978 to 1986. This is because 1978 saw the arrival of Tim Shaw as the head of R&D at Gibson. Les Pauls were returned to much closer to original specs during this time (though they still featured three-piece maple necks), and Shaw also hand-wound humbucking pickups that some players feel are very close to original PAFs in quality and tone.

As for the three-piece maple necks and different neck shapes used during that era, for some players they are demonic in nature, while others perceive a nice feel, slightly longer sustain, and slightly brighter tone with less midrange and bottom end. Keep in mind that many of Gibson's very high end and very highly regarded instruments, such as the L5, featured three-piece maple necks from when they were first introduced, way back in the 1930s.

Many other changes were also made in the Norlin years; Les Pauls became very heavy (up to 15 pounds!), extensive shielding was added to the control cavities, the Nashville Tune-o-matic bridge was introduced, and more. Some players love the Norlins, some hate them—it's all a matter of personal taste. It can also vary from individual guitar to individual guitar—there are certainly Norlin gems and Norlin dogs, as with any time in any guitar manufacturer's history.

Table 14.2   Gibson Les Paul Standard Characteristics

Body	One-piece mahogany with carved maple top.
	In certain production years in the 1970s, "pancake" bodies made of laminated slabs of mahogany were used.
	Some modern models have chambered or weight-relieved bodies.
Neck	Set-neck.
	Mahogany; maple during certain production years in the late 1970s and early 1980s.
Scale length	24-3/4 inches.
Fingerboard	Rosewood.
Fingerboard radius	12 inches.
Frets	22 nickel-silver.
Bridge pickup	Humbucker, usually in a metal cover.
Neck pickup	Humbucker, usually in a metal cover.
Bridge	Nashville or ABR-1 Tune-o-matic.
Tailpiece	Stop tailpiece.
	Lightweight aluminum on vintage units.
	Zinc/nickel/steel on many modern units.

Tuners	Three full-size tuners per side of headstock.
Finish	Nitrocellulose lacquer.
Electronics/Controls	3-position pickup selector.
	Bridge pickup volume.
	Neck pickup volume.
	Bridge pickup tone.
	Neck pickup tone.
Variations	Gibson has issued many models based on the Les Paul Standard, including the Les Paul Traditional, Les Paul Classic, Les Paul Studio, and many more. Some of these are chambered or weight relieved, others are not. There also have been many reissues of vintage Les Paul Standards, in particular of late 1950s models.

Les Paul Lovers

Les Paul	Peter Green	Gary Moore	Billy Gibbons
Eric Clapton	Joe Bonamassa	John Sykes	Al Dimeola
Slash	Jimmy Page	Ace Frehley	Pete Townshend
Zakk Wylde	Randy Rhoads	Alex Lifeson	Vivian Campbell
Tom Scholz	Neal Schon	Neil Young	Stone Gossard
Steve Jones	Mick Jones	Duane Allman	Warren Haynes
Dickey Betts	Buckethead	Peter Frampton	Steve Hackett
Paul Kossoff	Tak Matsumoto	Mick Ralphs	Brian Robertson
Mick Ronson	Gary Rossington	Alex Skolnick	Mick Taylor
Joe Walsh	Snowy White	Billy Joe Armstrong	Mike Bloomfield
Joe Perry	Scott Gorman	Gary Richrath	Steve Clark
John Fogerty	Robert Fripp	Steve Lukather	John McLaughlin
Steve Stevens	Jeff Watson	Leslie West	Nancy Wilson

Fender Stratocaster

Leo Fender scores not one, but two hits in our "Big 3" of iconic guitar models! In 1954, following the success of the Telecaster, Fender launched the Stratocaster, which some players feel was Leo's crowning guitar design achievement. Like the Telecaster, the Strat has been in continuous production ever since. It is perhaps the most copied guitar model ever made—even Gibson has made Strat-like guitars, including the Victory models of the 1980s, and, perhaps most amazing, a low-budget Jimi Hendrix tribute guitar that was manufactured but never released after a huge outpouring of public outrage. In fact, the word "Strat" has almost become a generic term for a guitar with similar contours to a Stratocaster, despite the fact that Fender has a trademark on the term.

Where the Telecaster has a flat alder or ash body with simple rounded corners that can be quickly cut out on a bandsaw, the Stratocaster features a sleek, contoured body (also made of alder or ash) that is shaped for the comfort of the player. Strat necks are maple, with either maple or rosewood fingerboards. Rosewood fingerboards were standard from 1959 to 1967, with maple fingerboards available via special order only. From 1959 to 1962, the rosewood fingerboards were "slab" designs, meaning a very thick (nearly 5mm or almost 1/4 inch), flat-bottomed slice of rosewood was glued to the neck, then radiused. From 1962 to 1979, the neck was pre-radiused, then a thinner layer of rosewood was laid on top, matching the radius of the neck.

But the two things that define the Stratocaster tone the most are the Fender Synchronized Tremolo bridge/tailpiece and the three pickguard-mounted single-coil pickups. On earlier Stratocasters, all three pickups were the same, but in the late 1970s, Fender began using reverse-wound/reverse-polarity middle pickups, which are hum canceling when combined with the bridge or neck pickup. Fender has also begun offering pickups that are specifically designed or calibrated to sound best in the bridge, middle, or neck positions. The body routing for the pickups has also changed, from specific routs for single-coil pickups, to "swimming pool" routs that basically remove all the wood in the pickup area, allowing for the installation of any combination of humbuckers and single-coils, to today's HSH rout, which allows for humbuckers or single-coils at the bridge and neck positions with a single-coil middle pickup. Removing the extra wood for the swimming-pool rout can definitely affect the resonance of the body.

Originally, the pickups were selected with a three-position switch, which allowed the player to choose any of the three pickups individually. Clever players soon learned to balance the switch between positions, allowing the bridge and middle or neck and middle pickups to be heard together. Fender followed in 1977 with a five-position switch that allowed those "in between" selections and cemented the versatile tones of the Strat. There is a master volume control and dedicated tone controls for the neck and middle pickups. Many players (led by Eric Johnson) began rewiring their Strats with one tone control for the bridge pickup and the other for the neck or the neck and middle pickups, and Fender has responded recently by releasing models with this "modern" wiring scheme.

In 1965, CBS purchased Fender. Many players feel that the guitars and amps of the Fender CBS era (which ended with the employee purchase of the company in 1985) are of lesser quality than "pre-CBS" instruments. There were many changes made to Stratocasters during the CBS years, ranging from larger headstocks to early '80s models with new pickups, new tremolo bridges, and a single tone control. As of the mid-'80s, the Strat had largely returned to its former glory, and most players feel that the quality had returned to its former high level.

Modern Strats are available that are direct reissues of vintage models or with modern features, such as two-point tremolo bridges, roller nuts, various types of noiseless pickups, mid-boost and other onboard EQ options, locking tuners, humbucking pickups, and even models equipped with special pickups for driving MIDI synthesizers.

Because of its bolted-together nature, the Stratocaster is one of the most modded guitars. In fact, an entire replacement-parts industry has sprung up around the Stratocaster and spread to the Telecaster and other models. Everything from replacement pickups and hardware to replacement bridges and pickguards, all the way to replacement bodies and necks made from exotic woods, are available for customizing a Fender Strat or for building a Strat-style guitar from the ground up.

Table 14.3 Fender Stratocaster Characteristics

Body	Alder or ash.
Neck	Bolt-on.
	Maple.
Scale length	25-1/2 inches.
Fingerboard	Maple or rosewood.
Fingerboard radius	7-1/4 inches (vintage).
	9-1/2 or 12 inches (modern).
Frets	21 nickel-silver (vintage and modern).
	22 nickel-silver (certain modern models).
Bridge pickup	Single-coil in plastic cover.
Middle pickup	Single-coil in plastic cover.
Neck pickup	Single-coil in plastic cover.
Bridge	Synchronized tremolo bridge/tailpiece or fixed "hardtail" bridge with bent or stamped metal bridge plate.
	Six bridge pieces.
	Some Strats come with "ashtray" metal bridge covers, which most players promptly remove and lose.
Tailpiece	On tremolo-equipped models, integrated with bridge.
	On fixed-bridge models, through-body stringing with metal ferrules in back of body to anchor strings.
Tuners	Six mini tuners on one side of headstock.
Finish	Nitrocellulose lacquer (vintage and certain modern models).
	Polyurethane or polyester (most modern models).
Electronics/Controls	3-position pickup selector (vintage).
	5-position pickup selector (modern).
	Master volume.
	Middle pickup tone.
	Neck pickup tone.
Variations	Numerous signature models, numerous variations, varying pickup types and configurations, and many more.

The Attack of the Super Strat!

Prior to the late '70s, a Strat was a Strat was a Strat. When you bought a Strat, it had three single-coil pickups, a master volume, and two tone controls. The only real variations were hard tail versus tremolo and maple fingerboard versus rosewood fingerboard—and the color. But in 1978 that all changed, when a Dutch-born kid from Southern California released an album with his band—an album where he played on a pieced-together Strat-style guitar painted with bicycle paint and featuring a single humbucking bridge pickup and a lone volume control. That kid, Eddie Van Halen, and his "Frankenstrat" started a revolution in the guitar world. Suddenly there were Strat variations galore. One humbucker, two humbuckers, a humbucker and two single-coils, a humbucker and one single-coil, P-90s, and other pickup combinations were and are available, with the pickups mounted into a pickguard or with the body "rear loaded" with no pickguard at all.

These Strat-style guitars, referred to as "super strats" and made by manufacturers such as Kramer, Jackson, Charvel, Hamer, Ibanez, and many more, were quickly adopted by hard rockers and metal-heads but have since become accepted beyond their 1980s hairband roots by fusion players, jazz artists, and anyone who is looking to combine the thick, chunky tone of a Gibson (especially the bridge pickup tone) with the feel, performance, and tremolo of a Strat.

Super strats also often feature different body woods—basswood, swamp ash, mahogany, and others being common—and are often fitted with Floyd Rose locking tremolos. Many feature slim neck profiles suited to shredding and are often strung with .009 gauge or lighter strings. Many early super strats also featured slanted bridge humbuckers, an orientation developed by Eddie Van Halen to get the pole pieces on the humbucker to line up with the wider spaced strings of the Fender bridge. These days, many super strats use either Trembucker or F-spaced humbuckers (which feature wider pole piece spacing, the same as a Fender single-coil) or special bridges featuring narrower humbucker-spaced bridge pieces.

Today, super strats are made by everyone from Fender to Ibanez, Jackson (now actually owned by Fender) to Godin, as well as by boutique manufacturers such as James Tyler, John Suhr, and many others.

Many players particularly enjoy being able to switch between the sound of a humbucker at the bridge—which might not be quite as thick sounding as a Gibson Les Paul, but which still delivers rich, round, punchy tone—and the chiming sound of a neck and/or middle single-coil pickup, finding that this combination allows them to cover a wide range of musical styles and situations. Many times the bridge pickup is set up with a coil split or tap switch, to change it to single-coil operation for brighter sounds or for Strat-like "in between" sounds when combined with a middle single-coil.

Strat-mongers

Ritchie Blackmore	John Mayer	Mark Knopfler	Eric Clapton
Eric Johnson	Jimi Hendrix	Stevie Ray Vaughan	Robert Cray
Buddy Guy	Dick Dale	David Gilmour	Rory Gallagher
Buddy Holly	Hank Marvin	Yngwie J. Malmsteen	Robin Trower
Richard Thompson	Bonnie Raitt	Ritchie Valens	Ron Wood
Tommy Bolin	The Edge	Randy Bachman	Scott Henderson
Allen Hinds	Oz Noy	John Frusciante	Jimmy Vaughan
Chris Duarte	Henry Garza	Lowell George	Robbie Blunt
Dave Murray	Janick Gers	Nile Rodgers	Gary Moore
Wayne Krantz	Ronnie Earl	Eric Gales	Ernie Isley
Ed King	Sonny Landreth	Nils Lofgren	Trevor Rabin
Richie Sambora	Steve Winwood	Carl Verheyen	Bill Carson
Jeff Healey	Greg Koch	Ike Turner	Frank Zappa

Gibson ES-335

What do you get when you cross a hollow-body with a solid-body? Why, another of Ted McCarty's great triumphs at Gibson, the ES-335, that's what! The ES-335, also known as the ES-335TD (the "ES" stands for "Electric Spanish," while the "TD" stands for "thinline, dual or double pickups") was the world's first thinline semi-hollow-body electric guitar. It featured a thin—specified at 1.75 inches thick, though actual guitars vary a bit from this—hollow body with a solid center block that runs from the neck to the endpin.

Two humbuckers—originally PAFs; later other Gibson pickups were used—at the bridge and neck positions provide the sweet, resonant tones. Like a Les Paul, a three-position switch allows for either pickup to be used alone or for both pickups to be combined. Each pickup has its own volume and tone controls.

All ES-335s feature Tune-o-matic bridges, though tailpieces have varied. The earliest 335s had stop tailpieces. Around 1965, the tailpiece was changed to a trapeze type. Reissues have generally featured stop tailpieces. Nickel plating is used on all hardware.

The ES-335 features a laminated maple top, back, and sides. Three or four laminations are used. The grain of the inside and outside lamination layers runs "horizontally," along the length of the body. The grain of the center laminations (between the inside and outside layers) runs perpendicular, "vertically," across the body. It is rumored that poplar may have been used for some inner lamination layers. The 335s of the late 1950s and early 1960s feature fat, thick necks. The neck carve changed to a faster, thin neck in the mid-1960s.

The ES-335 could be considered a direct descendent of Les Paul's original "Log" experimental guitar—perhaps more so even than the eponymous Les Paul solid-body model. The Log featured a solid 4×4 chunk of wood with a neck attached, to which "wings" made from an acoustic guitar's body—which had been sawn in half—were attached to give it a guitar-like shape. Like the Log, the 335 was intended to reduce the feedback problems associated with hollow-body guitars while still providing the tonal richness of a hollow-body. The result is a tremendously flexible guitar that can sound as warm as a hollow body with the sustain and feedback resistance of a solid body.

Introduced in 1958, the ES-335TD was officially discontinued in 1981, though the ES-335DOT reissue was introduced that same year, and various reissues have been available ever since.

Table 14.4   Gibson ES-335 Characteristics

Body	Thinline semi-hollow-body with violin-style "F" holes.
	Solid maple center block.
	Hollow body "wings."
Neck	Set-neck.
	Mahogany; maple during certain production years.
Scale length	24-3/4 inches.
Fingerboard	Brazilian rosewood from 1958 to 1966.
	Indian rosewood beginning in 1966.
Fingerboard radius	12 inches.
Frets	22 nickel-silver.
Bridge pickup	Humbucker, usually in a metal cover.
Neck pickup	Humbucker, usually in a metal cover.
Bridge	Nashville or ABR-1 Tune-o-matic.
Tailpiece	Stop tailpiece.
	Trapeze tailpiece replaced stop tailpiece in 1965.
	Maestro Vibrola or Bigsby tremolo tailpiece on certain models.
	Lightweight aluminum on vintage units.
	Zinc/nickel/steel on many modern units.
Tuners	Three full-size tuners per side of headstock.
Finish	Nitrocellulose lacquer.
Electronics/controls	3-position pickup selector.
	Bridge pickup volume.
	Neck pickup volume.
	Bridge pickup tone
	Neck pickup tone.
Variations	Over the years, Gibson has made a number of variations on the ES-335 semi-hollow-body theme, including:
	ES-345—gold hardware, split parallelogram inlays, stereo output, Varitone 6-position preset filter circuit.
	ES-347—coil tap on pickups, block fingerboard inlay, ebony fingerboard, TP6 fine-tuning stop tailpiece.

ES-355TD—fancier version of ES-335, with block inlays, front and back body binding, neck and headstock binding, optional stereo output, optional Varitone filter circuit.

CS-336—Custom Shop model, smaller size (close to a Les Paul), made from a single piece of carved mahogany, with multiple binding on body, neck, and headstock. The CS-356 was a fancier version featuring gold-plated hardware. The ES-339 is a less expensive production model, with laminate construction.

Trini Lopez Standard—signature model made from 1964 to 1970, featuring a Firebird-style neck with six-on-a-side headstock, and diamond-shaped "F" holes.

B.B. King Lucille—signature version of ES-345TD-SV, with standard stereo wiring and Varitone circuit, maple neck, and no "F" holes to further reduce feedback.

Semi-Hollow-Body Stars

B.B. King	Larry Carlton	Lee Ritenour	Alex Lifeson
Eric Johnson	Alvin Lee	Freddie King	Warren Haynes
Dave Grohl	Trini Lopez	Eric Clapton	Chuck Berry
Justin Hayward	Jorma Kaukonen	Roy Orbison	Carl Wilson
Otis Rush	Peter Banks	Jimmy Rogers	Elvin Bishop

Gibson Explorer and Flying V

Ted McCarty did it again in 1957, with the release of the most radical trio of solid-body electric guitars the world had ever witnessed. Designed in response to criticism that Gibson was stodgy in comparison to Fender, the arrow-shaped Flying V, lightning-bolt Explorer, and futuristic Moderne definitely turned heads at the time. The Moderne was never put into production, but the V and the Explorer were produced until 1959. They weren't exactly a commercial success their first time out of the gate, but there's no denying the impact they would have a few years down the road. Both models were reissued in 1967 and have enjoyed many reissues and variations ever since.

The Explorer and Flying V were originally made from limba, an African wood somewhat similar to mahogany. (The wood was referred to by its trademarked name, "korina," rather than as limba.) Both the body and neck were made from the same type of wood; rosewood was used for the fingerboards. Later reissue Flying Vs and Explorers have often been made from mahogany, for both the body and neck. In the case of both the Explorer and the Flying V, the body of the guitar is a massive slab of korina or mahogany, which contributes to a thick, rich tone with a lot of sustain.

Two PAF pickups provided the power for the original Flying V and Explorer, controlled by a volume control per pickup and a master tone control. A three-position switch allowed players to select either pickup by itself or both pickups combined.

It's no secret that the Flying V and Explorer were just a bit ahead of the curve when they were released in the late 1950s, but both models have made up for it with a big comeback over the past four decades—hard rockers and heavy metallers discovered these models, other manufacturers began making copies and variations on the originals, and both models are now quite popular. With somewhat more subtle lines than many of their descendants, both models have also managed to escape the stigma associated with the overly "pointy" models released by various manufacturers in the 1980s.

Table 14.5 Gibson Explorer and Flying V Characteristics

Body	Solid-body.
	Korina.
Neck	Set-neck.
	Mahogany.
Scale length	24-3/4 inches.
Fingerboard	Brazilian rosewood from 1958 to 1959.
	Indian rosewood beginning with 1967 reissues.
	Ebony on certain models.
Fingerboard radius	12 inches.
Frets	22 nickel-silver.
Bridge pickup	Humbucker, usually in a metal cover.
Neck pickup	Humbucker, usually in a metal cover.
Bridge	Nashville or ABR-1 Tune-o-matic.
Tailpiece	Explorer—stop tailpiece.
	Flying V—"V"-shaped flat metal tailpiece plate, stop tailpiece, or Maestro "short lyre" vibrola.
Tuners	Explorer—six full-size tuners on one side of headstock.
	Flying V—three full-size tuners per side of headstock.
Finish	Nitrocellulose lacquer.
Electronics/controls	3-position pickup selector.
	Bridge pickup volume.
	Neck pickup volume.
	Master tone.
Variations	Over the years, Gibson has made a number of variations on the Flying V and Explorer.
	Most famous are the Flying V II and Explorer II models, with walnut/maple laminated bodies, body contouring, and in the case of of the Flying V II, very strange boomerang-shaped single-coil pickups.
	Most infamous among the Gibson models would have to be the "Holy" V and Explorer, which featured large holes cut through the bodies, basically leaving a frame with pickups mounted on them.
	Gibson has also released a number of more or less faithful reissues, "designer" models, signature models, and more.

Radical Shape Shifters

Michael Schenker	Matthias Jabs	Albert King	Allen Collins
Rudolph Schenker	The Edge	Jimi Hendrix	James Hetfield
Matty Lewis	Lonnie Mack	Chris Spedding	Rickey Medlocke
Jeff Carlisi	Don Preston	Brendon Small	Billy Gibbons
Marc Bolan	K.K. Downing	J. Geils	Lenny Kravitz
Wolf Hoffman	Eddie Van Halen	Andy Powell	Ryan Peake
Rick Nielson	Chad Kroeger	Tom Dumont	Dave Davies

Gibson Firebird

As the 1960s dawned, Gibson was in something of a slump. The flagship Les Paul was discontinued in favor of the SG, the Flying V and Explorer had tanked, and the Moderne was never released. Then-president Ted McCarty was looking for something to bring a fresh spark to the company's lineup. Car designer Ray Dietrich was brought in to lend his vision to a new model. Taking inspiration from the tailfins found on 1950s cars and applying those curves to a tamed Explorer shape resulted in the Firebird, which was launched in 1963.

The mini-humbuckers in the Firebird were interesting in that, unlike other mini-humbuckers that used a single bar magnet and six iron polepieces, the Firebird pickups used six alnico polepiece magnets. In 1965, some Firebirds also used P-90 single-coil pickups. The Firebird pickups produce a clean, crisp tone that is different from other mini-humbuckers. Each pickup has its own volume and tone controls.

The Firebird was the first guitar from Gibson to offer neck-thru construction, featuring a neck/center body section made from nine alternating layers of mahogany and walnut. With its Fender-like six-on-a-side headstock, the string tension on the Firebird is different from other three-on-a-side Gibsons, creating a different feel.

Today, Gibson continues to manufacture Firebirds, and at this writing had just introduced the limited-run Firebird X, which incorporates digital electronics, bluetooth switching, and built-in effects.

Table 14.6   Gibson Firebird Characteristics

Body	Solid-body.
	Mahogany.
Neck	Neck-thru design on reverse models.
	Set neck on non-reverse models (1965–1969).
	Laminated construction; five layers of mahogany alternating with four layers of walnut.

Scale length	24-3/4 inches.
Fingerboard	Indian rosewood.
	Ebony on certain models.
Fingerboard radius	12 inches.
Frets	22 nickel-silver.
Bridge pickup	Mini humbucker, usually in a metal cover.
Neck pickup	Mini humbucker, usually in a metal cover.
Bridge	Nashville or ABR-1 Tune-o-matic.
Tailpiece	Stop tailpiece or Maestro vibrola.
Tuners	Six "banjo" tuners on one side of headstock.
Finish	Nitrocellulose lacquer.
Electronics/controls	3-position pickup selector.
	Bridge pickup volume.
	Neck pickup volume.
	Bridge pickup tone.
	Neck pickup tone

Variations: There were several variations on the original Firebird theme, each of which were available reverse (shaped like a rounded-off Explorer with the six tuners on the treble or bottom side of the neck) and, from 1965 to 1969, non-reverse (set neck construction, flipped over with the long body horn on top and the six tuners on the bass or top side of the neck):

Firebird I—one pickup, one-piece stop tailpiece/bridge combo.

Firebird III—two mini-humbucking pickups, stop tailpiece/Tune-o-matic bridge or Gibson Vibrola with Tune-o-matic bridge.

Firebird V—three mini-humbucking pickups, Maestro Vibrola with Tune-o-matic bridge, gold hardware.

Firebird VII—two mini-humbucking pickups, stop tailpiece/Tune-o-matic bridge or Maestro Vibrola with Tune-o-matic bridge.

Flame Throwers

Johnny Winter	**Warren Haynes**	**Clarence "Gatemouth" Brown**	**Allen Collins**
Eric Clapton	**Brian Jones**	**Phil Manzanera**	**Steve Winwood**
Jorma Kaukonen	**Steve Stills**	**Steve Van Zandt**	**Paul McCartney**

Gibson SG

The great irony of the "Golden Era" of Gibson Les Pauls—1958, 1959, and 1960—is that the popularity and sales of the guitar model were steadily dropping. By 1961, Gibson discontinued the traditional single-cutaway Les Paul model, replacing it with the double-cutaway SG Les Paul. The "Les Paul" was quickly dropped from the name, finally putting the single-cutaway solid-body on true hiatus. (Single-cutaway Les Paul reissues began to appear in 1968.) From a manufacturing standpoint, the SG ("Solid Guitar") had some big advantages for Gibson: The thinner body required smaller pieces of wood; there was no separate maple top to source, carve, and attach; and the thin neck and streamlined neck heel required less wood. From a player standpoint, the SG has actually proven itself the best-selling Gibson model of all time. More than 50 years later, it remains extremely popular.

Early SGs sported PAF humbucking pickups, controlled by a three-position switch and individual volume and tone controls. The thin, speedy neck joined the body three frets higher than on Les Pauls, at the 19th fret. This and the lack of a bulky neck heel can make the neck and neck joint somewhat less stable than other models, but it provides excellent access to the upper frets. With its thin body, the SG can tend toward neck heaviness. However, the thinner body and neck also make the sound less "chunky" than a Les Paul, helping it cut through a dense track or a live band. The sound carries good focus with a punchy midrange and good resonance due to the body's light weight. And, many players simply enjoy the comfort of the SG's more compact size and lighter weight.

Table 14.7   Gibson SG Characteristics

Body	Solid-body.
	Mahogany.
Neck	Set neck.
	Mahogany.
Scale length	24-3/4 inches.
Fingerboard	Indian rosewood.
Fingerboard radius	12 inches.
Frets	22 nickel-silver.
Bridge pickup	Humbucker, usually in a metal cover.
Neck pickup	Humbucker, usually in a metal cover.
Bridge	Nashville or ABR-1 Tune-o-matic.
Tailpiece	Stop tailpiece or Maestro vibrola.
Tuners	Three full-size tuners per side of headstock.
Finish	Nitrocellulose lacquer.
Electronics/controls	3-position pickup selector.
	Bridge pickup volume.
	Neck pickup volume.
	Bridge pickup tone.
	Neck pickup tone.

Variations	There were several variations on the SG theme, including:
	SG Jr.—stripped down, entry-level version.
	SG Special—two P-90 pickups.
	SG Custom—luxury model with three humbucking pickups, Vibrola tailpiece.

SG Screamers

Angus Young	**Eric Clapton**	**Frank Zappa**	**Tony Iommi**
Pete Townshend	**Derek Trucks**	**Duane Allman**	**John Cipollina**
Elliot Easton	**Robbie Krieger**	**Frank Marino**	**Daron Malakian**
Jerry Garcia	**Mick Box**	**Thom York**	

Gibson L-5 CES

Gibson first launched the L-5 archtop acoustic guitar in 1922, under the supervision of innovative master luthier Lloyd Loar. The L-5 was the first guitar to feature violin-style "F" holes, one of the first with an adjustable truss rod, and the first truss-rod equipped carved top to have 14 frets clear of the body. The body was reshaped with a cutaway in 1939, another first, at least for an American guitar. As the premier acoustic archtop of the day, it was the first-choice of big band rhythm guitarists.

When guitars moved into the electric age, the highly popular L-5 followed suit, receiving pickups in 1951. The first L-5 electrics featured P-90 single-coil pickups. In 1958, the pickups were changed to PAF humbuckers.

The L-5 CES was quickly adopted by jazzers including Wes Montgomery and continues to be popular with contemporary players, such as as Tuck Andress and Lee Ritenour. It was also used for some of the earliest electric guitar recordings, played by Scotty Moore on some of Elvis Presley's tracks, including "Mystery Train" and other RCA tracks.

Table 14.8   Gibson L-5 CES Characteristics

Body	Hollow-body.
	Carved solid spruce top.
	Solid maple sides and carved maple back.
Neck	Set neck.
	Maple.

Scale length	24-3/4 inches.
Fingerboard	Ebony.
Fingerboard radius	12 inches.
Frets	20 nickel-silver.
Bridge pickup	Humbucker, usually in a metal cover. Earliest models featured P-90 single-coil.
Neck pickup	Humbucker, usually in a metal cover. Earliest models featured P-90 single-coil.
Bridge	ABR-1 Tune-o-matic mounted to a wooden base.
Tailpiece	Trapeze tailpiece.
Tuners	Three full-size tuners per side of headstock.
Finish	Nitrocellulose lacquer.
Electronics/controls	3-position pickup selector. Bridge pickup volume. Neck pickup volume. Bridge pickup tone. Neck pickup tone.
Variations	There have been several signature editions of the L-5 released, including: Lee Ritenour—one "floating" mini-humbucker mounted to the end of the neck, with a volume control mounted to the pickguard. Wes Montgomery—one humbucker with volume and tone controls.

L-5 Lovers

Wes Montgomery	**Scotty Moore**	**Tuck Andress**	**Pat Martino**
Lee Ritenour	**Eddie Lang**	**Maybelle Carter**	**Jan Akkerman**

Gibson ES-175D

Launched in 1949, the Gibson ES-175 was positioned as a smaller archtop offering a more manageable and a more affordable alternative to the top-of-the-line L-5. (Trivia: The "175" in the name comes from the original price—$175.) The ES-175 was the first Gibson electric guitar to offer a "Florentine" cutaway (with a sharp point on the end of the cutaway, rather than a soft, smooth curve). Until 1953, the ES-175 featured a single P-90 single-coil in the neck position. In 1953, the ES-175D was released with two single-coil pickups. In 1957, the ES-175 and the ES-175D were updated with two humbucking pickups. The single-pickup ES-175 was discontinued in 1971, though it was semi-resurrected in 1991 as a Herb Ellis signature model (ES-165, with a single mini-humbucker). The ES-175D remains in production today.

Though it has less acoustic tone than an L-5 CES, the ES-175 produces an excellent, rich, archtop electric tone. And, to be fair, the 175 was designed from the beginning to be an electric model, it wasn't a modified acoustic archtop like the L-5.

It is still very popular with jazzers today. Though Steve Howe has made a career using the ES-175 for rock, its tendency toward feedback at high volume makes it difficult for most rockers to manage.

Table 14.9 Gibson ES-175D Characteristics

Body	Hollow-body archtop. Laminated maple/poplar/maple top, back, and sides. Mahogany back and sides from 1983 to 1990.
Neck	Set neck. Mahogany.
Scale length	24-3/4 inches.
Fingerboard	Rosewood.
Fingerboard radius	12 inches.
Frets	20 nickel-silver.
Bridge pickup	Humbucker, usually in a metal cover.
Neck pickup	Humbucker, usually in a metal cover. Earliest models featured one P-90 single-coil at neck position.
Bridge	ABR-1 Tune-o-matic mounted to a rosewood base.
Tailpiece	Trapeze tailpiece.
Tuners	Three full-size tuners per side of headstock.
Finish	Nitrocellulose lacquer.
Electronics/controls	3-position pickup selector. Bridge pickup volume. Neck pickup volume. Bridge pickup tone. Neck pickup tone.
Variations	There have been few variations on the ES-175; perhaps the most infamous was the ES-175T, a thinner bodied version that was made from 1976 to 1979. It was not well received.

ES-175 Aficionados

Steve Howe	**Pat Metheny**	**Joe Pass**	**Howard Roberts**
Kenny Burrell	**Joe Diorio**	**Jimmy Raney**	**B.B. King**
Wes Montgomery			

Gretsch G6120

Gretsch was founded in the late 1800s as small music store in Brooklyn and then became an import company specializing in musical instruments. Eventually, the company began making their own drums, and in 1954, they launched a line of hollow-body archtop guitars. The model 6120 (later known as the 6120 Chet Atkins Hollowbody and then as the 6120 Nashville) was quickly endorsed by Chet Atkins and then adopted by the rockabilly stars of the day, including Eddie Cochran and Duane Eddy. The 6120 was discontinued in the late 1970s; interest in the model was revived when Brian Setzer and the Stray Cats hit the scene in the early 1980s.

Though the G6120 is a true hollow-body archtop, it features internal bracing between the top and the back. Some models and years featured "trestle" braces, while others used simple sound posts as braces. The originals featured DeArmond pickups, which were replaced by Gretsch Filter'Tron pickups after Chet Atkins complained that the magnets in the DeArmonds were too strong. In 1961, Gretsch cut the body depth from three inches to around two inches. In 1962, the G6120 was completely redesigned with fake "F" holes, double cutaways, a padded back, and more. Further changes continued through the '60s, followed by even more after Baldwin purchased Gretsch in 1967. The model number was changed to 7660 in 1972. When Fred Gretsch III bought the company back, one of the first models to reappear was the classic G6120. In 2008, Gretsch gained the rights to use the Chet Atkins name on the 6120 again.

The G6120 has a very different sound from Gibson-style jazz-box hollow-bodies, such as the L-5 and the ES-175. It has a brighter, twangier tone that works well for rockabilly and roots styles, as well as alternative and punk styles.

Table 14.10 Gretsch G6120 Characteristics

Body	Hollow-body archtop.
	Laminated maple top, back, and sides.
Neck	Set neck.
	Maple.
Scale length	24.6 inches.
Fingerboard	Ebony or rosewood.
Fingerboard radius	12 inches.
Frets	22 nickel-silver.
Bridge pickup	DeArmond from 1954–1958.
	High-sensitive Filter'Tron humbucker.
	Dynasonic single-coil on certain models.
Neck pickup	DeArmond from 1954–1958.
	High-sensitive Filter'Tron humbucker.
	Dynasonic single-coil on certain models.
Bridge	Rocking bar bridge.
Tailpiece	Bigsby vibrato tailpiece.
Tuners	Three full-size tuners per side of headstock.

Finish	Nitrocellulose lacquer on early models.
	Gloss urethane on modern models.
Electronics/controls	3-position pickup selector.
	3-position tone selector.
	Bridge pickup volume.
	Neck pickup volume.
	Master volume.
Variations	There have been many different 6120 models—15 are in the current Gretsch catalog, including signature and left-handed models, plus there are additional lower-priced import models. Variations on the 6120 include the Filter'Tron versus single-coil versus TV Jones pickups, trestle bracing versus sound posts, rosewood versus ebony fingerboards, different inlays, and more.
	6120EC Eddie Cochran—Dynasonic single-coil bridge pickup, P-90 neck pickup, no tone switch, master tone control.
	6120SSL Brian Setzer—flame maple, TV Jones Classic pickups, trestle bracing, white dice control knobs.
	6120TV Brian Setzer Hot Rod—TV Jones classic pickups, no tone switch, pickup selector switch and master volume control only.

6120 Twangers

Chet Atkins	**Eddie Cochran**	**Duane Eddy**	**Pete Townshend**
Brian Setzer	**Rev. Horton Heat**	**Keith Scott**	**Chris Cheney**

Rickenbacker 360/12

The 1960s were very good to Rickenbacker, particularly after George Harrison took to using a 360/12 twelve-string semi-hollow-body guitar with the Beatles, beginning with *A Hard Day's Night* in 1964. The 360/12 was one of the first electric 12-string guitar models, building on the foundation of the Rickenbacker 360 six-string model. In fact, the big difference is the addition of six more tuners on the headstock placed at 90 degrees to the main six tuners, so that the headstock would not need to be elongated and to prevent the guitar from being neck heavy. The nut was changed to a twelve-slot type, but the bridge remained the standard model, with six adjustable bridge pieces. Likewise, the standard thin six-string neck was used, which made the 360/12 somewhat difficult to finger cleanly, as the strings were so close together. Interestingly, Rickenbacker reversed the order of the octave strings. On a standard twelve-string, the octave strings are on the bass side and are struck first when the player uses a down stroke with a pick. On the Rickenbacker 360/12, the octave strings are on the treble side, struck after the standard-tuned string.

The sides and top of the 360/12 are actually carved from a single slab of maple, to which the back is attached. Two single-coil pickups provide the trademark "jangly" tone made famous by Roger McGuinn and others. For those after that tone, the Rickenbacker 360/12 remains the only way to truly achieve it.

Table 14.11   Rickenbaker 360/12 Characteristics

Body	Semi-hollow-body.
	Carved maple.
Neck	Set neck.
	Maple/walnut/maple laminate.
Scale length	24-3/4 inches.
Fingerboard	Rosewood.
Fingerboard radius	10 inches.
Frets	21 nickel-silver frets until 1969.
	24 nickel-silver frets beginning in 1969.
Bridge pickup	Rickenbacker single-coil.
Neck pickup	Rickenbacker single-coil.
Bridge	Tune-o-matic-style six-saddle adjustable bridge.
Tailpiece	Trapeze tailpiece.
Tuners	Six full-size tuners per side of headstock.
Finish	Proprietary finish formulation.
Electronics/controls	3-position pickup selector.
	Bridge pickup volume.
	Neck pickup volume.
	Bridge pickup tone.
	Neck pickup tone.
	Bass pickup tone/mix.
Variations	360—the original six-string version.
	370/12—adds a third, middle pickup.
	450/12—solid body, two-pickup version.

Ricky Janglers

George Harrison	**John Lennon**	**Roger McGuinn**	**Mike Campbell**
Tom Petty	**Brian Jones**	**Mike Rutherford**	**Jeff Buckley**
Pete Townshend	**Chris Martin**	**Johnny Marr**	**Chris Walla**
Ed O'Brien	**Paul Kantner**	**Carl Wilson**	**Daniel Johns**

Iconic Amplifiers

I T TAKES MORE THAN JUST A GREAT ELECTRIC GUITAR to create stellar tone—the amplifier plays at least an equal part in the equation. And, just as with the iconic guitars we explored in the previous chapter, over the years certain amplifiers have emerged as true stars. These powerful tone-generation engines take the signal from a great electric guitar and not only make it louder but also add their own special tonal mojo, bringing the sound to life and magnifying whatever is played.

As with the guitars we examined, the list of iconic amps comes from just a few manufacturers, who in turn have been the basis for dozens, if not hundreds, of models from boutique and major manufacturers around the world. (This is not to say that these are the only great amps in the world—there are certainly many, many stellar new and vintage amps out there—but those included here have had the most impact on guitar amp design and on guitar amp tone.)

This plethora of options is both a blessing and a curse. It used to be, when you wanted an amp, you went to the store and tried out a few Marshalls, a few Fenders, maybe a Vox or an Orange, a few Peaveys—the number of choices was fairly defined and limited. Today, all that has changed. There are tons of choices offering any mix of features and sounds you could want, which is a wonderful thing. The problem is that there are tons of choices offering any mix of features and sounds you could want—how can you possibly make a decision as to which is the right one for you? Especially when it's difficult to find any place that carries even a fraction of the available options, so that you can actually play and hear them.

Internet discussion forums are a good source of information—at least if you can find denizens who are objective, experienced, and educated. And, every manufacturer, big and small, has a website filled with information for you to wade through. But perhaps a good place to start is with the roots of where so many of today's amplifier models come from, with the iconic amplifiers of the past.

Fender

The man behind the iconic guitars, Leo Fender, also springs to the top of our iconic amplifier list. Self-taught in electronics, Fender opened up a repair shop in 1938, where he also rented and sold his homemade PA systems and musical instrument amplifiers. By the late 1940s, the Fender Electrical Instrument Company business was rolling, and Fender's amps were being sold nationwide. Fender's tweed-covered amps gained a reputation as being highly reliable on the road and were also known as the most powerful amps available at the time. Through the years and decades that followed, many amp models, big and small, tube and solid-state, have been launched by the company. The most iconic are certainly the more "traditional" tube amps—and these are the amps that are the basis of so many amp models from so many other manufacturers. There have certainly been some successful Fender solid-state amps, and recently, even some very impressive and highly featured modeling Fender amps, but where the icons of Fender amp tone are concerned, tube amps are where it's at. Almost any of the "vintage" Fender tube amps could make the list, so perhaps it is most efficient to break the Fenders down into the different eras of production and then dig deeper into some individual models from there.

There are actually two ways to do this; the first is by cabinet type, which breaks down as is shown in Table 15.1.

Table 15.1   Fender Amp Eras by Cabinet Type

Years	Type	Characteristic
1946–1948	Woodies	Uncovered wooden cabinets. Mahogany, maple, and walnut finishes. Wooden carrying handle. Rear-facing control panel on back of amp.
1948–1953	TV front	Rectangular speaker/grille cut out with rounded corners; resembles vintage television set. Tweed covering that hid the finger-jointed cabinet design. Up-facing control panel on top rear of amp. Brown mohair speaker grille. Leather carrying handle.
1953–1955	Wide panel	Rectangular speaker/grille cut out with square corners. Wide tweed areas above and below speaker grille. Dark linen grille.
1955–1960	Narrow panel	Tweed areas above and below grille are thin, resulting in the grille encompassing much more of the front of the amp. Brown plastic grille "cloth."
1959–1963	Brownface	Control panel is moved to front of amp and colored brown. Tweed replaced with blonde (larger piggyback amp models) or brown (smaller combo amp models) vinyl know as "Tolex." Oxblood- or wheat-colored grille cloth. Black plastic carrying handle.
1963–1967	Blackface	Black control panel. Black Tolex covering. Reinforced black carrying handle. Silver sparkle grille cloth. Most models are enhanced with built-in reverb.
1967–1980s	Silverface	Silver control panel. Numerous circuit changes beginning after the purchase of Fender by CBS in 1965, though some early and "transitional" Silverface amps feature identical circuitry to Blackface amps. Silver grille with blue sparkle. Many amp models feature master volume controls after 1972.
1980–1982	Blackface	Return to black control panel, but circuits are the same as the late Silverface models.

This type of organization of the Fender amps works well for vintage amp collectors. However, for most players interested in how the tone and amp features have evolved over the years, it makes more sense to break down the amps into somewhat larger "eras" based on their major characteristic—the type of covering or the coloring of the control panels, which fairly accurately correspond to major redesigns of the amps' circuitries. For most players, these major eras begin in the late 1940s with the tweed-covered amps, progress to the brown control panel amps, to the black control panel amps, to the silver control panel amps, and then to the "modern" era amplifier models.

Tweed

The original amps released by Fender are known as "Woodies," cleverly named after their uncovered wooden cabinets. But Fender quickly found that the wooden cabs weren't especially resistant to the bumps, bruises, scrapes, and scratches of everyday life, plus the joinery at corners was visible. In 1948, the company began covering their pine amplifier cabinets with tweed suitcase material. This era lasted until 1959, when the Brownface amps made their first appearance.

The first tweed-covered amp on the market was the diminutive Champ, which, interestingly enough, was also the last amp in the line to keep its tweed, not going Tolex until 1964. (The other amp models went Tolex by 1960.) The Deluxe, Twin, Super, Bassman, and others followed throughout the late '40s and the '50s.

Tweed amps featured their chassis mounted "upside down," hanging from the top of the cabinet. The controls were accessible at the back of the top of the amp. Though Leo Fender designed the amps to play clean, they gained their renown as players discovered the amazing breakup, sensitivity, response, dynamics, and overdrive they produced when cranked up. The Tweed amps were quite simple in design, though there were numerous variations in the various circuits used. (See the upcoming "Fender Circuit/Amp Designations" sidebar.) Tube rectifiers were used, with simple tone and volume controls and no built-in reverb or other effects. In most cases, Jensen P8, P10, and P12 alnico speakers were used for the Tweed amps, but occasionally Oxford and Cleveland alnico speakers were used. The pine cabinets were quite lightweight and resonated freely with the speaker contributing to the tone produced, as opposed to later amps with much heavier and stiffer cabinet builds.

These amps were definitely a big part of the birth of rock 'n roll, with their sweet, greasy, saturated tone, loaded with rich harmonics. They've been used for countless recordings and continue to be used (either originals, reissues, or clones) by many guitarists. However, they're not the amp for you if you need a master volume, high gain, an effects loop, channel switching, or other modern features.

Fender Circuit/Amp Designations

When the Tweed era began, Fender came up with a numbering system for the circuit designs and amp models that was used consistently for model identification purposes through 1963. (Note: This designation did not indicate when a specific amp was manufactured; it simply showed when the circuit was designed. See the upcoming "When Was It Made?" sidebar for information on dating Fender amps.) Here's how it worked: The first number in the code indicated the decade in which the circuit was designed: 5 for the 1950s, 6 for the 1960s. Next came a letter indicating the year of the decade. (See Table 15.2.)

Table 15.2 Letter/Year Designations for Fender Amplifiers

Designation	Year of Circuit Design
A	1951 or 1961
B	1952 or 1962
C	1953 or 1963
D	1954
E	1955
F	1956
G	1957
H	1958
I	1959

Next, each amp model was given a number. (see Table 15.3.)

Table 15.3 Fender Amp Model Numbering

Number	Model	Year First Introduced
1	Champ (first released as the Champion)	1948
2	Princeton	1946
3	Deluxe (first released as Model 26)	1946
4	Super (first released as Dual Professional)	1947
5	Pro	1947
6	Bassman	1952
7	Bandmaster	1953
8	Twin	1953
9	Tremolux	1955
10	Harvard	1955
11	Vibrolux	1956
12	Concert	1959
13	Vibrasonic	1959
14	Showman	1960
15	Standalone Reverb Unit	1961
16	Vibroverb	1963

In some cases, the circuit was modified mid-year; in this case, a "-A" designation was added. Taken all together, you have 1950s designations such as 5G8 for the 1957 Twin circuit, 5E3 and 5C3 for the 1955 and 1953 Deluxes, and 5F1 for the 1956 Champ, with the 5F1-A 1956 Champ coming out later in the year with a modified circuit.

In 1963, Fender changed to using model names along with circuit designations that reflect the month and year of design, as well as the circuit revision. AA indicated the first circuit revision, AB indicated the second revision, and so on. The revision letters were followed with the month number, 1 through 12, corresponding to January through December. The last two numbers were the years, beginning with 63 for 1963, 64 for 1964, and so on. This resulted in circuit designations such as AA763, indicating a first circuit revision, created in July of 1963. AB1163 indicates a second revision, from November of 1963. AA1070 would be a first revision, created in October 1970.

Blonde/Brownface

The Blonde and Brownface eras ran nearly concurrently, with the Brownface amps available from 1959 to 1963, while the Blonde amps were available from 1960 to 1964. The big difference between the amps was the colors of the coverings and grille clothes. Both featured the same brown-colored control panel.

The Brownface amps were the first amps from Fender to use Tolex—a flexible vinyl covering that replaced the tweed cloth covering used previously. The Tolex used was brown in color. The grille cloth was typically oxblood (dark maroon), and the front control panel was brown (thus the Brownface moniker). Some influential models from the era include the 6G6-B-circuit Bassman, 6G2-circuit Princeton, 6G3-circuit Deluxe, 6G4-circuit Super, and the venerable standalone Brownface Fender Reverb unit. The 6G8-circuit Twin was the "big box" Blonde model, with four 6L6 tubes and much higher output power. (See the "Fender Circuit/Amp Designations" sidebar for how to decipher Fender's amp model/circuit nomenclature.)

Early Brownface amps actually had the volume control for the Normal channel placed to the right of the bass and treble controls; these early examples are referred to as "center volume" models. The volume knob was relocated to the left of the bass and treble controls in late 1960, which has since become the traditional position for it.

The Blonde amps featured cream-colored Tolex covering, with oxblood- (dark maroon) or wheat-colored grilles and brown control panels. (These brown control panels technically make them Brownface amps, but by popular usage, the Blonde moniker prevails.) The majority of the Blonde amps were larger, higher-power "piggyback" models, with separate heads and cabinets. Examples included the Bassman, the Showman, and the Bandmaster.

Sonically, most players describe the Blonde and Brownface amps as being sort of "bridges" between the Tweed and Blackface amps, with tighter low end than the Tweeds and more midrange tonal girth than Blackface models. Some players feel that the Blonde and Brownface amps share some sonic similarity with early Marshall amps, with more midrange depth or throatiness than the traditional twang of vintage Fenders, and smoother overdrive and breakup when the amp is cranked up.

Many players also feel that the tremolo circuits in the Blonde and Brownface amps are the pinnacle of that effect's implementation. There were actually two types of tremolo used by Fender on the Blonde/Brownface amps: The "harmonic" tremolo, which employs three tubes, was used on the larger amps, such as the Super, Bandmaster, and Concert. It has an almost Leslie-sounding rotating speaker/chorusy effect that some players describe as "swampy." It splits the high and low frequencies and processes them separately, resulting in a "phasey" sounding effect. The second type, the "bias-vary" tremolo, is a more traditional pulsating-volume sort of tremolo effect. It works by modulating or varying the bias voltage that is sent to the amp's power tubes, which results in the output level from the tubes changing up and down, creating the pulsating volume effect.

There are many notable recorded examples of Blonde/Brownface amps. Just a few oft-heard examples: Ted Nugent is rumored to have used a Brownface Deluxe (with an Electro-Voice SRO speaker) for "Cat Scratch Fever." Mark Knopfler is said to have relied on a Brownface Vibrolux for "Sultans of Swing" and other early Dire Straits material. Billy Gibbons from ZZ Top is also said to have recorded with Brownface Deluxes in the early days.

When Was It Made?

None of Fender's early circuit/model number schemes indicated the year of a specific amplifier's manufacture, just the year that the circuit used for it was designed or revised. A separate date code was stamped on each amp, indicating when that unit was actually built. Three types of manufacturing date codes were used:

▶ From 1951 to 1967, two-character codes were used to indicate the year a specific amp was made. Letters were assigned to each year of manufacture (A through Q—some early 1966 amps still used the 1965 O designation by mistake), with the month in which the amp was built indicated by a second letter (A through L for January through December). An amp stamped with CC, for example, was built in March of 1953. NA would indicate an amp made in January of 1964.

▶ Late in the 1960s through to the late '70s, codes such as F074469 were used, where 69 is the year of manufacture and 44 is the week of the year in which the amp was made.

▶ Beginning in the late 1970s, the amp chassis were stamped with a number such as 0842, which, when read backward, reveals the 24th week of 1980.

Blackface

For many players, the epitome of Fender amp goodness is the "Blackface" amps, which were made from 1963 through 1967. Identified by their black Tolex covering, silver sparkle grille cloth, and, of course, black-colored control panels, the Blackface era amps featured significant circuit changes, housed in cabinet designs from the Brownface era, except that the speaker baffle was changed from plywood to particle board (MDF—*medium density fiberboard*). Most Blackface amps came stock with Jensen alnico speakers, though CTS (*Chicago Telephone Systems*) and Oxford speakers were also used in some models.

The Blackface amps are non–master volume control designs; they feature clean preamps. To push the amps into breakup, they must be turned up loud enough for the power tubes to really begin to work hard—there's a definite sweet spot in terms of volume and drive and achieving a sweet, warm tone from the Blackfaces.

Interestingly, all of the Blackface amps use the same two-channel preamp design, with the exception of the smallest Champ and Princeton models. The main differences are in the output power and tubes used and the speaker configuration. Except for the Champ, the amps were Class AB designs, using two 6V6 or 6L6 power tubes or two pairs of 6L6 power tubes for push-pull operation. The same phase inverter was used in all the amps, and the same reverb tank/circuit was used (in most of the combo amps, not the heads). All the amps except the Bassman head and the Champ featured opto-coupler tremolo (labeled "vibrato") circuits. Fixed bias with an adjustment potentiometer was used. Smaller models used tube rectifiers while high-power models used solid-state rectifiers.

Some larger Blackface models add an adjustable midrange control on the Vibrato channel. For those with fixed midrange (no midrange control), the mids are wired to be equivalent to the adjustable midrange control set to 5. Most models feature Bright switches on both channels, which allows the high frequencies to bypass the volume control. The Bright switch has less and less effect as the amp is turned up. The Bassman replaced the Bright switch on the Normal channel with a Deep switch, which fattened the low end.

Tonally, Blackface amps produce tight low end, with reduced midrange, and sparkling top end. The amps are very responsive to touch, with punchy attack and good dynamics. As they are turned up, they begin to break up smoothly, reaching a sweet spot with good sustain and rich tone—the volume of that sweet spot, of course, depends on the model. With a Princeton, the volume can be manageable; with a Twin, getting to the sweet spot results in substantial output! While Blackface amps sound great when cranked, they are perhaps most renowned for creating the ultimate clean electric guitar tone.

Famous users of Blackface amps include Stevie Ray Vaughan, Eric Johnson, Dick Dale, countless country and blues players, and more. Blackface are among the most sought-after amps on the vintage market and have been cloned by many manufacturers, as well as reissued by Fender.

Silverface

In January of 1965, Leo Fender sold Fender Electric Instruments Company to CBS, which renamed the company Fender Musical Instruments. This gave rise to significant delineation, "pre-CBS" and "post-CBS," though technically, changes to the amps did not begin until 1967, with the Blackface era ending with the change to silverface control panels in that year. But even from that point, the early Silverface amps were still very similar, if not identical, to the Blackface circuits. And, even as the Silverface amps began to evolve, their circuits remained close enough to Blackface designs that a technician could still modify them back to Blackface specs quite easily.

However, beyond the early Silverface years, the amps had been changed so much from the Blackface specs that only serious (and expensive) modification could make them Blackface. In most cases, amps made prior to mid-1968 can be easily "Blackfaced." After that time, most Fender amps are too different from the Blackface designs to be effectively modded. By late 1968, the wiring used in the amps was changed from cloth-covered to PVC (plastic) covered. For most experts this change was the final, absolute end of the Blackface circuits. If nothing else, the lead dress (how the wires were routed and secured) was not as neat and precise with the PVC wires ("messy" is how one expert described it); some experts feel that this could affect the tone produced.

So, what's the big deal? Why are the Silverface amps so maligned? For many players, the reason is that the Blackface amps are perceived as the pinnacle of Fender tone—a high bar was set, and the Silverfaces couldn't reach that level. When CBS purchased the company and began meddling with the circuits, the sound changed. Beyond this, most believe that the components used in Silverface amps were of lesser quality and that the speakers weren't as good. The biasing was changed as well, from the bias adjustment pot found on Blackfaces to a pot that was used to balance the bias between the power tubes. This was done to allow the use of unmatched tubes, to compensate for the lower-quality tubes available at the time, and to reduce hum resulting from circuit design changes. The circuits were modified for higher voltages, in order to provide more clean headroom.

Beginning in 1972, even the cabinets were changed, from solid pine construction to laminated wood, with the planks required made by gluing 3- or 4-inch wide strips together. The cabinets were also rabbet joined instead of finger joined. Because the speaker baffle was mortised into the cabinet, a separate frame with the grille cloth stretched over it was attached using hook-and-loop fasteners.

By the '70s, Oxford and Utah speakers had taken over as the stock offering, displacing the Jensens that were primarily used earlier. In general, players do not find these speakers to sound as good as the Jensens. JBL D-series speakers were offered as an optional upgrade.

Tonally, compared to the Blackface amps, Silverface amps are often described as more "flabby" in the bottom end, with less detail in the top end, and with saggier and mushier response due to the use of different rectifier tubes (switched from GZ34 in the Blackfaces to the cheaper 5U4GB in the Silverfaces). Changes to the power transformers and changing from Mallory capacitors to "chocolate drop" capacitors are said to make the Silverfaces more two-dimensional feeling and sounding than the Blackfaces.

In 1972, Fender began adding master volume controls and pull-boosts to the amps to allow for distortion at lower volume. Many players feel that the distortion on these master volume–equipped amps is a failure; fortunately the master volume controls can be easily bypassed and removed from the circuit.

Yikes, based on all that, the Silverface Fenders must be the worst amps in the world! The reality isn't quite that dismal. With some exceptions, such as the "ultra-linear" high-power amps of the late '70s and early '80s, the Silverfaces sound like Fender amps. Not quite the same as the Blackfaces, but, depending on the year and circuit, there are many excellent-sounding Silverfaces—and you can get them at much more affordable prices than their Blackface brethren. The key is to know what you're getting, and in some cases what mods will bring the amp to life (such as swapping out the speakers).

Modern Fenders

Since the Silverface era, Fender has released many, many new models, some of which have done well and sound very good—their Hot Rod series of amps, for example, is said to be the best-selling tube amp on the market at the time of this writing. But perhaps their biggest success, from a tonal standpoint, has been a series of reissues of the vintage models, ranging from Tweed Champs, Princetons, Twins, and Deluxes, to Blackface Princetons, Twins, Deluxes, and Supers. Opinions vary among players as to how accurate these reproductions are. Some, such as the Tweed reissues, are perceived as very close to the originals. And the Custom Shop amplifiers, such as the Vibro King, have also been well received.

The Blackface reissues, which are based on printed circuit board construction, as opposed to hand wiring, seem to be more polarizing; some players feel they sound great, while others prefer the originals. In technical terms, some players believe that the biggest difference between the hand-wired originals and the printed circuit board reissues is that the originals are easier to repair. Others say that printed circuit boards don't have the same signal-carrying characteristics as point-to-point wires.

Many players suggest that changing the stock tubes on the Blackface reissues out for NOS tubes, changing out the speaker—even just seriously breaking in the stock speaker—and sometimes changing out the transformers can make a big difference in these amps. There is also a "bright" capacitor on the reverb channel of the Deluxe Reverb Reissue that most players recommend clipping to tame harsh top end.

In fairness, the only way to really objectively compare an original to a reissue would be to use the same tubes, make sure the biasing is correct (many Fenders I've seen have been biased cold from the factory, which definitely affects their performance), and use the same speaker and speaker cabinet. Then you can truly evaluate the comparison—though any aged components, such as capacitors, will still make a difference in the sound of the original.

Marshall

It's tough to dispute that Marshall is responsible for much of the sound of rock! But the company we know today as one of the major sources of rock 'n roll tone had very humble beginnings. Jim Marshall was a drummer and drum teacher who opened a small drum shop in the early 1960s. The story goes that the burgeoning guitar heros of the day—Ritchie Blackmore, Pete Townshend, and more—would come into the shop with their drummer cohorts and ask why Marshall wasn't also selling guitar gear. Marshall began importing Fender and Gibson guitars and Fender amps, but, in the true spirit of an entrepreneur, he decided he could make his own amplifiers and sell them for less money.

JTM45 and Bluesbreaker

With his repairman Ken Bran and tech Dudley Craven, Marshall began making prototypes of a tube amp based around the 5F6-A Fender Bassman (1956, first revision) circuit. In fact, the original prototypes copied this circuit exactly but substituted 12AX7 tubes for the tweed Bassman's 12AY7 tubes for more preamp gain. The tone stack in the prototypes and early amps was also very close to the 5F6-A, with different capacitor values for slightly different frequency points. The phase inverter is the same, and the power amp is similar, but with triple the amount of negative feedback, the Marshall prototypes had flatter response and lower gain than the Bassman.

Perhaps the biggest difference: Marshall decided to house the amp electronics in a separate head cabinet from the speaker cabinet. He also chose to use four 12-inch Celestion speakers in a closed-back cabinet instead of the four 10-inch Jensens in an open-back cabinet that Fender used. This created a very different tone from the Fenders, with bigger, chunkier bottom end, more punch, and less high-end sparkle.

An infusion of capital from his distributor, Rose-Morris, allowed Marshall to go into production for amps, with the first model released for production named the JTM45 (named for James and his son Terry Marshall and the amp's claimed 45-watt power rating). Unfortunately, the Rose-Morris deal didn't work out well, with Marshall feeling that the distributor priced his amps too high for most buyers. To counter this, he released amps under a variety of other names, including Park, Narb, Big M, Kitchen/Marshall, and CMI. Today, these rare other-named models are highly sought after.

To reduce production costs, Marshall began using tubes from England in 1964, notably the KT-66 in place of the 6L6. This resulted in a tougher, more aggressive tone that players such as Eric Clapton enjoyed. When he joined the Bluesbreakers, Clapton asked Marshall to build him a small combo amp with tremolo. Two models were created, the Model 1961 with four 10-inch speakers, and the Model 1962 with two 12-inch speakers—the latter, made in 1965 and 1966, gained more popularity and became known as the Bluesbreaker model.

These early Marshall amps, along with other models, such as the 1974 combo and 2061 head, will be surprisingly clean, low-gain designs for those familiar with only modern high-gain Marshalls. These amps are extremely dynamic and very touch sensitive, and they offer tremendous transient response for powerful note attack. Though these KT-66 powered Marshalls have good headroom and are capable of warm, rich clean tones, they really want to be cranked up to get their real sound—which means they're *loud*, even the seemingly low-powered 18-watt models. If you want a fat, gritty, grinding moderate-gain tone with articulate top end, these are the Marshalls for you.

The JTM45 amps feature four inputs feeding two channels, High Treble and Normal, each with its own Loudness control. It has become common practice for players to use short cables to jumper these two channels together and then tailor the overall gain and tone using the Loudness controls. The tube rectifier provides a softer sound, with nice "sag" that many players enjoy.

Plexi Amps

As loud as the JTM45 amps were, players such as Pete Townshend and John Entwhistle from the Who began requesting even bigger amplifiers for increased volume, as well as 8×12" cabinets for more projection and volume. Marshall responded with a new amp, the 100-watt Model 1959 Super Lead—with a gold plexiglas front panel—that immediately earned a place as one of the great rock amps. Soon after, KT-66 tubes went up in price, and Marshall switched to using EL34 power tubes, which gave a smoother sound with excellent harmonic content.

The big changes in these amps were larger power transformers and higher plate voltages. There was a specific reason for this: The PA systems of the day were, to be kind, lacking in power and quality. The idea behind the Super Lead and other amps was to provide an amp loud enough to make up for the shortcomings of the sound systems, especially when mated with a stack of two 4×12" cabinets. The higher power also gave them more headroom than earlier JTMs.

In 1968, the JMP series of amps came out, which used slightly smaller transformers and slightly lower plate voltages. This resulted in less clean headroom and more reliable performance from the amps. The main models in the JMP series included the Bass and Super Bass (50 and 100 watts, respectively) and Lead and Super Lead (also 50 and 100 watts, respectively). Marshall Major (200 screaming watts of gut-punching power) and Tremolo and Super Tremolo models (with built-in tremolo effects) were also released in much smaller numbers, as well as the eight-input P.A. and Super P.A. Models (which can be cranked up with a guitar for excellent Marshall tones).

Like the JTM-era amps, the Plexi amps have four inputs, which players often jumper together. These amps are also regularly modded—this was especially popular in the '80s—so many of the "vintage" units have added master volume controls, added effects loops, an extra preamp tube for gain, and/or an added cooling fan for better reliability. And, like the JTMs, these amps sound best when they are cranked. The 100 watters are a bit louder (though not as much as you might think) than the 50 watters, with tighter bottom end and increased headroom.

If you find an unaltered Plexi, it will have more crunch than a JTM but still wouldn't be considered a high-gain amplifier by most players. Plexi amps have a ton of punch and bright, articulate top end. They are very dynamic and provide rich, harmonic-laden tones. Keep in mind that these are not master volume amps (unless modded later). To drive them hard, you have to play hard and loud, use a booster, or use a guitar with high-output pickups.

There are countless examples of recorded Plexi tones, from Jimi Hendrix to Jimmy Page to Angus Young. The "Plexi tone" perhaps reached its apex with Eddie Van Halen's much-vaunted "Brown Sound" on the early Van Halen albums. Accounts vary as to how this tone was achieved, with Eddie claiming his Plexi was modded and run using a Variac to increase the wall voltage. Others dispute this, saying that Eddie got his tone using a stock Plexi and his specific guitar, pickups, and effects, including an Echoplex, which is known for the tone and boost of its preamp.

For many players, the Plexi-era amps are the pinnacle of Marshall, with their hand-wired construction and excellent transformers.

Metal Panels and the JCM800

In 1969, Marshall changed the control panels on their amps to gold-colored brushed aluminum, ending the Plexi era. However, through 1973, the circuits in the metal-panel amps remained the same as the equivalent plexi-paneled model, with the same hand wiring and components. However, the plate voltages were reduced to extend tube life, and the amps became a bit brighter, an ongoing trend for Marshall. In many cases, with a few component changes, it is possible to return an early metal panel Marshall to Plexi specs.

In 1973, printed circuit board construction began to replace hand wiring, and in 1976, master volume controls were introduced in new head and combo models, such as the Model 2204 (50 watts) and the Model 2203 (100 watts). Around this time, U.S. and Japan export models began to come equipped with 6550 power tubes at the request of the distributor, who felt that EL34s were not reliable. Players generally believe that amps from this time period are not as good as those prior to 1973, though these amps can be easily converted to use EL34s, making them much more similar to earlier models.

In 1981, Marshall saw the release of the JCM800 series master volume amps, which featured updated cosmetics. The Model 2203 and Model 2204 remained in the lineup under the new series and contained the same circuits as the similarly named JMP-era models. Beginning in 1985, the circuit for the 2203 100 watter was changed to cut costs. (The 50-watt 2204 was not changed.) Some players feel these changes resulted in the 2203 having a thinner, grainier tone with less punch and volume. Around this time, 2205 (50 watts) and 2210 (100 watts) channel-switching models were introduced as both heads and combos. Some players felt these amps lacked the fullness of earlier models, but other players enjoyed the ability to have a clean channel in their Marshall, paired with a distortion channel with a master volume control to keep things reined in.

Later JCM800s in Europe and Canada featured 6550 power tubes, as the supply of decent EL34s had dried up—and would remain dry until new tube factories came online in Russia in the mid-'90s. These were higher powered, somewhat fatter, more metallic-sounding tubes that have found favor with players such as Zakk Wylde with Ozzy Osbourne.

In 1987, Marshall celebrated their 25th anniversary—and Jim Marshall's 50th anniversary in the music business —with the release of the 25/50 Silver Jubilee amp, which featured silver panels and custom silver Tolex. These are very highly regarded amps, despite featuring some of the changed circuitry from the JCM800s, because the circuits were specially tuned by Marshall with unique tone stacks and increased gain. An effects loop, direct out, and channel switching increased the versatility. An extra gain stage using a diode for clipping was added, to the dismay of some players who immediately dismissed this solid-state addition to the all-tube Marshall design, but others found the tone and gain of the circuit to be spot on. Joe Bonamassa is one player who relies on a Silver Jubilee (often paired with various other complementary amps) as the basis of his tone.

Modern Marshalls

Since the 1990s, Marshall has faced strong competition in the rock amp market from a variety of manufacturers, including Mesa/Boogie, Soldano, Peavey, and newer "boutique" manufacturers ranging from those making clones of vintage Marshall models to those pushing the high-gain limits ever higher. Marshall has responded with signature amps from players such as Slash and Kerry King (Slayer), both of which were based on the JCM800. Early amps have also been reissued, such as the Model 1959, the Model 1974X, the JTM45, and the Bluesbreaker, and there have been special limited-run models, such as an excellent one designed after Jimi Hendrix's amps. The JCM900, DSL, TSL, and JVM series have expanded the tonal possibilities with additional channels, more flexible controls, and extensive features. Opinions vary on the tonal quality of the new amps, but these amps have been especially popular with high-gain metal players and shredders.

Vox AC30

With roots dating back to Tom Jennings' first music store in the 1940s, which imported accordions, the history of Vox amplifiers begins with a small portable amp released under the Univox name. The first actual Vox-labeled product, a volume pedal, appeared in 1954. Various amps were released under the JMI (*Jennings Musical Instruments*) name; then in 1957, the Vox AC2/30 appeared ("AC" for "alternating current," a new concept at the time). January 1958 saw the AC1/15 (later known as the AC15) and the G1/10 (which became the AC10) amps released. In the summer of 1959, the AC30 debuted. In the late 1950s and early 1960s, the new Vox amps became very popular with players in the nascent British rock scene. The company expanded the line quickly with models such as the AC50 and AC100 (as used by the Beatles and others), as well as with Phantom guitars, the wah-wah pedal, and much more.

Unfortunately, the business side of things did not go as smoothly as the gear design side of things. By the late 1960s, Tom Jennings and other key people were forced out of the company. Bad investments and business deals were made, and the company went into receivership. The brand passed through several different hands, including CBS (who also owned Fender at the time) and Rose Morris (distributor for Marshall) over the next two decades. The company continued to make amps, but the designs were changed, mostly for cost-cutting reasons. Then in 1993, Korg acquired Vox and set out to restore the AC30, the flagship amp of the line, to its former glory. Since then, hand-wired reissues of the AC15 and AC30 have been released, along with models featuring more modern features. New amps and a successful line of Valvetronix modeling amps have also been released. But the star of the company's line remains the venerable AC30, with its distinctive black Tolex/brown diamond grille cloth cosmetics.

The first generation Vox AC30s—or more accurately AC30/4, for its four inputs—had a TV front cabinet, much like early Fender amps. The Normal channel used an EF86 preamp tube, while the Bright channel used ECC83 tubes (known as 12AX7 tubes in the U.S.). The preamp had a single tone control. Two EL34 power tubes were used for power. These were soon replaced by four EL84 power tubes. Originally, the AC30 had a single 12-inch Goodmans 60-watt speaker; the AC30 Twin model used two 12-inch speakers. The Goodmans speakers were eventually replaced with Celestion G12 alnico speakers. By 1960, the TV front was gone, and the amps were covered in fawn-colored "Rexine" material.

In 1961, the AC30/6 was expanded to three channels—Normal, Brilliant, and Bass—with all three driven by ECC83/12AX7 preamp tubes. An option for the AC30, called the Top Boost, was also introduced. The Top Boost option mounted to the back of the amp and added a gain stage and bass and treble controls.

By 1963, the Top Boost was standard on AC30s (commonly referred to as AC30TB models), with its controls moved to the standard top-mounted control panel.

Though the circuit is usually described as a pure Class A design, it has many characteristics of a Class AB design, with cathode bias. A tube rectifier is used—the GZ34—but the power supply has little "sag," even when hit hard. No negative feedback is used in the design, which reduces clean headroom. There are actually numerous points in the circuit where the amp easily goes into distortion: the preamp, the power amp, the small output transformer, and the Celestion speakers. Like Fender and Marshall amps, there is a sweet spot, volume-wise, where the AC30 really begins to sing. Despite the fact that the amp is rated for 30 watts, that sweet spot is typically quite loud.

Today, Vox offers hand-wired reissues of the original Top Boost AC30, as well as modernized Custom Classic versions. JMI has also returned to business and offers clones of vintage AC30s, both two- and three-channel versions. The Top Boost circuit is an optional retrofit on the JMI amps. Many other manufacturers also make clones of the AC30.

The AC30 definitely has a one-of-a-kind sound compared to Fender and Marshall amps. "Jangle" and "chime" are two adjectives often applied to the amps. With the original EF86 preamp, the AC30 can take on some of the tonal characteristics of early Marshall amps. The Normal channel offers a warm, round tone, while the Top Boost adds substantial gain and top end. The amp's unique High Cut tone control allows the high frequencies to be rolled off, making the tone darker and warmer. While not high gain amps, AC30s can definitely get into heavy-distortion territory when pushed.

The list of players who have relied on the Vox AC30 range from country pickers such as Brad Paisley and Buddy Miller to rockers such as Brian Downy (Thin Lizzy and Pink Floyd), and from blues rockers such as Rory Gallagher to jazzers including John Scofield. But the iconic AC30 tones are in the hands of alt-rockers such as Peter Buck of REM, rockers Tom Petty and Mike Campbell, and, of course, U2's the Edge and Queen's Brian May (who was honored with a limited-edition signature model).

Roland Jazz Chorus

In 1975, Roland released one of the first truly successful solid-state amplifiers, the JC-120 Jazz Chorus. It is also one of the only amps (solid-state or tube) to continue in production today—with only minor differences between the current units and the originals. The Jazz Chorus was also the first stereo combo amplifier to reach the market. It contains two 60-watt amplifiers, each driving its own 12-inch speaker. The JC-120 has two channels, Normal and Effect, with a bright switch and a 3-band EQ on each channel. The Effect channel can access the built-in analog chorus to create the stereo effect. The chorus is actually mono, operating on just one of the amps/speakers, but when combined with the other amp running dry, the effect is a wide, lush stereo image. Reverb, distortion, and vibrato effects are also accessible from the Effect channel.

A number of Jazz Chorus siblings were released over the years, including heads and mono-only versions. See Table 15.4 for details on these various models.

Table 15.4 Roland Jazz Chorus Models

Model	Preamp Channels	EQ	Power Amp	Speakers	Effects Loop
JC-20 (Japan only)	1	3-band	2×10 watts	2×5"	No
JC-50	1	2-band	1×50 watts	1×12"	No
JC-55	1	3-band	2×25 watts	2×8"	No
JC-60A	1	3-band	1×60 watts	1×12"	No
JC-77	1	4-band	2×40 watts	2×10"	No
JC-80	1	3-band	1×60 watts	1×15"	No
JC-90	1	4-band	2×40 watts	2×10"	Mono send/ stereo return
JC-120A	2: Normal and Effect	3-band per channel	2×60 watts	2×12"	No
JC-120H	1	4-band	2×60 watts	—	No
JC-120E	2: Normal and Effect	3-band per channel	2×60 watts	2×12"	Stereo send/ stereo return
JC-160	2: Normal and Effect	3-band per channel	2×60 watts	4×10"	No
JC-200	2: Normal and Effect	3-band per channel	2×100 watts	—	No

Though the Jazz Chorus hasn't changed much, there have been a few changes over the years. For example, somewhere along the line, the amp gained a stereo effects loop that can be switched between series or parallel operation and between line or instrument level for matching the loop to stompboxes or pro rack gear. There are those who feel that the cabinets aren't built quite the same on newer models, and there was a brief period when different speakers were used. The original speakers were quickly reinstated and have remained the same since. The circuitry has also been changed from all discrete components to a mix of discrete components and integrated circuits. Still, most players feel that the tone of the Jazz Chorus has remained fairly consistent through these changes.

The Jazz Chorus did indeed find favor among jazz players such as Lee Ritenour and George Benson, but it has also proven popular among players of other styles of music. From Andy Summers of the Police to Metallica, from King Crimson to Joni Mitchell, the clean, chorused JC sound has appeared on many recordings and stages in many musical genres. The emphasis in that statement should definitely be on "clean"—you'll almost never hear a Jazz Chorus amp used for its distortion sound, which is often described as dry, sticky, and sterile. The Jazz Chorus is also popular with guitar synthesizer users because of the amp's pristine, hi-fi clean sound and powerful full-range output.

Mesa/Boogie

What started as a practical joke led to two breakthroughs on the way to a major music industry success—and perhaps the first boutique amplifier company. In the late '60s, Randall Smith, an employee at a small music store (that started as a Chinese restaurant) with second jobs rebuilding Mercedes-Benz engines and doing home repair, came up with an idea for putting one over on his friend Barry Melton of Country Joe and the Fish: He would take Melton's Fender Princeton amp and rebuild it with the guts from a Bassman and a JBL D-120 12-inch speaker—when his unsuspecting friend turned on his "Princeton," he'd be blown out the door by the super-loud little amp. Local players, including Carlos Santana, found out about the hot-rod Princeton and wanted one of their own. More than 200 of those Princeton "Boogie" amps (a name credited to Santana's response to hearing the first amp) were made.

The second breakthrough was Smith's idea for adding an extra tube gain stage to a preamp he was building to drive a player named Lee Michael's Crown power amp. Three volume controls were used in the circuit to control the preamp gain. This "cascaded" preamp design became the basis for Smith's first production amplifier, the Mark I, released in 1972. Since then, Mesa/Boogie has released dozens of amplifier models, but the Mark series has remained the flagship of the line.

Mark I

The original Mark I (the Mark I name actually was an afterthought; it wasn't used until later, after the Mark II came out) was a 60- or 100-watt all-tube design. Unlike later Boogie designs, both of the Mark I's gain stages occur before the tone controls, which is said to give the amp a "looser" sound. The amps have two channels, one said to be voiced like a Fender Bassman, the other with the Boogie "high gain" sound. There actually were separate input jacks for the two channels; there was no footswitching, though an A/B switch could be used to choose which jack your guitar was feeding.

Reverb was an option; later, other options such as onboard graphic EQ, and additional features such as Pull Bright and Pull Boost were offered. The speakers were Altec-Lansing or Electro-Voice models.

The Mark I was quickly adopted by Carlos Santana—perhaps their biggest proponent—along with Keith Richards and Ron Wood of the Rolling Stones, Larry Carlton, and many more. In addition to the massive (for the time) amounts of gain on tap in the amp, Boogies became known for their beautiful exotic wood cabinets, cane/ wicker grilles, and other custom options.

Mark II

The second generation of Boogie amps introduced such features as channel switching (Mark IIA) and an effects loop and lead drive and master controls (Mark IIB). The Mark IIB generation also saw the arrival of Boogie's proprietary Simul-class operation, where in a 100-watt amp two of the power tubes run in Class AB while the other two run in Class A. A Mark IIB could be configured with either a switch for Simul-class operation or a switch that took the amp from 100 watts down to 60 watts. Pull Bright, Pull Shift (midrange shift), and Pull Boost switches on the front-panel controls were standard equipment.

The Mark IIC had improved, quieter channel switching and a better reverb circuit. The Mark IIC+, the last of the Mark II series, had a better effects loop circuit and a more sensitive lead channel. The Mark IIC+ is widely regarded as having the best-sounding, sweetest lead channel in a Boogie amp, especially among hard rockers and metal players.

Mark III

The next generation Mesa/Boogie amps, the Mark III, added a "crunch" or "rhythm" channel, which shared the controls of the clean channel. Some players dislike this model because with the shared controls, the tone of each channel was a compromise. Make the lead channel sound good, and the crunch and clean channels suffered. Set up a great clean sound, and the crunch and lead channels are compromised. There could also be a volume drop when switching to the crunch channel on early Mark IIIs.

Mark IV

In 1990, Mesa launched the Mark IV, which expanded on the three-channel concept by adding independent controls for the clean, crunch, and lead channels. (The clean and crunch channels still shared bass and mid controls.) The A version, which was made through late 1993, did not have footswitch control over the reverb or effects loop. Its lead channel is said to sound like the one in the Mark IIIC. The B version, made until 2008, had a footswitchable reverb and effects loop and a slightly revoiced lead channel.

Mark V

The latest in the Mark series, the Mark V, offers three completely independent channels that feature switches that can change their voicing to tweed, Mark I, Mark IIC+, Mark IV, Marshall, and other tones. Graphic EQ is standard; it can be assigned to any or all channels, and there are "contour" switches for controlling the effect of the EQ on each channel. Each channel can also be set for 10 watts Class A, 45 watts Class AB, or 90 watts Simul-class output power. In addition to a master volume control, there is a footswitchable Solo master volume for setting a second level. The fixed power amp bias can be switched for either 6L6 or EL34 tubes. The effects loop can be assigned per channel. Then there are the extras, such as a tuner out, slave out, cooling fan, and more—in other words, it's the "kitchen sink" Boogie.

Tonally, any of the Mark series can cover a very wide range of sounds—though, of course, the newer models are even more flexible and gain-laden than the revolutionary originals. From sparkling clean to thick crunch to bright chime to harmonic soaked, super-sustain overdrive, the preamps offer many options. The tone stacks are powerful, even without the addition of a graphic EQ, and most of the models offer tons of tone-shaping options and features. The list of innovations and patents that Randall Smith and his crew have come up with is very impressive, and, though not everyone loves their tones, Boogies have certainly established themselves as benchmarks in many areas. The cascading gain idea alone would have been enough to lock in Boogie's place in amp history, let alone everything else the company has done. The biggest complaint that players have regarding these amps can be summed up as "too many knobs" or "too complicated."

Dumble Overdrive Special

Myth, rumor, misconception, and near-religious zeal—just type the words "Dumble" and "amp" into a message on any guitar forum, and you'll spark an almost instant debate filled with fervor and, unfortunately, probably vitriol. People seem to either love Alexander (formerly Howard) Dumble's amp creations passionately or to hate them with equal passion. But there's no denying, Dumble's amps—and the who's who of tone-centric guitarists that use them, such as Robben Ford, Larry Carlton, Sonny Landreth, John Mayer, Stevie Ray Vaughan, Carlos Santana, and Eric Johnson—have made a huge mark on guitar tone. Though Dumble's own amp manufacturing output is small in numbers (less than 200 or 300 are estimated to exist, depending on whom you ask), the void has been filled by clone amps, "inspired by" amps, and a cadre of pedals that attempt to emulate the tone of these controversial amplifiers.

All of this controversy is fueled by the reclusive and secretive nature of Dumble himself—who is either revered as an amp design genius or dismissed as someone who based his amps on Fenders, which were based on RCA tube application notes—and by the amazingly high prices his amps bring. New amps are said to be in the $20,000 range, with used amps selling for $50,000 or even more. For some reason, these high prices and rumors about Dumble cause highly polarized reactions among players, particularly among players who have never used one.

Perhaps the most widely known Dumble model is the Overdrive Special. This amp features two inputs, a "normal" input and a second input using a solid-state initial input stage. The input stage is followed by tube stages and passive EQ. Additional tube gain stages follow the EQ. Numerous switches, including bright, deep, mid, boost, and rock/jazz, allow the amp's tone and response to be tailored. Some models also allow the response to be tailored with trim pots inside the amp. Beyond this, Dumble is said to customize and personalize each amp for its intended owner/player. Various mods and updates, such as the Robben Ford mod (adds "sag" to the amp), the Skyliner EQ (re-voicing of the tone stack), and the HRM (Hot Rubber Monkey mod adds a second, internal tone stack after the overdrive stage), can additionally tailor the response of the amp.

Generally, Dumble amps do not include an effects loop. Rather, an external rackmount box, called a *Dumbleator*, is used to interface the amp with rack or stompbox effects. Most Dumble Overdrive Specials use 12AX7 preamp tubes and 6L6 power tubes, though a few use EL34 tubes. The amps are hand wired to eyelet boards, using components carefully specified by Dumble. The circuit boards and components in the amps are covered in epoxy "goop" to keep them secret from prying eyes or potential cloners. In the early days, Dumble also protected his circuits with a sort of nondisclosure document that purchasers were required to sign.

Fans of Dumble amps speak of the amps' fast response and touch sensitivity as well as the throaty, horn-like midrange tonal quality and extended sustain. There is a "bloom" to the mids and lows, with smooth high frequencies, open but not compressed. There is less crunch than a Marshall and less "sag" than a Fender. Those who love them, love them. Those who don't like them…they tend to hate them, and often dislike the players who use them—not necessarily personally, but just in regard to the tones and styles of music they prefer.

There's certainly no other amp that has inspired so much rhetoric!

Iconic Effects

JUST AS THERE HAVE BEEN CERTAIN ICONIC ELECTRIC guitars and amplifiers through the years, so have certain effects pedals established themselves as touchstones for producing certain tones. I'm not talking about the "flavor of the month" pedals that some Internet forum is raving about (until the next month, when a new flavor appears), but pedals that create or created a new, distinct, lasting sound—that have stood the test of time, that have been copied over and over (and over) and used as the inspiration for new pedals by major manufacturers and boutique manufacturers, and that have even been modeled repeatedly by digital effects manufacturers.

This list could be much longer—I'm sure someone will be asking, "Where is the Colorsound Tone Bender, MXR Distortion+, MuTron BiPhase or MuTron II, Fender Blender, A/DA Flanger, Foxx Tone Machine, Ross Compressor, Electro-Harmonix Small Stone…" or whatever might be his or her favorite vintage pedal. Then there will be those looking for the newer hot pedals—Klon Centaur, Hermida Zendrive, Analog Man King of Tone, DigiTech Whammy, or whatever. But since we don't have room to look at every one of the hundreds of great pedals on the market, we'll look at those stompboxes that made the most impact through the years, whether they are new or old, and the ones that have been imitated and copied the most.

BOSS CE-1 Chorus Ensemble

Though there were chorus-type effects before the BOSS CE-1 Chorus Ensemble (such as the Uni-Vibe, various flangers, and so on), the Chorus Ensemble was really the one that defined what "chorus" meant. Launched in 1976 and based on the chorus circuit found in Roland's JC-120 Jazz Chorus guitar amplifiers, the CE-1 is an all-analog device that offers a choice of either stereo chorus or stereo vibrato featuring true pitch shifting. ("Stereo" in this case means dry signal from one output and wet signal from the other output.) It was the first pedal released under Roland's new BOSS guitar pedal division brand. (Trivia: Legend has it that Roland's guitar division was originally named MEG, for Musical Engineering Group, until they realized that "Meg" was a girl's name.)

It was also the first pedal to use the then-new BBD (*bucket brigade driver* or *bucket brigade delay*) integrated circuit technology. The chorus is controlled by one level control, while the vibrato can be controlled with depth and speed knobs.

At first, the Chorus Ensemble was slowly adopted by guitarists as well as keyboard players for its ability to generate everything from shimmer to spacious, lush sounds to near-Leslie rotating speaker simulation. (More trivia: The CE-1 became known in some circles as the "Andy Summers in a Box" pedal, though both Pete Cornish and Andy Summers himself have asserted that he never used it—his original chorus sound came from a modified Electro-Harmonix Electric Mistress flanger.) Momentum picked up toward the end of the 1970s, and then BOSS scored a big hit with the first CE-1 descendant, the familiar compact blue CE-2 mono chorus. (There were two versions of the CE-2—the early ones made in Japan and those released after 1988, which were made in Taiwan. The earlier versions are slightly richer and smoother sounding.)

These days, the CE-1 seems somewhat limited to many players, and its size and weight make it less desirable for many pedalboard applications. It has also become known for tone suck when it is bypassed—the pedal was originally aimed at low-impedance signals, such as keyboards, and not at guitars—though there are mods to address this, or a buffered pedal in front of it will help. However, the CE-1 has been honored with both boutique re-creations and ongoing generations of descendants from BOSS and other manufacturers.

BOSS DD-2

Another effects coup for Roland/BOSS: The DD-2 was the first digital delay stompbox—digital delays had appeared before the DD-2, but there had never been a compact, guitar-centric digital delay pedal before. The DD-2 was introduced in 1984 and became an immediate hit. It offered up to 800 milliseconds of delay time, substantially more than the analog delays and tape-based delays of the day. But unlike the crystal-clear rack-mount digital delays available at the time, the DD-2's delay repeats managed to achieve an "organic," analog-like sound, which many players found blended with the dry signal better. In addition to straight echo/delay effects, the DD-2 had a sample/hold mode for repeating a short passage or creating a short loop. As with the CE-2 chorus discussed a moment ago, the original DD-2 units were made in Japan, with later DD-2s made in Taiwan. Many players prefer the sound of the Japanese DD-2s.

BOSS's DD line of delays continues to expand to this day—and remains among the most popular stompboxes—with the descendants of the DD-2 including the DD-3, DD-5, DD-6, DD-7, and larger-format DD-20. Several companies offer modifications to the various members of the DD series of delays, providing extended capabilities or improved tonality.

B.K. Butler Tube Driver

B.K. Butler began making tube overdrives for his own use in the mid-1970s and then went to work for Carvin. In 1979, he launched an early version of the Tube Drive, a tube-based overdrive pedal, with ads in *Guitar Player* magazine. While working as an engineer at Dean Markley in the early 1980s, he came up with a new tube overdrive design—the now familiar Tube Driver—which Chandler began marketing for him. At some point, there was a split from Chandler, resulting in unauthorized versions of the pedal that are not the same as what Butler designed. Butler designed the Tube Works Real Tubes rack preamp and MosValve amplifier, as well as a three-knob "entry-level" version of the Tube Driver. Around 1993 or 1994, he began making the 911, essentially a re-release of the four-knob Tube Driver.

According to Butler, when he was developing the Tube Driver, he voiced it by playing the chords from ZZ Top's "Tush" over and over again on a Rhodes piano. The pedal offers a rich, complex, tube-fueled overdrive, with a neutral tonality that you can shape using the bass and treble controls. It has plenty of gain and output on tap and can almost push into fuzz territory. The Tube Driver comes configured with a 12AX7 preamp tube, but other preamp tubes can be substituted for different gain levels and tones, such as the 12AT7, 12AU7, or others. (A 12AT7 would put out around 60 percent of the gain of a 12AX7, a 12AY7 would have around 45 percent the gain of a 12AX7, and a 12AU7 would only put out around 19 percent as much gain as a 12AX7.)

At this writing, B.K. Butler is making about six of these units per week, personally voicing and checking each one by hand. He also offers upgrades, such as NOS tubes and a bias knob that allows additional control over the tube saturation and tone. Prominent players who rely on the Tube Driver include Eric Johnson (see Chapter 26), Keith Urban, David Gilmour (see Chapter 22), and Billy Gibbons.

Dallas Arbiter Fuzz Face

The Fuzz Face fuzz box may be one of the simplest guitar effects ever designed—the originals had something like 11 electronic components total. And, it is also one of the most copied or "cloned" effects, which is interesting, since the Fuzz Face is also one of the least consistent and most temperamental of effects. Plug in two vintage units, and they could sound equally good and yet sound completely different from one another; which one should you clone?

Most experts recognize two distinct generations of the original Fuzz Face. The first generation, made by Arbiter Electronics (later Dallas Arbiter) beginning in 1966, used two germanium transistors to create distortion. Germanium has interesting tonal characteristics, with a thick, smooth tone without fizziness and generally with a low to moderate amount of gain. However, the consistency of germanium transistors varies wildly, with tolerances in values skewing as much as 50 percent! (This is one reason why two "identical" vintage Fuzz Faces can sound completely different.) Plus, germanium is affected by temperature and different types and strengths of batteries. Use a germanium Fuzz Face in a hot, sweaty club one night, and you'll get a certain tone. Use it the next afternoon for a rehearsal in a cool basement, and the sound may be totally different. Change the type of battery you're using or replace an old battery with a fresh one, and the tone will also change. (Most experts recommend non-alkaline batteries for germanium Fuzz Faces, as alkaline batteries will make the sound duller.) The "features" continue, such as the tendency for Fuzz Faces to break into wild, screaming oscillation when they are plugged in after certain other buffered pedals, such as most non-true bypass wahs. Using other pedals, such as a compressor, before a Fuzz Face will result in nastier fuzz tones.

The second generation of Fuzz Faces, those made beginning in 1969, used silicon transistors. Using silicon fixed many of the inconsistencies of the germanium transistors but produced a fuzz tone that's variously described as fuzzier, brighter, harsher, or edgier. Many users prefer the original germanium sound, but it's interesting that two notable guitarists relied on silicon Fuzz Faces for their most lauded sounds: Jimi Hendrix in his Band of Gypsies days (see Chapter 24) and Eric Johnson, who uses a silicon Fuzz Face as part of his dirty rhythm guitar signal chain.

Within these two generations of the original vintage Fuzz Faces, there are further variations, such as the type of transistor used. Original units used NKT-275 germanium transistors. (Some boutique manufacturers still have supplies of NOS—new old stock—NKT-275 transistors, and some even grade them for the gain levels and other specs so that their Fuzz Face "clones" can be custom tailored to a player's specific taste.) Some experts say that AC128 transistors were used in some early Fuzz Faces, while others dispute this. The original silicon Fuzz Faces used BC108C or BC109C small metal-can transistors. Modern boutique Fuzz Faces sometimes use BC182 and/or BC183 plastic-can transistors.

The original Fuzz Face was discontinued in 1974, with reissues from various companies such as Crest Audio (a descendent of Dallas Arbiter) beginning in 1976. Jim Dunlop purchased the name in the 1990s and now makes "official" Fuzz Faces (both silicon and germanium versions). Boutique manufacturers have created both vintage-accurate (to one degree or another) re-creations of the Fuzz Face and modern updates that strive to improve on the consistency and features of the original. These improvements may consist of everything from hand selecting and matching the transistors used, to adding an on/off status LED (there was none on the original), to even adding bias controls that can compensate for using germanium transistors in different temperature and battery situations. Some manufacturers will also add a power supply jack for using an AC adapter, though this can impact the tone and add noise.

Dallas Rangemaster

Back in the 1960s, many players felt that early British amplifiers were too dark; they wanted more gain and more top end so that they could cut through and be heard. (The advent of PA systems that could handle miked-up guitar amps was still a few years away.) The Dallas Rangemaster, a treble booster, was one device to which they turned for a tone and gain boost. Though it might seem as though using a treble booster might result in a harsh or shrill tone, in fact, a treble booster like the Rangemaster tightens up the bottom end, which gives the impression that there is more midrange and treble in the signal. The gain is also increased, overdriving the front end of the amplifier.

Popular myth (unconfirmed and unsupported by any evidence) has it that Eric Clapton (see Chapter 19) used a Rangemaster to overdrive his Marshall amp while recording at least a few of the tracks on the John Mayall *Blues Breakers* album. Players who were confirmed to have used the Rangemaster include Ritchie Blackmore (Deep Purple), Marc Bolan (T. Rex), Tony Iommi (Black Sabbath), Billy Gibbons (ZZ Top), George Lynch (Dokken), and Rory Gallagher. But perhaps the most prominent user of Rangemasters was Brian May (see Chapter 27), who used them to create thick overdrive tones with his Vox AC30 amps on the early Queen albums (up to *A Day at the Races*).

The original Rangemaster wasn't really a pedal; it was an "amp top" box with an on/off switch, a "set" knob (for gain control), an input jack, and an attached output cable to feed the amp. Various germanium transistors were used in the originals, including OC-44, OC-71, and probably NKT-275 transistors. Original units can be quite noisy, as the tolerances on the transistors were not tight; modern boutique manufacturers have addressed this by hand selecting the transistor used in each unit and carefully biasing it for the best performance.

Ibanez TS-808 Tube Screamer Overdrive Pro

Between the much-venerated Ibanez Tube Screamer itself, its Ibanez variants, and the myriad copies, tributes, knock-offs, wannabees, and "improved" versions, Tube Screamer–style overdrive is in all likelihood the most popular effect ever. There are even guitarists who don't settle for using just one—they'll load two on their pedalboard for even more Tube Screamer goodness!

The Tube Screamer is a low- to moderate-gain overdrive pedal that is often used as a true overdrive—as a boost to push the input of an amplifier into distortion. Though considered a transparent-sounding overdrive, Tube Screamers typically have a strong mid-boost that helps guitars punch more and cut through a mix. The pedal was designed by Mr. S. Tamura for Ibanez in the late 1970s. To improve the dynamics and clarity of the pedal, the design features some clean signal mixed back in with the clipped signal; this also helps the Tube Screamer avoid sounding muddy even when cranked. The TS-808 Tube Screamer is a simple-to-operate pedal, with just overdrive, tone, and level controls.

The lore of the Tube Screamer excites considerable interest in some circles; variations in the op amp used (original TS-808s might use Malaysian Texas Instruments RC4558P or Japanese JRC4558, or rarely, TL4558P chips, which were also used in early BOSS OD-1 pedals), whether or not there is a nut on the power input jack, European narrow box versus U.S. regular-sized box, and more are discussed and studied endlessly—along with debates over how much each of those things affect (or don't affect) the tone.

In 1982, Ibanez repackaged the TS-808 as the TS9, using a slightly different case and changing the output circuit a bit, resulting in a brighter, less smooth sound. Some players, such as U2's the Edge, prefer this version. As the years passed, different op amps were also used, such as the JRC2043DD. Let's just put it this way: Most players prefer the original RC4558 chips.

In 1985, the TS9 (and the rest of the Ibanez 9 series) was discontinued, replaced by various plastic-cased pedals that strayed from the classic Tube Screamer design. In 1993 the TS9 was reissued, though the op amp used did not meet with favor compared to the original. In 1998, the TS9DX Turbo Tube Screamer was released, which featured more gain and four modes with increased low end.

In 2004, the original TS-808 Tube Screamer was reissued. Though it is not a 100-percent accurate re-creation of the original, it did use the correct RC4558 chip and the correct output circuit. In 2009, the hand-wired TS-808 Tube Screamer was issued, giving Ibanez its own "boutique" version of the Tube Screamer to compete with the many knockoffs and variations.

The list of artists who have used Tube Screamers and Tube Screamer–style pedals is tremendously long, from Stevie Ray Vaughan (see Chapter 31) to Trey Anastasio, from Kenny Wayne Shepherd to John 5, to…well, just about any guitarist you could mention has used one at one time or another. Some players run the overdrive knob almost off with the level cranked, and others turn up the overdrive and set the level to a more moderate output, but regardless, the Tube Screamer and its siblings and cousins have gotten a lot of play time over the years.

Maestro Echoplex

Tape echoes—where an incoming sound is recorded to a piece of magnetic tape and then played back after a certain amount of time by a playback head—were developed in the early 1950s, but it wasn't until Mike Battle and Don Dixon designed the Echoplex in 1959 that the effect really came into its glory. The big advance with the Echoplex was that the playback head could be physically slid back and forth, allowing the delay time to be adjusted from short to long and anywhere in between. In 1962, Maestro began distributing the Echoplex. For many years, it was the only echo game in town for guitar players.

The first Echoplexes, later designated the EP-1, were tube-based, as were the second-generation EP-2 models, which featured minor upgrades. In the 1970s, the EP-3 Echoplex introduced transistor circuitry and several enhancements. This was followed by the EP-4, which added LED metering, tone controls, and a compander for reducing noise. Unfortunately, the compander wasn't installed correctly, so modifications were required to make the EP-4 sound like the earlier models—later manuals even included instructions for how to remove the compander board. Two other offshoots were also issued: the budget Sireko and the 4-channel EM-1. In the late '70s, the EP-3, EP-4, and EP-6t (basically a tube EP-2) were reissued by Harris Teller using NOS (new old stock) parts. In 1991, the Echoplex was discontinued. The Echoplex name has since resurfaced on a line of loopers made by Gibson under the Oberheim brand.

The Echoplex was extremely popular with guitarists as an echo effect, but it has almost as much appeal as a preamp/tone shaper—the preamp circuitry in the Echoplexes does something very nice to guitar signals. Many players, including Eddie Van Halen (see Chapter 30), Eric Johnson, and Ritchie Blackmore, have put this preamping effect to use as part of their tone. At this writing, companies such as Xotic and ClinchFX had released clean boost pedals containing preamp circuitry based on the Echoplex.

Some players still rely on vintage Echoplexes (at this writing, Eric Johnson is using two for his live rig), though it is increasingly difficult to find parts and even tape cartridges for them. The units were never designed for the rigors of the road, plus whenever an Echoplex is powered up, the tape runs constantly, so ongoing maintenance is always required to keep these now-aging devices in action. Lovers of vintage gear prize them and find the sound worth the work to keep their Echoplexes alive. For those looking for a more modern solution, Fulltone recently put out their TTE, a tube-based tape echo unit for those who want the tape echo sound without the maintenance worries associated with a decades-old mechanical device.

MXR Dyna Comp

The MXR Dyna Comp is an interesting box; it's very simple, with just two knobs and an on/off footswitch. As a compressor, it does not have a lot of subtlety or range—it basically grabs the guitar signal and throttles it. (To be tweaky, the Dyna Comp isn't a compressor; it's a limiter that sets a ceiling above which the signal can't pass.) But for the players who use it, there really is no substitute—though a number of clones and variations have been introduced. The Dyna Comp can be used as a boost for leads and for smoothing out clean picking, but it is probably most favored by country guitarists for chicken-picking duty—if you have a Tele and play country in Nashville, odds are that you've at least tried to use a Dyna Comp with your rig.

Jim Dunlop now produces both new MXR Dyna Comps as well as a limited-edition reissue of the '76 script logo version, which uses an NOS CA3080 "metal can" integrated circuit for quieter, smoother performance.

Whirlwind, which is owned by Michael Laiacona, one of the cofounders of the original MXR, has also put out their own Rochester Series version that is said to be a vintage-correct replica of the '76 Dyna Comp. (The Whirlwind Red Box adds a few modern amenities, such as an on/off status LED, true bypass circuitry, and an AC power adapter jack.)

There are a few mods that some players prefer to add to their Dyna Comps, such as changing out certain capacitors for better, more even and high-fidelity high- and low-frequency response. Another common mod is the "tired battery" mod, which simulates what happens to a Dyna Comp when an older, worn-out battery is used—the attack gets a bit slower, which lightens up the compression a small amount. Boutique manufacturers have also added their own touches. One popular feature is a "blend" knob, which allows the clean signal to be mixed in with the compressed signal. This helps maintain a more natural feel to the note attack by allowing pick transients to get through without being squashed by the compressor.

MXR Phase 90

Released in 1974, the Phase 90 was the first pedal produced by MXR. The Phase 90 is a four-stage phase shifter that has preset depth and feedback, with a single knob to control speed. In 1977, the Phase 90 changed to a block logo with slightly different circuitry—a feedback path was added for a more intense phase shift effect. Later block-logo Phase 90s also used three dual op amps instead of six single op amps. The Phase 45 was two-stage version with a less intense phase shift sound, while the Phase 100 adds a second control knob for selecting among four preset waveforms/intensities for more flexibility.

The pedal stopped production in 1984 when MXR went bankrupt. Jim Dunlop now makes three models: the MXR Phase 90, a special Eddie Van Halen signature version, and a script-logo '74 Vintage version, which features a hand-wired board and hand-selected components. There is also an MXR Custom Shop version with an on/off status LED and improved headroom and clarity. As with their version of the Dyna Comp, Whirlwind has also released the Orange Box, a vintage-correct replica of the original 1974 Phase 90.

One prominent user of the Phase 90 was Eddie Van Halen, who put the effect to work for both special effect swooshiness and to add treble boost, movement, and character to his solos on the first two Van Halen records.

Roger Mayer Octavia

If you've heard Jimi Hendrix's "Purple Haze" (and what guitar player hasn't), then you've heard an Octavia. Originally designed by acoustician and tech wiz Roger Mayer in 1967, the Octavia combines a frequency doubler (produces a note an octave higher than the note being played) with some filtering and other processing to create a unique effect. Later versions included built-in harmonic drive and other changes as Mayer continued collaborating with Hendrix to further develop the effect. Because a final version was never reached before Hendrix passed away, Mayer did not commercially release the pedal at the time, though units were given to Peter Frampton and Steve Marriott of Small Faces, Syd Barrett of Pink Floyd, and other artists. Early units had germanium transistors and used ferrite transformers; later versions switched to silicon transistors. The later silicon version was released by Tycobrahe (Roger Mayer's website calls it an "inaccurate copy" of the 1969 24-volt type made for Keith Relf of the Yardbirds), and a unit of this generation was later replicated by Jim Dunlop (see below).

Roger Mayer makes two versions of the Octavia—one in a rocket-ship enclosure and the other, the Vision Octavia, in a rectangular, wedge-shaped enclosure. Chicago Iron now owns the Tycobrahe name and is producing several varieties of Octavia. Jim Dunlop is also making the Jimi Hendrix Octavio, said to duplicate one of Hendrix's wedge-shaped silicon Octavias, which is on display at the Experience Music Project in Seattle. (Mayer says he never labeled any of the Octavias he made for Hendrix, so someone else labeled that one.) There are also numerous clones and "inspired by" octave divider/doubler effects on the market.

Roland RE-201 Space Echo

Roland's RE family of tape echoes was launched in 1973 with the RE-100 and RE-200, though the roots of the company reach back to Ace Tone, which was founded in 1960 and which produced the EC-1, EC-10, and EC-20 Echo Chamber tape echoes. Like the Echoplex, the RE-100 family used a loop of analog tape; incoming sound was recorded to the tape and then played back after a short time by a series of playback heads. The RE-100 featured six "mode" settings for different delay times. Controls were available for the echo volume, for the number of repeats, and for setting the bass and treble in the output signal. A unique feature was the "standby" switch, which stopped the tape movement when no delay was required, in order to extend the tape and tape head life. The RE-150 was a straight-ahead tape echo, without the bass and treble EQ. The RE-200 was the "deluxe" model, with 11 delay mode settings and the addition of a built-in spring reverb.

The RE-100 and RE-200 were soon replaced by the RE-101 and RE-201, respectively. The RE-101 featured improved noise and sonic performance and also offered six to fifteen times longer tape life. Like the RE-200, the RE-201 is the "deluxe" model, with the addition of spring reverb. A later model, the RE-301 Chorus Echo, featured the addition of built-in chorus as well as an additional "sound-on-sound" playback head that allowed for very long delay times. It (and later RE models) also utilized IC chips, where the earlier RE models all used discrete electronics. This resulted in quieter operation and more flexibility, but it did change the sound compared to earlier models. The RE-501 Chorus Echo added longer delay times, better noise performance, and balanced XLR inputs and outputs that allowed it to be used for professional PA and recording studio applications. A rackmount version of the RE-501, the SRE-555, was also made. Its chassis mounted into its rackmount case on small wheels so the "guts" of the unit could be easily rolled out (without removing it from the rack) when it was time to change the tape.

The RE-201 Space Echo was widely appreciated for its warm, round, rich sound, which helped the echos sit properly with respect to the dry signal. The reverb tank is quite short—after all, it had to fit inside the table-top RE-201—but it provides a decent ambience. High-tech guitarists and electronic musicians enjoyed the RE-201 for its ability to self-oscillate—to create wacky, sci-fi sounds even when nothing was connected to its input jack. Artists such as David Gilmour and Randy Rhoads relied on the Space Echo for its unpredictable behavior, semi-random echo effects, and "spacey" sound.

Original units are highly sought after and still used by bands such as Portishead and Radiohead and guitarists such as Brian Setzer. Roland has released the RE-20 Space Echo pedal that uses digital modeling to re-create the sound of the original Space Echo, and Universal Audio has created a software plug-in version of the Space Echo for their computer-based UAD effects card.

TC Electronic TC 2290 Dynamic Digital Delay

First introduced by TC Electronic in 1986, the rackmount 2290 became *de rigueur* for high-tech guitarists building rack rigs. The unit provides many types of mono and stereo delay effects, chorus, looping/sampling (stock memory was four seconds, expandable to 64 seconds), flange, tremolo, panning, gating, and more. It also featured five effects loops for connecting external effects, which could be switched into and out of the signal path. With these effects loops and MIDI control, the 2290 could become the centerpiece for a complex, highly flexible processing rig. Extensive front-panel control and sophisticated tap tempo options made the unit fairly easy to use, given how many features it offered.

A big part of the 2290's appeal was its "dynamic" processing ability, where the effects would be automatically turned down or suppressed when the guitarist was playing and then would automatically increase in volume in the spaces between the notes. This allowed the player to use heavy effects but not have the effects interfere with the notes as they were being played.

TC Electronic has released several descendants of the 2290, based on its circuitry and capabilities, including the D-Two rackmount delay and the Nova Delay stompbox. Though long discontinued, the 2290 remains a must-have item for many guitarists as well as for recording studio effects processing.

Thomas Organ Company Crybaby, Vox Clyde McCoy, and Vox V846

It may seem hard to believe, but the much-loved wah-wah pedal may have been the result of a happy accident. One story explaining its origin goes something like this: Warwick Electronics, which owned the Thomas Organ Company, purchased the Vox name, hoping to sell gear based on the popularity of the Beatles and their association with the Vox brand. While an engineer named Brad Plunkett was working on a midrange boost circuit intended for brass instruments, someone came up with the bright idea of mounting the mid-boost electronics into a volume pedal from a Vox Continental Organ and playing an electric guitar through it. Thinking that the effect sounded like a Harmon mute used on a trumpet, the pedal was named the Clyde McCoy. (Clyde McCoy was a famous trumpet player who had a hit, "Sugar Blues," in 1931, where he used a Harmon mute on his trumpet to create "wah" and other tonal effects.) When the pedal was first commercially released in February 1967, it featured a picture of McCoy on the bottom. Later models deleted the picture but included McCoy's signature. The pedal was manufactured in Italy and used an English-made halo inductor or an Italian-made 80-5048-7 Fasel inductor in its circuit.

The Thomas Organ Company (the U.S. distributor) also needed a unique wah pedal they could sell in their market. (JMI, the European distributor, wanted the Vox Clyde McCoy kept in Europe.) To serve this need, a pedal labeled "Crybaby" was made for the American market, though there are reports of a few Vox Crybaby-labeled pedals being produced around this time. At the same time (circa April 1967), Vox introduced the V846 wah, which used a Japanese TDK 5103 cube inductor and had many other circuit changes (the Crybaby and Vox King wah of that time period shared this same circuit), which experts feel dramatically changed the sound of the pedal.

Unfortunately, the Crybaby was never trademarked, and JEN elettronica Pescara (which made the Vox/Thomas Organ units in Italy) also used the same design to make very similar wah pedals under a wide range of brands and names. By the late '60s, some 40 to 50 companies made or sold wah pedals. The effect fell out of favor in the '80s, with only Thomas Organ, Morley, and a few others still making wah pedals.

Today, the effect has made a comeback, and wahs are made by a wide range of manufacturers. Jim Dunlop owns the Crybaby name and makes a number of Crybaby wah models. Vox has reissued their classic wahs as well as come out with new models. Then there are the "boutique" manufacturers, such as Fulltone, RMC (Real McCoy Custom), Budda, and many more, who each have their own take on the wah pedal. Some include extra options, such as switchable volume boosts, controls for adjusting the voicing of the wahs, and even multiple inductors, which can be switched in and out to change the sound of the wah.

Univox Uni-Vibe

The Univox U-915 Uni-Vibe was developed by Japanese engineer Fumio Mieda for the Shin-Ei company and released in the United States in 1969. (The Uni-Vibe was also sold as the Jax Vibra-Chorus outside the United States and was also known as the U-915 Shiftee Uni-Vibe and the Lafayette Electronics Roto-Vibe—not to be confused with the current Dunlop JD-4S Rotovibe.) The idea was to create a rotating speaker/Doppler effect for keyboardists and organists—prior to the Uni-Vibe, the only way to get that pulsating, shimmery, watery effect was to use a large, bulky, and heavy mechanical speaker cabinet featuring a rotating treble horn and rotating cylinder around the bass speaker. Though few would mistake the sound of a Uni-Vibe for that of a Leslie rotating speaker, there's no denying that the result was a very cool effect.

The Uni-Vibe is essentially a four-stage phase shifter using a pulsing light bulb surrounded by four photo-resisters to almost semi-randomly stagger the filters (instead of aligning them, as in a more conventional phase shifter). Plus, unlike a regular phase shifter, the filters in the Uni-Vibe aren't all tuned to the same frequency. The resulting sound is often referred to as "wobbly," or described as the "heartbeat" of the Uni-Vibe.

The Uni-Vibe consisted of a large rectangular box with a separate, complementary foot-controlled expression pedal that could be used to control the speed of the modulation effect and to turn off the effect. The originals were switchable from chorus to vibrato and featured intensity and volume controls, dual inputs, and a single output.

Jimi Hendrix was the first guitarist to shine the spotlight on the Uni-Vibe. (He used the Chorus setting on "Machine Gun" and "The Star Spangled Banner" and the Vibrato setting on "Dolly Dagger" and other songs.) He was followed by David Gilmour, Frank Marino, Grand Funk Railroad (the solo on "The Locomotion"), Stevie Ray Vaughan, and many others, though perhaps the biggest post-Hendrix proponent of the Uni-Vibe was Robin Trower, who featured it prominently on *Bridge of Sighs* and other albums.

The original units were large (compared to other pedals, not compared to the nearly refrigerator-sized Leslie cabinet it was designed to replace!), were not especially reliable, and were notorious for tone suck. That last one, though, is also due to the aging of the capacitors in vintage units—there are 19 electrolytic caps in the original units that do not age especially gracefully—which makes them sound darker than modern, "new" units. And, of course, the originals could vary considerably from unit to unit depending on when each was manufactured and what components were available and used at the time.

Part II

The Icons
of Tone

As A MUSICIAN, THERE ARE FEW THINGS MORE DIFFICULT—or more important—than finding your own voice. Part of your "voice" is the musical side of your playing: the notes you choose, the phrasing you use, your use of dynamics, and so on. But a big part of what makes you unique as a player is your sound; the tone or tones that you alone create, that set you apart as a guitar player, and that comprise the distinct sonic fingerprint that your audience can use to identify you, your playing, and your music. The gear you choose is key to achieving your unique tone, of course. The problem is that few of us have the opportunity to try every single piece of gear that is on the market to find out what is best for us and our style of music. Nor would we have the time to listen to or to try all the thousands of tone tools—new, old, and vintage—that are on the market, even if we did have the opportunity to be in the same room with all of them.

Given that there is no way any of us can try every piece of gear, we need some sort of starting point from which we can launch our tone quest, some way to narrow down the universe of gear to items that potentially could do the job for us. There are several ways to do this. Reviews in gear magazines and online user reviews and forum discussions are all useful resources for learning more about gear. But, as with many things in life, learning from those who were or are successful in what you want to accomplish is a great way to start.

In our tone quest, this means checking out the gear other players use for various styles. Once you have an idea of the types of gear that work for other players for what you want to do, and for what the "standard" items are in each style, then you can extrapolate to arrive at the exact items that you need to make the sound you want. Or at least you can use information about the gear that those other players find works as a starting point for embarking on your own quest.

If you're going to look at the gear that other players use, then why not focus on the gear that the best players —which for our purposes doesn't mean the "best" players in terms of playing ability, but rather those with the most identifiable sounds—are using. It means examining the pieces of gear famous players with instantly recognizable sounds use and looking at how they use their gear to create those iconic tones.

You have to be careful of several things when doing this, though.

▷ "Celebrity" players have been known to receive free gear in exchange for the use of their name or photo as an endorsement for a product—and we're interested in what gear provides the tone, not in which manufacturer provided the best "deal" for the artist. To be fair, just because a player appears in an ad doesn't mean you should assume they are "for sale." Many players like to support the makers of the gear they use. And, not all manufacturers give away gear for free—if a player is using it, he may well have paid for it.

Still, if a popular player suddenly appears as an endorser in many ads in a magazine, you can't help but wonder if he's more interested in the compensation than in the gear. There are also many "endorsement" examples where a player appears in ads for a product but never actually uses it in the studio or onstage.

▷ Big-name players often have gear budgets that are greater than the average guitar player can muster. It's all well and good if your favorite player uses a $50,000 amp and a $300,000 vintage guitar, but unless you have unlimited funds at your disposal, knowing which over-the-top guitar or amp he or she has might be an interesting bit of information, but it isn't very applicable to our more real-world situations.

▷ It's difficult to get a realistic idea of the sound of a piece of gear from a finished studio recording. In today's studio world, it is possible to massage a tone to make it better or even to shape it into something completely different. And, by the time a recording has gone through various stages of mixing, mastering, editing, and processing, it may not sound the same as it did when it was first tracked.

In some cases, an artist's playing may even be replaced by another player's—and the artist may not even know it. Or, a "ringer" may be brought in to bolster what an artist does with additional playing and tones. Live recordings are no more helpful than studio recordings; some "live" albums have everything but the audience applause replaced later with "better" studio recordings—you're not going to discern much about a player's live tone from that.

▷ What an artist uses in the studio may not be the same as what he uses on the stage. Some things work great in the rarified air of the recording studio but can't cut it in a high-volume stage situation. Or, they may be too valuable or fragile to take out on the road for a tour. Or a range of rental gear, or gear belonging to a producer or engineer, may have been used during recording to achieve particular sounds.

▷ There's no way to tell whether the gear a player uses is stock. Even if a guitar looks stock, the pickups or any number of other things may have been replaced with different components. Who knows what changes may have been made to the circuits of an amp or an effects pedal?

▷ What a player appears to be using onstage may not be what you're really hearing. Those stacks of 4×12 cabinets across the back of the stage? They could be fake, empty boxes or a simple backdrop, while the actual sound is coming from an amp placed somewhere offstage. Sometimes, the amps onstage are simply for the player to hear, while the actual sound is coming from another source and being fed to the PA system.

▷ Just because a player says something in an interview doesn't mean it's true. Eddie Van Halen and Billy Gibbons are notorious for giving misleading information about their rigs, sometimes in fun and sometimes to put those who want to copy them off the trail. Others make statements as jokes, which then take on a life of their own via the Internet or careless reporting.

▷ No matter how close you get to copying another player's rig, you'll never exactly get their sound—at least not without transplanting their hands onto your arms and their brain into your head (which might make things a bit crowded and uncomfortable). And even then, you might not get all the way there. We've all heard two guitarists play through the exact same rig with exactly the same settings, yet still sound quite different—it's that whole "the tone is in the fingers" thing.

All of this would seem to make it somewhat pointless to even consider the gear that other players, especially famous players, use to get their tones. But, there are ways to get close to what those players use and to get close to their sound. For example, there are sometimes ways to achieve results similar to what an expensive rig gets while using more affordable gear, or to capture the sound of rare vintage items by using more available modern gear—or, increasingly, by using digital models of that vintage gear. So, just because your favorite player uses a super-expensive, rare, or vintage item doesn't mean that you can't pursue his tone with more commonly available (and affordable) gear.

But, unless you are in a tribute band or you have an obsession with sounding like someone else, exactly duplicating another player's tone really isn't the point. The point (in my mind, at least) is to learn from how others get their tones, particularly those who have identifiable tones associated with them, and to take what you can from this to apply it to your own rig and your own tone quest. Maybe you'll learn one little thing about the guitar a player uses that you can "steal" to use with your own guitar to further your tone quest. Maybe a particular combination of amps, effects, and guitars a player uses will suddenly click for you and will change how you approach your own rig. Maybe it will work in reverse: You'll realize that a particular speaker is part of what creates a tone you *don't* like, so you can avoid it in your own rig. Learning what *not* to do can be as important as learning what *to* do.

For all these reasons, along with many more, it is worth it to examine the rigs of players with distinctive tones and gear approaches. It's not the only method you should use to decide on gear—and it may not even be the primary method you should use—but combined with reading magazine and online reviews and articles, visiting discussion forums, talking to other players, trying as much gear as you can, and listening a *lot* (and, of course, reading this book), you'll be able to gather the information you need to assemble a rig that will provide you with your own voice.

With that in mind, let's dive into the rigs of some well-known, instantly identifiable players. The players in the pages that follow are certainly not the only ones who have their own unique tones. But they are the players who seem to come up over and over again among players discussing tone, and they provide a firm grounding in a lot of different gear and tone approaches.

Jeff Beck

FOR MANY PLAYERS, JEFF BECK IS THE BE-ALL AND END-ALL of guitar wizardry. From his groundbreaking work with the Yardbirds (where he replaced Eric Clapton; Jimmy Page also joined on bass, later moving to co-guitar), to his groundbreaking work as a fusion pioneer, to his current return to prominence with his successful solo albums and tours, his tone, touch, feel, and highly musical phrasing have garnered him legions of fans. He was among the first pop/rock guitarists to incorporate intentional distortion into his tone and feedback into his bag of tricks.

His tone through those different stylistic periods has also been a benchmark for many players who seek to emulate his expressiveness and sound. A big part of his approach, honed through the past few decades (since the '80s), is foregoing a pick in favor of using his thumb and fingers to pluck the strings. A second major component is his extensive use of the vibrato arm to shape notes and phrases. Seemingly more than just about any other guitar player, Jeff Beck's tone comes from his hands and his approach to playing.

From a gear standpoint, Beck has always kept it fairly simple and straightforward—depending on the time period, as simple as a Strat into a wah or fuzz and into a Fender or Marshall amp. He's never been one to always use the same gear, though. Aside from his signature Stratocasters, his gear changes on a very frequent basis. He has never been shy about modding his gear, frequently swapping necks and other components among his various instruments.

Guitars

In the early days, Beck relied on a blonde 1954 Fender Esquire with a two-piece ash body with an offset seam, and a maple neck and fingerboard. Jeff purchased the Esquire second-hand for $60. The body had already been reshaped with Stratocaster-like body contours at that point. The steel bridge saddles were replaced with brass saddles. Beck gave this Esquire to Seymour Duncan when Duncan built the Tele-Gib. (See the "Tele-Gib" section later in this chapter.) Fender has since released a Tribute-series version of this guitar.

Gibson Les Paul

During his fusion phase, Jeff began relying on a 1954 Gibson Les Paul—it can be seen pictured on the cover of 1975's *Blow by Blow*. The guitar was originally a goldtop with a standard wraparound aluminum bridge (no separate tailpiece). Beck repainted it "oxblood" (a deep chocolate-brownish color) and changed its original P-90 pickups out for PAF humbuckers. The neck was also shaved down to a slimmer profile, and the tuners were updated to newer units. Gibson recently released a "tribute" version of this guitar.

Tele-Gib

In 1974, Seymour Duncan built a guitar for Jeff based on a 1958 Fender Telecaster that had previously been heavily (and poorly) modified. Duncan replaced the Tele's rosewood fingerboard with a 3/16-inch slab of maple with a flatter 13-inch radius. He hand slotted the board and installed larger Gibson frets. A hand-cut pickguard was attached to the light ash body, and Duncan hand-wound two humbucking pickups, using the PAF coils and magnets from a '59 Gibson Flying V (once owned by Lonnie Mack) and wire from a motor repair shop. These pickups were later used as the basis for Duncan's popular Jazz and JB model humbuckers. The bridge is a cut-down Telecaster unit, with brass saddles from the early 1950s. (Seymour built himself a similar guitar with a Les Paul–style Tune-o-matic bridge and stop tailpiece. This guitar was recently offered as a limited-edition model by Duncan.)

According to Duncan, Beck's Tele-Gib guitar was used to record tracks on *Blow by Blow*, such as "'Cause We've Ended as Lovers" and "Freeway Jam."

Fender Jeff Beck Signature Stratocaster

After his fusion period, Beck began playing Strat-style guitars, such as Charvels and Jacksons. He also began using "real" Strats, leading Fender to release a few versions of Jeff Beck Signature Strats, some with thicker neck profiles and some with Lace sensor pickups. The current signature model Strat features an alder body with a urethane finish and a C-shaped maple neck with a rosewood fingerboard and 22 medium-jumbo frets. The guitars utilize Fender Special Design dual-coil Noiseless "stacked" pickups with ceramic magnets. For electronics, a standard five-way pickup selector switch is used, with a master volume, a neck pickup tone control, and a middle/bridge pickup tone control. A two-point vibrato bridge with stainless-steel bridge pieces, a metal LSR roller nut, and locking tuners round out the hardware.

Beck's main current Strat is a hybrid of several different Stratocasters. It features a neck from the Fender Custom Shop on a basswood Strat body, with Bill Turner–designed noiseless single-coil pickups with around 11k output measurement.

He uses Ernie Ball .009 to .052 strings, which get heavier as a tour proceeds and his hands get stronger. Beck sets the vibrato bridge to a steep angle—with the back of the bridge tilted away from the face of the guitar. This allows him to press down with the heel of his hand or to pull up on the bar to get vibrato and pitch-bend effects. Three springs are used in the guitar's claw to set the bridge angle.

Amps

In the Yardbirds, Beck usually used two Vox AC30 amps, wired in series. The amps were raised up, sitting on chairs.

In the '80s and '90s, for a higher gain and more strident tone, Beck relied on a prototype of the Marshall JCM2000 DSL. Beck's amp is said to be different from what ended up being the production models; despite their best efforts, apparently Marshall has been unable to duplicate the sound of this particular amp.

For his tribute album to Gene Vincent and his early guitarist, Cliff Gallup (*Crazy Legs*, 1993), he used a late-'50s Gretsch Duo Jet through a reissue Fender Bassman amplifier. He was also known to use Fender Twin amps, and for a time he used very small amps onstage, including Fender Pro Juniors.

His main amp for the *Live at Ronnie Scott's* performances was a 50-watt Marshall JTM45 "plexi" head, set for a fairly clean tone. Beck rolls all the low end off of his amps and turns up the mid, treble, and presence controls for his tone. The rest of his tone shaping comes from his guitar's controls (the amount of treble is constantly adjusted using the tone controls on the guitar) and his fingers.

Much of his album, *Emotion & Commotion* (2010), was recorded using a '50s (Tweed) Fender Champ amplifier.

Effects

Through the years, Beck has been known to use a number of fuzz pedals, including a Tone Bender and a Pro Co Rat, plus other "vintage" pedals, such as Crybaby wahs, Colorsound boosters and overdrives, Ibanez Tube Screamers, the Bag (an early talk box), a Roland Space Echo, and more.

On the *Ronnie Scott's* performances, Beck got his distortion from a Klon Centaur overdrive set for a clean, somewhat gritty boost into his JTM45. His effects include a Hughes & Kettner Rotosphere, a Maestro ring modulator (given to him by Jan Hammer), a Boss flanger, an EBS OctaBass, a Snarling Dogs Whine-O Wah, and a Lexicon Alex rackmount reverb.

Benchmark Recordings

Jeff Beck Group, *Truth* (1968)

Jeff Beck, *Blow by Blow* (1975)

Jeff Beck, *Wired* (1976)

Jeff Beck, *Live at Ronnie Scott's* (CD and DVD, 2008)

Getting the Sound

To achieve a tone similar to Jeff Beck's current sound, try this:

▷ A Strat-style guitar with three single-coil high-output noiseless pickups, with one of the tone controls wired to the bridge and a vibrato tailpiece. A Fender Jeff Beck signature Stratocaster will get you a good head start, but any single-coil equipped Strat with a tremolo will get you on the path.

▷ A low-gain overdrive/clean boost, such as a Klon or one of the many others on the market.

▷ A wah pedal.

▷ A lower-gain, "plexi" Marshall-style amp head.

▷ A Marshall-style 4×12 cabinet loaded with Greenback speakers.

Larry Carlton

L ARRY CARLTON MAY BE ONE OF THE MOST-RECORDED GUITARISTS of all time—thousands of sessions for albums, television, and soundtracks, then his work with the Crusaders and Fourplay, and of course, his many albums as a solo artist. He also may just have one of the sweetest guitar tones ever, well evidenced on solos played on Steely Dan songs and tracks for countless other artists, as well as in his own work.

Guitars

Few guitar players have ever been as closely associated with a single model of a guitar as Larry Carlton—there's a reason for his nickname, "Mr. 335"! Although he strayed a bit in the '80s, the vast majority of Carlton's recordings and live appearances feature his early 1969 (sometimes also identified as a 1968) Gibson ES-335, which features its tailpiece significantly farther away from the Tune-o-matic bridge than other 335s and a single-piece mahogany neck. (Single-piece mahogany necks were not offered on ES-335s in 1969; this neck must have been left over from 1968.) Gibson has released a signature version of this guitar, with the same tailpiece/bridge spacing, graphite nut, fingerboard radius, neck profile, Schaller tuners, and other details of his original. He uses D'Addario light-top/heavy-bottom strings, gauged .010 to .052. He uses a heavy-gauge teardrop-shaped pick.

For a short time, around the recording of *Last Nite*, Carlton became enamored of Valley Arts solid-body guitars, playing several Strat- and Tele-style instruments, some featuring EMG single-coil pickups, and some featuring Gibson P-100 stacked P-90-style pickups. (Various reports suggest that the P-100s may have been swapped out for regular P-90s or custom Seymour Duncan P-90-style pickups.) Despite being 7/8-sized Strat and Tele shapes, Larry's Valley Arts guitars used set-neck construction, Gibson-style 24.75-inch scale lengths, and separate Tune-o-matic bridges and stop tailpieces. Valley Arts released the Tele-shaped version as Larry Carlton Standard and Custom signature models.

On his 335, Larry often places the pickup selector in the middle position and then balances the volume and tone of each pickup using the guitar's controls to achieve the tone he wants. For more aggressive playing or for tonal variety, he does switch to the bridge or neck pickup alone.

Amps

During much of his L.A. studio career, Carlton relied on small amps, such as a Fender Princeton or a Tweed Deluxe (such as the one used for "Kid Charlemagne" by Steely Dan), some modified by Paul Rivera. He also was an early adopter and longtime user of the Mesa/Boogie Mark I amplifier.

But for many years, Larry has used a 100-watt Dumble Overdrive Special amp head with 5881 power tubes (for a darker, "slower," warmer tone compared to 6L6s), driving a 1×12 sealed and ported Dumble cabinet loaded with an Electro-Voice EVM-12L speaker. In recent years, he has also been known to use a Bludotone amplifier (basically a clone of his Dumble). Carlton primarily runs on the clean channel of the amp, turned up just to the point of breakup. He can switch to the overdrive channel of the amp or use the amp's preamp boost if he chooses, but the broken-up clean channel is his main sound.

Effects

Carlton's pedalboard during his L.A. studio heyday was a large, complex affair. For most of the past few decades, as he has concentrated on Fourplay and solo gigs and albums, he has moved toward a much simpler rig.

In concert, Larry uses an interesting wet/dry/wet guitar rig that is designed to re-create the sound that he hears when recording in the studio—the dry guitar in the center, with reverb and effects in stereo on the left and right. Live, he creates this effect by miking his Dumble speaker cabinet with a Shure SM57 microphone, routing the microphone to a Mackie 1604-VLZ Pro mixer with TC Electronic 1210 Stereo Chorus/Spatial Expander, TC Electronic M2000 stereo reverb, and Roland SDE-3000 delay rackmount effects plugged in. The output from the Mackie mixer is sent to the front-of-house (PA) mixer and to two JBL Eon powered speakers, which Larry places to either side of his amp onstage.

In addition to this stereo ambience system, Larry runs a Sho-Bud volume pedal (modded by Alexander Dumble for consistent tone as the volume is turned down) and a Crybaby wah pedal.

Studio Tricks

Needless to say, after decades of recording nearly every day in the world's top studios, Carlton has his recording approach dialed in. In the studio, Larry's Dumble amp is recorded using a Royer R-121 ribbon microphone and a Shure SM57 dynamic microphone feeding Neve 1073 microphone preamps/EQs and Universal Audio LA-3A compressor/limiters.

Benchmark Recordings

Steely Dan, *The Royal Scam* (1976)

Larry Carlton, *Larry Carlton* (1978)

Larry Carlton, *Last Nite* (1986)

Larry Carlton with Robben Ford, *Live in Tokyo* (2007)

Getting the Sound

To achieve a tone similar to Larry Carlton's, try this:

▷ A semi-hollow-body 335-style guitar. A Gibson Larry Carlton Signature LC-335 model will get you as close as possible to the instrument Larry plays, but any semi-hollow-body with humbuckers and a stop tailpiece will get you in the ballpark.

▷ A volume pedal—no one rides a volume pedal like Larry does.

▷ A wah-wah pedal.

▷ Dumble amplifiers are very difficult to come by (and super expensive), so you could try one of the many clones on the market, such as a Glaswerks, a Bludotone, a Ceriatone, a Fuchs, a Two-Rock, or any of the number of others.

▷ A sealed, ported 1×12 speaker cabinet with an Electro-Voice EVM-12L speaker.

▷ Another option is a pedal designed to create a Dumble-type tone, such as a Hermida Audio Zendrive, a Custom Tones Ethos, a Menatone Howie, or one of the dozens of other "Dumble" pedals on the market, paired with a blackface-style amplifier.

▷ Keep the gain down. Carlton does not often use a high-gain setting. Rather, he sets his amp on the verge of breakup, so that it is very dynamic and distorts when he digs in hard.

▷ A wet/dry/wet rig featuring separate stereo chorus, mono tap-tempo delay, and stereo 2.2-second hall reverb effects.

▷ Alternatively, a cranked Tweed Deluxe- or Princeton-style amp with a 335-style guitar will approach Larry's Steely Dan tone from the '70s.

Eric Clapton

FEW GUITARISTS HAVE INFLUENCED AS MANY OTHER PLAYERS as Eric Clapton has. Likewise, few have reinvented themselves as completely or as many times as Clapton has. From his early days with the Yardbirds to the prototypical blues rock of John Mayall and the Bluesbreakers, from Cream to Delaney and Bonnie, from Derek and the Dominos to his extensive solo *oeuvre*, Clapton's body of work covers a broad range of styles, playing approaches, philosophies, and tones.

Bluesbreakers

Though Clapton had already recorded tracks and established himself as the U.K.'s leading blues-rock guitarist in the early '60s with his playing in the clubs of London and with the Yardbirds, it was when he joined John Mayall's Bluesbreakers that he made his first serious tonal mark. After using a Telecaster and Vox with the Yardbirds, and after immersing himself in the blues as preparation for playing with John Mayall, EC was looking for a bigger sound with more sustain—a search that led him to the now standard rock and blues combination of Les Paul and Marshall.

Guitars

In the early 1960s, the Les Paul we all know and love had actually been discontinued by Gibson due to lack of sales. It was replaced by the double-cutaway SG/Les Paul model. Clapton, along with Peter Green and other artists, adopted late-'50s Les Pauls and through their example helped to establish that model as a premier rock axe. Clapton became interested in playing a Les Paul after seeing blues legend Freddie King pictured on an album cover playing a goldtop. He was a big factor in the late-'50s Les Paul Standard becoming the Holy Grail of solid-body electric guitars and in Gibson's decision to reissue the Les Paul in the late '60s.

For the John Mayall and the Bluesbreakers *Blues Breakers with Eric Clapton* album (which became known as the "Beano" album because of the comic book Eric is pictured reading on the cover), Clapton used a sunburst Gibson Les Paul equipped with stock PAF humbucking pickups. The guitar may have been a '59 or a '60; there are no photos or documentation to verify one date or the other, though Clapton has stated that he liked the guitar's thin neck, which would seem to indicate a '60, and the "reflector" control knobs also point toward it being a '60. Clapton removed the pickup covers revealing the coils and probably opening up the treble a small amount. The tuners were also changed. Sadly, the Les Paul that Clapton used to record the "Beano" album was stolen in 1966 and was never recovered or seen again.

There's an interesting subtext to Clapton's use of this guitar. Many players point to the "aged" wood in vintage instruments as contributing to their tonal superiority, but clearly that was not the case here—the '59 Les Paul he used was only six years old when this album was recorded, yet it had a depth of tone, richness, resonance, and sustain that was simply outstanding.

Amps

Clapton used a mid-'60s "Series II" Marshall Model 1962 JTM45 combo amplifier with a script logo for the recording of the *Blues Breakers* album. Jim Marshall has stated that his company began making combo amps at Clapton's request—the guitarist wanted an amp that he could easily transport in the trunk of his car.

The amp was equipped with KT66 power tubes and a GZ34 rectifier tube. (Very early versions of this amp used 5881 power tubes, and later Marshall switched to using EL34 power tubes.) It is likely the amp was loaded with two 12-inch, alnico 20-watt Celestion Greenback speakers, although it is possible that it had heavy-duty ceramic 25-watt Greenbacks. This amp model has since become known as the "Blues Breaker" amp. Clapton is said to have cranked the amp all the way up and to have told the engineer to place the microphone across the room for the recording.

Clapton was actually in John Mayall's Bluesbreakers at two different times; in the later stint, he was known to use a JTM45 head with a 4×12 cabinet instead of the combo.

Effects

Rumor has it that EC used a Dallas Rangemaster treble booster to push his Marshall combo harder for additional overdrive and sustain. However, no photos from the sessions document this, and there is no verification from Clapton or anyone else involved that one was ever used.

Cream

After leaving John Mayall's Bluesbreakers (for the second time), Eric Clapton began rehearsing with bassist Jack Bruce and drummer Ginger Baker. The three musicians formed the first "supergroup," Cream. It was during the Cream days that Clapton began developing his famous "woman tone," created by rolling off his guitar's tone control all the way to create a smooth, dark, singing, sustaining sound. (Check out "I Feel Free" off of *Fresh Cream* and "Sunshine of Your Love" off of *Disraeli Gears* for great examples of the "woman tone.")

Despite being together for just three years, Cream established the concept of extended improvisation and virtuosity in a rock context, did some of the first "headlining" tours of America that weren't "package" shows, and received some of the highest fees paid up until that time. They paved the way for heavy rock bands and jam bands alike. Clapton's playing and tone during this time was a tremendous influence on countless players, including such future stars as Eddie Van Halen, Eric Johnson, and many more.

Guitars

Clapton's "Beano" Gibson Les Paul Standard was stolen during Cream's early rehearsals. To record the group's first album, *Fresh Cream*, he borrowed another sunburst Les Paul (some experts date the guitar as a '59 based on its deeply flamed top), which had a Bigsby tailpiece and had the covers in place on both pickups.

He borrowed a third late-'50s sunburst Les Paul from Andy Summers (later of the Police), which had a stop tailpiece, uncovered pickups, and a missing switch plate. Eventually he purchased the guitar from Summers; some reports say that this guitar was also stolen in 1967. In 1968, Clapton was photographed playing yet another sunburst Les Paul at Cream concerts.

Spring 1967 saw the arrival of an iconic guitar in Clapton's arsenal: a Gibson SG that was painted with fluorescent colors by a pair of famous Dutch artists known as "The Fool." The guitar was initially identified as a '61 SG/Les Paul, but experts now state that it was a '64 SG Standard. Originally, the guitar was equipped with a tremolo tailpiece, which was later changed to a stop tailpiece. The tuners were swapped from the stock Klusons to Grovers. The pickups in this guitar would have been "patent number" humbuckers. PAFs had given way to patent-numbered pickups beginning in 1962, so even though these were not PAFs, they probably would still have been quite similar to the older pickups.

The "Fool" SG was used extensively for *Disraeli Gears* and *Wheels of Fire*, as well as *Goodbye, Live,* and *Live II*. It was also Eric Clapton's most used live guitar during this time period. Clapton later gave the guitar to George Harrison, who gave it to vocalist Jackie Lomax, who sold it to Todd Rundgren. Rundgren sold it at auction to a collector in 2001.

Clapton was also known to use a black, three-pickup Gibson Les Paul Custom (probably a '58 or '59) as a backup for the "Fool" SG, as well as for recording "Strange Brew" and other songs on *Disraeli Gears*. It later made appearances when he played with Blind Faith and Delaney and Bonnie.

The guitars played by Clapton during the final tours of the Cream era included a single-pickup mid-'60s Gibson Reverse Firebird I and a red block-inlay '64 Gibson ES-335, which he had purchased prior to joining the Bluesbreakers. The 335 is actually a very important guitar for Clapton; he used it with the Yardbirds and continued to use it regularly for the next 40 years. His former tech, Lee Dickson, has stated that it was one of Clapton's best-sounding guitars. It was kept mostly stock, aside from necessary repairs and maintenance and changing the stock Kluson tuners to Grovers. Clapton auctioned this guitar for charity in 2004. It brought $847,000, the highest figure any Gibson guitar has ever sold for.

Amps

During the Cream years, Clapton was a devoted Marshall user. In the early days of Cream, Jim Marshall was making amps by special order only; he had not yet opened a factory for mass production. Clapton had moved on from his "Bluesbreaker" combo and was probably using JTM100 model 1959 Super Lead heads, with four KT66 tubes for 100 watts of output. He used two 4×12 Marshall cabinets as a stack, loaded with 20-watt Alnico Celestion Greenbacks. (Jack Bruce used two 200-watt Marshall Major stacks to keep up with Clapton's volume level.) As time passed, his crew replaced the oft-blown 20-watt Celestions with the more durable 25-watt ceramic Celestions, which would have had a cleaner tone with less compression. On later Cream tours, newer Super Leads powered by EL34 tubes were used, and Clapton added a second stack for even more stage volume, sustain, and on-demand feedback.

Of importance: Clapton plugged into the Normal channel of his Marshalls. He did not use the brighter "Brilliant" channel as Jimi Hendrix and Pete Townshend did, nor did he jumper the two channels together. His goal seems to have been a clear, rich, powerful sound with a lot of sustain, but without harshness or excess piercing treble despite what had to be *substantial* volume levels.

Effects

Along with Hendrix, Clapton was among the earliest prominent users of the Vox wah-wah pedal. He has stated that he first heard the effect on Hendrix's "Burning of the Midnight Lamp" and purchased one for himself in the spring of 1967. It was famously used on "White Room" and "Tales of Brave Ulysses" from *Disraeli Gears*, which the band was recording at the time he bought the pedal.

1970 to 1985: Blackie and Brownie

After leaving Cream, Clapton was ready for a complete change, not just in the style of music he played and in his approach to soloing, but also in his tone. In fact, he went to the polar opposite, for a while stepping into the background as a sideman with Delaney and Bonnie and also working with Steve Winwood in Blind Faith, moving on to Derek and the Dominos, and ultimately launching his solo career. To facilitate the move from the heavy, super-loud, stack-driven free improvisation of Cream to the more structured song approach manifested by these other musical situations, he changed his gear and tone selection radically. First, he went from the big, sustaining humbucker tone of his Gibsons to the brighter, thinner tone of Fenders—a change that was influenced by Clapton hearing Buddy Guy, Jimmy Hendrix, and Steve Winwood playing Fender Strats. Second, he shifted from a heavy-sounding Marshall amp rig to a cleaner Fender-style system.

Brownie

Clapton's first Fender Stratocaster was "Brownie," a '56 Strat he purchased in 1967, reportedly for $400—it's the guitar that can be seen on the cover of his first solo album. Brownie has an alder body and a maple neck, with a well-worn tobacco sunburst nitrocellulose lacquer finish. It originally had a three-way pickup selector switch, which was changed to a five-way switch at some point in the mid- to late-'70s. Before that change, Clapton achieved the in-between pickup settings by balancing the three-position switch carefully between positions 1 and 2 or between 2 and 3. The tremolo arm was removed, and the claw was screwed down so the bridge was pulled tight and flush against the body.

Clapton used Brownie as his main guitar up to the early 1970s, most famously for Derek and the Dominos' *Layla and Other Assorted Love Songs*, as well as for his first solo album and for some of the tracks on *461 Ocean Boulevard*. After 1971, Brownie became Clapton's backup Strat. He auctioned it for charity in 1999; it went for nearly half a million dollars, the most a guitar had sold for up to that point. Some feel that Brownie was the best-sounding Strat that Clapton ever used.

Blackie

In the early '70s, Clapton was in a Nashville guitar shop and came across a rack of old '50s Strats. They were out of fashion at the time and priced for just a few hundred dollars each, so he bought all of them. Some he gave away to friends, such as Steve Winwood, George Harrison, and Pete Townshend, but he kept a few for himself, which he took apart and reassembled to create a hybrid made from the best bits of each. The result, christened "Blackie," became perhaps the most famous electric guitar of all time. Eric first used Blackie onstage in 1973 at the Clapton Rainbow Concert, then took it into the studio and used it on *461 Ocean Boulevard*. It became his number-one instrument for the next 12 years and appeared on 13 of his solo albums.

Blackie was retired in 1985 after the neck became too worn to comfortably function. He did use it twice over the next decade (for a Honda commercial in Japan and for a brief appearance at the Royal Albert Hall concerts), but he ultimately auctioned it for charity in 2004 for nearly $960,000, the highest price ever paid for a guitar. Before it was auctioned, Blackie served as a template for Fender's Eric Clapton signature model (see next section). In 2006, the Fender Custom Shop offered a "Tribute" replica edition of Blackie, limited to 275 pieces, which sold out in less than 24 hours.

Blackie has a three-piece alder body finished in black nitrocellulose lacquer with a one-piece V-shaped maple neck from a '57 Strat. The tremolo is pulled tight down to the body using five springs, with the claw screwed down. (Some reports say that a small chunk of wood was wedged into the back of the guitar to "block" the tremolo from moving.) Aside from normal maintenance, Blackie was kept in its "stock" condition, with its original vintage parts.

Amps

During this period, Clapton used larger Fender amps onstage, such as the Dual Showman. In the studio, when recording the *Layla* album, he used a small practice amp—a '50s Tweed Fender Champ. He also used a Leslie rotating speaker cabinet, with a switch that selected his regular guitar amp, the Leslie by itself, or both combined.

Later in the '70s, Eric began using Music Man HD-130 Reverb amps developed by Leo Fender. Some reports state that these amps were modified, though it is not clear in exactly what way. These "hybrid" amplifiers featured solid-state preamps and tube power amps, and offered a Fender-y clean/breakup tone. Clapton used them to drive custom open-back cabinets. In 1983, he used a Tweed '57 Fender Twin amp.

Effects

During this period, Clapton maintained his focus on a more pure guitar tone. Aside from the Leslie rotating speaker cabinet, the only effect he used with any regularity was a wah-wah pedal.

Mid-'80s to Mid-'90s

The recording of the *Behind the Sun* album and the subsequent tour marked a new tonal era for Eric Clapton. During this period, he went for a much more "processed" stereo tone, with heavier distortion and many more effects.

Guitars

When Clapton decided to retire Blackie, Fender set about creating a signature Stratocaster model that would fill the huge void left by the absence of his favorite guitar. The result was the Eric Clapton Signature guitar, which features an alder body finished in urethane; a soft V-shaped neck with a maple fingerboard, 22 frets, and a 9.5-inch radius; three Vintage Strat Noiseless pickups (early models had Lace Gold Sensors); a five-way pickup selector switch; a "blocked" vintage-style tremolo bridge and vintage-style tuning machines; and a synthetic "bone" nut. The electronics consist of a master volume control; a passive TBX (treble/bass expander) tone control, which is off when it is set to 5 and which cuts the bass when turned in one direction and the treble when turned in the other; and an active MDX mid-boost control with 25 dB of gain centered at 500 hertz. The mid-boost can drive and shape the pickups' output into a much thicker, fuller sound than a single-coil can usually produce. You can hear this fat tone on many of Clapton's solos from this period.

The Fender signature models were Eric's primary guitars through this period. The Noiseless pickups served him well in the face of his use of higher gain and heavier effects processing but still provided a vintage-pickup basis for his sound.

Amps

Clapton switched back to Marshalls for much of the '80s, using 50-watt JCM 800s (probably Model 2203) to drive 4×12 Model 1960 cabinets. Some reports describe these cabinets as having Electro-Voice EVM12L speakers replacing two of the stock Celestion speakers and having ports cut into the front baffles.

Somewhere around the *August* sessions, Clapton was influenced by Steve Lukather (Toto guitarist and L.A. studio musician) to switch to Soldano SLO-100 amplifiers. The amps were modified for him by Mike Soldano at the request of pedalboard wizard Peter Cornish, who redesigned Clapton's effects rig around this time. Cornish wanted an extra circuit added to the amps to accommodate the studio-level +4 dBm/low-impedance operation of Clapton's rackmount effects processors, which was not correct for interfacing with the amp's effects loop. During this time, his Marshall cabinets were reported to be loaded with four EVM12L drivers.

Effects

For his effects-laden tone in this time period, Clapton began using a large, complex rack effects system controlled by a Bradshaw switching system. His effects included a Dunlop Crybaby wah wah, a Boss CE-1 chorus and HM-2 Heavy Metal distortion, a Dyna-My-Piano Tri-Stereo Chorus, a dbx 160 studio rackmount compressor, a Roland SDE-3000 digital delay, an Ibanez HD-1500 Harmonics Delay, and even a Roland GR-700 guitar synthesizer.

When Clapton switched to the Soldano amps and his Pete Cornish/Bradshaw effects routing/switching system, he was using a Drawmer Model 1960 studio tube compressor, a TC Electronic 1210 Spatial Expander and a 2290 digital effects, a Roland SDE-3000 digital delay, a Yamaha SPX90 and a GEP50 digital effects, a Dyno-My-Piano Tri-Stereo Chorus, and a Dynacord CLS 222 Leslie speaker simulator. All of this was controlled by a large Cornish-designed foot controller. Cornish also designed a custom power stabilizer to maintain a strict 117 volts of AC power (within +/−0.5% accuracy).

The New Millennium

Since the mid-1990s, Clapton has returned to a straight-ahead, simplified vintage-based rig. During this period, he has also returned to his blues roots musically and has used a cleaner, less saturated tone with few effects other than an occasional Leslie speaker and wah.

Guitars

Onstage, Eric continues to rely on his Fender Eric Clapton Signature Stratocasters, although he has used a wide range of vintage, new, and custom instruments alongside his signatures while in the studio recording his albums. As he has for many years, Clapton uses Ernie Ball .010 through .046 strings and Ernie Ball heavy-gauge picks.

Amps

Fender Custom Shop '57 Twin reissue. He also uses a Leslie speaker cabinet. A footswitch allows him to select either the Fender, the Leslie, or both.

Effects

After the effects excesses of the '80s and early '90s, Clapton has come full circle back to the effects he used with his '60s and '70s rigs—just a Vox wah-wah pedal.

Benchmark Recordings

The Yardbirds, *Five Live Yardbirds* (1964)

John Mayall and the Bluesbreakers, *Blues Breakers with Eric Clapton* (1966)

Cream, *Fresh Cream* (1966)

Cream, *Disraeli Gears* (1967)

Cream, *Wheels of Fire* (1968)

Derek and the Dominos, *Layla and Other Assorted Love Songs* (1970)

Eric Clapton, *461 Ocean Boulevard* (1974)

Eric Clapton, *Slowhand* (1977)

Eric Clapton, *Behind the Sun* (1985)

Eric Clapton, *From the Cradle* (1994)

Getting the Sound

To achieve a tone similar to Eric Clapton's, first you must decide which one you want to emulate!

▷ **Bluesbreakers.** Use a Les Paul–style guitar with a JTM45-style combo amp. You could also experiment with a treble-booster pedal.

▷ **Cream.** If you want the classic rich, sustaining tone heard on the Cream-era recordings, you'll need a Les Paul– or SG-style guitar, with PAF-style pickups, through a Marshall Plexi-style amp and 4×12 cabinets loaded with Greenback-style speakers. Add a wah wah for color and roll back the guitar's tone control for that "woman tone."

▷ **Derek and the Dominos.** A '50s-style Strat-type guitar with three single-coil pickups and the tremolo bridge screwed down tight or blocked with a small piece of wood, played through a small Tweed-type Fender-style amp and optionally a Leslie-style rotating speaker cabinet or simulator, along with a wah-wah pedal, will get you there.

▷ **Modern.** Choose a Strat-style guitar with noiseless pickups and midrange boost, Tweed-style amplifier, and a wah-wah pedal.

The Edge

DRONES AND DELAYS...WHEN U2 BURST ON THE SCENE, the Edge was suddenly catapulted into the consciousness of guitar players, which was unusual, given his almost anti–guitar hero approach to the instrument. Eschewing the traditional guitar solo, the Edge developed a style based on melody, rhythm, and texture and learned to play his effects as much as he learned to play his guitar—his effects aren't necessarily used to "color" the signal, they're used as an integral part of the musical line or pattern. This is especially true with his use of delays.

His textural, rhythmic, and melodic work with U2 has spawned many admirers and imitators. In the last few years, his style has also become a powerful influence on guitarists in the Christian-rock genre.

The list of gear used by the Edge is overwhelmingly long—far beyond what almost any of us could put together in our wildest dreams.

Guitars

The first of the two guitars that the Edge is the most closely associated with is a 1976 Gibson Limited Edition Explorer—the original is said to be a bright-sounding guitar with a very thick neck; it has since been retired and replaced with three similar-vintage guitars. Second is a black 1973 Fender Stratocaster with a maple neck, another very bright-sounding guitar used for songs such as "Where the Streets Have No Name." Live, he also often uses Fender Eric Clapton signature Strats with Lace Sensors.

He used a '75 Alpine White Gibson Les Paul for recordings such as "New Year's Day" and "When Love Came to Town." He auctioned the original for charity, but Gibson later made him an exact replica of it.

The Edge has used untold other guitars during the course of his career—he's been known to take out nearly 50 guitars for a tour, using upward of 20 for a given show—from Fender Telecaster to Gretsch 6122 Country Gentleman, Rickenbacker 330/12 to Epiphone Casino.

The Edge uses Herdim picks, which have a "dimpled" area that is designed to improve the player's grip on the pick. An important contributor to his tone is that he reverses the pick and holds the part that is normally meant to strike the strings while hitting the strings with the dimpled area. This creates a different texture on the attack of each note than the smooth pick surface would. He uses D'Addario strings of various gauges for different guitars.

Amps

The Edge generally uses several amps to create a richer sound with more depth, although his early work was recorded with a single amp. He is most associated with the Vox AC30TB, of which he is said to own more than 30. His favorite is a 1964, which has been used in the recording of every U2 album. This amp has been re-housed in a '70s-era cabinet and has one Jensen Blue alnico speaker and one Jensen Silver alnico speaker. It has been re-capped and repaired with components from various Marshalls and Fenders, making it a singular amplifier.

He has also been known to use Fender amps alongside his Voxes, such as Tweed Deluxes (including a '58 with a speaker taken from a Vox and a '57 with a Jensen speaker), and a mid-'50s Harvard. Other amps include a newer Marshall 1987X head with a 4×12 cabinet (formerly owned by Mick Ralphs of Bad Company). But the basic platform upon which he builds his tone is the Vox AC30 Top Boost.

Effects

Delays are a huge part of the Edge's sound. He uses many types, such as the Electro-Harmonix Deluxe Memory Man (*Boy* and *October*), the Korg SDD-2000 and SDD-3000 (beginning in the mid-'80s), the TC Electronic 2290 (he has used a pair since *The Joshua Tree*), and the Line 6 Delay Modeler (since 2004). His delays are usually set to be in-tempo with the song. Those in-tempo delays may be eighth notes or quarter notes, and he also uses a delay time equal to three sixteenth notes or a dotted eighth note. He often uses modulation with his delays to increase the depth and texture of the sound and sets the delay feedback for three or four repeats. He also commonly runs a short delay and a long delay at the same time, both with modulation, creating a complex, rich sound.

In addition to delays, the Edge uses most other types of effects as well, including EQs, wahs, overdrives, boosts, fuzzes, filters, multi-effects boxes, Whammy pedals, pitch shifters, and more, from companies such as AMS, Lexicon, DigiTech, Eventide, Durham Electronics, Death By Audio, Boss, and Skrydstrup. His massive effects control/switching system was built by Skrydstrup.

Benchmark Recordings

U2, *Boy* (1980)

U2, *The Unforgettable Fire* (1984)

U2, *The Joshua Tree* (1987)

Getting the Sound

To achieve a tone similar to the Edge's, try this:

▷ A bright-sounding guitar. This could be a Strat-style guitar with single-coils and a vibrato tailpiece. Or an Explorer-style guitar, or a Tele-style guitar, or a Les Paul-style guitar, or a Gretsch hollow-body, or...just about anything bright-sounding.

▷ Two or more delays, preferably with modulation ability. Tap-tempo ability makes it easier to match the delay time to the song tempo.

▷ Various other effects to taste—just about anything goes.

▷ A multi-effects device or modeler could also be used to create complex effects routings and setups.

▷ A bright-sounding Class A amp loaded with alnico speakers, such as a Vox AC30 or one of the many clones or similar models.

Robben Ford

BLUES GUITARIST ROBBEN FORD HAS HAD AN ENVIABLE CAREER, recording and performing with the likes of Jimmy Witherspoon, Miles Davis, Larry Carlton, Charlie Musselwhite, Tom Scott and the L.A. Express, Joni Mitchell, and many more. Along the way, he has developed an instantly recognizable—and for many players, a very desirable—tone using a minimal (though very expensive) guitar rig.

Guitars

Ford relies heavily on just a few guitars. He is often seen playing a 1960 (some reports say a '61) rosewood-fingerboard Fender Telecaster that is said to have an extra-hot bridge pickup and steel bridge saddles. No one is sure whether the body is ash or alder. The bridge pickup was rewound by Lindy Fralin (some reports say the neck pickup was the one that was rewound or that both were rewound), and the frets have been replaced with a larger size. He also uses a goldtop 1954 Gibson Les Paul with P-90 pickups and a '57 goldtop with humbuckers, which is on long-term loan to him from Larry Carlton. A Gibson ES-335 appears with him frequently.

In the 1980s, Fender created a Robben Ford signature model based on their Esprit model, a double-cutaway guitar with two humbuckers. As with many of Ford's humbucker-equipped guitars, the signature models featured coil splitting; he often splits a pickup for his rhythm tone and then switches back to humbucker mode for soloing. He also played custom models made by Gene Baker, who worked for the Fender Custom Shop and who has since built guitars under his own name. The late Taku Sakashta built Ford a gorgeous NouPaul, a guitar based on the Gibson Les Paul model with J.M. Rolph pickups and coil splitting. Aside from the Sakashta, Ford does not play his signature or custom guitars much onstage, instead sticking with the Tele, a Les Paul, or a 335.

Amps

Few players have become as closely associated with a single amplifier as Robben Ford has with his Dumble Overdrive Special—in fact, he may have been the inspiration for the amp's creation. As the story goes, Ford needed an amplifier. He rented a Dumble (some versions of the story say to record his album *Inside Story*), and eventually he connected with Alexander Dumble and bought an Overdrive Special amp of his own. About 10 years later, Dumble told him the rest of the story: The Overdrive Special was designed to capture the tone that Robben was getting using a cranked-up Blackface Fender Bassman (other versions of the story suggest it was a Blackface Super Reverb) in the early days when he was playing with Jimmy Witherspoon—Ford's tone inspired Dumble to create the amplifier that Ford later bought and has used ever since. (Maybe it's just an urban legend, but it's still a good story....)

Ford runs his Overdrive Special head, which reportedly has Dumble's Skyliner EQ mod, into a Dumble open-back 2×12 cabinet loaded with Celestion G12-65 speakers. He creates a wet/dry rig using a second amplifier, often a Fender combo such as a Super Reverb or a Twin Reverb.

For smaller gigs or for "fly" gigs where it isn't practical to take the Dumble, Ford uses a rental Fender amp, usually a Super Reverb or a Twin with a Hermida Zendrive as an overdrive pedal. (The Zendrive was supposedly developed by Alf Hermida to duplicate Robben's Dumble tone.)

Effects

For ambience with his wet/dry setup, Ford takes a feed off of his Dumble using a Dumbleator—a tube interface designed to mate effects properly with the amp's send/return loop. A TC Electronic 2290 rackmount processor provides reverbs and delay effects. He uses a basic pedalboard (sometimes just the pedals on the floor) with a Crybaby wah wah, an Ernie Ball volume pedal, the Dumble's footswitch, and a footswitch for selecting presets on the TC 2290.

With his band with Michael Landau, Renegade Creation, Robben uses a more substantial board, including his standard Zendrive/volume pedal/wah setup, but also featuring a Line 6 DL4 delay modeler, an Arion SCH-1 chorus, and a G-Lab reverb.

Benchmark Recordings

Robben Ford, *Talk to Your Daughter* (1988)

Jing Chi, *Jing Chi* (2002)

Robben Ford, *Truth* (2007)

Getting the Sound

To achieve a tone similar to Robben Ford's, try this:

▷ A Les Paul– (with P-90s or humbuckers), Tele-, or ES-335-style guitar—or, if you can find one, a Fender or Baker Robben Ford signature model.

▷ A Dumble Overdrive Special would be ideal, but they're super expensive and quite rare, so you could try one of the many clones, such as a CeriaTone, a Fuchs, a Bludotone, a Glaswerks, a Two-Rock, a Carol Ann, or one of the many others.

▷ A second clean amp for a wet/dry rig.

▷ A reverb/delay for wet/dry ambience, a wah-wah pedal, and a volume pedal.

▷ If your budget can't swing a Dumble-style amp, try a Blackface-style amp (a Fender Super Reverb or Twin is what Robben would use) and a Hermida Zendrive, a Custom Tones Ethos, or another Dumble-inspired pedal.

David Gilmour

Born in Cambridge, England, David Gilmour began learning to play guitar during school lunch hours, along with Syd Barrett. Years later, in 1967, he was asked to join Pink Floyd to help stabilize the guitar parts as Barrett became more and more undependable. Eventually, Barrett was "let go" from the group (they simply didn't pick him up for a gig one night) and Gilmour became the sole guitarist. He remained with Pink Floyd through the group's last album. He also has had a successful solo career, launched with his first album, *David Gilmour*, in 1978. Gilmour has elevated the tone of a Stratocaster to its pinnacle—players point to his tracks on Pink Floyd's records as well as his solo albums as examples of the prototypical Fender Strat sound.

Guitars

David Gilmour has always played Fenders, beginning with Telecasters in the late '60s prior to and after joining Pink Floyd. Once he was in Floyd, he became a faithful Stratocaster player throughout the rest of his career, though he has strayed to other models here and there. In particular, he has relied on two Strats, one black and one red, for most of his recording and live-performance needs.

The Black Strat

The most storied guitar used by Gilmour is his infamous Black Strat, which is so iconic among his fans that an entire book was written about it. The famous Black Strat is actually the second black Stratocaster Gilmour owned. The first was purchased while Pink Floyd was on tour in New York in 1970; that guitar was stolen and then replaced by a second black Strat, which became Gilmour's most recognizable guitar. He began using it in June of 1970.

The Black Strat was originally completely stock, with a late-'60s alder body, with the exception of black paint over the original sunburst finish. The guitar has been modified many times, from its replacement black pickguard to a three-pin XLR jack installed in the side and later removed, with the empty hole filled back in with wood and painted black. At various times, the guitar had a mini switch installed (to combine the neck and bridge pickups), a humbucking pickup added between the bridge and middle pickups, a rosewood fingerboard maple neck, a replacement bridge assembly, a DiMarzio FS-1 bridge pickup, a couple of different Jackson/Charvel maple necks, a custom-wound Seymour Duncan bridge pickup, a locking Kahler tremolo system, Kluson tuners, a 22-fret Charvel neck, a Fender '57 reissue Strat neck, and many more modifications.

Today, the guitar has a 1983 '57 reissue C-shaped maple neck with a maple fingerboard, Fender tuners, a black pickguard, 1971 Fender neck and middle pickups, a custom-wound Seymour Duncan SSL-1C bridge pickup, the original Fender tremolo bridge (the hole from the Kahler was filled in), a five-way pickup selector, a mini switch for combining the bridge and neck pickups, and a short 4.25-inch tremolo arm. The guitar's grounding was improved, and shielding was added to help keep it quiet. Gilmour uses three springs in the tremolo and has David Gilmour signature GHS strings, gauged .010 to .048.

The Black Strat was used on many of Pink Floyd's albums, from *Atom Heart Mother* all the way to *The Final Cut*, including *Dark Side of the Moon* and *The Wall*. It was loaned to the Hard Rock Cafe for a number of years, where reportedly it was scratched and dinged and lost two of its control knobs. On its return, it has once again become Gilmour's go-to guitar and was used for his more recent solo albums, such as *On an Island*.

The Red Strat

The story goes that in 1984, Gilmour purchased a large number of new Strats from Fender's London warehouse to take on tour in place of his increasingly valuable older guitars. One of these, a 1983 '57 reissue Strat in red with a C-shaped maple neck, became his favorite guitar for nearly 20 years, until he began using the Black Strat again. This guitar has an alder body and a nitrocellulose lacquer finish, and it was fitted with EMG SA single-coil pickups with alnico V magnets and EMG's EXP bass and treble boost and SPC midrange boost. (EMG later branded and now sells this as the DG20 pickup system.) It has appeared on *A Momentary Lapse of Reason*, *The Division Bell*, and other recordings and tours, as well as parts of *On an Island*, up until the return of the Black Strat.

Other Guitars

Early in his tenure with Pink Floyd, Gilmour used a blonde Telecaster given to him by his parents, which was lost by an airline in 1968. He has also been known to use a late-'50s brown Telecaster, a '59 Telecaster Custom, a '55 Esquire, and various reissue and new Teles. When his original blonde Tele was lost, the band gave him a white Stratocaster, probably a '66 or '67, with a rosewood fingerboard, which was stolen in early 1970.

Although he is clearly a Fender devotee, Gilmour has used Gibson guitars as well, including a late-'50s Les Paul TV and a late-'50s, three-pickup "Black Beauty" Les Paul Custom. But perhaps the most notable of his Gibsons is his 1955 goldtop Les Paul, with P-90 pickups. This guitar is most famous as the one used for the solo on "Another Brick in the Wall (Part 2)." It was also used throughout the '80s and '90s for tracks on *A Momentary Lapse of Reason*, *The Division Bell*, and other recordings. A very similar '56 goldtop with a Bigsby tailpiece was used for parts of *On an Island*.

A custom guitar made by the late Canadian luthier Bill Lewis is used prominently on *Echoes* and *Dark Side of the Moon*. Among its distinguishing features are dual humbucking pickups (invented and patented by Jack Lewis) that can be switched to single coil, a 24-fret fingerboard, and other interesting and forward-thinking features, such as dual steel bars in the neck for extra rigidity and stability. Jimmy Page and Eric Clapton have also been known to use Bill Lewis guitars.

Though the aforementioned guitars are his main recording and performing guitars, Gilmour also owns a large collection of guitars. Perhaps the jewel of the collection is a 1954 Fender Stratocaster with serial number 0001. While not the first Strat ever made, it is a unique instrument with many distinctive features.

Amps

Gilmour has used a few different amplifiers and combinations of amplifiers over the years.

▷ For 1968's *A Saucerful of Secrets*, he used a Selmer Stereomaster amplifier with Selmer 1×12 and 2×12 cabinets.

▷ By 1969, he had added Hiwatt DR103 amp heads and WEM Super Starfinder 200 4×12 cabinets. A Leslie 147 rotating speaker was added in 1969 as well.

▷ In 1972, he was using the Hiwatts and WEM cabs and the Leslie, along with Blackface Fender Twin amps.

▷ By '77, the Twins had become a Dual Showman head with a 2×15 cabinet. For *The Wall* tour, his amps included the Hiwatt DR103s, a Mesa/Boogie Mark I head, an Alembic F-2B tube preamp, Yamaha RA-200 rotating speakers, and WEM Super Starfinder cabinets.

▷ For his 1978 tour in support of his first solo album, he was using the Mesa/Boogie as a preamp, splitting it to stereo with a Boss chorus, and then using Fender Twin amps to drive WEM or Marshall cabinets. In the studio, he also used Gallien-Krueger 250 ML Mk II and Marshall JCM 800 amps.

▷ 1987 saw the return of the Hiwatts and WEM cabinets, alongside two Fender Twin Reverb II amps, the Alembic F-2B tube preamp, and a Mesa/Boogie Mark III Simul-Class head and Hiwatt 4×12 cabinets.

▷ In 1994, for *The Division Bell*, Gilmour relied on the Hiwatts and WEMs, Marshall JCM 800 4×12 cabinets, Hiwatt STA-100 "slave" amps, the Alembic preamp, and Doppola rotating speaker cabinets.

▷ For his tours in the early 2000s, he was using mid-'50s Tweed Fender Deluxe and Twin combo amps.

▷ More recently, he has been using a variety of amps, depending on the size of the venue, such as the Hiwatts and WEMs, an Alessandro Blue Tick, Yamaha RA-200 rotating speakers, a Magnetone 280-A combo, and a '56 Tweed Fender Twin combo.

Effects

David Gilmour's effects rig has steadily expanded over the years. His effects are a huge part of the tones that he creates.

▷ In 1968, he was using a Dallas Arbiter Fuzz Face (at different times he has used NKT275 versions as well as BC108 versions), a Crybaby wah wah, and a Binson Echorec delay unit.

▷ By *Meddle* in 1971, he had added a DeArmond volume pedal.

▷ In 1972, he began using a Colorsound Power Boost and a Univox Uni-Vibe.

▷ For the *Dark Side of the Moon* sessions, he added a Kepex Tremolo and an EMI Synthi Hi-Fli effects box.

▷ In 1977, his Pete Cornish–built touring pedalboard contained a Fuzz Face; a Crybaby wah; a Morley EVO-1 echo/volume pedal; a Colorsound Power Boost; Cornish fuzz, tone, and volume pedals; MXR Phase 90 phaser, Dyna Comp compressor, and noise gate/line driver pedals, and a Digital Delay System I; Electro-Harmonix Big Muff fuzz and Electric Mistress flange pedals; a Uni-Vibe; and a Binson Echorec II delay.

▷ For *The Wall*, his pedalboard included many of the earlier pedals as well as an Electro-Harmonix Small Stone phaser, a Cornish treble and bass boost pedal, and a Boss CE-2 chorus.

▷ In 1984, he adopted a Boss SCC-700 system, which could control up to seven Boss pedals and had 32 presets. He used Boss SD-1 overdrive, GE-7 EQ, DD-2 digital delay, CS-2 compressor/sustainer, HM-2 distortion, and CE-3 chorus pedals with the SCC-700. Additionally, he used MXR digital delays.

▷ By 1987 and '88, for the *A Momentary Lapse of Reason* tours, his rig expanded dramatically, with Boss stomp boxes, TC Electronic Sustain/Parametric EQ pedals (several, with each one dedicated to a Big Muff, Boss, or other distortion pedal), two Yamaha SPX-90 II digital effects, a TC Electronic 2290 digital effects, a Roland DEV-5 digital delay, a Korg DRV-3000 digital delay, a Lexicon PCM-70 digital reverb, MXR digital delays, Rane SM-26 splitter/mixers, and more, all contained in a pedalboard and two large racks and controlled with a Bradshaw switching system.

▷ For *The Division Bell* tours, Gilmour's rig changed again. This time, he used a Boss CS-2 compressor and four GE-7 EQs, Rat and Pete Cornish distortions, two BK Butler Tube Driver tube overdrives (one for clean boost, one for overdrive), along with other pedals such as Big Muffs, a Heil Talk Box, and an MXR Dyna Comp. His rack gear (once again, two large racks full) included a TC 2290, an MXR digital delay, a Lexicon PCM-70, a rackmount Uni-Vibe, a DigiTech ISP-33B pitch shifter, a Dynacord CSL-222 rotating speaker simulator, an Electro-Harmonix Electric Mistress flanger, and two Boss CE-2 choruses, which were always on and feeding certain amplifiers.

For this rig, Pete Cornish designed a routing system that was controlled by a Bradshaw switcher. He also modified many of the effects for better performance and for impedance and level matching.

▷ By 2002, Gilmour had scaled his live rig back substantially. Among his effects were a Boss CS-2; a Cornish G-2 (high-gain germanium distortion), SS-2 (dual G-2 distortion), stereo chorus, tube 6-band EQ, and Tape Echo Simulator; a Big Muff; and a BK Butler Tube Driver; plus a Roland SDE-3000, an MXR Digital Delay, and an Ernie Ball volume pedal.

▷ More recently, Gilmour has been using another custom Cornish pedalboard, loaded with a Demeter Compulator compressor; a DigiTech Whammy pedal; a Boss GE-7; Cornish P-1 Precision Fuzz and G-2 distortion, and Tape Echo Simulator pedals; two BK Butler Tube Drivers; a Crybaby wah; an Ernie Ball volume pedal; along with rack effects such as Roland and MXR digital delays, a Cornish "Sound On Sound" looper, a DigiTech pitch shifter, and a rackmounted Uni-Vibe.

Benchmark Recordings

Pink Floyd, *Dark Side of the Moon* (1973)

Pink Floyd, *The Wall* (1979)

Pink Floyd, *The Division Bell* (1994)

David Gilmour, *Live in Gdansk* (2008)

Getting the Sound

To achieve a tone similar to David Gilmour's, try this:

▷ A Strat-style guitar with three single-coils (early '70s Fender-style or EMG SA pickups) and a tremolo bridge.

▷ Electro-Harmonix Big Muff and a BK Butler Tube Driver or other tube overdrive, or other overdrive, fuzz, and distortion boxes.

▷ Compressor, chorus, flanger, phaser, wah, and digital delay effects.

▷ Clean-ish, punchy, Hiwatt-style tube amps with 4×12 cabinets. For a more current tone, Fender Tweed-style amps may be desirable. A rotating speaker or simulator is a useful addition.

Warren Haynes

I S WARREN HAYNES THE HARDEST-WORKING MAN in the music biz?
Between his gigs with the Allman Brothers, Gov't Mule, Phil Lesh & Friends, and the
Grateful Dead, and as a solo artist, the man is always either playing a gig or on his
way to play a gig. In each of those different band situations, he uses a slightly different
rig, although regardless of what he plays, his thick, rich tone is always upfront, singing
the blues.

Guitars

No matter where he is playing or whom he is playing with, Haynes is almost always
found with a Gibson guitar in hand—a Les Paul, a 335, a Firebird, or sometimes an SG.
He has stated that although he enjoys hearing other players using single-coil-equipped
guitars, he is a dyed-in-the-wool humbucker man, and his guitar choices bear this out.

One of his main recording guitars is a 1961 Gibson ES-335. Other than replacing the
original Bigsby tailpiece with a stop tailpiece, this guitar is stock. He also has a '67
ES-335 that formerly belonged to Gregg Allman, who played it for more than 20 years.

His main Les Paul was formerly a 1989 R9—an '89 reissue 1959 Les Paul Standard
loaded with Seymour Duncan Pearly Gates pickups. Recently, however, his main live
guitar has been a limited-edition Gibson "Inspired by Warren Haynes" model Les Paul.
Special features on this guitar, which is based on a '58 reissue Standard, include
Burstbucker 1 (neck) and Burstbucker 2 (bridge) pickups, Schaller strap locks, and a
built-in Custom Audio Electronics preamp, which does not add gain but instead keeps
the tone consistent as the guitar's volume control is turned down. The Inspired by
Warren Haynes model has no pickguard. There is also a Gibson Warren Haynes Signature
Les Paul Standard, which features Burstbucker 2 (neck) and Burstbucker 3 (bridge)
pickups and a TonePros bridge and tailpiece. Like the Inspired By model, it has no pickguard.

Warren also has a mid-'90s reissue '58 Les Paul Standard with a Duncan Antiquity in the bridge position and a 1998 '59 Les Paul Standard reissue with a Duncan JB in the bridge. One of his most unusual guitars is a 12-string Les Paul (one of only two ever made), which features a coil-tap switch for splitting the pickups to single-coil. He uses that guitar in a drop-D tuning.

Haynes uses a 1964 Gibson Firebird III with a Duncan Alnico II Pro mini humbucker in the neck. His '97 Firebird has a Duncan Alnico II Pro mini humbucker in the bridge. He also plays a non-reverse Firebird with P-90 pickups.

With Phil Lesh & Friends, he often plays a 2000 Gibson SG, which is loaded with a Duncan-made custom copy of the neck pickup in Peter Green's Les Paul (with the reversed magnet) and a custom-made copy of the bridge pickup from Clapton's "Fool" SG made by Duncan.

He sets his action high so that he can play both regular lead and slide on the same guitar. For standard-tuned guitars, Haynes uses GHS Burnished Nickel Rocker strings gauged .010 to .046; when he tunes down, he goes up a gauge to .011 to .050. For certain drop tunings, he uses .010 to .058 gauge strings. He keeps a Gordie Johnson model SG (one of only 50 made) loaded with Gibson P-94 humbucker-sized P-90-style pickups in his "crazy" C tuning (C, C, G, C, G, C) and strings it with .014 to .058 gauge strings. His picks are D'Andrea 347 Delrex teardrop-shaped mediums. His cables are Planet Waves.

Amps

Haynes uses a variety of amplifiers, especially when recording. But there is one constant: his Díaz CD-100, a 100-watt tube head made by the late César Díaz. (Díaz was well known for working on amps for Stevie Ray Vaughan, Eric Clapton, and other artists.) The OD-100 is loaded with 6550 power tubes and is said to have two 100-watt transformers running in series. It is rated at 130 or 140 watts of output power. This amp always forms the basis of his tone, which he enhances and shapes by adding another amplifier to create a "composite" sound. The Díaz amp often drives a Marshall 4×12 cabinet loaded with 65-watt Celestions.

The amp he chooses as the second amp in each situation defines the subtleties and the "size" of his tone with that particular band. For example, with the Allman Brothers, he often uses a 50- or 100-watt Marshall Super Lead Plexi head or a Soldano SLO-100 head (modified with a switch to bypass the bright cap on the overdrive channel) along with the Díaz. Lately he has been using a PRS amplifier, a Dallas model, with the Allmans, in place of the Soldano or Marshall.

With Phil Lesh & Friends, he used a CAE (Custom Audio Electronics, Bob Bradshaw's company) head or sometimes a Fender Super Reverb. In recent years, he has been using a PRS amplifier, a Dallas model, with the Grateful Dead.

With Gov't Mule, Warren often uses the Díaz along with both the Soldano SLO-100 and a PRS Super Dallas prototype, which is an amp that Doug Sewell and Paul Smith reverse engineered from a '68 Marshall owned by Eric Johnson. The Díaz is on all the time, and he switches between the Soldano and PRS amps, which both feed the same Marshall 4×12 cab. For cross-stage monitoring, the bass player listens to Haynes through a Category 5 Andrew 50-watt combo amplifier while the drummer listens to a Category 5 Tempest 45-watt combo amplifier.

For his tour in support of his *Man in Motion* solo album, Warren used the Díaz amp along with two PRS "30" combo amps.

Haynes reportedly can hear the difference between amps operating at 115 volts and 120 volts, and he prefers the sound at 115 volts. His amps are run on a Variac variable transformer to ensure that the voltage is consistent at that level.

His cabinets include a Tone Tubby 4×12 and a Marshall 4×12. His usual speakers of choice are Celestion Vintage 30s. His cabinets are miked up using Shure KSM32 condenser microphones on the top speakers and Shure SM57 or Sennheiser e609 dynamic microphones on the bottom speakers.

Effects

With certain of his projects, Haynes uses more effects than others. For example, when he plays with the Allman Brothers, which is a bigger band with more players and more going on, Haynes uses fewer effects—a Boss DD-2 digital delay and a Crybaby wah pedal.

With Gov't Mule he tends to use more effects for additional colors and textures. His processors of choice include a Boss OC-2 Octaver, a Custom Audio Electronics Super Tremolo, a Díaz Texas Tone Ranger (used to boost the level of his Firebirds to the same volume as his Les Pauls), a Klon Centaur overdrive, a Hughes & Kettner Rotosphere rotating-speaker simulator, a Dunlop Crybaby wah wah, a Chandler SDE-2 digital delay, an EMMA DiscomBOBulator envelope filter, and an Ernie Ball volume pedal. He has been known to use a Dunlop Jimi Hendrix Fuzz Face on occasion.

His effects are switched using a Bradshaw switching system. He runs 20 feet of cable from the switcher to his Crybaby and 20 feet of cable back to the switcher in order to attenuate the high frequencies slightly.

Benchmark Recordings

Allman Brothers, *Live at the Beacon Theatre* (DVD, 2003)

Gov't Mule, *Dose* (1998)

Gov't Mule, *Deja Voodoo* (2004)

Gov't Mule, *Mulennium* (2010)

Warren Haynes, *Man in Motion* (2011)

Getting the Sound

To achieve a tone similar to Warren Haynes', try this:

▷ You've got to have humbuckers, in a Gibson-style guitar—a Les Paul–, ES-335–, or Firebird-style axe.

▷ At least one Marshall-style amplifier, cranked up loud for power amp distortion but without pushing the preamp too far into gain territory.

▷ An overdrive, a wah wah, an octave divider, a delay, and a rotating speaker effect, each used sparingly for color here and there.

Jimi Hendrix

J IMI HENDRIX MAY BE THE MOST ICONIC ELECTRIC GUITARIST EVER. During the short duration of his career, from 1967 to 1970, he impacted countless guitarists with his music, his recordings, his performances, and, of course, his tones. From Eric Johnson to Stevie Ray Vaughan, other artists have covered his songs and attempted to capture the spirit of his sound. Even other artists in the tone pantheon, such as Eric Clapton, have been influenced by his gear choices.

Entire books have been written about Hendrix's gear—and it is great fun to delve into all the minute details of his gear throughout his career, in search of those elusive pieces of "magic" that others might have missed. But we can summarize what we need to know in much less space if we focus on what he used as the basis for his most famous tones.

Guitars

Jimi Hendrix began playing Fender guitars early in his career, in 1964, when he was with the Isley Brothers. He played a Duo-Sonic with the Isleys and a Jazzmaster with Little Richard. But the most famous Hendrix tones are primarily based on Fender Stratocasters; he bought his first one in 1966 from Manny's in New York and used a few different rosewood-fingerboard Strats in '66 and '67. Following those years, when he was with the Experience, he mostly chose maple-fingerboard Strats. Later in his career he also played a hand-painted Gibson Flying V, and he was seen playing other guitars, such as Gibson Les Pauls and SG Customs at various times. Still, for most listeners, the classic Jimi tone is Strat-based.

Some theorize that Hendrix played mostly CBS-era Strats made in the mid- and late '60s because he liked the way the larger headstock on these guitars (compared to pre-CBS Strats) contributed to enhanced sustain and how the slightly lower-output single-coils of that era produced a clearer, more articulate tone with more dynamics. It's hard to imagine that the small amount of extra mass in the headstock would add very much sustain, though there could be some truth to why he preferred the lower output pickups.

But Hendrix didn't just stick to CBS Strats. He used both pre-CBS and CBS Strats. Those close to him who worked on his gear, such as Roger Mayer, state that Jimi bought Strats out of necessity. Whatever was available was what he used, and because the selection that was available was quite limited in those days, particularly in England, he took what he could find. Also keep in mind that, at that time, pre-CBS Fenders weren't necessarily regarded as the Holy Grail–level vintage guitars they are now. They would simply have been used guitars, a few years old. Most players did not seek them out as "special" guitars compared to the new (CBS) instruments made at the time.

What probably made a bigger difference to his tone than the vintage of his guitars was that Hendrix famously used right-handed Stratocasters but flipped them over and restrung them to play them left handed. This also placed the controls on the top, where he preferred having them. According to Mayer, because things were so hectic, the only mod that was made was flipping or replacing the nut.

Stringing a right-handed Strat left handed changes a few things:

> The low E string now has the longest span of string on the headstock (between the nut and the tuning machine), while the high E has the shortest. This affects the tension on the string and could subtly affect the tone. The low E and A strings were passed under the string tree.

> The angle on the bridge pickup would be reversed, with the low E side closest to the bridge and the high E side farthest away from the bridge. This makes the low strings sound twangier, while the high strings sound a bit fatter and less bright.

> On all three pickups, the pole piece heights will be flipped relative to the strings. At that time, the pole piece for the G string was the highest to compensate for the wound G many players used. The B pole piece would have been the lowest, and so on. Flipped over and restrung left handed, the tallest pole piece would be under the D string, and the shortest would be under the A string, and so on. This would affect the relative volume balances among the strings.

It has been said that one of the reasons Hendrix used a .015 G string was to help keep the string balances more even, compared to the more-standard .017 G string. However, he used Fender 150 Rock 'n' Roll Light strings, which in those days were gauged .010, .013, .015, .026, .032, and .038. Today's Fender 150R strings run .010, .013, .017, .026, .036, and .046.

Rumors abound about his strings of choice. And players who met/knew Hendrix and who played his guitars report different things. Bob Kulick has stated that Jimi told him he used an E string for his B string, which would have made a very light B. Buddy Miles, however, states that Hendrix used a very heavy E string. Mike Bloomfield played Hendrix's Strats and also stated that they were strung with mixed gauges because Jimi felt it helped his guitars stay in tune better.

One source states that Hendrix used all five springs in the tremolo block on his Strats and that the bridge was pulled flat against the body, so the strings could only be lowered in pitch, not raised. For his first album, *Are You Experienced*, he tuned to standard pitch. Beginning with *Axis: Bold as Love*, he tuned down a half step, to E♭.

For those who place all their Hendrix eggs in the Strat basket, several sources state that Jimi actually used Noel Redding's Fender Telecaster to record two of his most famous songs, "Purple Haze" and "Hey Joe." Assuming he restrung the guitar for left-handed use, this still would have resulted in the string lengths on the headstock, the staggering of the pole pieces, and the angle of the bridge pickup being reversed, just as when he played a right-handed Strat upside down.

Hendrix used medium picks of whatever type was available. Of more interest from a tonal standpoint is his use of "coily" cables. These cables, which were common at that time, were not made from the best quality materials and probably had an effect on the top end of his signal—more than likely he was losing treble due to these cables, which would have given his Strat a warmer sound.

Amps

Hendrix is most often associated with using 100-watt Marshall JMP100 "Plexi" Super Lead amplifiers. With his low-output single-coil pickups, these would have produced a fairly clean, crunchy tone, with most of the distortion coming from the power tubes in the amp—he ran the amps at extremely high volume levels. He used Marshall 4×12 cabinets, the 1982 slant cab and the 1982 B straight cab, which was taller than today's standard Marshall 4×12s. Ultimately, he ended up with three heads and six cabinets on stage. Marshall made a "signature" limited-edition reissue of the heads and cabs that he used, featuring those larger cabinet dimensions. Only 600 units of this amp, the Marshall Super 100JH and accompanying 1982/1982B cabinets, were made.

In the early days, his cabinets were stock, loaded with G12M Greenback Celestion speakers (some of which may have been 20-watt versions). Later, he switched to 30-watt G12H-30 speakers, probably the 55-Hz resonant-frequency version, which were originally intended for use in bass amps. These speakers would have reduced speaker breakup for a cleaner sound, and they would have had increased bass and lower mid response.

Marshalls were not the only amps that Hendrix used, of course. He was known to use a Leslie speaker for chorus-type effects. In the early days—1965 and 1966—he used a Fender Twin amplifier. He also had a deal after the Monterey Pop Festival where he was using Sunn amplifiers for around 14 months—he moved back to Marshalls and Fenders from these fairly quickly. These amps were apparently used with cabinets loaded with a JBL D-130F 15-inch speaker and a PA-style horn driver, not the best choice for amplifying electric guitar. He also used Fender Dual Showman amps with 2×15 cabinets alongside his Marshalls and Sunns in 1968.

According to techs working at West Coast Organ and Amp Repair, who were said to have prepared Hendrix's amps for touring in 1969, his cabs at the time were loaded with 75-watt Celestions, and his amps were powered with 6550 tubes instead of EL34 tubes. They further state that he preferred the 6550s running at high plate voltages. His Dual Showman amps were stock.

Effects

Many players assume that Hendrix used tons of effects. But compared to the acre-covering pedalboards, refrigerator-sized racks, and sophisticated computer-controlled switchers used by some of today's guitarists, Hendrix used very few effects. In fact, in the early days, there were just three pedals found onstage: a Dallas-Arbiter Fuzz Face, a Vox (later Crybaby) wah wah, and a custom, Roger Mayer–made Octavia, an octave-doubler that created a note an octave above the guitar's original pitch. (You can hear it in action during the solo on "Purple Haze.") Hendrix ran the Octavia after the Fuzz Face, which creates a different sound than running the pedals in the reverse order.

Interestingly, one source says that Hendrix began using a wah pedal after hearing Clapton on "Tales of Brave Ulysses." However, Clapton has stated that he began using wah after hearing Hendrix on "Burning of the Midnight Lamp." Other sources state that Hendrix first saw/heard the wah pedal when meeting Frank Zappa in mid-1967.

Later in his career, Jimi also used a Univox Uni-Vibe to create warbly rotating speaker-style effects. ("Machine Gun" has great examples of the Uni-Vibe in use.)

Studio Tricks

Eddie Kramer, the engineer who made most of Hendrix's recordings, used a lot of studio trickery to help him achieve the sounds he was after. For example, two slightly out-of-sync tape machines were used to create flanging effects. Tapes were also flipped over to create backward effects. Studio reverb, tape delay, and other studio effects were all employed at various times.

Benchmark Recordings

Jimi Hendrix Experience, *Are You Experienced* (1967)

Jimi Hendrix Experience, *Axis: Bold as Love* (1967)

Jimi Hendrix Experience, *Electric Ladyland* (1968)

Jimi Hendrix/Band of Gypsys, *Band of Gypsys* (1970)

Various Artists, *Woodstock: Music from the Original Soundtrack and More* (1970)

Getting the Sound

To achieve a tone similar to Jimi Hendrix's, you won't need a ton of gear, but there are some specifics that can help you get closer to his sound:

▷ A Strat-style guitar with three single-coil pickups and a vibrato bridge. To get even closer, try a left-handed guitar if you are right handed or a right-handed guitar if you are left handed. If you'd rather have your guitar body "right side up," with the controls in the usual places, use a reversed headstock/neck (left-handed headstock/neck on a right-handed guitar and vice versa), low-output single-coil pickups, and a reverse-angle bridge pickup.

▷ For early Hendrix tones, a Fuzz Face, Crybaby wah wah, and an Octavia are essential (wired in that order). For later tones, you'll also want a Uni-Vibe. A number of companies make "signature" versions or reissues of the vintage models he used that will provide appropriate tones.

▷ A flanger will help you re-create some of the studio effects applied to Jimi's guitars during recordings. A volume pedal or envelope effect may be used to create backward guitar effects.

▷ For best results, use 100-watt Marshall-style amps, of the late-'60s Plexi variety, combined with two 4×12 cabinets per head, and cranked *way* up. For the early tones, use Greenbacks. For later tones, try G12H-30s.

▷ A big component of the Hendrix sound is massive, extreme volume, which amplified various noises he made on the guitar and made feedback effects easy to achieve.

Allan Holdsworth

THERE ARE "SHREDDERS" WHO CAN REEL OFF HUNDREDS of notes in a second, but few have the talent to transcend being simply fleet-fingered technicians to ascend to the level of true musicianship. Allan Holdsworth is definitely one exception to the "shredder" rule. While he has astounding technique, it's his one-of-a-kind approach to his instrument, combined with his exceptional musicality, that never fails to amaze and intrigue. As a guitarist, he is in his own league.

Though he has never achieved the commercial mainstream success that some of the other "Icons of Tone" have enjoyed, for decades Allan Holdsworth has reigned as a "musician's musician"—a guitar player that others point to as one of the purest of the breed. His credits include a stellar list of groundbreaking fusion groups and collaborations, including Tempest, Bruford, U.K., Soft Machine, the New Tony Williams Lifetime, Gong, Jean Luc Ponty, Gordon Beck, Frank Gambale, i.o.u., and many more, as well as a long and distinguished solo career featuring many important recordings.

Unique in every way, from his "outside" chordal/harmonic sense to his intervallic melodic choices, from his sophisticated use of the vibrato arm to his stunningly fluid legato technique, from his compositions to his instantly identifiable clean and lead tones, Holdsworth has been a tremendous influence on many guitar players. Much of his approach is aimed at diminishing the traditional attack and percussiveness of the guitar in favor of a more horn-like articulation, pianistic block chords, and soft-attack articulations reminiscent of strings or synthesizer.

Holdsworth changes his gear quite often, though his tones have remained remarkably consistent throughout all of these changes. But the sound produced by his gear is only part of his tonal equation. His touch and approach also have a big impact—few players have developed their legato technique as intensely as Holdsworth has, and equally few are as adept at shaping notes with the vibrato arm. Equally important are the actual notes he chooses, with wide interval leaps and unusual rhythmic groupings, and the often-dissonant chords that he plays, with close, keyboard-style voicings.

Guitars

Some sources have said that early on Holdsworth was influenced by Clapton during the Cream days (which is interesting, as it is difficult to discern any connection between how the two play or sound), which led to him playing a Gibson SG during the first part of his career. Allan, however, says that he initially played Stratocasters after hearing Hank Marvin and the Shadows. But about six months later, he tried an SG and fell in love with it. He ended up using SGs for a number of years. He also played a Gibson ES-335 for a short time, while he was with Tempest.

Modded Strats

Holdsworth was using an SG when he joined the New Tony Williams Lifetime (1975). But in 1976 he began using Fender Strats modded with humbuckers—PAFs he took from his SGs, which were later replaced with DiMarzio PAFs and then finally with Seymour Duncan '59s. He may have predated Eddie Van Halen installing humbuckers in Strats (or at least independently began modding his guitars in this way at around the same time).

In the '80s he met luthier Grover Jackson (of Charvel/Jackson), who built him three "test" Strat-style guitars using different woods. The first had a basswood body, a maple neck, and an ebony fingerboard with a custom-wound Duncan humbucker at the bridge. The second used jelutong from Malaysia for the body with a maple neck and fingerboard with a Duncan '59 neck humbucker at the bridge. The last had a spruce body with a one-piece maple neck/fingerboard with a custom-wound DiMarzio humbucker at the bridge.

In the mid-'80s he worked with Ibanez on the Allan Holdsworth Signature AH-10 and AH-20, which had Strat-style shapes with basswood bodies and a hollow area under the pickguard for increased resonance. Like Allan's Strats and Jacksons, these guitars featured Fender-style vibrato tailpieces and either a single humbucker in the bridge position or two humbuckers, one at the bridge and the other at the neck.

Headless

As his solo career progressed, Allan began to use headless Steinberger guitars, which were often modified by luthier Bill Delap with flatter fingerboards and huge Dunlop 6000 frets. Eventually, his association with Steinberger resulted in the GL2TA-AH signature model. This guitar was equipped with passive Seymour Duncan SH-AH1 humbucking pickups and Steinberger's unique Trans-Trem vibrato system.

Holdsworth continues to use Steinbergers today, though he plays them less than he used to. For headless guitars, he has been using custom guitars built for him by Bill Delap. These feature slightly more substantial bodies than the original Steinbergers. Delap also built him several baritone guitars. At this writing, he was still using one with a 38-inch scale length.

In mid-2009 he began working with Rick Canton of Canton Custom Guitars on new instruments. These guitars generally feature very large frets (Dunlop 6000 fret wire), a Steinberger Trans-Trem, a flat fretboard, a hollow-body design for extra resonance, and either custom-wound pickups or a Seymour Duncan Allan Holdsworth signature humbucking pickup, which features 12 adjustable pole pieces. Reports indicate that while these guitars have been a success in the studio, he has not been able to use them live due to feedback problems.

Fatboy

In the late 1990s, Holdsworth worked with Carvin to create two signature models, the H2 and the HF2 "Fatboy." The H2 has a 1-3/4-inch-thick chambered alder body with a set alder neck, while the HF2 has a thicker, 2-3/8-inch chambered alder body with a maple set neck with an ebony fingerboard. (Carvin offers other types of body woods, including maple tops and exotic woods, neck woods, and fingerboard woods as options on these guitars. Holdsworth's personal Fatboys typically have figured maple tops.) Both guitars use Carvin's Allan Holdsworth H22N (neck) and H22B (bridge) humbucking pickups, which feature alnico 5 magnets and vintage-style enameled wire. A Tune-o-matic bridge and stop tailpiece are standard, with Strat-style vibrato tailpieces optional.

Though his signature Carvin guitars have dual humbuckers, Allan has stated his preference for single-humbucker guitars, based on his feeling that the magnetic pull from neck pickups reduces sustain and vibration in the strings. It has also been stated that he uses 250k-ohm potentiometers with his humbuckers, which would result in a darker sound than the usual 500k-ohm pots. He also uses his guitar's tone control to remove some high frequencies for a smoother sound.

Strings and Picks

Allan's touch is light, both with his right and his left hand. He uses very light strings—La Bella .008 gauge (.008, .011, .013, .018 wound, .024, .036)—and relies on drive from his amp or his effects for sustain. On his Carvin Fatboy, he uses .009 gauge strings. He uses Dunlop 1-mm picks for melodies and solos but tends to pluck chords using his bare fingers, so that the notes sound simultaneously, piano-style, rather than with the traditional guitar pick strum.

Amps

Holdsworth has used many, many different amps throughout his career, ranging from Vox AC30s in the early years to Marshall stacks, from Pearce to Hartley Thompson (used with i.o.u.), from Mesa/Boogies in the late '80s to Johnson amps—note that many of his amps have been solid-state designs. He relied on Yamaha DG80 digital modeling combo amplifiers for quite a while but lately seems to favor Hughes & Kettner zenTera and TriAmp MK II amps. He typically has one amp set for his clean sound and one amp set for his lead sound. He runs the output of his amps into a dummy load, such as the Rocktron Juice Extractor or the "Harness," which he designed himself. The dummy load reduces the speaker level output from the amps to line level. The line-level signal can then be routed through his effects chain, on to a stereo power amp, and into his speaker cabinets. He also uses preamps, such as the Mesa/Boogie Quad preamp and the Yamaha DG-1000 modeling preamp, the latter of which was used for recording *Sixteen Men of Tain* (2000).

His sound is quite midrange-centric; several observers have reported that he turns the bass control on his amps all the way off. Others have stated that he also turns down the highs, leaving just the midrange. In '80s interviews, he described his approach as making the amp bright sounding and then turning down the treble from his signal using the guitar's tone control.

His clean tone is quite clean, with no breakup. His lead tone has a lot of sustain but not a lot of distortion. He has stated that distortion is a "necessary evil" and that his approach has always been to try to achieve as much sustain as possible with as little distortion as possible. His is more of a mid-gain sound without fuzziness; the lack of highs helps to keep the "fizz" to a minimum in his tone, even when the gain is higher for increased sustain.

For touring, Holdsworth often relies on whatever rental amps are available in each town or venue—on any given night he could be playing through a Fender Twin, a Marshall cabinet, or whatever else has been provided. His effects system is designed to allow him to get his tones no matter what amp he is playing through.

Effects

Allan Holdsworth's clean and lead tones are heavily processed with effects. He uses a stereo clean tone run through a number of delays to create a rich ambience. His distorted lead tone uses completely different effects (and even different amps and speakers) than his clean tone.

During the i.o.u. years, he used an A/DA Stereo Tapped Delay for his stereo clean sound with the Hartley Thompson amps. He also used a Yamaha E-1010 analog delay for longer echoes. For many years, he used a large rack of delays and EQs to create his sound, including two Rocktron Intellifexes. Then Allan collaborated with Yamaha to create the UD Stomp, which he has described as a rack full of delays (eight delays in parallel) in one box. He carried two (one for his clean sounds and one for his distorted leads), claiming that this allowed him to pack his entire effects rig into a suitcase and carry it onto an airplane.

When Yamaha discontinued the UD Stomp, Holdsworth switched to using their MagicStomp—actually, he uses six, with each dedicated to a particular effect. Three are used for his clean tone (eight-voice chorus often created with eight modulated delays, delay, pitch shift, and so on) and three for his lead tone.

He has stated that he sometimes uses a booster in the recording studio, such as the Custom Audio Electronics Boost/Overdrive or the TC Electronic Booster+Line Driver & Distortion. He uses TC Electronic 1140 rackmount parametric equalizers to shape his post-amp sounds. He has also used the Roland VG-8 virtual guitar system for certain synth-like sounds.

Holdsworth runs his effects in stereo for a rich, wide effect that is somewhat similar to a synthesizer in many cases. (He has also used real synthesizers extensively in the past, driven by a Synthaxe guitar-style controller.) He uses volume pedals both to "swell" the front of notes and chords, removing the pick attacks, as well as to balance effects levels and blends. In some cases, the volume swells are programmed into his effects boxes and do not require a volume pedal.

Benchmark Recordings

U.K., *U.K.* (1978)

i.o.u., *i.o.u.* (1982)

Allan Holdsworth, *Metal Fatigue* (1985)

Allan Holdsworth, *Live at Yoshi's* (DVD, 2007)

Getting the Sound

To achieve clean and lead tones similar to Allan Holdsworth's, try this:

▷ A lightweight, resonant solid-body or chambered solid-body guitar with a single, moderate-output humbucker at the bridge and a tremolo bar, strung with very light strings.

▷ Either a multi-tap delay or several delays that can be combined for a chorused/ambient stereo tone.

▷ A volume pedal for swelling into clean chords with no pick attack.

▷ Either separate amplifiers for clean and for dirty, or an amp that can be switched from clean to dirty, with dedicated EQ and effects switching for each channel.

▷ Alternatively, a modeling preamp, amp, or pedal—Allan has used them himself—will help you create his clean and dirty tones.

Eric Johnson

I F THERE IS ONE PLAYER WHO IS A POSTER BOY FOR TONE OBSESSION, it would have to be Austin-based guitarist Eric Johnson. Few go to the lengths that he does to achieve the tones that he desires, and even fewer possess the ears that he is said to have. Over the years some have mocked his perfectionism and his claims, such as being able to hear the difference between various types of batteries in certain pedals —which has since been proven to be true—but he has maintained his sense of humor and his dedication to his art and his pursuit of tone. He is well known for his sparkling, bright, echo-laden clean sounds; full, punchy rhythm tones; and smooth "violin-like" lead sounds.

His multi-amp approach has remained constant through many years, with a few side trips into effects routings and various amps here and there. He often chooses vintage amps and effects to create his tones. Likewise, his choice of guitars has remained constant for a number of years, often centering on vintage models.

Guitars

Johnson is most closely associated with the Fender Stratocaster guitar. He has played several vintage Strats from the '50s. He has been known to change out the bridge pickup for a DiMarzio HS-2, which is a stacked humbucking single-coil. Johnson only connects one coil on the HS-2 so it is not humbucking. However, the output is higher than a vintage Strat pickup, and even with one coil disconnected, the HS-2 still provides a fatter sound than the stock pickup.

He also says he installs larger frets and rewires the electronics so that the second tone knob controls the bridge pickup. (On a standard-wired Strat, there is no tone control on the bridge pickup.) Over the years, photos have shown other mods to his guitars, such as replacing a steel high-E bridge saddle with a brass saddle, B-string pole pieces pushed into the pickup to reduce the volume level of that string (not a recommended mod as you can easily destroy the pickup), and more.

Eric also worked with Fender to develop two versions of a signature Stratocaster, which he uses regularly. As with all things Eric Johnson, the details of these signature models have been tweaked to his exact specifications. The first signature Eric Johnson Strat features a lightweight alder body with '57-era deep contours and cavities. It has a one-piece quartersawn maple neck and fingerboard with a flatter-than-vintage 12-inch radius. Other special touches include a thin nitrocellulose finish on the body and neck, a vintage-style tremolo tailpiece with '57 recesses in the string block and no paint between the base plate and the string block, staggered vintage-style tuners, and more.

The pickups are custom-wound to Johnson's specs, with each one set up for a different sound. The bridge pickup uses an alnico 5 magnet and measures over 7k-ohms. The middle pickup is reverse-wound for hum canceling when combined with the bridge or neck pickup and has an output around 6.7k-ohms. It is voiced like a '63 Strat single-coil. The neck pickup is voiced like a '54 Strat pickup with an alnico 3 magnet; it measures nearly 6k-ohms. The guitar uses a five-way pickup selector switch and has the two tone controls wired to the neck and bridge pickups; there is no tone control on the middle pickup.

The more recent Eric Johnson signature model is similar except that it has a quartersawn maple neck with a bound rosewood fingerboard. Both guitars come set up with five tremolo springs and .010 to .046 Fender 250R strings, although Johnson has a signature pure-nickel rollerwound string set from GHS gauged .010 through .050.

But Strats are not the only guitars that Johnson uses. He also plays Gibson ES-335, Les Paul, and SG models. In fact, one of his biggest hits, "Cliffs of Dover," was recorded using a 335, not a Strat, as most players assume. Eric also has signature humbucking pickups from DiMarzio, which were developed to provide a more Gretsch-like tone from his Gibson '59 reissue Les Paul Standard. These pickups have a PAF-like output level but are voiced to be brighter and clearer than PAFs, with single-coil-like top end.

Amps

Eric Johnson uses a three-amp setup, with separate amps and speakers for clean, crunch/rhythm, and lead tones. Some pictures show his amps/cabinets on small risers to decouple them acoustically from the stage. Some pictures also show his speaker cabinets with one caster cup removed from the top, which would "unseal" the cabinet, with the resulting hole acting as a vent or a sort of port.

Clean Amps

Johnson relies on Fender amps for his cleans, most recently a pair of Blackface Twin Reverbs run in stereo. He uses either combos or units that have been rehoused in head cabs. The rehoused amps each drive two speakers in a Marshall 4×12 cabinet that is wired for stereo operation and that has been converted to an open back. Recently, he has been loading one side (whether one of the combos or two speakers in the 4×12) with JBL D120F speakers and the other side with the stock Jensens.

Crunch/Rhythm Amp

For his rhythm tone, Johnson mostly uses late '60s 100-watt Plexi Marshalls, although he has experimented with the Marshall Hendrix signature JTM 45 100-watt head. In the late '80s through the early '90s, he used a

Dumble Overdrive Special for his rhythm tone. His rhythm amps drive a Marshall 4×12 loaded with vintage 30-watt (G12H) Celestions. Early on, he was also known to use a Mesa/Boogie Mark I, and he has experimented with new Fulton-Webb amplifiers. Fulton-Webb's DR45 (Dirty Rhythm) amp head is a collaboration between the company and Johnson, although he does not seem to be using it himself with any regularity.

Lead Amp

For lead, Johnson uses either 50- or 100-watt late '60s Plexi Marshall heads. Recently, he has been using a new Marshall handwired '69 Plexi reissue through a Marshall 4×12 cabinet loaded with vintage 25-watt (G12M) Celestions.

Effects

With the triple amp setup and his large, well-loaded pedalboard, Johnson's rig seems complex. But in fact, what he has are three fairly simple signal paths, one for each amp, brought together onto one board. In other words, each amp has its own discrete effects chain. From the guitar, two A/B switches feed the effects and are used to select among the clean, rhythm, and lead amps.

He uses George L's cables with brass plugs as well as some low-priced cables, with many of the cable runs longer than necessary to help attenuate the highs in the signal. Some pedals are run off of AC power, while others use batteries. Johnson is very specific about how the pedals are placed and mounted on his pedalboard —his Tube Driver is mounted on an elevated block of wood, for example—which is said to have an effect on his tone.

Clean Effects

From one side of the first A/B switch, the guitar feeds an old MXR Dyna Comp compressor (a recent addition to his chain) and then into either an Echoplex tape echo or a Boss DD-2 digital delay followed by an Electro-Harmonix Deluxe Memory Man. From there the signal goes through a TC Electronic Stereo Chorus/Flanger, which splits it to stereo to feed the two Fender Twin amps.

Crunch/Rhythm Effects

Another output from the A/B switches selects the Marshall amp used for rhythm, which is set for a crunchy, Hendrix- or Keith Richards–style rhythm tone. A vintage Dallas Arbiter Fuzz Face or a modern Dunlop Fuzz Face can be used to punch up the gain and add sustain for melody and some lead parts. (Dunlop is rumored to be developing a signature EJ Fuzz Face.) Recently, Johnson added an Ibanez Tube Screamer that is used for heavier power chords to his rhythm signal chain, as well as a ToadWorks Barracuda Howard Leese signature flanger.

Lead Effects

Johnson's lead effects have remained the same for many years: The last output from the A/B switches feeds a B.K. Butler Tube Driver and an Echoplex tape echo, and the lead amp. He also uses a Crybaby wah wah.

Post Effects

In some cases, Eric also mikes his amps and routes the signal through other effects, such as an MXR 1500 digital delay. These effects are sent through a powered PA speaker system, such as a JBL EON, to create a wet/dry effect, adding echo or flanging without muddying up the sound of the main amps.

Benchmark Recordings

Eric Johnson, *Tones* (1986)

Eric Johnson, *Ah Via Musicom* (1990)

Eric Johnson, *Venus Isle* (1996)

Getting the Sound

To achieve a tone similar to Eric Johnson's, try this:

▷ A vintage Strat-style guitar with three single-coils and a tremolo. It is important to have a tone control wired to the bridge pickup. A Fender Eric Johnson signature model will provide the necessary features, but any '50s-vintage-style Strat-type guitar will be a good start.

▷ Either separate amps and speakers for stereo clean, crunch/rhythm, and lead, or an amp with three discrete channels or presets that can be set for different tones and gain levels.

▷ Separate effects for stereo clean, crunch/rhythm, and lead that can be switched either with each amp or using a bypass looper, switched at the same time as the channels are changed on the amp.

▷ A modeling amp with built-in effects, or a modeling effects device could be used to create the three separate sounds and the different effects variations Johnson uses.

Brian May

WITH HIS LONG, CURLY HAIR AND TALL, SLIM FRAME, Brian May might just be the prototypical rock star—though he's probably also the only rock star who holds an advanced degree in astrophysics, the only to be named Chancellor of Liverpool John Moores University, and one of very few to be a named a Commander of the Order of the British Empire. But it's his unique tone and approach to playing that sets him apart from other guitarists. Using an unusual blend of homemade, customized, and off-the-shelf gear, he creates a tone that is instantly recognizable. In fact, he claims to have had his exact sound in his head when he began playing—it was just a matter of finding the right gear to achieve that sound.

Guitars

Brian May has used a few different guitars for certain songs during his career, such as a 1967 Fender Telecaster owned by Queen drummer Roger Taylor for the solo on "Crazy Little Thing Called Love"—Freddie Mercury played the rhythm part for the song on the same Telecaster. But aside from single-song anomalies such as the Tele, he has a near-exclusive relationship with the "Red Special," a guitar he built at age 16 with his father. The pair used materials that were available around their house to make the Red Special, such as wood from a fireplace surround (neck and center block), pearl buttons (position markers), shelf edging (binding), and motorcycle parts (vibrato tailpiece).

The guitar is semi-solid, built around an oak center block with mahogany "wings" that have been routed out to create chambers. The thick, wide neck is mahogany with an oak fingerboard with 24 frets and a 24-inch scale length. Originally the guitar had homemade pickups, but May switched them out for Burns Tri-Sonic single-coils. Each pickup has its own on/off switch and its own phase switch. The pickups are wired in series rather than in parallel, which is part of what gives the Red Special its unique tonal capabilities. May potted the pickups in epoxy resin to cut down on microphonic squealing.

Brian uses a British sixpence coin as a pick, stating that plastic picks are too flexible. The sixpence has a ser-rated edge, which adds "grind" to each note's attack. May's right-hand touch is very light. He uses Optima (formerly Maxima) Gold strings, gauged .009 through .042 and plated with 24k gold; with the Red Special's short scale length, the string tension is very low. On the Red Special, his action is set low: 1.5mm (a little more than 1/16 inch) at the twelfth fret for the high E string, and 2mm at the twelfth fret for the low E string.

The Burns pickups on his Red Special are set quite close to the strings; apparently, these pickups do not suffer from the string pull issues for which single-coils such as Fender Strat pickups are famous. For the bridge pickup, the high E side is 2.5mm away and the low E is 2.75mm away. The middle is 3mm from the high E and 3.25mm from the low E. The neck is 3.25mm from the high E and 3.5mm from the low E. All his pickup heights are measured with the strings un-fretted. (For reference, 3mm is slightly less than 1/8 inch.)

In the early '70s, May used Fender Stratocasters as backup guitars onstage, and for a few years in the mid-'70s he even used Gibson Les Paul Deluxes and a Gibson Flying V as backups. He has also used various "Brian May" model guitars—essentially replicas of his Red Special—as backups for concert work, such as one made by luthier John Birch (this guitar was smashed at a concert in 1982 in a fit of frustration), the Brian May signature models made by Guild in the '80s and '90s, and most recently, exact duplicates of the Red Special custom made by Greg Fryer (whom May also entrusted to restore his original Red Special in 1998). Various other companies have also made copies of the Red Special, such as Burns and Guyton, as well as numerous others. Brian May Guitars, his own company, even took over production of the Guyton Red Special when that company ceased making them.

Amps

Just as he is faithful to his Red Special, Brian has also maintained a near-exclusive relationship with Vox AC30 amps. He was influenced in his amp choice by seeing and meeting the late Irish guitarist, Rory Gallagher. Many of his most famous tracks were cut with a 1963 Vox AC30 Bass.

Today, he uses both vintage and new AC30TBX Top Boost amplifiers loaded with Celestion "Blue" alnico speakers. He plugs into the Normal channel and cranks all the settings up full. Vox made a 500-piece run of a Brian May Edition AC30, which has only one control: a volume knob. Other features of the Brian May Edition amp include a built-in treble booster and a half-power switch. This amp is equipped with a Celestion "Blue" alnico speaker.

Onstage, May uses nine AC30s, arranged into three groups of three amps. He uses these banks of amps in two ways. First, he switches among them using a switcher made by Pete Cornish to reduce the wear and tear each amp receives. Second, he uses them with delays to create his signature harmony guitar effects. One amp group receives the dry guitar signal, while the other two are each fed by a different delay, creating an echo 1/dry/echo 2 system for delay effects and harmonies on songs such as "Brighton Rock." His road amps are said to be modified with all unused tubes and electronics removed—including the electronics for the second, Top Boost channel—and certain components beefed up. This is reported to increase the gain (estimated at a 6-dB increase) and to change the tone slightly.

May is said to be extremely picky about his vacuum tubes because he drives them so hard with all of his con-trols cranked and because he demands complete consistency. His EL84 power tubes are put through a battery of intense tests that simulate full-blast stage conditions. Those that survive (apparently the survival rate is quite low) are deemed consistent and reliable for May's purposes. Likewise, the ECC83/12AX7 preamp tubes he uses are thoroughly tested for hum, noise, microphonics, and exact gain level.

Deacy

In the studio, May often uses a small combo amp he calls the "Deacy," which was made by Queen bassist John Deacon. Built from a hi-fi amplifier circuit board inside of a bookshelf speaker cabinet containing a 6.5-inch Elac twin-cone speaker, the Deacy is a solid-state amp using germanium transistors. The amp is battery powered and has no controls at all—just plug in and play! Brian pushes it with a treble booster to create his signature smooth overdrive. Some sources report that when he records the Deacy, he covers it with a coat to reduce the treble.

The Deacy was primarily used for the layered "guitar choir" or "symphonic" parts found in many Queen songs, because the AC30 didn't layer as well. The Deacy was first heard on "Procession" and "The Fairy Feller's Master-Stroke" from *Queen II* (1974). It can be heard prominently on "God Save the Queen" from *A Night at the Opera* (1975), as well as on numerous other Queen recordings.

Vox also made a signature version of the Deacy amp, called the Brian May Special. It was a solid-state 10-watt amp with a 6.5-inch speaker. Unlike the original Deacy, it had volume and EQ controls. The Brian May Special amp had a built-in treble-booster circuit; an output jack following the treble booster could be routed out of the Special for use as a preamp to overdrive another amp, such as an AC30.

Effects

An integral part of Brian May's tone is his use of a treble booster to push his AC30s into overdrive. Originally he used a Dallas Rangemaster, but his original was lost in the early '70s after being used on all of the Queen albums up to *A Day at the Races*. His father built him a replacement unit. Later, Pete Cornish made him an improved version, the TB-83, which had 32 dB of gain boost. It was subsequently replaced by a custom treble booster made by Greg Fryer in 2000. Fryer now offers several versions of his treble booster for sale, duplicating the gain levels and booster voicings that May used in the '70s and '80s.

Brian uses two delay units in conjunction with his triple-bank amp rig. Originally, he used two Echoplex EP3 tape echoes (modified by May for longer delay times for songs such as "Stone Cold Crazy"), but due to reliability problems with the Echoplexes, he switched to using two digital delays, ultimately settling on Rocktron Intellifex XL units. His dry guitar signal feeds one bank of three amps, and each delay feeds its own set of three amps. This system allows for maximum clarity for each signal and gives the effect of three guitarists playing simultaneously, in harmony, and allows him to re-create the layered sounds on Queen's recordings. The echoes are set at multiples of one another. For example on "Brighton Rock," the first delay is set to 800 milliseconds, and the second is set to 1,600 milliseconds.

Among his other effects are a fOXX phaser, used on "Bohemian Rhapsody," "We Will Rock You," and others. He uses a Dunlop rackmount Crybaby wah wah, but as a fixed filter for tone shaping, not to create the traditional wah-wah effects. In the early years, he used a Boss CE-1 chorus and later a CE-5 chorus. In more recent years, he has used a TC Electronic G-Force for chorus to thicken his sound and for pitch shifting to create harmony lines. A Hughes & Kettner Rotosphere is employed for rotating speaker effects.

Benchmark Recordings

Queen, *Queen II* (1974)

Queen, *Sheer Heart Attack* (1974)

Queen, *A Night at the Opera* (1975)

Queen, *The Game* (1980)

Getting the Sound

To achieve a tone similar to Brian May's, try this:

▷ A key ingredient in the Brian May tone is his unorthodox homemade Red Special guitar. A chambered guitar with a mahogany body and neck would provide a good start. The Seymour Duncan Custom Shop will make replicas of the Burns Tri-Sonic single-coil pickups, and Adeson in the U.K. manufactures Tri-Sonic reproductions. Otherwise, a guitar with three single-coil pickups that can be switched for series operation and with independent phase switches for each pickup, plus a vibrato tailpiece, will get you in the ballpark.

▷ Use light-gauge strings and a coin with a serrated edge as a pick. Keep your touch light.

▷ Amp-wise, there is only one authentic choice: a cranked up Vox AC30TBX with Celestion Blue alnico speakers, using the Normal channel. But, any of the AC family amps (or other similar Class A tube amps) could be used. If you can find a Vox Brian May amp, you won't need a treble booster; otherwise, a treble booster will be necessary to get the drive and tonal shaping required.

▷ To create May's layered effects, a Vox Brian May Special amp is the truest option, if you can find one. Greg Fryer is said to be working on a replica of the Deacy as well.

▷ To create May's live harmony/three-guitar effects, you'll need a delay capable of long delay times. For maximum clarity, the two echo repeats should be routed to separate amplifiers from the dry signal.

▷ A phaser will be required for certain songs.

▷ Another solution would be to use a "Brian May" pedal, such as the DigiTech Artist Series Brian May Red Special, which uses modeling to re-create Brian's signature tones.

Jimmy Page

THERE MUST HAVE BEEN SOMETHING IN THE WATER in England in the early to mid '60s that led to an onslaught of talented guitarists. How else can you explain the near simultaneous appearance of the Peter Green, Jeff Beck, Eric Clapton, Pete Townshend, Mick Taylor, David Gilmour, Ritchie Blackmore, Keith Richards, Ron Wood, Tony Iommi, Jimmy Page, and many others? Of these, Jeff Beck, Eric Clapton, and Jimmy Page form the Holy Trinity of British Rock Guitarists—the three that have influenced more players than any others.

And of the Trinity, Page holds the distinction of playing in perhaps the world's most important hard rock band, Led Zeppelin. During the 12 years or so that the band was around, they were the biggest thing going in rock. Page's earlier work with the Yardbirds (where he initially played bass and later played lead alongside Beck) was enough to cement him a spot in the rock 'n roll annals—actually, the myriad studio sessions he did in the mid-'60s was probably enough to earn him a spot on the roll. Some sources credit him with playing on 50 to 90 percent of the sessions done in England at the time! But it was his groundbreaking composing, arranging, and playing with Led Zeppelin that established him as a true superstar.

Guitars

Jimmy Page has had a career that can be divided into a few different musical eras: his mid-'60s studio session player period, the Yardbirds, Led Zeppelin, and post-Zeppelin. But guitar-wise, there are only three real eras: studio, Yardbirds, and Zeppelin/post Zeppelin.

The Session Years

During his "studio" period, 1963 to 1966, Page played on countless sessions—often as a "ghost" for other established bands, even such bands as the Who. During this time, he predominantly played a 1960 Gibson Les Paul Custom "Black Beauty," which had three humbucking pickups (stock, it would have been equipped with PAFs) and a Bigsby vibrato tailpiece. Unfortunately, this guitar was stolen while Led Zeppelin was on tour in 1971 and was never seen again. Page even ran an ad in *Rolling Stone* requesting information about it, to no avail. The Gibson Custom Shop made a replica of this guitar, limited to 25 pieces, in 2008.

The Yardbirds

With the Yardbirds, Page often played a 1958 (sometimes identified as a 1959) Fender Telecaster, which was given to him by Jeff Beck in 1966. (Some sources report that Beck "abandoned" this guitar when he left the Yardbirds.) This Tele went on to feature prominently during the early Led Zeppelin years. He also used a 1961 Danelectro 3021, which he used in the Yardbirds from '67 to '68. Like the Tele, his Danelectro figures into later use with Led Zeppelin. In addition to these two guitars, Page continued to rely heavily on his 1960 Les Paul Black Beauty during the Yardbird years.

Led Zeppelin

During the Led Zeppelin years, Jimmy Page is most strongly associated with what has become the classic hard rock combination: a Les Paul Standard through a Marshall stack. However, Page used a variety of guitars during his time with Zeppelin, and in fact, some of those massive tones that people long assumed were coming from a Les Paul/Marshall were played using guitars and amps from the opposite end of the spectrum.

A great example of this "I thought it was a Les Paul" confusion is the entire first Led Zeppelin album, where Page played the '58 Telecaster he had used with the Yardbirds. He later modified it with a Parsons/White B-Bender in 1976. Page also painted it with a psychedelic dragon, and for a short time it had a maple neck (see below). This guitar was used to record what has been voted "The Greatest Guitar Solo of All Time," the one on "Stairway to Heaven." (Some conflicting reports say that a 1961 Telecaster was used for this famous solo.) The '58 Tele remained a stalwart for many years, until it was ruined by a friend who refinished it as a "surprise" for Page—the neck ended up on a Tele Page used with the Firm many years later. Around 1977, Page also began using a 1953 Telecaster with a B-Bender, finished in "Botswana Brown." For a short time, he swapped this guitar's maple neck for the '58 Tele's rosewood neck.

In addition to the Telecaster, Jimmy used the 1961 Danelectro 3021 he played in the Yardbirds retuned to BADGAD for "White Summer." It was also tuned to DADGAD and used for "Black Mountain," "Kashmir," and "In My Time of Dying." A 1958 Danelectro 3021 was also used during the Zeppelin years.

Toward the end of Led Zeppelin, Page was known to use a 1964 Fender Stratocaster finished in Lake Placid Blue. (He had also used black and white Strats at earlier points in his career.) This guitar was played onstage for songs such as "Over the Hills and Far Away" and "In the Evening." Fender Electric XII and Vox 12-string guitars were used for recording various songs, such as "Thank You," "Stairway to Heaven," and "When the Levee Breaks," and for live performances.

Then, of course, there was the 1971 Gibson EDS-1275 double-neck guitar, with its 6-string and 12-string necks. This guitar is stock except for the removal of the pickup covers. He most famously played the double-neck onstage for "Stairway to Heaven," but he also used it for "Tangerine," "The Rain Song," and "The Song Remains the Same." One of his tricks was to set the double-neck's three-position neck selector switch to the middle position so that both necks were on. When set like this, the unused neck would resonate and ring sympathetically along with what Page was playing on the other neck. (This double-neck is sometimes credited as the guitar used to record "Stairway to Heaven," but this is incorrect—a Telecaster and a Fender Electric XII were used for that song, along with a Harmony acoustic guitar.)

Les Pauls

But, despite the fact that Jimmy Page has used many different guitars during his career, most would point to the Les Paul as "his" guitar. Along with Eric Clapton, he is perhaps the player who most influenced other guitarists to "rediscover" the Les Paul and to bring it back to prominence after it was discontinued in the early 1960s. Along with Clapton (and Keith Richards, Peter Green, and Mike Bloomfield), he was also a big part of why late-'50s Les Pauls have become Holy Grail instruments for so many guitarists and collectors. Interestingly, his "vintage" Les Pauls (they were just used Les Pauls when he got them, the "vintage" designation came later) were not prime examples of flamed tops; his guitars had quite plain tops—which they made up for by producing stellar tones!

1959 Les Paul Standard "Number One"

Purchased from Joe Walsh in 1969 (some reports say Walsh gave it to Page as a gift), this 1959 Gibson Les Paul Standard quickly became known as Page's "Number One." This guitar had its neck shaved down to make it slimmer, which occurred before Page acquired it. It was also modified with a push/pull potentiometer on the bridge pickup's tone control, which put the two pickups out of phase when used together. (Some sources report that the two pickups are always wired out of phase and that the push/pull pot is a coil tap.) The stock Kluson tuners were replaced with gold-plated Grovers (the rest of the guitar's hardware is chrome plated), and the jackplate was replaced several times. In 1972, the original PAF bridge pickup was replaced with a covered '70s "T-top" Gibson humbucking pickup when the original stopped working while Zeppelin was on tour in Australia. (The story goes that Number One's pickup was damaged when the cover came off after being smacked with Page's violin bow during "Dazed and Confused.") The T-top was replaced in the early '80s with a custom-wound, uncovered Seymour Duncan pickup.

Page's Number One Les Paul has been cloned a few times; luthier Roger Giffin (formerly of the Gibson Custom Shop) made a copy of it in 1991. In the mid-'90s, Gibson released the first Jimmy Page Signature Les Paul, which was based on Number One. In 2004, Gibson began making replicas of Number One as the Custom, Art, and Historic division's "Jimmy Page Signature Les Paul 'Number One.'" Jimmy received the first one, and he played and autographed the next 24, which were aged by luthier Tom Murphy. The next 150 were released as a "Limited Edition Aged" version, with the same Murphy aging but no autograph. A non-limited-edition "Custom Authentic" version was also available until 2007.

Number One became Page's primary guitar onstage, supplanting the 1958 "Dragon" Telecaster. It was used for Led Zeppelin recordings beginning with Led Zeppelin *II*.

1959 Les Paul Standard "Number Two"

Acquired in 1973, this '59 Les Paul was used as a backup for Number One and also was tuned to DADGAD for songs such as "Moby Dick." Its tuners were replaced with Grovers, and its neck was shaved down to be closer to the shape of the neck on Number One, though Number Two is reportedly not as slim as Number One.

Later, Number Two was modified with push/pull pots on its volume and tone controls for splitting the guitar's humbucking pickups and for putting each pickup's coils in series or parallel. Two push-button switches were added under the pickguard for switching the pickups out of phase and for connecting them in series or parallel. Page's goal was said to be to configure the electronics so that he could explore all the tonal possibilities a dual-humbucker guitar could offer. He used this guitar throughout the Led Zeppelin era, and later brought it back out for the '90s Firm and Page/Plant tours, as well as for the O2 reunion concert in 2007.

Gibson made three versions of the Custom Shop "Jimmy Page 'Number Two' Les Paul." The first, a run of 25 guitars, was Murphy aged and was signed by Page. The second version, a run of 100 guitars, was Murphy aged, but not signed. The third version, a run of 200 guitars, was "VOS" (vintage old stock), without aging.

Other Les Pauls

Page has also played a number of other Les Pauls during his career, including various Gibson signature models. For *The Song Remains the Same* live recording and concert film, he used a cherry refinished 1973. This guitar had a B-Bender installed. In the '70s, he used two Les Paul Deluxes that were refitted for full-size T-top Gibson humbuckers. One of these Les Paul Deluxes, a '69, was deemed "Number Three." In the '90s, with Coverdale/Page and on the Plant/Page tour, Jimmy played several Les Paul Classic Premium Plus models.

Strings and Picks

Jimmy Page has consistently relied on Ernie Ball Super Slinky strings throughout his career. These are nickel-wound strings, gauged .009 through .042. He uses Herco heavy-gauge nylon picks (now made by Dunlop). Page prefers a very low action on his guitars.

Amps

During his studio session days and with the Yardbirds, Jimmy Page relied on Vox amplifiers. He mostly played AC30/6 models, although he was also known to use the AC-100 MK II with the Yardbirds. In the early days of Led Zeppelin, a Vox UL4120, which used four KT88 power tubes to crank out 120 watts of power, was used. He has stated that although he liked the AC30s with Yardbirds, they were not loud enough to keep up with John Bonham's drums in Led Zeppelin.

Supro

Opinions vary as to which Supro combo amp was used by Page for recording the first Led Zeppelin album and for the solo on "Stairway to Heaven." Page has stated that he used a "little Supro with a 12-inch speaker." For many, this points to a model 1624TN, which is the only Supro that had a 12-inch speaker. But other sources suggest that he actually used a 1958 or 1959 model 1690TN, which had 6L6 power tubes and that came with dual 10-inch speakers, and that Jimmy replaced the dual 10s with a single 12-inch speaker. An amp displayed at the Rock and Roll Hall of Fame seems to confirm this.

Marshall

Page discovered Marshall amps and cabinets early on and used them in the early days of Led Zeppelin, often in combination with other amps. By the end of 1971, he had settled on using 100-watt Marshall 1959 SLP Plexi Super Lead amps onstage; the other amps were history. He also used his Plexi Marshalls for recording in the studio. One of his Super Leads was said to have belonged to Hendrix. Some of Page's Marshalls were modified with new transformers and KT88 power tubes for 200 watts of output and a cleaner tone. Some sources say this occurred around 1975; others suggest it happened earlier. Some sources also report that other mods were done to Page's Marshalls to increase preamp gain and to change the tone stack response, but this has never been verified.

Other Amps

Toward the end of the Yardbirds, Page used a Fender Dual Showman amp, which was later traded for PA equipment for Led Zeppelin. He also used a '68 Fender Super Reverb near the end of the Yardbirds and for early Led Zeppelin gigs.

At gigs in '68 and '69, with Led Zeppelin, Page was seen playing an Arbiter Power 100 amp, which had KT88 power tubes and resembled a Marshall but was said to be more like a Hiwatt in sound. The Arbiter was replaced by Hiwatt Custom 100 amps, which he used through 1971. The Hiwatts were custom versions with DR103 power sections but with higher-gain preamps. During these early days, he sometimes mixed Marshalls with these other amps. He was also known to use a Selmer Treble 'n Bass amp and Goliath cabinet around this time.

In the studio, he used a Leslie 147 rotating speaker cabinet borrowed from John Paul Jones to record the solo for "Good Times, Bad Times."

A variety of other amps were seen onstage with Page, such as Orange, Univox, Wizard, and various other Marshalls. It is likely that these amps were used for his Theremin, not for his guitar.

For the Plant/Page tours, Page used 100-watt Fender Tonemaster heads with Fender 4×12 cabs loaded with Celestion Vintage 30 speakers. He also used a Fender Vibro-King combo around this time. In 1999 and 2000, when he toured with the Black Crowes, Page used Orange AD30 amplifiers.

Cabinets and Speakers

In 1969, with Led Zeppelin, Page began using Marshall 1982A (angled front) and 1982B (straight front) cabinets loaded with 30-watt Celestion G30H speakers. He has stuck with these cabinets throughout the rest of his career.

In recent years (such as at the O2 reunion concert), Page has also used Engl 4×12 speaker cabinets.

Effects

There are several effects that have been mainstays for Page throughout his career. The first is the Vox Crybaby wah. (He also used a Vox King wah, a Vox V846, and an early gray Vox wah for short periods at different points in his career.) The second is the Sola Sound Tonebender Fuzz MK II, which he employed with his Supro and other amps for his classic overdriven sound with the Yardbirds and early on with Led Zeppelin. During his session days, he sometimes used a Maestro FZ-1 Fuzz-Tone (the pedal used by Keith Richards for "Satisfaction").

His echo with Led Zeppelin beginning in 1970 was a Maestro Echoplex EP2, which replaced the Vox CO2 Deluxe Echo "Long Tom" tape echo he had used previously. In 1972, he replaced the EP2 with a Maestro Echoplex EP3. He used a script-logo MXR Phase 90 for a number of Led Zeppelin songs.

Page also used a number of other effects, such as an Eventide H910 Harmonizer, which he used for his "noise" solos during late '70s Zeppelin concerts. An MXR Blue Box was used to create the sub-octave effect in "Fool in the Rain."

With the Firm, Page began using a Pete Cornish pedal board that contained a Boss CE-2 chorus and SD-1 over-drive, as well as a DigiTech WH-1 Whammy Pedal, a Roger Mayer Voodoo fuzz, a Crybaby wah, a booster, and a send/return loop for his Echoplex.

Studio Tricks

Jimmy Page is a strong believer in the studio maxim, "distance equals depth." He frequently mixes a close microphone on his amp with another microphone placed some distance from the amp—as much as 20 feet away—capturing the ambience and tone in the room. This is blended with the close mic to create a big, deep sound.

While he used his 100-watt Marshall Plexi amps in the studio, many sources recount that he preferred to use small combo amps. These smaller amps could be cranked up for a big tone at a much more manageable volume level.

Among the studio tricks that Page invented was reverse echo, where the tape is flipped backward, an echoed guitar part is played, and then the tape is flipped back in the proper direction. When played, the echo comes before the original guitar part.

Benchmark Recordings

Led Zeppelin, *Led Zeppelin* (1969)

Led Zeppelin, *II* (1969)

Led Zeppelin, *IV* (1971)

Getting the Sound

To achieve a tone similar to Jimmy Page's, try this:

> ▷ A Telecaster-style or a Les Paul–style guitar.

> ▷ A few simple effects: a wah wah, an echo, and perhaps a phaser.

> ▷ Either a small, cranked tube combo amp pushed by an overdrive or a Marshall-style amp.

Brad Paisley

SINCE 1999, BRAD PAISLEY HAS EXPERIENCED a meteoric rise to success in the music industry. Though he is widely known as a vocalist and songwriter, he is also hailed as a tremendous guitar player. He combines traditional country twang with hints of southern rock and rock 'n roll, all blended with dazzling technique, highly evolved note selection, and a rich, punchy tone. In the midst of an avalanche of "modern country" that sounds more like '70s rock, Paisley is, along with Vince Gill, Keith Urban, and other Nashville stars, bringing the focus of country music back to great chicken pickin' guitar playing.

Paisley has long been a gear hound, playing a ton of great guitars in his concerts and in the studio. Unfortunately, along with many other artists, he lost nearly all of his gear in the 2010 Nashville floods. He quickly rebuilt his rig in time to hit the road for a tour and has not looked back since.

Guitars

Teles, Teles, and more Teles! Paisley's number-one guitar is a 1968 Fender Telecaster with an (appropriately) paisley finish. The guitar has an alder body, a maple neck and a maple fretboard, and Dunlop 6105 frets. The guitar has a Lindy Fralin Blues Special bridge pickup and an overwound Fralin neck pickup. It is equipped with a Glaser G-bender. Fortunately, Paisley had this guitar at home, and it was spared from damage in the Nashville flood. This guitar was used to record the vast majority of his tracks.

He also plays a number of custom-built, paisley-finished Tele-style guitars in concert, made by luthier Bill Crook. Some of Paisley's Crook guitars have alder bodies; others have ash bodies. Most have maple necks and fingerboards with 6105 fret wire. He uses compensated vintage Tele-style bridges on his guitars. His guitars feature pickups by Seymour Duncan, Adder, Ron Ellis, and Voodoo. One of his more unusual Crooks is a reverse Firebird shape, with a Tele bridge and bridge pickup and a neck P-90. Other unusual Crooks include a baritone Tele and a 12-string Tele.

Paisley also plays a 1963 Tele with a rosewood fingerboard that is stock, aside from being refinished. Among his many other guitars, he has a '52 Tele that is stock except for a refret with 6105 wire and a Glaser G-bender.

Though he rarely is seen playing anything other than a Tele, he does own several Fender Strats, along with various other models. He uses a refinished '65 Strat for one song, "She's Everything," in his shows. He has also used Gretsch Country Gentleman and Gibson ES-335 guitars in the studio for various tracks.

But ultimately, the Brad Paisley tone is all about Teles.

Amps

Class A, all the way. Paisley's number-one amplifier is a fawn-colored '62 Vox AC30. He has a number of other AC30s, as well as AC30-style amps made by Tony Bruno, including several Underground 30 amps. Paisley is a firm supporter of Dr. Z and owns Mini Z, Stingray, Maz 38 and Maz Jr., Prescription, and other Dr. Z amps—he is said to have lost as many as 24 Dr. Z amps in the Nashville floods. He has worked with the company on several amp models, including the Z-Wreck, which is based on a collaboration between Dr. Z and the late Ken Fischer of Trainwreck amps. (Paisley also owns an original Trainwreck amp.) He also has a number of Fender amps, including a Vibro-King, a Deluxe, and others.

On tour, Paisley uses four amps, each of which is set for a different gain level. Rather than step on an overdrive, he simply switches to another amp when he wants more gain or distortion. He can use the amps individually or switch them on in whatever combination he desires. The amps he uses live include a Dr. Z Z-Wreck, two Bruno Underground 30s, one run with reverb, and an Underground 45, which is Tony Bruno's version of a Trainwreck Rocket amp.

Paisley uses Vox-style Dr. Z 2×12 cabinets loaded with one Celestion Gold alnico and one Celestion Blue alnico speaker.

Effects

For his reverb, Paisley uses a Dr. Z Z-Verb, which is a tube-driven outboard spring reverb unit. Beyond this, Paisley has two effects racks, a smaller one for "fly" and television appearances, and a larger one for concerts. At concerts, the fly rack serves as a backup to the main rack.

Fly Rack

The pedals in Paisley's "small" rack include a Way Huge Aqua Puss analog delay, a Wampler Analog Echo, a Wampler Ego Compressor, a Boss TR-2 tremolo (modded by Robert Keeley), a Boss DD-3 digital delay (Keeley modded), an Empress Superdelay, and an Ibanez TS808 Tube Screamer (Keeley modded). The effects and Paisley's four amps are switched and routed using an RJM Music Effects Gizmo loop switcher controlled by a Voodoo Lab Ground Control.

Concert Rack

The pedals in Paisley's larger rack include a Way Huge Aqua Puss analog delay, a Wampler Analog Echo, a Wampler Ego Compressor, a Wampler Paisley Drive, a Boss DD-2 digital delay, a Maxon AD999 analog delay, an Ibanez TS808 Tube Screamer (modded by Keeley), and a block-logo MXR Phase 90. He also uses a Line 6 M13 multi-effects modeler, which replaced three rackmount Line 6 effects he lost in the flood. He uses it for pitch effects as well as for long delays and for combinations of short and long delays. Two RJM Music Effects Gizmos are used to control these effects and to switch his four amps. A Voodoo Lab Ground Control switches presets in the Effects Gizmos. He runs his rack off of a Furman power conditioner and an APC UPS (uninterruptible power supply).

Studio Tricks

Paisley recorded his first few albums with the '68 Tele, a '60 and/or a '62 Vox AC30, and a Way Huge Aqua Puss analog delay set for a short slapback echo. Later, various Dr. Z amps, such as the Maz 38 and a Z-28 loaded with a JBL D130, started to creep into his studio rig, as did other effects, such as a Boss CS-1 compressor and an MXR Dyna Comp. His song "Ticks" used a rackmount Line 6 Filter Pro; he also used the Filter Pro to create fixed wah-type filter effects on other songs.

Benchmark Recordings

Brad Paisley, *Part II* (2002)

Brad Paisley, *5th Gear* (2007)

Brad Paisley, *Play* (2008)

Getting the Sound

To achieve a tone similar to Brad Paisley's, try this:

  ▷ You'll definitely need a Tele-style guitar!

  ▷ An analog delay.

  ▷ Optionally, a compressor and an overdrive.

  ▷ A Class A tube amplifier, such as a Vox AC30, a Dr. Z, a Bruno, or one of the many other AC30-style amps, loaded with alnico speakers.

Eddie Van Halen

RANKENSTRATS, VARIACS, AND MODDED MARSHALLS. None of these were on the radar when Van Halen's first album hit the streets in February of 1978…to say nothing of two-handed tapping, tapped harmonics, whammy tricks, and the "brown sound." You could debate whether Eddie Van Halen "invented" any of these things, but one thing is for sure: On his band's first record, he synthesized a new sound and a new approach to the electric guitar that changed everything for many players—some have likened his impact on guitarists to that of Jimi Hendrix. Over the next several decades, his influence remained huge, with countless players striving to achieve his tone, his feel, and his style.

Tonewise, EVH set the standard for many players with his much-vaunted "brown sound," which is described as thick, warm, round, dirty, and comfortable to listen to, even at high volume levels. The Van Halen sound is not as high gain as many players seem to assume it is, and it is largely based on power-amp distortion rather than preamp over-drive. How did he get that sound? Opinions vary, and much misinformation has been spread—mostly by Eddie himself, who liked to keep the players who were attempting to emulate him guessing.

Guitars

Eddie is most famous for his "Frankenstrat," a mutt made from inexpensive parts. His goal was to achieve a thick Les Paul–type tone, but with the feel and vibrato arm of a Stratocaster. The guitar has been researched to death as players and manufacturers seek to duplicate Van Halen's early tone.

The Frankenstrat (as it came to be known) featured an unfinished maple neck and fingerboard with a wider than standard width and Gibson jumbo frets, and a body made from northern ash that had been routed to accommodate a humbucking pickup in the bridge position. The medium-weight, two-piece body was a "second" due to a knot in the wood. It was painted black using acrylic lacquer bicycle paint and then taped off and painted with white stripes.

The guitar had a vibrato tailpiece from a late '50s or early '60s Strat, with a steel trem block. The bridge was set flush against the body so that it would only drop in pitch. Three vibrato springs were installed. The neck had a brass nut with extra-wide slots that was oiled to keep the strings from sticking when the vibrato arm was abused. Schaller mini tuning machines were used.

Van Halen used a single Gibson PAF humbucking pickup mounted in the bridge position. It was taken from a 1961 ES-335 and rewound at Seymour Duncan's facility to Eddie's specs. The pickup was screwed directly into the wood instead of mounted to the pickguard. Because the bridge of the guitar was Fender spaced, the pickup was angled so that the front-coil pole piece would catch the high E string and the back-coil pole piece would see the low E string. The pickup height was about 1/8 inch from the strings. Van Halen potted the pickup in paraffin wax (he used surfboard wax melted in an old can) to cut down on microphonic squealing at high volume levels. A single Gibson 500k volume pot completed the electronics.

Eddie used Fender pure-nickel XL150 strings, with gauges from .009 to .040, tuned down to E♭. He boiled the strings for 10 to 20 minutes prior to installing them to help keep the tuning more stable. The action on the guitar was said to be high, but with the light strings dropped in pitch, it was still easy to play. These factors also contributed to the tone produced. Van Halen held a Fender medium pick (0.71mm) between his middle finger and thumb; he later changed to very thin picks.

Over the years, the guitar evolved with the addition of red bicycle paint, with a Floyd Rose bridge (and a 1971 quarter screwed under the bridge to maintain contact with the body), and with a replacement maple neck from Kramer during the years Van Halen was endorsing that brand (beginning around 1984). The pickguard was removed, and a non-functioning single-coil pickup was added to the neck position along with a similarly non-functioning five-way switch stuffed into the empty middle pickup route. Reflectors were added to the back of the body.

Ibanez Destroyer

Though the Frankenstrat gets all the press and attention (especially after EVH/Fender released a $25,000 limited-edition reproduction of it), in fact around half of the first Van Halen album was recorded with an Ibanez Destroyer guitar (a knock-off of a Gibson Explorer). These guitars had a "korina" finish and were often described as korina instruments, but in fact most were made from "sen," a Japanese wood that is lighter than korina and that generally has a softer tone. It is unclear whether the guitar had its original "Super 70" Ibanez humbucker in the bridge position during the recording of the first album or whether a custom-wound PAF was used—photos from the era seem to support the PAF. Otherwise, this guitar was stock at the time. Later, Eddie used a saw to cut a chunk of wood out of the body behind the bridge so that it resembled a cross between a Flying V and an Explorer. Eddie felt this ruined the instrument's tone, and it was retired (though it made an appearance on the *Women and Children First* album cover).

VH II and Later

For *Van Halen II*, Eddie built a new yellow and black striped Strat-style guitar using Charvel parts and featuring a DiMarzio humbucking pickup into which he had put a Gibson PAF magnet, then had it rewound to his specs. (This guitar was later buried with the late Dimebag Darrell from Pantera.) On later tours, he played guitars ranging from Kramer re-creations of the Frankenstrat, to Steinbergers with striped paint, to six-channel Ripley guitars (made by Kramer), to double-neck Kramers. Needless to say, Van Halen has used a wide range of guitars throughout his career. But despite this, most of his tone is built around the Frankenstrat and his more recent signature guitars. (See the next section.)

Signature Guitars

Van Halen worked with Ernie Ball (beginning in 1991) and Peavey (beginning in 1996), and he later formed his own company, EVH, to make signature "Wolfgang" guitars and amplifiers. The current Wolfgangs have 1.5-inch thick basswood bodies with 1/2-inch thick carved maple tops and quarter-sawn maple necks with bird's-eye maple fingerboards. These guitars feature two custom-wound humbucking pickups and Floyd Rose bridges with "D-Tuna" levers for instantly dropping the tuning to D on the low E string. Other features include small "vintage" stainless steel frets, low-friction 500k volume and 250k tone Bourns potentiometers, and a three-way pickup selector switch. Other variations on the model were also introduced, including one with a stop tailpiece and Tune-o-matic style bridge. Van Halen played these guitars on his tours in the late '00s.

Amps

In the early days, Van Halen was Marshall all the way—a '67 100-watt Super Lead, serial number 12301 to be exact—which he purchased from the Rose Palace, where it was the "house" amp, around 1974. The amp is a 1959 SLP model, with four inputs and no master volume control. He stated in some interviews that his amps were heavily modded. In others, he stated that they were "beefed up" with bigger transformers by Jose Arredondo. However, techs who have worked on or maintained the amp state that it is stock, and Eddie has since verified this. He used Sylvania 6CA7 (a heavy-duty USA-made EL34 variant) tubes in the amps and claims to have run them with the bias cranked all the way up. His settings on the amp are easy to duplicate: everything on 10.

Another place where the truth may have been stretched is in Eddie's use of an Ohmite Variac variable transformer to change the AC voltage running the amp. In one interview, he stated that he liked to crank the Variac up to 130 or 140 volts and watch the tubes glow and/or melt—he held that the amps only lasted for about 10 hours of play, had to be re-tubed daily, and so on. (Using a Variac in this way is not recommended!) Techs have stated that he actually ran the Variac at around 90 volts, which would starve the amp for AC voltage and make the tubes last longer. Regardless of whether it was cranked up or turned down, the use of a Variac was likely a contributor to the tone he achieved.

Van Halen usually used one Marshall 4×12 cabinet per amp head, the bottom cabinet in the stack. The '60s-era basket-weave cabinet used for recording the first Van Halen album is said to have featured two Celestion Greenbacks and two JBL D120Fs. Many of his early cabinets were "peeled"—their covering was removed to display the bare wood.

In later years, Van Halen began using 5150 amps from Peavey, which were two-channel, all-tube amps that he helped design. Later, Peavey updated these to the 5150 II, which added separate EQ control for each channel and an additional preamp tube. These amps were also adopted by many other players, including Ted Nugent, Brad Whitford, Joe Satriani, and others. When the relationship between Peavey and Van Halen ended, the amps were renamed the 6505 and continued to be popular with many hard rock and metal players.

After leaving Peavey, Van Halen launched a partnership with Fender, under the brand name EVH, to make a new amp, the 5150 III. These are three-channel heads, 100-watts, all-tube, with separate EQ for each channel. Matching 4×12 cabinets featured EVH speakers, made by Celestion and patterned after Heritage G12M Greenbacks.

Onstage, the speaker out from the 5150 was fed into a Palmer speaker simulator/dummy load, sent through a Bradshaw effects rig, then routed to a stereo H&H power amp and into two 4×12 cabinets. The dry sound from the amp itself was sent into another 4×12 cabinet to create a wet/dry/wet rig. (Some sources suggest he may have been using a dummy load/power amp setup very early on; see the sidebar "Alternate Take.")

In the studio, Eddie is said to have used his "Holy Grail" Super Lead Plexi Marshall for every album except *Van Halen III*.

Effects

In the classic days of the original "brown sound," Eddie's effects were pretty simple, though they had a huge impact on his tone. From his guitar, he used a 30-foot guitar cable plugged into an MXR Flanger followed by an MXR script Phase 90. (MXR now makes EVH "signature" reissues of both of these pedals.) Following these, he plugged into an EP-3 Echoplex (some reports say two Echoplexes), which is a big part of the sound—these old tape echoes preamp the signal even when they are bypassed and can significantly color the tone. Last in the chain was a Univox EC-80, another tape delay that used cassette tapes. This delay was used to re-create some of the special effects on the first album. Van Halen modified this unit by building it into an old practice bomb and by installing a new motor that allowed for slower tape speeds and therefore longer delay times.

In some cases, Van Halen is said to have used either an MXR 6-band EQ or a Boss GE-10 10-band EQ between the phase shifter and the Echoplex or after the Echoplex for extra tone shaping and possibly for a slight boost. These don't seem to have been used all the time, just when some extra help was needed for a particular venue.

In some studio situations, such as during the recording of Brian May's *Star Fleet* and on his solo on Michael Jackson's "Beat It," Van Halen simply played his Frankenstrat through an Echoplex into his Marshall, with no other effects.

Studio Tricks

On the first record, Van Halen's guitar was recorded using two Shure SM57 microphones (one aimed straight at the center of the speaker, the other at an angle, both pulled off the speaker about 1.5 inches) and a vintage Universal Audio 610 console. On later albums, Neve consoles were used. The dry, or unprocessed, guitar was panned hard to one side of the stereo field, while a split from that signal was run through an Eventide processor for a very short delay and then through an EMT plate reverb. This effected signal was panned hard to the opposite side of the stereo field—sort of an early precursor to the wet/dry effects rigs some players, such as Robben Ford and Jimmy Herring, use today. Later (beginning around the Sammy Hagar days), Van Halen went for a much more stereo amp tone in the studio, which replaced the original wet/dry effects processing.

Benchmark Recordings

Van Halen, *Van Halen* (1978)

Van Halen, *Fair Warning* (1981)

Van Halen, *5150* (1986)

Getting the Sound

To achieve a tone similar to Eddie Van Halen's early sound, try this:

▷ A Strat-style guitar with an angled, low-to-moderate output humbucker in the bridge position and a tremolo tailpiece.

▷ An MXR flanger. (The MXR EVH signature version will get you there even faster.)

▷ A script MXR Phase 90. (The MXR EVH signature version has a switch that instantly calls up Eddie's setting.)

▷ An Echoplex or other tape delay, or a modeled tape echo that can simulate an Echoplex. With a modeled delay, add a preamp such as the Xotic EP Booster for coloration.

▷ Optionally, a 6-band or 10-band graphic EQ, set for a "frown" shape, with the mids boosted.

▷ A Plexi-style amplifier, such as a Marshall 1959 SLP or one of the many clones. Dime the controls—you may need an attenuator to control the volume level if the amp doesn't have a master volume control.

▷ A 4×12 speaker cabinet loaded with Celestion Greenbacks.

▷ For a more recent-vintage EVH tone, substitute a Wolfgang guitar and a 5150 amplifier and matching cabinet, and consider running a wet/dry/wet rig with stereo effects processing.

Stevie Ray Vaughan

W HEN STEVIE RAY VAUGHAN BURST ON THE SCENE IN 1983, it was not easy to find blues on the airwaves—the genre was ready for a new champion, and Vaughan took up the mantle and established his home of Austin as the center of Texas blues and as a wellspring of gifted guitar players. Known for his fiery, physical brand of guitar playing, Vaughan was a huge influence on many players and spawned legions of imitators in the short seven years between the release of his first album and his death in 1990.

Guitars

Stevie Ray Vaughan was associated almost exclusively with Fender Stratocasters through his career, though he did use a few other guitars here and there. Vaughan *attacked* the strings with ferocity—with both his right and his left hands. Because of these factors, he was very hard on his guitars and had to replace frets and other parts much more often than other players.

Number One

Stevie played through many different guitars in his early years before finding "Number One" (also known as his "First Wife"), a Fender Strat he purchased in 1973 or 1974. This tobacco-sunburst Strat quickly became his main guitar. He played Number One until it was very heavily worn.

Though Vaughan referred to the guitar as a '59, when the Fender Custom Shop disassembled it, they found it had an alder '62 body and a '63 neck. The pickups, however, were dated from a '59 Strat. The guitar has a full "D" neck shape with a thin veneer (not thick slab) rosewood fingerboard with large frets and a bone nut. The guitar was re-fretted several times, the last time with Dunlop 6100-sized frets (Stevie referred to them as bass frets, though this wasn't true), which resulted in the fingerboard being flatter than its original 7.25-inch radius. Vaughan preferred a high action: 5/64 inch on the high E string and 7/64 inch on the low E string for ringing sustain and clear tone.

He used very heavy strings: GHS Nickel Rockers, gauged .013 to .058 when his hands were in shape, .011s or .012s when they were not. He always tuned down a half step, ostensibly for vocal reasons, but also to reduce the string tension.

The guitar had a left-handed vintage-style tremolo, in imitation of Jimi Hendrix's use of upside-down Strats. Because he broke tremolo arms so often, his father made him thick stainless-steel replacements (which he still broke). He used all five springs in the back of the guitar to counterbalance the pull of the heavy strings. The saddles were vintage replacements that did not all match. Short pieces of plastic tubing were slipped over the strings to help keep them from breaking in the tremolo block. The bridge plate and bridge saddles were also ground with a Dremel tool to smooth off sharp edges to reduce string breakage. The tuning machines were replaced at least twice. In the mid-'80s, the hardware was changed to gold-plated items.

Vaughan set his pickups very high (close to the strings). According to techs who have examined the guitar, the treble side of the bridge pickup touched a straight-edge laid along the fingerboard, with the middle pickup slightly lower and the neck pickup slightly lower yet, around 1/16 inch down. The bass side of each pickup was around 1/32 inch lower than the treble side. According to some sources, the guitar had a dummy coil installed to reduce hum and buzz from the single-coil pickups. A push-pull switch on the bottom tone control could be used to bypass the dummy coil.

The neck on Number One was retired in 1990, as it was too worn to be refretted again. It was replaced with the neck from "Red," another of his Strats, but this neck was broken by a falling piece of stage rigging. A new Fender neck was installed at that point. After Vaughan's death, the original Number One neck was reinstalled.

Lenny

In the early '80s, Vaughan found a Stratocaster in a pawn shop that he liked. His wife and his friends pooled their money and bought the guitar for him; he named it "Lenny" after his wife, Lenora (whose nickname was "Lenny"). The guitar was a '63 or '64. Originally, it had a rosewood fingerboard neck, but Stevie replaced it with a maple fingerboard neck given to him by his brother, Jimmy. This guitar was used to record "Lenny" (off of *Texas Flood*) and "Riviera Paradise" (off of *In Step*). Fender later released a limited-edition replica of this guitar.

Other Guitars

Stevie played a variety of other guitars, mostly Stratocasters, such as Red, a stock 1962 Stratocaster purchased in 1984. Its neck was later moved over to Vaughan's Number One and was subsequently broken. A left-handed Strat neck was installed on Red.

"Yellow" was an old Strat that had been routed for four humbuckers before Vaughan acquired it. It was painted yellow and loaded with a single neck pickup.

In 1984, Billy Gibbons from ZZ Top presented Stevie with a guitar made by James Hamilton with Vaughan's name inlaid on the ebony fingerboard. This guitar, nicknamed "Main," featured a two-piece maple body with through-neck construction. It originally was loaded with EMG active pickups, but these were replaced with vintage Strat pickups.

Also in 1984, Charley Wirz of Charley's Guitar Shop gave Stevie a guitar he had made with an alder body and ebony fingerboard, loaded with "lipstick" pickups and a non-tremolo hard-tail bridge. This guitar can be seen on the cover of *Couldn't Stand the Weather*. Wirz and Vaughan guitar tech Rene Martinez made 33 replicas of this guitar and sold them as a limited-edition run. Like all of his Strats, it had a five-way pickup selector switch.

Vaughan was also known to play a 1958 Gibson ES-335 and a Gibson Johnny Smith hollow-body archtop.

Amps

Vaughan rarely played through just one amplifier. Rather, he chained together multiple amps to create a composite tone—and ear-splitting volume levels. He ran his amps clean but cranked them up to get power-tube distortion. One of his techs recalls Stevie setting his amp by running his hand along the bottom of the controls to turn them all to 10. Others recall the amp volumes set around 7, though these settings would increase through the set until the volumes were dimed by the time he played "Voodoo Chile."

In the early 1980s, Stevie used one Marshall amp, a Model 4140 Club and Country 100-watt combo loaded with two Celestion G12-80 speakers, and two Fender Vibroverb 1×15 combos, which were early examples, sequentially serial-numbered 5 and 6. He was also known to use a 100-watt Marshall Super PA and a Marshall Major 200-watt head.

By the mid-'80s, he was using two Fender Super Reverbs loaded with four 10-inch Electro-Voice EVM speakers, as well as the two Vibroverbs, one of which ran a Fender Vibratone cabinet that featured a Styrofoam cylinder that rotated around the speaker. The Vibroverbs were said to have their tremolo circuits disconnected and their Normal channel disconnected from the phase inverter. Some reports say the Fender amps were all modified with thicker baffle boards to support the heavier E-V speakers and that their transformers were upgraded and moved to allow space for the larger E-V speaker magnets. The Supers provided the clean top end while the Vibroverbs provided the fat bottom end.

In some cases, the Super Reverbs were replaced with two much-louder 150-watt Dumble Steel String Singer heads with 4×12 cabinets loaded with Electro-Voice EVM-12L speakers. And sometimes, the Vibroverbs, Supers, and Dumbles were all combined together. Toward the end of his life, Vaughan also used a pair of reissue Fender Bassman amps with four 10-inch speakers. A custom 1-in/6-out splitter was used to distribute his guitar's output to all the amplifiers without signal loss.

Effects

An Ibanez Tube Screamer was a mainstay in Stevie's rig. Some sources suggest he used several versions, including the TS-808, TS-9, and TS-10 Classic; others suggest he relied on vintage TS-808 models. He set his overdrive as a clean boost, with the gain down and the output up. In some cases he cascaded two Tube Screamers together for extra drive. A '60s Vox wah wah was also a mainstay in his equipment list (he was even said to have chained two wahs together and rocked them in opposite directions for a "phased" effect), along with a Dallas-Arbiter Fuzz Face (later modified by his tech with germanium transistors) and a Roger Mayer or Tycobrahe Octavia. Occasionally, he added a Uni-Vibe.

Benchmark Recordings

Stevie Ray Vaughan and Double Trouble, *Texas Flood* (1983)

Stevie Ray Vaughan and Double Trouble, *Couldn't Stand the Weather* (1984)

Stevie Ray Vaughan and Double Trouble, *In Step* (1989)

The Vaughan Brothers, *Family Style* (1990)

Getting the Sound

To achieve a tone similar to Stevie Ray Vaughan's, try this:

▷ A Strat-style guitar with three '50s-style single-coil pickups and a tremolo bridge. One key to getting a tone like Stevie's with a Strat-style guitar is to use very heavy strings and a high action, and to drop the guitar's tuning down by half a step from standard pitch.

▷ A Tube Screamer–style overdrive and a wah pedal.

▷ A Fender-style tube amp, set clean but cranked up to get power tube distortion.

▷ For an even thicker tone, run the guitar into several cranked tube amps simultaneously.

Tonal Resources

Magazines

Guitar Aficionado, www.guitaraficionado.com

Guitar Edge, www.guitaredge.com

Guitar Player, www.guitarplayer.com

Guitar Techniques, www.guitar-techniques.com

Guitar World, www.guitarworld.com

Guitarist, www.guitarist.co.uk

Premier Guitar, www.premierguitar.com

ToneQuest Report, www.tonequest.com

Total Guitar, www.totalguitar.co.uk

Vintage Guitar, www.vintageguitar.com

Selected Books

Bacon, Tony, *The Les Paul Guitar Book* (Backbeat Books, 2009)

Bacon, Tony, *The Fender Electric Guitar Book* (Backbeat Books, 2007)

Bacon, Tony, *50 Years of Gretsch Electrics* (Backbeat Books, 2005)

Bacon, Tony, *The Ultimate Guitar Book* (Alfred A. Knopf, 1997)

Balmer, Paul, *The Fender Stratocaster Handbook* (Voyageur Press, 2007)

Balmer, Paul, *The Fender Telecaster Handbook* (Voyageur Press, 2010)

Balmer, Paul, *The Gibson Les Paul Handbook* (Voyageur Press, 2008)

Burrluck, Dave, *The PRS Guitar Book* (Backbeat Books, 2007)

Carter, Walter, *Classic Electrics* (Jawbone Press, 2008)

Denyer, Ralph, *The Guitar Handbook* (Knopf, 1992)

Doyle, Michael, *The History of Marshall* (Hal Leonard, 1993)

Erlewine, Dan, *How To Make Your Electric Guitar Play Great* (Backbeat Books, 2001)

Erlewine, Dan, *The Guitar Player Repair Guide* (Backbeat Books, 2007)

Fjestad, Zachary R., *Blue Book of Electric Guitars* (Blue Book, 2009)

Hoover, Will, *Picks!* (Backbeat Books, 1995)

Hunter, Dave, *Guitar Amplifier Handbook* (Backbeat Books, 2005)

Hunter, Dave, *The Guitar Pickups Handbook* (Backbeat Books, 2009)

Marx Jr., Wallace, *Gibson Amplifiers 1933–2008* (Blue Book Publications, 2009)

Molenda, Michael, *The Guitar Player Book* (Backbeat Books, 2007)

Pittman, Aspen, *The Tube Amp Book* (Backbeat Books, 2003)

Schiller, David, *Guitars* (Workman Publishing Company, 2008)

Wheeler, Tom, *The Stratocaster Chronicles* (Hal Leonard, 2004)

Wheeler, Tom, *The Soul of Tone* (Hal Leonard, 2007)

Discussion Forums

Many manufacturers host "official" forums for the discussion of their own products; these can usually be reached through the manufacturer's website. The following sections consist of a selection of some of the more popular independent forums that are by and for those interested in a particular electric guitar topic.

General Guitar Forums

Axaholics, www.axaholics.com

The Fret, www.thefret.net

The Gear Page, www.thegearpage.net

Guitars101, www.guitars101.com/forums

Guitar Diner, www.guitardiner.com

Guitar Notes Discussion Forum, www.guitarnotes.com/forum

Guitar Nuts 2, www.guitarnuts2.proboards.com/index.cgi

Harmony Central, www.harmony-central.com

Vintage Guitar and Bass Discussion Forum, http://forums.vintageguitars.org.uk

VintAxe Guitar Forum, www.vintaxe.com/boards

Non-Manufacturer Forums for Specific Guitars

BC Rich Players, www.bcrichplayers.com

Birds and Moons (PRS), www.birdsandmoons.com

Fender Discussion Page, www.fenderforum.com

Fenderpick, www.fenderpick.com

Fender-Forum, www.fender-forum.com

FenderTalk, forum.fendertalk.com

Gibson Talk (Gibson and Epiphone Guitar Forum), www.gibson-talk.com

Gretsch Talk, www.gretsch-talk.com

The Gretsch Pages, www.gretschpages.com

Hamer Fan Club, www.hamerfanclub.com

Hofner Guitars Internet Community, www.hofner.co.uk

Jemsite (Ibanez), www.jemsite.com

Kramer Guitar Forum, www.kramerforum.com

My Les Paul, www.mylespaul.com

Les Paul Forum, www.lespaulforum.com

Schecter Guitar Forum, www.schecterforum.com

Strat-Talk, www.strat-talk.com

Telecaster Electric Guitar Central, www.tdpri.com

Amplifiers and Effects Forums

Amp Workshop, www.ampworkshop.yuku.com

The AMPAGE Music Electronics Forum, music-electronics-forum.com/home.php

The Boogie Board, forum.grailtone.com

Guitar Amp Modeling, www.guitarampmodeling.com

Huge Racks, Inc. (no, it's not porn—this one is for rackmount and other guitar gear), www.hugeracksinc.com

The Marshall Amp Forum, www.marshallforum.com

Marshall Vintage Modern Forum, www.marshallvintagemodern.com

Mesa Boogie Amp Forum, mesaboogieampforum77319.yuku.com

MTS Forum (Randall and Egnater modular amps), mtsforum.grailtone.com

Solid State Guitar Amp Forum, www.ssguitar.com

VGuitar Forums (Roland V guitar systems), www.vguitarforums.com

Vintage Amps Forum, www.vintageamps.com

Wattkins Amp Forums (18-watt, JTM45/Bassman, push-pull, and single-ended amp forums), www.wattkins.com

Index